William Nelson Hutchinson

Dog Breaking

The most Expeditious, Certain and Easy Method

William Nelson Hutchinson

Dog Breaking
The most Expeditious, Certain and Easy Method

ISBN/EAN: 9783337337391

Printed in Europe, USA, Canada, Australia, Japan

Cover: Foto ©Lupo / pixelio.de

More available books at **www.hansebooks.com**

DOG BREAKING.

THE MOST EXPEDITIOUS, CERTAIN, AND EASY METHOD,

WHETHER GREAT EXCELLENCE OR ONLY MEDIOCRITY BE REQUIRED,

WITH ODDS AND ENDS FOR THOSE WHO LOVE

THE DOG AND GUN.

BY MAJOR-GENERAL W. N. HUTCHINSON,

LATE COLONEL GRENADIER GUARDS.

FOURTH EDITION, REVISED AND ENLARGED.

NEAR WALTHAM ABBEY.—*Sept.* 1, 1847.

LONDON:
JOHN MURRAY, ALBEMARLE STREET.
1865.

PREFACE TO FOURTH EDITION.

A FOURTH preface, Mr. Murray!!!

There are not sufficient materials, although there is some fresh matter, and undeniably, many excellent sketches, thanks to the clever artist F. W. KEYL, and the talented amateur John M——n, who, contrary to the advice of many friends, has determined that the sword shall be his profession rather than the pencil.

Well!—another party shall speak for me, and much surprised will he be to find the duty his words are performing; but they advocate so good a cause that I feel sure of his forgiveness. He writes in the third person, for we are perfect strangers to each other.

" Captain T——r has all his life been a most enthu-
" siastic sportsman, but never broke a dog, until a year

"ago, when he happened to come across the Major-
"General's work on 'Dog-breaking.' Since then he has
"trained two *entirely* on the system laid down in the
"book. People say they have never before seen dogs
"so well-broken—certainly the owner never has."

"Always an ardent disciple of St. Hubert, Captain
"T——r is now still more so from the increased grati-
"fication he derives from the performance of animals
"trained entirely by himself."

Reader, why not give yourself a similar gratification?

W. N. H.

GOVERNMENT HOUSE, DEVONPORT,
December, 1864.

PREFACE TO THIRD EDITION.

I CANNOT help congratulating my canine friends, (and may I not their masters also ?), on the circulation of two large impressions of this work; for I trust that many of the suggestions therein offered have been adopted, and that their education has consequently been effected in a much shorter period, and with far less punishment, than that of their forefathers.

I have endeavoured in the present edition to render more complete the lessons respecting Setters and Pointers. I have added somewhat on the subject of Spaniels, Retrievers, and Bloodhounds. It has been my aim, also, to give a few useful hints regarding the rearing and preservation of Game; and I shall be disappointed if the youngest of my readers does not derive, from the perusal of what I have written, an assurance that he need not take the field wholly ignorant of all sporting matters, or without any knowledge of the best method of "handling arms."

W. N. H.

PREFACE TO SECOND EDITION.

WHEN Colonel Hawker, who has been styled the "Emperor of Sportsmen," writes to me, (and kindly permits me to quote his words), "I perfectly agree with you in everything you have said, and I think your work should be preached in a series of lectures to every dog-breaker in the profession, as all these fellows are too fond of the whip, which hardens the animal they are instructing, and the use of their own tongues, which frighten away the birds you want to shoot," I feel some confidence in the correctness of what I have put forth. But there may be points that have not been noticed, and some things that require explanation, especially as regards Spaniels and Retrievers. In endeavouring to supply these deficiencies, I hope my additional prosing may not send the dog-breaker to sleep, instead of helping to make him more "wide-awake."

W. N. H.

PREFACE NO PREFACE.

(FOR FIRST EDITION.)

My respected Publisher has suggested that a Preface may be expected. His opinion on such a subject ought to be law; but as I fear my readers may think that I have already sufficiently bored them, I will beg them, in Irish fashion, to refer any formalist, who considers a Preface necessary, to the *conclusion* of the work, where a statement will be found of the motive which induced me to write.

W. N. H.

CONTENTS.

CHAPTER I.
PRELIMINARY OBSERVATIONS. QUALIFICATIONS, IN BREAKER,— IN DOG 1

CHAPTER II.
INITIATORY LESSONS WITHIN DOORS. SHOOTING PONIES . . . 9

CHAPTER III.
INITIATORY LESSONS CONTINUED. SPANIELS 20

CHAPTER IV.
LESSONS IN "FETCHING."—RETRIEVERS 57

CHAPTER V.
INITIATORY LESSONS OUT OF DOORS.—TRICKS . . 76

CHAPTER VI.
FIRST LESSON IN SEPTEMBER COMMENCED. RANGING . . . 99

CHAPTER VII.
FIRST LESSONS IN SEPTEMBER CONTINUED. CAUTION.—NATURE'S MYSTERIOUS INFLUENCES , ... 111

CONTENTS.

CHAPTER VIII.

FIRST LESSON IN SEPTEMBER CONTINUED. CUNNING OF AGE.—RANGE OF FROM TWO TO SIX DOGS 129

CHAPTER IX.

FIRST LESSON IN SEPTEMBER CONTINUED. "POINT" NOT RELINQUISHED FOR "DOWN CHARGE" 150

CHAPTER X.

FIRST LESSON IN SEPTEMBER CONTINUED. ASSISTANT.—VERMIN 165

CHAPTER XI.

FIRST LESSON IN SEPTEMBER CONCLUDED. BAR.—LEG STRAP.—SPIKE-COLLAR 176

CHAPTER XII.

SHOOTING HARES. COURAGE IMPARTED.—"BACKING" TAUGHT 194

CHAPTER XIII.

HINTS TO PURCHASERS. PRICE OF DOGS.—SHEEP KILLING . . 210

CHAPTER XIV.

A REST BEYOND "HALF-WAY HOUSE." ANECDOTES OF DOGS ON SERVICE AT HOME 230

CHAPTER XV.

ANECDOTES OF DOGS ON SERVICE ABROAD. RUSSIAN SETTERS . 249

CHAPTER XVI.

DISTINGUISHING WHISTLES. "BACKING" THE GUN. RETREAT FROM AND RESUMPTION OF POINT. RANGE UNACCOMPANIED BY GUN. HEADING RUNNING BIRDS 278

CONTENTS. xiii

CHAPTER XVII.

PAGE

SETTER TO RETRIEVE. BLOODHOUNDS. RETRIEVERS TO "BEAT." WOUNDED WILD-FOWL RETRIEVED BEFORE THE KILLED . . 294

CHAPTER XVIII.

BECKFORD. ST. JOHN. CONDITION. INOCULATION. VACCINATION. CONCLUSION 307

POSTSCRIPT : MR. L——G'S LETTER 322

APPENDIX :

 COVERS, SHOOTING, LOADING 328

 TRAPPING.—OWL AS DECOY.—HEN HARRIER.—KEEPER'S VERMIN-DOGS.—STOATS 331

 REARING PHEASANTS.—CANTELO.—PHEASANTRIES.—MR. KNOX 335

 SETTERS.—POACHERS.—KEEPERS.—NETTING PARTRIDGES.—BLOODHOUNDS.—NIGHT-DOGS 344

INDEX, *in which the figures refer to the numbers of the paragraphs, and not to the pages* 349

LIST OF ILLUSTRATIONS.

VARIOUS RETRIEVERS	*Frontispiece.*
SCENE NEAR WALTHAM ABBEY, 1st Sept. 1847 . .	*Title-page.*
OLD-FASHIONED ENGLISH SETTER,—RETRIEVERS, ONE A CROSS WITH BLOODHOUND. (Lesson VIII. Par. 141)	*Page* 25
THE CHECK—'HOLD HARD!'	30—
A FOUR-LEGGED WHIPPER-IN	33
CLUMBERS. (Lesson III. Par. 141)	43
WILD SPANIELS. (Lesson XII. Par. 141)	47
IRISH WATER SPANIEL. (Lesson I. Par. 141)	53
INCLINED TO 'RAT'.	77—
BROACHING A BARREL	84
DEAF TO THE VOICE OF PERSUASION	90—
A SOLICITOR	91—
REPLETE WITH GOOD THINGS	95 -
BACKING THE GUN AGAINST THE BIRD	117
SAFELY MOORED, 'STEM' AND 'STERN'	121
"STIFF BY THE TAINTED GALE WITH OPEN NOSE OUTSTRETCHED AND FINELY SENSIBLE"	124—
A DOG-FISH	125
"SMALL, ACTIVE POINTER." (Lesson IX. Par. 141) . . .	131
"SHORT-LEGGED STRONG-LOINED SUSSEX SPANIEL." (Lesson XV. Par. 141)	137

LIST OF ILLUSTRATIONS.

	PAGE
"DUKE OF GORDON'S BLACK AND TAN SETTERS." (Lesson XIV. Par. 141)	141
LARGE HEAVY POINTER. (Lesson X. Pars. 141 and 266)	157
CARRYING A POINT, AND CARRYING A POINTER	173
THE FIRST COURSE	197
FASHIONABLE (ENGLISH) SETTER, AND OLD-FASHIONED POINTER. (Lesson XIII. Par. 141)	215
IRISH RED SETTER. (Lesson II. Par. 141)	221
SCENE FROM 'CRIPPLE-GAIT.'—'GAME' TO THE LAST	237
DOMINI AND 'DOMINOS'	245
THE MIGHTY KING	254
COOL AS A CUCUMBER	255
A REGULAR BORE	259
THERE ARE BOUNDS TO SPORT	263
WARM GREETING OF A GREAT 'BORE'	266
INVITATION TO A 'WHITE-BAIT' DINNER	267
BRINGING HOME THE BRUSH	269
SCENE ON THE 'THLEW-ÉE-CHOH-DEZETH'	272
RUSSIAN SETTER. (Lesson XI. Pars. 141 and 266)	275
TELL ME MY HEART (HART) IF THIS BE LOVE	283
DIVISION OF PROPERTY	297
"EXAMPLE BETTER THAN PRECEPT"	303
PORTRAIT OF BRISK	321
'FOUL' FEEDING	336
A WELL-TRAINED BLOODHOUND	045

*** *The Frontispiece, Vignette Title, and the Lessons, are designed and drawn on Wood by* F. W. KEYL. *See 4th Preface.*

DOG-BREAKING.

CHAPTER I.

PRELIMINARY OBSERVATIONS. QUALIFICATIONS, IN BREAKER,—
IN DOG.

1. Dog-breaking an Art easily acquired.—2. Most expeditious Mode of imparting every Degree of Education. Time bestowed determines Grade of Education. In note, Col. Hawker's opinion.—3. Sportsmen recommended to break in their own Dogs.—4. Men of property too easily satisfied with badly-broken Dogs. Keepers have no Excuse for Dogs being badly broken.—5. Great Experience in Dog-breaking, or Excellence in Shooting, not necessary. Dispositions of Dogs vary.—6. What is required in an Instructor.—7. Early in a Season any Dog will answer, a good one necessary afterwards. Hallooing, rating Dogs, and loud whistling spoil Sport. In note, Age and choice of birds. Several shots fired from Stooks at Grouse without alarming them. American Partridges and our Pheasants killed while at roost.—8. What a well-broken Dog ought to do.—9. Severity reprobated.—10. Astley's Method of teaching his Horses.—11. Franconi's *Cirque National de Paris.*—12. *Initiatory* Lessons recommended—to be given when alone with Dog—given fasting.—13. Success promised if rules be followed. Advantages of an expeditious Education. September shooting not sacrificed.

1. DOG-BREAKING, so far from being a mystery, is an art easily acquired when it is commenced and continued on rational principles.

2. I think you will be convinced of this if you will have the patience to follow me, whilst I endeavour to explain what, I am satisfied, is the most certain and rapid method of breaking in your dogs, whether you require great proficiency in them, or are contented with an inferior education. No quicker system has yet been devised, however humble the education may be. The education in fact, of the peasant, and that of the future double-first collegian, begins and proceeds on the same

B

principle. You know your own circumstances, and you must yourself determine what time you choose to devote to tuition; and, as a consequence, the degree of excellence to which you aspire. I can only assure you of my firm conviction, that no other means will enable you to gain your object so quickly; and I speak with a confidence derived from long experience in many parts of the world, on a subject that was, for several years, my great hobby.*

3. Every writer is presumed to take some interest in his reader; I therefore feel privileged to address you as a friend, and will commence my lecture by strongly recommending, that, if your occupations will allow it, you take earnestly and heartily to educating your dogs yourself. If you possess temper and some judgment, and will implicity attend to my advice, I will go bail for your success; and much as you may now love shooting, you will then like it infinitely more. Try the plan I recommend, and I will guarantee that the Pointer or Setter pup which I will, for example sake, suppose to be now in your kennel, shall be a better dog by the end of next season (I mean a more killing dog) than probably any you ever yet shot over.

4. Possibly, you will urge, that you are unable to spare the time which I consider necessary for giving him a high education, (brief as that time is, compared with the many, many months wasted in the tedious methods usually employed), and that you must, perforce,

---

* It may be satisfactory to others to know the opinion of so undeniable an authority as Colonel Hawker. The Colonel, in the Tenth Edition of his invaluable Book on Shooting, writes, (page 285)—"Since the publication of the last edition, Lieutenant-Col. Hutchinson's valuable work on 'Dog-breaking' has appeared. It is a perfect *vade mecum* for both Sportsmen and Keeper, and I have great pleasure in giving a cordial welcome to a work which so ably supplies my own deficiencies."

content yourself with humbler qualifications. Be it so. I can only condole with you, for in your case this may be partly true; mind I only say *partly* true. But how a man of property, who keeps a regular gamekeeper, can be satisfied with the disorderly, disobedient troop, to which he often shoots, I cannot understand. Where the gamekeeper is permitted to accompany his master in the field, and hunt the dogs himself, there can be no valid excuse for the deficiency in their education. The deficiency must arise either from the incapacity, or from the idleness of the keeper.

5. Unlike most other arts, dog-breaking does not require much experience; but such a knowledge of dogs, as will enable you to discriminate between their different tempers and dispositions (I had almost said characters)—and they vary greatly—is very advantageous. Some require constant encouragement; some you must never beat; whilst, to gain the required ascendancy over others, the whip must be occasionally employed. Nor is it necessary that the instructor should be a very good shot; which probably is a more fortunate circumstance for me than for you. It should even be received as a principle that birds ought to be now and then missed to young dogs, lest some day, if your nerves happen to be out of order, or a cockney companion be harmlessly blazing away, your dog take it into his head and heels to run home in disgust, as I have seen a bitch, called Countess, do more than once, in Haddingtonshire.

6. The chief requisites in a breaker are:—Firstly, command of temper, that he may never be betrayed into giving one unnecessary blow, for, with dogs as with horses, no work is so well done as that which is done cheerfully; secondly, consistency, that in the exhilaration of his spirits, or in his eagerness to secure a bird,

he may not permit a fault to pass unreproved (I do not say *unpunished*) which at a less exciting moment he would have noticed—and that, on the other hand, he may not correct a dog the more harshly, because the shot has been missed, or the game lost; and lastly, the exercise of a little reflection, to enable him to judge what meaning an unreasoning animal is likely to attach to every word and sign, nay to every look.

7. With the coarsest tackle, and worst flies, trout can be taken in unflogged waters, while it requires much science, and the finest gut, to kill persecuted fish. It is the same in shooting. With almost any sporting-dog, game can be killed early in the season, when the birds lie like stones, and the dog can get within a few yards of them; but you will require one highly broken, to obtain many shots when they are wild. Then any incautious approach of the dog, or any noise, would flush the game, and your own experience will tell you that nothing so soon puts birds on the run, and makes them so ready to take flight, as the sound of the human voice, especially now-a-days, when farmers generally prefer the scythe to the sickle, and clean husbandry, large fields, and trim narrow hedges, (affording no shelter from wet) have forced the partridge—a *short-winged* * bird—

---

* Rounded, too, at the extremities—the outer feathers not being the longest—a formation adverse to rapid flight. The extreme outer feather of *young* birds is pointed, and, until late in the season, accompanies soft quills, weak brown beaks, and yellow legs. These (beaks and legs) become grey on maturity, or rather of the bluish hue of London milk—and the quills get white and hard—facts which should be attended to by those who are making a selection for the table. Hold an old and a young bird by their under beaks between your fore-finger and thumb, and you will soon see how little, comparatively, the old beak yields to the weight. This rule applies equally to grouse, the legs of which birds when young are not much feathered, but late in the season it is difficult to determine their age. Yet a knowing hand will find a difference, the old birds' legs will still be the more feathered of the two; and

unwillingly to seek protection (when arrived at maturity) in ready flight rather than in concealment. Even the report of a gun does not so much alarm them as the command, "Toho," or "Down charge," * usually, too, as if to make matters worse, hallooed to the extent of the breaker's lungs. There are anglers who recommend silence as conducive to success, and there are no experienced sportsmen who do not acknowledge its great value in shooting. Rate or beat a dog at one end of a field, and the birds at the other will lift their heads, become uneasy, and be ready to take wing the moment you get near them. "Penn," in his clever maxims on Angling and Chess, observes to this effect, "if you wish to see the fish, do not let him see you;" and with respect to shooting, we may as truly say, "if you wish birds to hear your gun, do not let them hear your voice." Even a loud whistle disturbs them. Mr. O——t of C——e says, a gamekeeper's motto ought to be,—" No whistling

its feet will be more worn and extended. If you spread open the wing of any game bird, you will find the upper part (near the second joint) more or less bare. The less that part is covered with feathers the younger is the bird.

A poulterer once told me that at the end of the season he judged much of the age of birds by the appearance of their heads.

"Ware" sunken eyes, and tainted or discoloured vents—they have been too long out of the kitchen.

* The following facts are strong evidences of the correctness of this assertion. Late in the season far more grouse *than ought to be* are shot by "gunners," to use an American expression,—" true sportsmen" I can hardly term them— who conceal themselves in large stooks of grain, to fire at the birds which come from the hills to feed; and, curious to say, several shots are often obtained before the pack takes wing. The first few reports frequently no more alarm them, than to make the most cautious of the number jump up to look around, when, observing nothing that ought to intimidate them, they recommence feeding. By commencing with the undermost birds, the Americans sometimes shoot in daylight all the Partridges (as they erroneously call them) roosting on a tree; and poachers in this country, by making a similar selection, often kill at night (using diminished charges) several Pheasants before those that are on the topmost branches fly away. A strong breeze much favours the poacher by diminishing the chance of the birds much hearing him.

—no whipping—no noise, when master goes out for sport."

8. These observations lead unavoidably to the inference, that no dog can be considered perfectly broken, that does not make his point when first he feels assured of the presence of game, and remain stationary *where he makes it*, until urged on by you to draw nearer—that does not, as a matter of course, lie down without any word of command the moment you have fired, and afterwards perseveringly seek for the dead bird in the direction you may point out,—and all this without your once having occasion to speak, more than to say in a low voice, "Find," when he gets near the dead bird, as will be hereafter explained. Moreover, it must be obvious that he risks leaving game behind him if he does not hunt every part of a field, and, on the other hand, that he wastes your time and his strength, if he travel twice over the same ground, nay, over any ground which his powers of scent have already reached. Of course, I am now speaking of a dog hunted without a companion to share his labours.

9. You may say, " How is all this, which sounds so well in theory, to be obtained in practice without great severity?" Believe me, with severity it never can be attained. If flogging would make a dog perfect, few would be found unbroken in England or Scotland, and scarcely one in Ireland.

10. Astley's method was to give each horse his preparatory lessons alone, and when there was no noise or anything to divert his attention from his instructor. If the horse was interrupted during the lesson, or his attention in any way withdrawn, he was dismissed for that day. When perfect in certain lessons by himself, he was associated with other horses, whose education

was further advanced. And it was the practice of that great master to reward his horses with slices of carrot or apple when they performed well.

11. Mons. A. Franconi in a similar manner rewards his horses. One evening I was in such a position, at a performance of the *Cirque National de Paris*, that I could clearly see, during the *Lutte des Voltigeurs*, that the broad-backed horse held for the men to jump over was continually coaxed with small slices of carrots to remain stationary, whilst receiving their hard thumps as they sprang upon him. I could not make out why the horse was sniffing and apparently nibbling at the chest of the man standing in front of him with a rein in each hand to keep his tail towards the spring-board, until I remarked that a second man, placed in the rear of the other, every now and then, slily passed his hand under his neighbour's arm to give the horse a small piece of carrot.

12. Astley may give us a useful hint in our far easier task of dog-breaking. We see that he endeavoured by kindness and patience to make the horse thoroughly comprehend the meaning of certain words and signals before he allowed him any companion. So ought you, by what may be termed "initiatory lessons," to make your young dog perfectly understand the meaning of certain words and signs, before you hunt him in the company of another dog—nay, before you hunt him at all; and, in pursuance of Astley's plan, you ought to give these lessons when you are alone with the dog, and his attention is not likely to be withdrawn to other matters. Give them, also, when he is fasting, as his faculties will then be clearer, and he will be more eager to obtain any rewards of biscuit or other food.

13. Be assured, that by a consistent adherence to the simple rules which I will explain, you can obtain the perfection I have described, (8) with more ease and expedition than you probably imagine to be practicable; and, if you will zealously follow my advice, I promise, that, instead of having to give up your shooting in

September, (for I am supposing you to be in England) while you break in your pup, you shall then be able to take him into the field, provided he is tolerably well bred and well disposed, perfectly obedient, and, except that he will not have a well-confirmed, judicious range, almost perfectly made; at least so far made, that he will only commit such faults, as naturally arise from want of experience. Let me remind you also, that the keep of dogs is expensive, and supplies an argument for making them earn their bread by hunting to a *useful* purpose, as soon as they are of an age to work without injury to their constitution. Time, moreover, is valuable to us all, or most of us fancy it is. Surely, then, that system of education is best which imparts the most expeditiously the required degree of knowledge.

CHAPTER II.

INITIATORY LESSONS WITHIN DOORS. SHOOTING PONIES.

14. One Instructor better than two.—15. Age at which Education commences.—In-door breaking for hours, better than Out-door for weeks.—16. To obey all necessary Words of Command and all Signals before shown Game.—17. Unreasonableness of not always giving Initiatory Lessons—leads to Punishment—thence to Blinking.—18. Dog to be *your* constant Companion, not another's.—19, 21, 22. Instruct when alone with him. Initiatory Lessons in his Whistle—in "Dead"—"Toho"—"On"—20. All Commands and Whistling to be given in a low Tone.—23 to 26. Lessons in "Drop"—Head between fore-legs—Setters crouch more than Pointers.—24. Slovenly to employ right arm both for "Drop" and "Toho."—27. Lessons in "Down-charge"—Taught at Pigeon-match—Rewards taken from Hand.—28. Cavalry Horses fed at discharge of Pistol—Same plan pursued with Dogs.—29. Dog unusually timid to be coupled to another.—30. Lessons at Feeding Time, with Checkcords.—31. Obedience of Hounds contrasted with that of most Pointers and Setters.—32. Shooting Ponies—how broken in.—33. Horse's rushing at his Fences cured—Pony anchored.

14. IT is seldom of any advantage to a dog to have more than one instructor. The methods of teaching may be the same; but there will be a difference in the tone of voice and in the manner, that will more or less puzzle the learner, and retard rather than advance his education. If, therefore, you resolve to break in your dog, do it entirely yourself: let no one interfere with you.

15. As a general rule, let his education begin when he is about six or seven months old,* (although I allow

---

* But from his very infancy you ought not to have allowed him to be disobedient. You should have made him know—which he will do nearly intuitively—that a whip can punish him, though he ought never to have *suffered* from it. I have heard of pups only four months old being made quite *au fait* to the preliminary drill here recommended. This early exercise of their intelligence and observation must have benefited them. The questionable point is the unnecessary consumption of the instructor's time.

that some dogs are more precocious than others, and bitches always more forward than dogs,) but it ought to be nearly completed before he is shown a bird (132). A quarter of an hour's daily in-door training—called by the Germans "house-breaking"—for three or four weeks will effect more than a month's constant hunting without preliminary tuition.

16. Never take your young dog out of doors for instruction, until he has learned to know and obey the several words of command which you intend to give him in the field, and is well acquainted with all the signs which you will have occasion to make to him with your arms. These are what may be called the initiatory lessons.

17. Think a moment, and you will see the importance of this preliminary instruction, though rarely imparted. Why should it be imagined, that at the precise moment when a young dog is enraptured with the first sniff of game, he is, by some mysterious unaccountable instinct, to understand the meaning of the word "Toho?" Why should he not conceive it to be a word of encouragement to rush in upon the game, as he probably longs to do; especially if it should be a partridge fluttering before him, in the sagacious endeavour to lure him from her brood, or a hare enticingly cantering off from under his nose? There are breakers who would correct him for not intuitively comprehending and obeying the "Toho," roared out with stentorian lungs; though, it is obvious, the youngster, from having had no previous instruction, could have no better reason for understanding its import, than the watch-dog chained up in yonder farm-yard. Again he hears the word "Toho"—again followed by another licking, accompanied perhaps by the long lecture, "'Ware springing

birds, will you?" The word "Toho" then begins to assume a most awful character; he naturally connects it with the finding of game, and not understanding a syllable of the lecture, lest he should a third time hear it, and get a third drubbing, he judges it most prudent, (unless he is a dog of very high courage) when next aware of the presence of birds, to come in to heel; and thus he commences to be a blinker, thanks to the sagacity and intelligence of his tutor. I do not speak of all professional dog-breakers, far from it. Many are fully sensible that comprehension of orders must necessarily precede all but accidental obedience. I am only thinking of some whom it has been my misfortune to see, and who have many a time made my blood boil at their brutal usage of a fine high-couraged young dog. Men who had a strong arm and hard heart to punish,— but no temper and no head to instruct.

18. So long as you are a bachelor, you can make a companion of your dog, without incurring the danger of his being spoiled by your wife and children; (the more, by-the-bye, he is your own companion and no other person's the better) and it is a fact, though you may smile at the assertion, that all the initiatory lessons can be, and can best be, inculcated in your own breakfast-room.

19. Follow Astley's plan. Let no one be present to distract the dog's attention. Call him to you by the whistle you propose always using in the field. Tie a slight cord a few yards long to his collar. Throw him a small piece of toast or meat, saying, at the time, "Dead, dead." Do this several times, chucking it into different parts of the room, and let him eat what he finds. Then throw a piece (always as you do so saying, "Dead"), and the moment he gets close to it, check

him by jerking the cord, at the same time saying, "Toho," and lifting up your right arm almost perpendicularly. By pressing on the cord with your foot, you can restrain him as long as you please. Do not let him take what you have thrown, until you give him the encouraging word, "On," accompanied by a forward movement of the right arm and hand, somewhat similar to the swing of an under-hand bowler at cricket.

20. Let all your commands be given in a low voice. Consider that in the field, where you are anxious not to alarm the birds unnecessarily, your words must reach your dogs' ears more or less softened by distance, and, if their influence depends on loudness, they will have the least effect at the very moment when you wish them to have the most. For the same reason, in the initiatory lessons, be careful not to whistle loudly.*

21. After a few trials with the checkcord, you will find yourself enabled, without touching it, and merely by using the word "Toho," to prevent his seizing the toast (or meat), until you say "On," or give him the forward signal. When he gets yet more perfect in his lesson, raising your right arm only, without employing your voice, will be sufficient, especially if you have gradually accustomed him to hear you speak less and less loudly. If he draw towards the bread before he has obtained leave, jerk the cord, and *drag him back to the spot from which he stirred.* He is not to quit it until you order him, occupy yourself as you may. Move about, and occasionally go from him, as far as you can, before you give the command "On." This

---

* It may be fancy, but I have imagined that coveys hatched near railway stations have less than other birds regarded the sportsman's whistle.

will make him less unwilling hereafter to continue steady at his point while you are taking a circuit to head him, and so get wild birds between him and your gun, (265, 284.) The signal for his advancing, when you are facing him, is the "beckon" (see 37).

22. At odd times let him take the bread the moment you throw it, that his eagerness to rush forward to seize it may be continued, only to be instantly restrained at your command.

23. Your *left* arm raised perpendicularly, in a similar manner, should make the young dog lie down. Call out "Drop," when so holding up the left hand, and press him down with the other until he assumes a crouching position. If you study beauty of attitude, his fore-legs ought to be extended, and his head rest between them. Make him lie well down, occasionally walking round and round him, gradually increasing the size of the circle—your eyes on his. Do not let him raise himself to a sitting posture. If you do, he will have the greater inclination hereafter to move about: *especially when you want to catch him, in order to chide or correct him.* A halt is all you require for the "Toho," and you would prefer his standing to his point, rather than his lying down,* as you then would run less risk of losing sight of him in cover, heather, or high turnips, &c. Setters, however, naturally crouch so much more than Pointers, that you will often not be able to prevent their "falling" when they are close to game. Indeed, I have heard some sportsmen argue in favour of a dog's dropping, "that it rested him." An advantage, in my

* This is one reason for giving initiatory lessons in the "Toho" before the "Drop." Another is that the dog may acquire the "Toho" before he has run the chance of being cowed in learning the "Drop." If the latter were taught first, he might confound the "Toho" with it.

opinion, in no way commensurate with the inconvenience that often attends the practice.

24. If you are satisfied with teaching him in a slovenly manner, you can employ your right arm both for the "Toho" and "Drop;" but that is not quite correct, for the former is a natural stop, (being the pause to determine exactly where the game is lying, preparatory to rushing in to seize it,) which you prolong by art,* whilst the other is wholly opposed to nature. The one affords him great delight, especially when, from experience, he has well learned its object: the latter is always irksome. Nevertheless, it must be firmly established. It is the triumph of your art. It insures future obedience. But it cannot be effectually taught without creating more or less awe, and it should create awe. It is obvious, therefore, that it must be advantageous to make a distinction between the two signals,—especially with a timid dog,—for he will not then be so likely to blink on seeing you raise your right hand, when he is drawing upon game. Nevertheless, there are breakers so unreasonable as not only to make that one signal, but the one word "Drop" (or rather "Down") answer both for the order to point, and the order to crouch! How can such tuition serve to enlarge a dog's ideas?

25. To perfect him in the "Down," that difficult part of his education,—difficult, because it is unnatural,—practise it in your walks. At very uncertain, unexpected times catch his eye, (having previously stealthily taken hold of the checkcord—a long, light one,) or whistle to call his attention, and then hold up your left

---

* I know of a young man's reading the first edition of this book, and taking it into his head to teach his Terrier to point according to the method just recommended. He succeeded perfectly. Some Terriers have been made very useful for cover shooting.

arm. If he does not *instantly* drop, jerk the checkcord violently, and, as before, drag him back to the exact spot where he should have crouched down. Admit of no compromise. You must have *implicit, unhesitating, instant*, obedience. When you quit him, he must not be allowed to crawl *an inch* after you. If he attempt it, drive a spike into the ground, and attach the end of the checkcord to it, allowing the line to be slack ; then leave him quickly, and on his running after you he will be brought up with a sudden jerk. So much the better: it will slightly alarm him. As before, take him back to the precise place he quitted,—do this invariably, though he may have scarcely moved. There make him again "Drop"—always observing to jerk the cord at the moment you give the command. After a few trials of this tethering, (say less than a dozen) he will be certain to lie down steadily, until you give the proper order or a signal (21), let you run away, or do what you may to excite him to move. One great advantage of frequently repeating this lesson, and thus teaching it *thoroughly*, is, that your dog will hereafter always feel, more or less, in subjection, whenever the cord is fastened to his collar. He must be brought to instantly obey the signal, even at the extreme limit of his beat.

26. Most probably he will not at first rise when he is desired. There is no harm in that,—a due sense of the inutility of non-compliance with the order to "Drop," and a wholesome dread of the attendant penalty, will be advantageous. Go up to him,—pat him,—and lead him for some paces, "making much of him," as they say in the cavalry. Dogs which are over-headstrong and resolute, can only be brought under satisfactory command by this lesson being indelibly implanted,—and I think a master before he allows the keeper to take a

pup into the field to show him game, should insist upon having ocular demonstration that he is perfect in the "Drop."

27. When he is well confirmed in this all-important lesson, obeying implicitly, yet cheerfully, you may, whilst he is lying down, (in order to teach him the "down charge,") go through the motions of loading, on no account permitting him to stir until you give him the forward signal, or say "On." After a few times you may fire off a copper cap, and then a little powder, but be very careful not to alarm him. Until your dog is quite reconciled to the report of a gun, never take him up to any one who may be firing. I have, however, known of puppies being familiarized to the sound, by being at first kept at a considerable distance from the party firing, and then gradually, and by slow degrees brought nearer. This can easily be managed at a rifle or pigeon match, and the companionship of a made-dog would much expedite matters. Whenever, in the lessons, your young dog has behaved steadily and well, give him a reward. Do not throw it to him; let him take it from your hands. It will assist in making him tender-mouthed, and in attaching him to you.

28. In some cavalry regiments in India, the feeding-time is denoted by the firing off of a pistol. This soon changes a young horse's first dread of the report into eager, joyous, expectation. You might, if you did not dislike the trouble, in a similar manner, soon make your pup regard the report of a gun as the gratifying summons to his dinner, but coupled with the understanding that, as a preliminary step, he is to crouch the instant he hears the sound. After a little perseverance you would so well succeed, that you would not be obliged even to raise your hand. If habituated to wait patiently

at the "drop," however hungry he may be, before he is permitted to taste his food, it is reasonable to think he will remain at the "down charge," yet more patiently before he is allowed to "seek dead."

29. If your pupil be unusually timid, and you cannot banish his alarm on hearing the gun, couple him to another dog which has no such foolish fears, and will steadily "down charge." The confidence of the one, will impart confidence to the other. Fear and joy are feelings yet more contagious in animals than in man. It is the visible, joyous animation of the old horses, that so quickly reconciles the cavalry colt to the sound of the " feeding-pistol."

30. A keeper who had several dogs to break, would find the advantage of pursuing the cavalry plan just noticed. Indeed, he might extend it still further, by having his principal in-door drill at feeding-time, and by enforcing, but in minuter details, that kennel discipline which has brought many a pack of hounds to marvellous obedience.* He should place the food in different parts of the yard. He should have a short checkcord on all his pupils; and, after going slowly through the motions of loading, (the dogs having regularly "down-charged" on the report of the gun,) he should call each separately by name, and by signals of the hand send them successively to different, but designated feeding-troughs. He might then call a dog to him, which had commenced eating, and, after a short abstinence, make him go to another trough. He might bring two to his heels and make them change troughs, and so vary the lesson, that, in a short time, with the

* There is often such a similarity in the names of hounds, that a person cannot but be much struck, who for the first time sees them go to their meals, one by one as they are called.

aid of the checkcords, he would have them under such complete command, that they would afterwards give him comparatively but little trouble in the field. As they became more and more submissive, he would gradually retire further and further, so as, at length, to have his orders obeyed, when at a considerable distance from his pupils. The small portion of time these lessons would occupy, compared with their valuable results, should warn him most forcibly not to neglect them.

31. All keepers will acknowledge that, excepting a systematic beat, there is nothing more difficult to teach a Pointer or Setter than to refrain from "pursuing Hare." They will concede that there is a natural tendency in the breed to stand at game; and, as a necessary consequence, they must admit that they would have far more trouble in weaning a young foxhound from the habit, whose every instinct urges him to chase. And yet these keepers may daily see not merely one hound, but a whole pack in the highest condition, full of energy and spirits, drawing a cover alive with Hares, not one of which a single dog will even look at. Should not this fact convince a keeper, that if he is often obliged to speak loudly to the brace of dogs *he calls* broken, there must be something radically wrong in his management? Is he satisfied that he began their education sufficiently early, and that he has been uniformly consistent since its commencement?

32. If you have to break in a shooting pony, you must adopt some such plan as that named in 27 and 28 to make him steady. Your object will be never to alarm him, and gradually to render him fond of the sound of the gun. To effect this, you will keep the pistol, or whatever arms you use, for a long time out of his sight. Commence by burning but little powder, and fire * at some distance from him. Always give him a slice of carrot or apple immediately after he hears the report, and, if you act judiciously and patiently, he will soon love the sound. You may then fire in his presence *(turning your back upon him, as if he were not a party in any way concerned)*, and, by degrees, approach nearer and nearer; but do not go quite into his stall,—that would make him shrink or start, and you wish to banish all nervousness; the least precipitation would undo you; therefore begin in the stable, with only using a copper cap. Need I caution you against firing if near any straw?

33. Confidence being fully established, pursue the same plan when you ride the pony. Again commence with a copper cap, only

---

* It would expedite matters much if the groom did this while you remained near the pony to feed him, or *vice versâ*.

by slow degrees coming to the full charge. As before, always reward him after every discharge, and also at the moment when you pull up and throw the reins on his neck. If he finds he gets slices of carrot when he stands stock-still, he will soon become so anxious to be stationary that you will have to ride with spurs to keep him to his work. By such means you could get him to lead over fences and stand on the other side until you remount. Many years ago I had in Ireland a chestnut which did not belie his colour, for I purchased him far below his value on account of his great impetuosity with hounds. He had a sad habit of rushing at his leaps, but riding him in a smooth snaffle, and often giving him slices of carrot, gradually cured his impatience, and he ultimately became very gentle and pleasant. A naval officer, well known to a friend of mine, finding he could not by other means make his pony stand when the dogs pointed, used, sailor like, to anchor the animal by "heaving overboard" (as he expressed it) a heavy weight to which a line from the curb-bit was attached. The weight was carried in one of the holster pipes,—in the other was invariably stowed away a liberal allowance of "Grog and Prog."

CHAPTER III.

INITIATORY LESSONS CONTINUED. SPANIELS.

34, 35. Initiatory Lessons in "Dead" and "Seek," continued.—36. In Signals to hunt to the "right"—"left"—"forward."—37. In the "Beckon." Woodcock Shooting in America.—38. In looking to you for instructions.—39. In "Care."—40. Always give a reward.—41. In "Up."—saves using Puzzle-peg.—42. Dog to carry Nose high.—43. Initiatory Lesson in "Footing" a Scent.—44. In "Heel." —45. In "Gone" or "Away."—46. In "Fence" or "Ware-fence."—47. "No" a better word than "Ware."—48. Accustomed to couples.—49. Initiatory Lessons in-doors with a Companion—when one "drops" the other to "drop."—50. Makes "Backing" quickly understood.—51. Initiatory Lessons with a Companion in the Fields.—52. Initiatory Lessons save Time—make Dogs fond of hunting.—53. Checkcord described. Wildest Dogs possess most energy.—54. Advantages of Checkcord explained—Spaniels broken in by it.—55. Lad to act as Whipper-in. —56. Retriever that acted as Whipper-in.—57. Jealousy made him act the part. Might be taught to Retriever.—58. Instead of "down charge" coming to "heel." —59. As Puppies kept close to you, not to "self-hunt"—"broke" from hare.— 60. Blacksmith straps Horse's Leg above Hock—Dog's similarly confined—Shot-belt round the necks of wildest.—61. Hunted in Gorse.—62. Age when shown Game. Example of good Spaniels advantageous.—63. Perfected in "Drop"— taught to "seek dead"—to "fetch"—entered at Hedge-rows and lightest Covers. Bells to Collars.—64. To hunt farther side of Hedge.—65. How Sportsmen may aid Keeper. In note, Covers for Pheasants. Hints to Tyros on Shooting and Loading (See *Appendix*).—66. Experienced Spaniels slacken Pace on Game.— 67. Difficult to work young ones in Silence.—68. Spaniels that Pointed.— 69.—Game first accustomed to, most liked.—70. Principal requisites in Spaniels. —71. The signal "to point with finger."—72. Following Cockers a Young Man's work.—73. Education differs in different Teams.—74. One and a half couple of large Spaniels sufficient. One of the Team to retrieve.—75. Clumbers procuring more Shots in Turnips than Pointers.—76. Lord P——n's highly-broken Team.—77. Of small Cockers three couple a Team. What constitutes Perfection.—78. Retriever with Team. Duke of Newcastle's Keepers.—79. Some Teams allowed to hunt Flick.—80. Rabbits shot to a Team in Gorse. Shooting to Beagles described—81. Markers necessary with wild Spaniels.—82. Cover beat with wildest Dogs before shot in. Woodcocks.—83. Old Sportsmen prefer mute Spaniels.—84. Babblers best in some Countries. Cock-shooting in Albania. —85. Hog and deer in ditto.—86. Glorious month's sport in the Morea.— 87. Handy old Setters capital in light cover. Attention necessary when first entered.—88. C——e's Pointers as good in cover as on the stubble. 89. Pointer that ran to opposite side of Thicket to flush Game towards Gun.—90. Water Spaniels, how broken.—91. Shepherd's Forward Signal best for Water Retrievers.—92. Wild Fowl reconnoitred with Telescope.—93. Qualities required in Water Retriever. In note, Poachers in Snow. Beast or man of one uniform colour easily detected.—94. Ducks emit a tolerable scent—"Flint" and Mr. C——e's Setter.—95. Steady Spaniels in Rice Lakes.

34. WHEN your young dog is tolerably well advanced in the lessons which you have been advised to practise,

hide a piece of bread or biscuit. Say "Dead, dead." Call him to you. (44.) Let him remain by you for nearly a minute or two. Then say " Find," or " Seek." Accompany him in his search. By your actions and gestures make him fancy you are yourself looking about for something, for dogs are observing, one might say, imitative, creatures.* Stoop and move your right hand to and fro near the ground. Contrive that he shall come upon the bread, and reward him by permitting him to eat it.

35. After a little time (a few days I mean), he will show the greatest eagerness on your saying, at any unexpected moment, "Dead." He will connect the word with the idea that there is something very desirable concealed near him, and he will be all impatience to be off and find it; *but make him first come to you,* (for reason, see 269.)—Keep him half a minute.—Then say " Find," and, without your accompanying him, he will search for what you have previously hidden. Always let him be encouraged to perseverance by discovering something acceptable.

36. Unseen by him, place the rewards (one at a time), in different parts of the room,—under the rug or carpet, and more frequently on a chair, a table, or a low shelf. He will be at a loss in what part of the room to search. Assist him by a motion of your arm and hand. A wave of the right arm and hand to the right, will soon show him that he is to hunt to the right, as he will find there. The corresponding wave of the left hand and arm to the left, will explain to him, that he is to make

---

* "Imitative creatures!" who can doubt it? If you make an old dog perform a trick several times in the sight of a young one who is watching the proceedings, you will be surprised to see how quickly the young one will learn the trick, especially if he has seen that the old dog was always rewarded for his obedience.

a cast to the left. The underhand bowler's swing of the right hand and arm, will show that he is to hunt in a forward direction.* Your occasionally throwing the delicacy (in the direction you wish him to take), whilst waving your hand, will aid in making him comprehend the signal. You may have noticed how well, by watching the action of a boy's arm, his little cur judges towards what point to run for the expected stone.

37. When the hidden object is near you, but between you and the dog, make him come towards you to seek for it, beckoning him with your right hand. When he is at a distance at the "Drop," if you are accustomed to recompense him for good behaviour, you can employ this signal to make him rise and run towards you for his reward, (and, according to my judgment, he should always join you after the "down charge," 271). By these means you will thus familiarise him with a very useful signal; for that signal will cause him to approach you in the field, when you have made a circuit to head him at his point (knowing that birds will then be lying somewhere between you and him), and want him to draw nearer to the birds and you, to show you exactly where they are. This some may call a superfluous refinement, but I hope *you* will consider it a very killing accomplishment, and being easily taught, it were a pity to neglect it. When a Setter is employed in cockshooting, the advantage of using this signal is very

---

* Obedience to all such signals will hereafter be taught out of doors at gradually increased distances: and to confirm him in the habit of sniffing high in the air (41) for whatever you may then hide, put the bread or meat on a stick or bush, but never in a hedge (175). With the view to his some day retrieving, as instanced in 277, it will be your aim to get him not to seek immediately, but to watch your signals, until by obeying them you will have placed him close to where the object lies, at which precise moment you will say energetically "Find," and cease making any further signs.

apparent. While the dog is steadily pointing, it enables the sportsman to look for a favourable opening, and, when he has posted himself to his satisfaction, to sign to the Setter (or if out of sight tell him), to advance and flush the bird: when, should the sportsman have selected his position with judgment, he will generally get a shot. I have seen this method very successfully adopted in America, where the forests are usually so dense that cocks are only found on the outskirts in the underwood.

38. After a little time he will regularly look to you for directions. Encourage him to do so; it will make him hereafter, when he is in the field, desirous of hunting under your eye, and induce him to look to you, in a similar manner, for instructions in what direction he is to search for game. Observe how a child watches its mother's eye; so will a dog watch yours, when he becomes interested in your movements, and finds that you frequently notice him.

39. Occasionally, when he approaches any of the spots where the bread lies hidden, say "Care," and slightly raise your right hand. He will quickly consider this word, or signal, as an intimation that he is near the object of his search.

40. Never deceive him in any of these words and signs, and never disappoint him of the expected reward. Praise and caress him for good conduct; rate him for bad. Make it a rule throughout the whole course of his education, out of doors as fully as within, to act upon this system. You will find that caresses and substantial rewards are far greater incentives to exertion than any fears of punishment.

41. Your pup having become a tolerable proficient in these lessons, you may beneficially extend them by

employing the word "Up," as a command that he is to sniff high in the air to find the hidden bread or meat, lying, say on a shelf, or on the back of a sofa. He will, comparatively speaking, be some time in acquiring a knowledge of the meaning of the word, and many would probably term it an over-refinement in canine education; but I must own I think you will act judiciously, if you teach it perfectly in the initiatory lessons; for the word "Up," if well understood, will frequently save your putting on the puzzle-peg. For this you would be obliged to employ, should your dog prove disobedient and be acquiring the execrable habit of "raking" as it is termed, instead of searching for the delicious effluvia with his nose carried high in the air. Colonel Hawker much recommends the puzzle-peg, but I confess I would not fetter the dog by using it, unless compelled by his hereditary propensity to hunt-foot.

42. Whenever birds can be sought for in the wind, the dog should thus hunt the field (and the higher he carries his nose the better), for, independently of the far greater chance of finding them, they will allow the dog to come much nearer, than when he approaches them by the foot: but of this more anon. (185, 186.)

43. Setters and Pointers naturally hunt with their noses sufficiently close to the ground,—they want elevating rather than depressing. Notwithstanding, you will do well to show your pupil a few times out of doors, how to work out a scent, by dragging a piece of bread unperceived by him *down wind* through grass, and then letting him "foot" it out. Try him for a few yards at first; you can gradually increase the length of the drag. You must not, however, practise this initiatory lesson too frequently, lest you give him the wretched custom of pottering.

OLD-FASHIONED ENGLISH SETTER,—RETRIEVERS, ONE A CROSS WITH BLOODHOUND.

Heel.—"A backward low wave of the right hand."– Par. 44.

44. The word "Heel," and a backward low wave of the right hand and arm to the rear, (the reverse of the underhand cricket-bowler's swing,) will, after a few times, bring the dog close behind you. Keep him there a while and pat him, but do not otherwise reward him. The object of the order was to make him instantly give up hunting, and come to your heels. This signal cannot be substituted for the "beckon." The one is an order always obeyed with reluctance (being a command to leave off hunting), whereas the "beckon" is merely an instruction in what direction to beat, and will be attended to with delight. The signal "heel," however, when given immediately after loading, is an exception; for the instructions about "Dead," in xi. of paragraph 171, will show that without your speaking, it may be made to impart the gratifying intelligence of your having killed. See also 277.

45. To teach him to attach a meaning to the word "Gone," or "Away," or "Flown,"* (select which you will, but do not ring the changes,) you may now rub a piece of meat (if you have no one but your servant to scold you) in some place where the dog is accustomed frequently to find, and when he is sniffing at the place say "Gone," or "Away." This he will, after some trials, perceive to be an intimation that it is of no use to continue hunting for it.

46. You will greatly facilitate his acquiring the meaning of the command "Fence," or "Ware fence," if, from time to time, as he is quitting the room through the open door or garden window, you restrain him by calling out that word.

---

* The least comprehensive and logical of the expressions, yet one often used. A dog being no critical grammarian, understands it to apply to "fur" as well as "feather."

47. Whenever, indeed, you wish him to desist from doing anything, call out " Ware," (pronounced " War "), as it will expedite his hereafter understanding the terms, " Ware sheep," " Ware chase," and " Ware lark." The last expression to be used when he is wasting his time upon the scent of anything but game—a fault best cured by plenty of birds being killed to him. However, the simple word "No," omitting " Chase" or "Fence," might be substituted advantageously for "Ware." All you want him to do is to desist from a wrong action. That sharp sound,—and when necessary it can be clearly thundered out,—cannot be misunderstood.

48. That your young dog may not hereafter resist the couples, yoke him occasionally to a stronger dog, and for the sake of peace, and in the name of all that is gallant, let it be to the one of the other sex who appears to be the greatest favourite.

49. When he is thus far advanced in his education, and tolerably obedient, which he will soon become if you are consistent, and *patient, yet strict,* you can, in further pursuance of Astley's plan, associate him in his lessons with a companion. Should you be breaking in another youngster, (though one at a time you will probably find quite enough, especially if it be your laudable wish to give him hereafter a well-confirmed scientific range,) they can now be brought together for instruction. You must expect to witness the same jealousy which they would exhibit on the stubble. Both will be anxious to hunt for the bread, and in restraining them alternately from so doing, you exact the obedience which you will require hereafter in the field, when in their natural eagerness they will endeavour, unless you properly control them, to take the point of birds from one another; or, in their rivalry,

run over the taint of a wounded bird, instead of collectedly and perseveringly working out the scent. You can throw a bit of toast and make them "Toho" it, and then let the dog you name take it. In the same way you can let each alternately search for a hidden piece, after both have come up to you, on your saying "Dead." I would also advise you to accustom each dog to "drop," without any command from you, the moment he sees that the other is down.

50. Those lessons will almost ensure their hereafter instantly obeying, and nearly instantly comprehending the object of the signal to "back" any dog which may be pointing game.

51. When you take out two youngsters for exercise, while they are romping about, suddenly call one into "heel." After a time again send him off on his gambols. Whistle to catch the eye of the other, and signal to him to join you. By working them thus alternately, while they are fresh and full of spirits, you will habituate them to implicit obedience. When the birds are wild, and you are anxious to send a basket of game to a friend, it is very satisfactory to be able merely by a sign, without uttering a word, to bring the other dogs into "heel," leaving the ground to the careful favourite. Teach the present lesson well, and you go far towards attaining the desired result.

52. I trust you will not object to the minutiæ of these initiatory lessons, and fancy you have not time to attend to them. By teaching them well, you will gain time,— much time,—and the time that is of most value to you as a sportsman; for when your dog is regularly hunting to your gun, his every faculty ought to be solely devoted to finding birds, and his undisturbed intellects exclusively given to aid you in bagging them, instead of

being bewildered by an endeavour to comprehend novel signals or words of command. I put it to you as a sportsman, whether he will not have the more delight and ardour in hunting, the more he feels that he understands your instructions? and, further, I ask you, whether he will not be the more sensitively alive to the faintest indication of a haunt, and more readily follow it up to a sure find, if he be unembarrassed by any anxiety to make out what you mean, and be in no way alarmed at the consequences of not almost instinctively understanding your wishes?

53. In all these lessons, and those which follow in the field, the checkcord will wonderfully assist you

THE CHECK—'HOLD HARD!'

Indeed, it may be regarded as the instructor's right hand. It can be employed so mildly as not to intimidate the most gentle, and it can, without the aid of any whip, be used with such severity, or, I should rather say, perseverance, as to conquer the most wild and headstrong, and these are sure to be dogs of the greatest travel and endurance. The cord may be from ten to twenty-five * yards long, according to the animal's disposition, and may be gradually shortened as he gets more and more under command. Even when it is first employed you can put on a shorter cord, if you perceive that he is becoming tired. In thick stubble, especially if cut with a sickle, the drag will be greater, far greater than when the cord glides over heather. The cord may be of the thickness of what some call strong lay-cord, but made of twelve threads. Sailors would know it by the name of log-line or cod-line. To save the end from fraying it can be whipped with thread, which is better than tying a knot because it is thus less likely to become entangled.

55. Hunted with such a cord, the most indomitable dog, when he is *perfectly obedient to the " drop,"* is nearly as amenable to command, as if the end of the line were in the breaker's hand. By no other means can

SPANIELS

be *quickly* broken in. The general object of the trainer is to restrain them from ranging at a distance likely to spring game out of gun-shot, and to make them perfect to the "down charge." If one of these high-spirited animals will not range close when called to by whistle

---

* With a resolute, reckless, dashing dog you may advantageously employ a *thinner* cord of double that length,—whereas, the shortest line will sometimes prevent a timid animal from ranging freely. By-the-bye, the thinner the cord the more readily does it become entangled,—as a rule, a checkcord cannot be too firmly twisted,—a soft one quickly gets knotted and troublesome. (See note to 262.)

or name, the breaker gets hold of the cord and jerks it; this makes the dog come in a few paces; another jerk or two makes him approach closer, and then the breaker, by himself retiring with his face towards the spaniel, calling out his name (or whistling), and occasionally jerking the cord, makes him quite submissive, and more disposed to obey on future occasions.

55. In training a large team it is of much advantage to the keeper to have a lad to rate, and, when necessary, give the skirters a taste of the lash, in short, to act as whipper-in. The keeper need not then carry a whip, or at least often use it, which will make his spaniels all the more willing to hunt close to him.

56. Lord A——r's head gamekeeper was singularly aided :—he possessed a four-legged whipper-in. A few years ago while Mr. D—s (M.P. for a South Eastern County) was with a shooting party at his Lordship's, the keeper brought into the field a brace of powerful retrievers, and a team of spaniels, among which were two that had never been shot over. On the first pheasant being killed, all the old spaniels dropped to shot, but one of the young ones rushed forward and mouthed the bird. The person who had fired ran on to save it, but the keeper called aloud, and requested him not to move. The man then made a signal to one of the retrievers to go. He did so instantly, but, instead of meddling with the bird, he seized the spaniel, lifted him up, and shook him well. The moment the pup could escape, he came howling to the "heels" of the keeper, and lay down among his companions. The keeper then confessed that a couple of the spaniels had never been shot to,—but he confidently assured the sportsmen, they would see before the day was over, that the pups behaved fully as steadily as the old dogs, and explained to the

A FOUR-LEGGED WHIPPER-IN.—Par. 56.

party, how the retriever did all the disagreeable work, and indeed, nearly relieved him of every trouble in breaking in the youngsters. On the next few shots this novel schoolmaster was again deputed to show his pupils that he would not allow his special duties as a retriever to be interfered with. Both the young dogs, having been thus well chastised, became more careful,—made only partial rushes to the front, when a recollection of their punishment, and a dread of their four-footed tutor brought them slinking back to their older companions. As the keeper had averred, they soon learned their lesson completely,—gave up all thoughts of chasing after shot, and quietly crouched down with the other dogs.

57. I can easily imagine that it was a feeling of jealousy, which first prompted the retriever to thrash some spaniel who was endeavouring to carry off a bird, and that the clever keeper encouraged him in doing so, instantly perceiving the value of such assistance. It is worth a consideration whether it would not be advisable to train the retriever employed with a team to give this assistance. A dog of a quarrelsome disposition could be taught, by your urging him, to seize any spaniel who might be mouthing a bird, in the same manner you would set on a young terrier to fly at a rat.

58. Doubtless it is the *highest* training to teach a team to "down-charge," but most breakers make their spaniels come into " heel," or rather gather close around them, (by the word "round") whenever a gun is discharged. This plan, though so injudicious in the case of pointers or setters, is but little objectionable in the case of spaniels, for spaniels in their small sweep inwards, are not likely to spring game while the guns are unloaded. It certainly possesses this merit, that it is

readily taught to puppies, (with the aid of a whipper-in) by the trainer's giving them some delicacy on their rejoining him. It may be urged, too, that the method much removes any necessity for noise in calling to a dog,—whereas, with a team trained to the "down-charge," however highly broken, it will occasionally happen that the keeper (or assistant) has to rate some excited skirter for not instantly "dropping." Moreover, in thick cover an infraction of the irksome rule to "down charge" may sometimes escape detection, which might lead to future acts of insubordination. The lamented Prince Albert's team of Clumbers "down-charge," but the greatest attention could be given, and was given to them. They were admirably broken, and I might add, were shot over by a first-rate hand.

59. When exercising young spaniels it is a good plan to habituate them, even as puppies, never to stray further from you than about twenty yards. With them, even more than with other kinds of dogs trained for the gun, great pains should be taken to prevent their having the opportunity of "self-hunting." If it is wished to break from hare, the method to be followed is mentioned in 334, &c., for with spaniels as with setters (or pointers) it is always advisable to drag them back to the spot from which they started in pursuit.

60. Occasionally you may see a country blacksmith, when preparing to shoe the hind-legs of a cart-horse that appears disposed to make a disagreeable use of his heels, twist the long hair at the end of his tail,—raise the foot that is to be shod,—pass the twisted hair round the leg immediately above the hock, and by these means press the tendon close to the bone. The tail assists in retaining the leg in position, and thus for the time the limb is rendered powerless. Acting much upon this

coercive principle, but discarding the aid of the tail, some breakers *slightly* confine a hind-leg of their most unruly spaniels with a soft bandage, shifting it from one leg to the other about every hour. Possibly a loop of vulcanized india-rubber, being elastic, would best answer the purpose. Restrained in this manner a dog is less likely to tumble about, and become injured, than if one of his fore-legs had been passed through his collar. Other breakers when hunting many couples together, fasten a belt with a few pounds of shot round the necks of the wildest. But the sooner such adjuncts to discipline can be safely discarded the better; for "brushing" a close cover is severe work. Gorse is the most trying. Its prickles are so numerous and fine, that the ears and eyes of every spaniel hunted in it ought to be separately examined on returning home, and well bathed in warm water. Their eyes are peculiarly liable to be injured by dust and gravel from their hunting so close to the ground.

61. To give young spaniels sufficient courage to face the most entangled cover, a judicious trainer will occasionally introduce them to thick brakes, or gorse, early in the morning, or in the evening, when the noise of his approach will have made the pheasants feeding in the neighbourhood, run far into it for shelter. The effluvia of the birds will then so excite the young dogs, especially if cheered with good companionship, (which always creates emulation,) that they will utterly disregard the pricks and scratches of the strongest furze.

62. If the time of year will permit it, they should be shown game when about nine or ten months old. At a more advanced age they would be less amenable to control. Happily the example of a riotous pup will not be so detrimental to the discipline of the rest of the team, as the example of an ill-conducted companion would be

to a pointer (or setter), for the influence of thoroughly steady spaniels makes the pup curtail his range sooner than might be expected. Finding that he is not followed by his associates he soon rejoins them.

63. A judicious breaker will regard perfection in the " drop" (23 to 26) as the main-spring of his educational system. He will teach his young spaniels to "seek dead," (34, 35, 43) where directed by signs of the hand. He will instruct them in "fetching," (109, 107, &c.) with the view to some of them hereafter retrieving. He will accustom them to hunt hedge-rows, and light open copses,—because always under his eye,—before taking them into closer cover. Nor until they are under some command, and well weaned from noticing vermin and small birds, will he allow them to enter gorse or strong thickets,—and then he will never neglect (though probably he will have used them before) to attach bells of *different sounds* to the collars of his several pupils (one to each), so that his ear may at all times detect any truant straying beyond bounds, and thus enable him to rate the delinquent by name. In this manner, he establishes the useful feeling elsewhere spoken of (383), that whether he be within or out of sight, he is equally aware of every impropriety that is committed.

64. Young spaniels, when they have been steadily broken in not to hunt too far ahead on the instructor's side of the hedge, may be permitted to beat on the other;—and this when only one person is shooting, is generally their most useful position, for they are thus more likely to drive the game towards the gun.

65. If a keeper is hunting the team, while you and a friend are beating narrow belts or strips of wood,* should

---

* The printer finds this note on covers, shooting, and loading, so long that he will place it in an Appendix.

you and he be placed, as is usual, on the outside, a little ahead of the keeper (one to his right, the other to his left), you would much aid him in preventing the young spaniels from ranging wildly, were you to turn your face towards him whenever you saw any of them getting too far in advance, for they will watch the guns as much as they will him. They should never range further than thirty yards from the gun.

66. Among spaniels the great advantage of age and experience is more apparent than in partridge-dogs. A young spaniel cannot keep to a pheasant's tail like an old one. He may push the bird for forty or fifty yards if judiciously managed. After that he is almost sure from impatience, either to lose it, or rush in and flush out of shot, whereas an old cocker, who has had much game shot over him, is frequently knowing enough to slacken his pace, instead of increasing it, when he first touches on birds, apparently quite sensible that he ought to give the gun time to approach, before he presses to a flush.

67. Even good spaniels, however well bred, if they have not had great experience, generally road too fast. Undeniably they are difficult animals to educate, and it requires much watchfulness, perseverance, and attention at an early age, so to break in a team of young ones that they shall keep within gun range, without your being compelled to halloo or whistle to them. But some few are yet more highly trained.

68. Mr. N——n, when in France, had a lively, intelligent, liver and white cocker, which would work busily all day long within gun-shot; and which possessed the singular accomplishment of steadily pointing all game that lay well, and of not rushing in until the sportsman had come close to him. But this is a case of

high breaking more curious than useful, for spaniels are essentially *springers*, not *pointers*, and the little animal must frequently have been lost sight-of in cover. The Messrs. W——e, alluded to in 551, had also a cocker that regularly pointed. Our grandfathers used to apply the term springers solely to large spaniels,—never to the Duke of Marlborough's small breed, which was greatly prized.

69. A dog is generally most attached to that description of sport, and soonest recognises the scent of that game, to which he has principally been accustomed in youth. He will through life hunt most diligently where he first had the delight of often finding. The utility therefore is obvious of introducing spaniels at an early age to close covers and hedge-rows, and setters and pointers to heather and stubble.

70. In spaniels, feathered sterns and long ears are much admired, but obviously the latter must suffer in thick underwood. The chief requisite in all kinds of spaniels, is, that they be good finders, and have noses so true that they will never overrun a scent. Should they do so when footing an old cock pheasant, the chances are, that he will double back on the exact line by which he came. They should be high-mettled,—as regardless of the severest weather as of the most punishing cover, and ever ready to spring into the closest thicket the moment a pointed finger gives the command.

71. A comprehension of the signal made by the finger, (which is far neater than the raising of the hand described in 34, but not so quickly understood) might with advantage be imparted to all dogs trained for the gun, in order to make them hunt close *exactly* where directed. It is usually taught by pointing with the forefinger of the right hand to pieces of biscuit, previously

concealed, near easily recognised tufts of grass, weeds, &c. It is beautiful to see how correctly, promptly, yet quietly, some spaniels will work in every direction thus indicated.

72. Breasting a strong cover with cockers, is more suited to young, than to old men. The gun must follow rapidly, and stick close when a dog is on the road of feather. A shot will then infallibly be obtained, if a good dog be at work; for the more closely a bird is pressed, the hotter gets the scent. If a pheasant found in thick cover on marshy ground near water,—a locality they much like in hot weather,—is not closely pushed, he will so twist, and turn, and double upon old tracks, that none but the most experienced dogs will be able to stick to him.

73. The preceding observations respecting spaniels apply to all descriptions employed on land-service, whether of the strong kind, the Sussex breed and the Clumber, or the smallest cockers, Blenheims and King Charles'.* But whether they are to be trained not to hunt flick,† (the most difficult part of their tuition, and in which there is generally most failure), and whether they shall be bred to give tongue, or run mute, will depend much upon the nature of the country to be hunted, and yet more upon the taste of the proprietor.

---

* These fetch immense *fancy* prices when well shaped,—black and tan, without a single white hair, and long eared. But this breed is nearly useless to the sportsman, whereas the Blenheim is a lively diligent little fellow in light cover, and from his diminutive size threads his way through low thick brushwood more readily than might at first be imagined, being incited to great perseverance by a most enthusiastic enjoyment of the scent. In strong high turnips, he is employed with much advantage to spring the partridge. He creeps under, where a larger dog would be constantly jumping.

† For the benefit of those who have the good fortune, or the bad fortune, as the case may be, of always living within the sound of Bow bells, "Flick," be it observed, is a synonym for "Fur," thereby meaning Hare, or Rabbit.

No fixed rules can be given for a sport that varies so much as cover-shooting.

74. Of the large kind, most sportsmen will think a couple and a half a sufficient number to hunt at a time. Certainly one of them should retrieve: and they ought to be well broken in not to notice flick. These dogs are most esteemed when they run mute. If they do, they must be hunted with bells in very thick cover; but the less bells are employed the better, for the tinkling sound, in a greater or smaller degree, annoys all game. Such dogs, when good, are very valuable.

75. I once shot over a team of Clumber spaniels belonging to Mr. D——z. The breed (the Duke of Newcastle's, taking their name from one of his seats), are mostly white with a little lemon colour, have large sensible heads, thick, short legs, silky coats, carry their sterns low, and hunt perfectly mute. The team kept within twenty or twenty-five yards of the keeper, were trained to acknowledge Rabbits, as well as all kinds of game; and in the country Mr. D——z was then shooting over afforded capital sport. One of the spaniels was taught to retrieve. He would follow to any distance, and seldom failed to bring. A regular retriever was, however, generally taken out with them. Mr. D——z told me that they required very judicious management, and encouragement rather than severity, as undue whipping soon made them timid. They are of a delicate constitution. He rather surprised me by saying that his spaniels from working quietly and ranging close, (therefore, alarming the birds less,) procured him far more shots in turnips than his pointers; and he had three that looked of the right sort. He explained matters, however, by telling me, that it was his practice to make a circuit round the outskirts of a turnip or potato field before hunting the inner parts. This of course greatly tended to prevent the birds breaking (401). A juvenile sportsman would rejoice in the services of the spaniels, for many a rabbit would they procure for him without the aid of powder and shot.

76. When Colonel M——, who died in Syria, was stationed with his troop of Horse Artillery at Pontefract, he was asked to shoot partridges at Lord P——n's seat in Yorkshire. On meeting the gamekeeper, according to appointment, he found him surrounded by a team of Clumber spaniels. Colonel M——, in some surprise at seeing no setters or pointers, remarked that he had expected some *partridge* shooting. "I know it," answered the man, "and I hope to show you some sport." To the inquiry why one of the spaniels was muzzled, the keeper said that his master had threatened to shoot it should it again give tongue, and, as it possessed a par-

CLUMBERS.

"All the Clumbers dropped instantly."—Par. 76.

ticularly fine nose, he (the keeper) was anxious not to lose it. They walked on, and soon the man told M—— to be prepared, as the spaniels were feathering. A covey rose. The Colonel, who was a good shot, killed right and left. All the Clumbers dropped instantly. When he was reloading, the keeper begged him to say which of the dogs should retrieve the game. M—— pointed to a broad-headed dog lying in the middle, when the keeper directed by name the spaniel so favoured to be off. It quickly fetched one of the birds. The keeper then asked M—— to choose some other dog to bring the remaining bird—a runner. He did so, and the animal he selected to act as retriever, performed the duty very cleverly; the rest of the team remaining quite still, until its return.

The Colonel had capital sport, killing nearly twenty brace, and the dogs behaved beautifully throughout the day. When afterwards relating the circumstances, he observed that, although an old sportsman, he had seldom been so gratified, as it was a novel scene to him, who had not been accustomed to shoot over spaniels.

77. Of small cockers, three couples appear ample to form a team. Some teams of small springers greatly exceed this number, and many sportsmen shoot over more than a couple and a half of the larger spaniels; but it is a question whether, in the generality of cases, the gun would not benefit by the number being diminished rather than increased. The smaller in number the team, the greater is the necessity that none of them should stick too close to "heel." The difficulty is to make them hunt far enough, and yet not too far. At least one of the number should retrieve well. If they give tongue, it ought to be in an intelligible manner; softly, when they first come on the haunt of a cock, but making the cover ring again with their joyous melody, when once the bird is flushed. A first-rate cocker will never deceive by opening upon an old haunt, nor yet find the gun unprepared by delaying to give due warning before he flushes the bird. When cocks are abundant, some teams are broken, not only to avoid flick, but actually not to notice a pheasant, or anything beside woodcock. Hardly any price would tempt a real lover

of cock-shooting, in a cocking country, to part with such a team. Hawker terms the sport, "the fox-hunting of shooting." Some sportsmen kill water-hens to young spaniels to practise them in forcing their way through entangled covers, and get them well in hand and steady against the all-important cocking season.

78. When a regular retriever can be constantly employed with spaniels, of course it will be unnecessary to make any of them fetch game, (certainly never to lift any thing which falls out of bounds), though all the team should be taught to "seek dead." This is the plan pursued by the Duke of Newcastle's keepers, and obviously it is the soundest and easiest practice, for it must always be more or less difficult to make a spaniel keep within his usual hunting limits, who is occasionally encouraged to pursue wounded game, at his best pace, to a considerable distance.

79. Other teams are broken no more than to keep within range, being allowed to hunt all kinds of game, and also rabbits; they, however, are restricted from pursuing wounded flick further than fifty or sixty yards. Where rabbits are abundant, and outlying, a team thus broken affords lively sport,—nothing escapes them.

80. In the large woods that traverse parts of Kent and Sussex, a kind of hunting-shooting is followed, that affords more fun, where there are plenty of rabbits and but few burrows, than might at first be imagined. The dogs employed are the smallest beagles that can be obtained. The little creatures stick to a hare, rabbit, or wounded pheasant with greater pertinacity than most spaniels, probably because they (the beagles) are slower, and hunt so low. Three or four couples make most animating music in the woodlands, and procure many shots, but they awfully disturb game. Mr. D——z has gorse covers through which openings or rides are cut. He shoots rabbits in them to a team of beagles trained not to notice hare. The burrows are ferreted the preceding day, and regularly stopped. The sport is excellent and most animating. Plenty of snap shots. An old buck rabbit once or twice hunted becomes extremely cunning. He is soon on the move, and will work round beyond the dogs, so as to double back upon the ground already hunted.

WILD SPANIELS.—Par. 81

81. Wild spaniels, though they may show you most cock, will get you fewest shots, unless you have well-placed markers. There are sportsmen who like to take out one steady dog to range close to them, and a couple of wild ones to hunt on the flanks, one on each side, expressly that the latter may put up birds for the markers to take note of.

82. Mr. O——n, who is devoted to shooting, acts upon this system, but upon a more enlarged scale. Having previously posted his markers, he has each cover, immediately before he shoots it, well hunted by the wildest of the dogs: he then takes a steady animal to the several spots pointed out, and is thus enabled to kill annually thrice as many cock as any other man in the country. The aptness of this bird, when a second time flushed, to return (397) to its old haunt, and when again put up to take wing in the direction of its first flight, much tends to its destruction.

83. An old sportsman knows *mute* spaniels to be most killing; a young one may prefer those which give tongue, (if true from the beginning owning nothing but game,) because, though undeniably greater disturbers of a cover, they are more cheerful and animating. The superiority of the former is, however, apparent on a still calm day, when the least noise will make the game steal away long before the gun gets within shot. But it is not so in all countries.

84. Wild as is the woodcock with us after it has recovered from its fatiguing migratory flight, and been a few times disturbed, there is not, perhaps, naturally, so tame a game-bird, and one more difficult to flush in close cover where rarely alarmed. Officers quartered at Corfu frequently cross in the morning to the Albanian coast,—a two hours' sail or pull,—and return the same evening, having bagged from fifty to sixty couples to half-a-dozen good guns. Their boat is directed to meet them at some head-land, towards which they shoot. An attendant to carry the game, and a relay of ammunition, &c., is told off to each sportsman, and *he* of the party who best knows the country, is chosen captain for the day, and walks in the centre of the line, the rest conforming to his movements. There is generally an agreement to halt for a minute, but not a second more, to allow a man to look for any cock he may have knocked over; therefore the possessor of a first-rate retriever is an

E

envied character. The strength and density of the bush occasionally there encountered, is more than we in England can imagine: and in such situations, experience has shown the sportsmen the superiority of spaniels which give tongue. On hearing the warning cheerful music, the line halts for a few seconds, as, notwithstanding all the noise, some little time may pass before the cock is sprung, for he is frequently so protected by a wall of impervious thicket, (though sure to have a clear opening overhead for unimpeded flight) that the keenest dogs cannot immediately get at him.

85. Although the country abounds with deer and boar, it is almost needless to observe, that the cock-shooters are too noisy a party often to bag such noble game, unless some ambitious and bold man (for being alone he risks having a long barrel covertly pointed at him) take up a favourable position far in advance. Captain Best, a fellow-student of mine, about a dozen years ago, gives a spirited account of this shooting, in his entertaining book, entitled "Excursions in Albania."

86. In the northern part of the Morea, about twenty-five miles from Patras (near Ali Tchelepi, a dilapidated monastery inhabited by only three monks—near Monolada, and Pera Metochi), Mr. O——n and Captain B——y, between the 14th of January, 1843, and the 11th of the following month (both days inclusive), killed 862 woodcocks, 11 hares, 11 duck, and 11 snipe. Not bad sport!

87. In very thick covers it is obvious, the height of setters being greatly against them, that spaniels are far preferable: but in light covers, and when the leaves are off the trees, *handy* old setters (if white, all the better) that will readily confine themselves to a restricted range, and will flush their game when ordered (IV. and VII. of 141 and 284) afford quite as much sport, if not more. Setters do not, to the same degree, alarm birds; and there is, also, this advantage, that they can be employed on *all* occasions, excepting in low gorse or the closest thickets, whereas spaniels, from their contracted "beat," are nearly useless in the open when game is scarce. You will be prepared, when first you hunt a setter in cover, to sacrifice much of your sport. There must be noise; for it is essential to make him at once thoroughly understand the very different "beat" required of him, and this can only be effected by constantly checking and rating him, whenever he rages beyond the prescribed

limits. He should hunt slowly and carefully to the right and left, and never be much in advance of the guns. In a short time he will comprehend matters, if you are so forbearing and judicious as invariably to call him away from every point made the least out of bounds. A less severe test of your consistency will not suffice. The few first days will either make or mar him as a cover-dog. You must naturally expect that hunting him much in cover, will injure his range in the open, and make him too fond of hedge-rows.

88. But there is a man in Yorkshire, who will not willingly admit this. C——e, Sir George A——e's gamekeeper,—and a good one he is,—for he has a particularly difficult country to protect, one intersected with "rights of way" in every direction,—makes his pointers as freely hunt the cover as the open. You never lose them, for they are sure to make their appearance when they think they have given you ample time to go to them if you choose. This cover work does not the least unsteady them, but it is right to state, that C—— is an unusually good breaker, and works his dogs with singular temper and patience. They are very attached to him, and appear to listen anxiously to what he says when he talks to them,—which, I own, he does more than I recommend.

89. Pointers, however, are manifestly out of place in strong cover, though an unusually high-couraged one may occasionally be found, who will dash forward in defiance of pricks and scratches; but it is not fair to expect it. In a very light cover I have often shot over one belonging to a relation of mine, which was so clever, that when I came close to her as she was pointing, she would frequently run round to the other side of the thicket, and then rush in to drive the game towards me. This killing plan had in no way been taught her; she adopted it solely of her own sagacity. Having been much hunted in cover when young, she was so fond of it (69) as to be, comparatively speaking, quite unserviceable on the stubbles.

WATER SPANIELS, (OR WATER RETRIEVERS.)

90. A young water spaniel might, with advantage, occasionally be indulged with a duck-hunt in warm weather. It would tend to make him quick in the water, and observant. The finishing lessons might

conclude with your shooting the bird and obliging him to retrieve it. He should be made handy to your signals (IV. to VII. and X. of 141), so as to hunt the fens and marshes, and "seek dead" exactly where you may wish.

91. This obedience to the hand is particularly required; for when the spaniel is swimming he is on a level with the bird, and therefore is not so likely to see it,—especially if there is a ripple on the water,—as you are, who probably may be standing many feet above him on the shore. As you may frequently, while he is retrieving, have occasion to direct his movements when at a considerable distance from him, you probably would find it more advantageous to teach him the forward signal used by shepherds (143), than the one described in IV. of 141.

92. A water spaniel should also be taught to fetch (96, 98, 106 to 109),—be accustomed to follow quietly close to your heels,—be broken in, not to the "down charge" (27), but to the "drop" (23 to 26), the instant you signal to him, while you are noiselessly stalking the wild-fowl previously reconnoitered, with the aid of your Dollond, from some neighbouring height; nor should he stir a limb, however long he and you may have to await, ensconced behind a favouring bush, the right moment for the destructive raking discharge of your first barrel, to be followed by the less murderous, but still effective flying shot. On hearing the report, it is his duty to dash instantly into the water, and secure the slain as rapidly as possible.

93. A really good water retriever is a scarce and valuable animal. He should be neither white nor black, because the colours are too conspicuous, especially the

IRISH WATER SPANIEL.

"Our good Irish friend."—Par. 95.

former, (a hint by-the-bye for your own costume);* he should be perfectly mute; of a patient disposition, though active in the pursuit of birds; of so hardy a constitution as not to mind the severest cold,—therefore no coddling while he is young near a fire,—and possess what many are deficient in, viz., a good nose: consequently, a cross that will improve his nose, yet not decrease his steadiness, is the great desideratum in breeding. He should swim rapidly, for wild-fowl that are only winged, will frequently escape from the quickest dog, if they have plenty of sea-room and deep water. (See also 113, 553, 567.)

94. Wild-fowl emit a stronger scent than is, I believe, generally supposed. At Mr. G——r's, in Surrey, Mr. L——g was shooting one day last season, when his pointer "Flint" drew for some time towards the river, and brought the sportsmen to the stump of an old tree. They could see nothing, and the dog must be standing at a moorhen; but on one of the beaters trying with a stick, out flew a mallard like a shot from a gun. As Mr. L——g levelled his tubes, it is unnecessary to observe that it fell; but probably it would have been lost had not "Flint," when encouraged, jumped into the water and brought the bird to land. A Mr. C——e, living near Edinburgh, whom I have the pleasure of knowing, has a white setter that is a capital hand at finding ducks, and sets them steadily.

95. In the wild-*rice* lakes, as they are commonly called, of America, a brace of highly-trained spaniels will sometimes, on a windy day, afford you magnificent

* But when the moors are covered with snow, poachers, who emerge in bands from the mines, often put a shirt over their clothes, and manage to approach grouse at a time when a fair sportsman cannot get a shot; but this is the only occasion on which one uniform colour could be advantageous. A mass of *any* single colour always catches, and arrests the eye. Nature tells us this; animals that browse, elephants, buffaloes, and large deer, as well as those which can escape from their enemies by speed, are mostly of one colour. On the contrary, the tiger kind, snakes, and all that lie in wait for, and seize their prey by stealth, wear a garment of many colours, so do the smaller animals and most birds, which are saved from capture by the inability of their foes to distinguish them from the surrounding foliage or herbage. The uniform of our rifle corps is too much of one hue.

sport. The cover is so good that, if it is not often beaten, the birds will frequently get up singly, or only a couple at a time. The dogs should keep swimming about within gun-shot, while you are slowly and silently paddling, or probably poling your canoe through the most likely spots. Relays of spaniels are requisite, for it is fatiguing work. If, by any rare chance, you are situated where you can get much of this delightful shooting, and *you are an enthusiast in training*, it may be worth your while to consider whether there would not be an advantage in making the dogs perfect in the "down charge," as they would then cease swimming the instant you fired. But this long digression about spaniels has led us away from your pup, which we assumed (3) to be a pointer or setter, very unlike our good Irish friend, well represented in the last engraving.

CHAPTER IV.

LESSONS IN "FETCHING."—RETRIEVERS.

96. Lessons in "fetching" recommended.—97. Dog not taught to retrieve bringing dead Bird he had found.—98. Taught to deliver into your hand; never pick up a Bird yourself; Dog which often lost winged Birds she had lifted.—99. Colonel T——y.—100. Retriever killing one Bird in order to carry two.—101. "Fau's" sagaciously bringing to firm ground Bird that had fallen in a swamp.—102. "Dove's" *spontaneously* fetching one from River, though not accustomed to retrieve.—103. Retrievers taught to carry something soft; injudiciousness of employing a stone.—104. How encouraged to plunge into Water; evil of deceiving a Dog instanced.—105. Diving, how taught.—106. "Fetching" taught with a Pincushion: with a Bunch of Keys.—107. Made to deliver instantly.—108. Practised to carry things of the size and weight of a Hare.—109. "Fetching," how taught at commencement. - 110. Brace of Setters taught with an old bone.—111. "Fetching" often taught unskilfully.—112. Regular Retrievers taught to fetch Birds; to "foot" Rabbits and Winged Game.—113. Retriever observes when a Bird is struck; a quality particularly useful in a Water Retriever. 114. Pigeons and small Birds shot to Retrievers.—115. Injudiciousness of aiding a young Dog when Retrieving; makes him rely on Gun rather than his own Nose.—116. Fatigue of carrying Hare tempts young Retriever to drop it; taught to deliver quickly by rewards of hard boiled liver.- 117. If he taste blood, put on Wire Snaffle; how made.—118. Retriever how taught to pursue faster: should commence to "road" slowly, but "follow up" rapidly.—119. Why Land Retrievers should "down charge."—120. Some Retrievers may "run on shot," but those for sale should "down charge."—121. Fine retrieving instanced in "Ben."—122. Anecdote showing his great sagacity.—123. Benefit derived from a Seton; another instance of "Ben's" superior retrieving qualities.—124. With "Ben's" good nose, certain advantage of "down charge."—125. Retrievers not to be of a heavy build, yet strong and thick-coated.—126. Cross between a Newfoundland and Setter makes best Retriever; the real Newfoundland described.—127. Cross from heavy Setter best Retriever.—128. Most Dogs can be taught more or less to Retrieve.—129. Young Retriever to lift Woodcock and Landrail.—130. Retrievers never to kill Rats; lift vermin, or wounded Herons, &c.

96. THOUGH you may not wish your young pointer (or setter) to perform the duties of a regular retriever, (536) still you would do well to teach him, whilst he is a puppy, to fetch and deliver into your hand anything soft you may occasionally throw for him, or leave behind you in some place where he will have observed you deposit it, while he is following at your heels. In

a little time you can drop something *without* letting him see you, and afterwards send him back for it. A dog thus made, who is your intimate companion, becomes so conversant with every article of your apparel, and with whatever you usually carry about you, that, should you accidentally drop anything, the observant animal will be almost certain to recover it. On receiving your order to be "off and find" he will accurately retrace your footsteps for miles and miles, diligently hunting every yard of the ground. Of course, the distances to which you at first send your dog will be inconsiderable, and you should carefully avoid persevering too long at a time, lest he get sick of the lesson. Indeed, in all his lessons,—as well in-doors as out,—but particularly in this, let it be your aim to leave off at a moment when he has performed entirely to your satisfaction; that you may part the best of friends, and that the last impression made by the lesson may be pleasing as well as correct, from a grateful recollection of the caresses which he has received. In wild-duck shooting you may be in situations where you would be very glad if the dog would bring your bird; and when it is an active runner in cover, I fear you will be more anxious than I could wish (322) that the dog should "fetch." It is probable that he will thus assist you if he be practised as I have just advised; and such instruction may lead, years hence, to his occasionally bringing you some dead bird which he may come across, and which you otherwise might have imagined you had missed, for its scent might be too cold, and consequently too changed, for the dog to have thought of regularly pointing it.

97. When I was a boy, I recollect seeing such an instance in Kent. As a great treat, I was permitted (but merely as a spectator)

to accompany a first-rate shot, Mr. C——h, who was trying a gun he thought of purchasing for his keeper. The dogs soon came upon a covey. He killed with his first barrel, but apparently missed with his second. He found fault with the gun for not shooting strongly; and I well remember impertinently fancying,—but I dared not say so,—that perhaps he was as much to blame as the gun. Soon afterwards, to our mutual surprise, we saw one of the dogs trotting up with a bird, still warm, in its mouth; thus tacitly reproving me for not having done justice to Mr. C——h's unerring eye and steady hand.

98. Mark my having said, "deliver into your hand," that your young dog may not be satisfied with only dropping, within your sight, any bird he may lift, and so, perhaps, leave it on the other side of a trout stream, as I have seen dogs do more than once, in spite of every persuasion and entreaty. With a young dog, who retrieves, never pick up a bird yourself, however close it may fall to you. Invariably, make him either deliver it into your hand or lay it at your feet. The former is by far the better plan. If the dog has at one moment to drop the bird at *your* will, he is likely to fancy himself privileged to drop it at another time for his *own* convenience. In other respects, too, the former is the safest method. I have a bitch now in my recollection, who frequently lost her master slightly winged birds, (which she had admirably recovered) by dropping them too soon on hearing the report of a gun, or coming on other game,—for off they ran, and fairly escaped, it being impracticable, by any encouragement, to induce her to seek for a bird she had once lifted.

99. This error, I mean that of allowing a wounded bird to regain its liberty, was once beautifully avoided by a pretty black retriever, belonging to Colonel T——y, a good sportsman and pleasant companion, who, not long since, told me the circumstance; and I am glad to be able, on such authority, to relate an anecdote evincing so much reflection and judgment, for I know not by what other terms to characterise the dog's sagacity.

100. Colonel T——y's avocations constantly take him from his neat bachelor's cottage in Kent, to travel abroad. Shooting in

Hungary he once knocked down two partridges at a shot,—one was killed outright, the other only slightly wounded. "Venus" soon hit off the trail of the latter,—quickly overtook it, and, while carrying it to her master, came upon the dead bird. She stopped, evidently greatly puzzled; and, after one or two trials, finding she could not take it up without permitting the escape of the winged bird, she considered a moment,—then, deliberately murdered it, by giving it a severe crunch, and afterwards brought away both together. It is due to the lady to observe that she is naturally as tender-mouthed as her name would imply her to be tender-hearted, and that this is the only known instance of her ever having wilfully injured any game.

101. Sometimes a dog's sagacity will induce him, *however little taught*, to assist you in your hour of need; but you must not trust to this. An intimate friend of mine, shooting in Ireland to a pointer-bitch that was totally unaccustomed to fetch and carry, but well instructed to seek for a dead bird, killed a snipe. It fell in soft, boggy ground, where he could not get at it to pick it up. After some vain efforts to approach it, he hied on the bitch, who was still steadily "pointing dead," with "Fetch it, Fan; fetch it." The bitch seemed for a moment puzzled at such an unusual proceeding, and looked round, inquisitively, once or twice, as if to say, "What can you mean?" Suddenly, my friend's dilemma seemed to flash upon her. She walked on, took the bird, quite gently, in her mouth, and carried it to where the ground was firm; but not one inch further would she bring it, despite all the encouragement of her master, who now wished to make her constantly retrieve. This was the first and last bird she ever lifted.

102. "Dove," a white setter, belonging to a near relation of mine, (the left-hand dog in the engraving illustrating 540, is considered extremely like her,) did, spontaneously, that which "Fan" only consented to do after much entreaty. My relation, shooting on the banks of the Forth, killed a partridge that was flying across the river. As he had no retriever with him he almost regretted having fired; but, to his surprise, "Dove" volunteered jumping into the water; made her way to the bird with a sort of steamboat paddle action,—for I verily believe it was the first time she had attempted to swim,—seized it, and, returning with it to the shore, deposited it safely on the bank. She never had retrieved before, and is not particularly good at "seeking dead."

102. I observed it was something soft which you should teach your dog to fetch. Probably you have seen a retriever taught to seek and bring a stone, upon which, in a delicate manner, the tutor has spit. Does it not stand to reason that the stone must have tended to give his pupil a hard mouth? And what may, later

in life, cause him much misery in dashing at a bounding stone, he may split a tooth. Dogs of an advanced age suffer more in their mouths than most of us suspect.

104. Should your pup be unwilling to enter water, on no account push him in, under the mistaken idea that it will reconcile him to the element,—it will but augment his fears (320). Rather, on a warm day, throw some biscuit for him, when he is hungry, close to the edge of the bank, where it is so shallow as merely to require his wading. Chuck the next piece a little further off, and, by degrees, increase the distance until he gets beyond his depth, and finds that nature has given him useful swimming powers. On no occasion will the example of another dog more assist you. Your youngster's diving can never be of service; therefore throw in only what will float. Otherwise he might have a plunge for nothing, and so be discouraged; and evidently it should be your constant aim to avoid doing anything likely to shake his confidence in the judiciousness of your orders.

A person I know, taught a dog many good tricks,—among others, to extinguish the papers thrown upon the ground that had served to light cigars. A booby of a fellow, very wittily, took in the dog, once, by chucking a red-hot coal to him. "A burnt child," says the old adage, "dreads the fire:" so does a burnt dog: and, of course, no subsequent encouragement would induce him, ever again, to approach a lighted paper.

105. If you ever have occasion to teach a dog to dive and retrieve, first accustom him, on land, to fetch something heavy, of a conspicuous colour. When he brings it eagerly, commence your diving lesson by throwing it into the shallowest parts of the stream. Only by slow degrees get to deep water, and let your lessons be very short. Never chuck in a stone. The chances are twenty to one that there are several at the bottom not very dissimilar, and the young dog ought not to be subjected

to the temptation of picking up one of them in lieu of that he was sent for. Should he on any occasion do so, neither scold nor caress him; quietly take what he brings, lay it at your feet, to show him that you want it not, and endeavour to make him renew his search for what you threw in ; do this by signs, and by encouragement with your voice, rather than by chucking stones in the right direction, lest he should seek for them instead of searching for what you originally sent him.

106. Some teachers make a young dog fetch a round pin-cushion, or a cork ball, in which needles are judiciously buried ; nor is it a bad plan, and there need be no cruelty in it, if well managed. At least it can only be cruel once, for a dog's recollection of his sufferings will prevent his picking up the offending object a second time. Others, after he is well drilled into "fetching," and takes pleasure in it, will make him bring a bunch of keys. There are few things a dog is less willing to lift. Most probably they gave him some severe rebuffs when first heedlessly snatching at them ; and the caution thereby induced tends to give him a careful, tender mouth. A fencing master, I knew in France, had a spaniel, singularly enough for a Frenchman, called "Waterloo," that would take up the smallest needle.

107. When your dog has picked up what you desired, endeavour to make him run to you quickly. Many who teach a dog to fetch, praise and encourage him while he is bringing what he was sent after. Clearly this is an error. It induces the dog to loiter and play with it. He thinks he is lauded for having it in his mouth and carrying it about. Reserve your encomiums and caresses until he has delivered it. (see 153.)—If you walk away, the fear of your leaving him, will induce him to hurry

after you. Let a dog retrieve ever so carelessly, still, while on the move, he will rarely drop a bird.

108. Dogs that retrieve should be gradually brought to lift heavy, flexible things, and such as require a large grasp, that they may not be quite unprepared for the weight and size of a hare; otherwise they may be inclined to drag it along by a slight hold of the skin, instead of balancing it across their mouths. Thus capacious jaws are obviously an advantage in retrievers.

The French gamekeepers, many of whom are capital hands at making a retriever (excepting that they do not teach the "down-charge"), stuff a hare or rabbit skin with straw, and when the dog has learned to fetch it with eagerness, they progressively increase its weight by burying larger and larger pieces of wood in the middle of the straw: and to add to the difficulty of carrying it, they often throw it to the other side of a hedge or thick copse. If the dog shows any tendency to a hard mouth they mix thorns with the straw.

109. I ought to have mentioned sooner, that you should commence teaching a puppy to "fetch," by shaking your glove (or anything soft) at him, and encouraging him to seize and drag it from you. Then throw it a yard or two off, gradually increasing the distance, and the moment he delivers it to you, give him something palatable. It is easier to teach a dog to retrieve as a puppy than when he is older. From teething his gums are in a state of slight irritation, and it gives him pleasure to employ his teeth and gums. Should you, contrary to every reasonable expectation, from his having no inclination to romp or play with the glove, not be able to persuade him to pick it up, put it between his teeth,—force him to grasp it by tightly pressing his jaws together, speaking all the while im-

pressively to him,—scold him if he is obstinate and refuses to take hold of the glove. After a little time retire a few paces, keeping one hand under his mouth (to prevent his dropping the glove), while you lead or drag him with the other. When you halt, be sure not to take the glove immediately from him,—oblige him to continue holding it for at least a minute, (lest he should learn to relinquish his grip too soon) before you make him yield at the command "give;" then bestow a reward. Should he drop it before he is ordered to deliver it, replace it in his mouth, and again retreat some steps before ordering him to "give." He will soon follow with it at your heels. If you have sufficient perseverance you can thus make him earn all his daily food. Hunger will soon perfect him in the lesson. Observe that there are four distinct stages in this trick of carrying,—the first, making the dog grasp and retain, —the second, inducing him to bring, following at your heels,—the third, teaching him not to quit his hold when you stop,—the fourth, getting him to deliver into your hands on your order. The great advantage of a sporting dog's acquiring this trick, is, that it accustoms him to deliver into your *hands ;* and it often happens that you must thus teach a dog to "carry" as a preparative to teaching him to "fetch." It certainly will be judicious in you to do so, if the dog is a lively, riotous animal; for the act of carrying the glove (or stick, &c.) quietly at your heels will sober him, and make him less likely to run off with it instead of delivering it when you are teaching him to fetch. As soon as he brings the glove tolerably well, try him with a short stick. You will wish him not to seize the end of it, lest he should learn to "drag" instead of to "carry." Therefore fix pegs or wires into holes drilled at right angles to each other at the extremities of the stick. He will then only grasp it near the middle.

110. On one occasion I had a brace of setters to instruct, which had come to me perfectly untaught, at far too advanced an age to make their education an easy task; they had also been harshly treated, and were consequently shy and timid. This obliged me to proceed with much caution and gentleness. I soon won their confidence, I may say, their affections; but I could not persuade them to play with my glove, nor to lift anything I threw before them. I was hesitating how to act, when I saw one of them find an old dry bone and bear it off in triumph. I encouraged him in carrying it,—threw it several times for him, and when he was tired of the fun, I brought the old bone home as a valuable prize. Next day I tied a string to it,—I frequently chucked it to a short distance, and when the dog had seized it I dragged it towards me, *generally turning my back to the dog.* As soon as I regained it, I made him attach a value to its being in my hands, by employing it as a plate on which to offer him some delicacy. In a few days I could dispense with the string, and I soon ventured to substitute for the bone the string rolled up as a ball; afterwards I employed a stick. Ultimately the dog fetched very promptly. His companion also took up the trick from the force of good example. (See note to 34.)

111. I have dwelt thus long on "carrying" and "fetching," because they are frequently taught so injudiciously, that the result is a complete failure.

112. This drill should be further extended if a

REGULAR LAND RETRIEVER

be your pupil. Throw dead birds of any kind for him to bring (of course one at a time), being on the alert to check him whenever he grips them too severely. If he persists in disfiguring them, pass a few blunted knitting needles through them at right angles to one another. When he fetches with a tender mouth, you will be able to follow up this method of training still further by letting him "road" (or "foot," as it is often termed) a rabbit in high stubble, one (or both, if a strong buck) of whose hind legs you will have previously bandaged in the manner described in 60. Be careful not to let him see you turn it out, lest he watch your proceedings and endeavour to "hunt by eye." Indeed, it might be

F

better to employ another person to turn it out. Keep clear of woods for some time:—the cross scents would puzzle him. If by any chance you have a winged pheasant or partridge, let him retrieve it. You will not, I presume, at the commencement select a morning when there is a dry cold wind from the north-east, but probably you will wish to conclude his initiatory lessons on days which you judge to possess least scent. The more he has been practised as described in 43, the better will he work; for he cannot keep his nose too perseveringly close to the ground. With reference to the instructions in that paragraph I will here remark, that before you let the dog stoop to hunt, you should have placed him by signal (35) near the spot from which you had begun dragging the bread. In paragraph 277 an instance is given of the manner in which a dog who retrieves should be put upon a scent; and why that mode is adopted is explained in 271.

113. It is quite astonishing how well an old dog that retrieves knows when a bird is struck. He instantly detects any hesitation or uncertainty of movement, and for a length of time will watch its flight with the utmost eagerness, and, steadily keeping his eye on it, will, as surely as yourself, mark its fall. To induce a young dog to become thus observant, always let him perceive that *you* watch a wounded bird with great eagerness; his imitative instinct will soon lead him to do the same. This faculty of observation is particularly serviceable in a water retriever. It enables him to swim direct to the crippled bird, and, besides the saving of time, the less he is in the water in severe weather, the less likely is he to suffer from rheumatism.

114. As an initiatory lesson in making him observant of the flight and fall of birds, place a few pigeons (or

other birds) during his absence, each in a hole covered with a tile. Afterwards come upon these spots apparently unexpectedly, and, kicking away the tiles, (or, what is better, dragging them off by a previously adjusted string,) shoot the birds for him to bring; it being clearly understood that he has been previously tutored into having no dread of the gun. As he will have been taught to search where bidden (IV. to VIII. of 141), nothing now remains but to take him out on a regular campaign, when the fascinating scent of game will infallibly make him search (I do not say deliver) with great eagerness. When once he then touches upon a scent, leave him entirely to himself,—not a word, not a sign. Possibly his nose may not be able to follow the bird, but it is certain that yours cannot. Occasionally you may be able to help an old retriever (544), but rarely, if ever, a young one. Your interference, nay, probably your mere presence, would so excite him as to make him overrun the scent. Remain, therefore, quietly where you are, until he rejoins you.

115. When we see a winged pheasant racing off, most of us are too apt to assist a young dog, forgetting that we thereby teach him, instead of devoting his whole attention to work out the scent, to turn to us for aid on occasions when it may be impossible to give it. When a dog is hunting *for* birds, he should frequently look to the gun for signals, but when he is *on* them, he should trust to nothing but his own scenting faculties.

116. If, from a judicious education, a retriever pup has had a delight in "fetching" rapidly, it is not likely he will loiter on the way to mouth his birds; but the fatigue of carrying a hare a considerable distance may, perhaps, induce a young dog to drop it in order to take a moment's rest. There is a risk that when doing so

he may be tempted to lick the blood, and, finding it palatable, be led to maul the carcase. You see, therefore, the judiciousness of employing every means in your power to ensure his feeling anxious to deliver *quickly*, and I know not what plan will answer better,—though it sounds sadly unsentimental,—than to have some pieces of hard boiled liver * at hand to bestow upon him the moment he surrenders his game, until he is thoroughly confirmed in an expeditious delivery. Never give him a piece, however diligently he may have searched, unless he succeed in bringing. When you leave off these rewards do so gradually. The invariable bestowal of such dainties during, at least, the retriever's first season, will prevent his ever dropping a bird on hearing the report of a gun (as many do), in order to search for the later killed game.

117. Should a young retriever evince any wish to assist the cook by plucking out the feathers of a bird; or from natural vice or mismanagement before he came into your possession,† show any predisposition to taste blood, take about two feet (dependent upon the size of the dog's head) of iron wire, say the one-eighth of an inch in diameter, sufficiently flexible for *you*, but not for *him*, to bend. Shape this much into the form of the letter U, supposing the extremities to be joined by a straight line. Place the straight part in the dog's mouth, and passing the other over his head and ears, retain it in position by a light throat lash passed through a turn in the wire, as here roughly repre-

---

* A drier and cleaner article than you may suppose, and which can be carried not inconveniently in a Mackintosh, or oil-skin bag,—a toilet sponge bag.

† If a retriever has the opportunity, while prowling about, of gnawing hare or rabbit-skins thrown aside by a slovenly cook, it will not be unnatural in him, when he is hungry, to wish to appropriate to himself the hide, if not the interior of the animals he is lifting.

sented. The flexibility of the wire will enable you to adjust it with ease to the shape of his head. When in the kennel he ought to be occasionally thus bitted, that he may not fret when he is first hunted with it. It will not injure his teeth or much annoy him, if it lies on his grinders a little behind the tushes.

118. Sometimes a retriever, notwithstanding every encouragement, will not pursue a winged bird with sufficient rapidity. In this case associate him for a few days with a quicker dog, whose example will to a certainty animate him and increase his pace. It is true that when he is striving to hit off a scent he cannot work too patiently and perseveringly; but, on the other hand, the moment he is satisfied he is on it, he cannot follow too rapidly. A winged bird when closely pressed, seems, through nervousness, to emit an increasing stream of scent; therefore, though it may sound paradoxical, the retriever's accelerated pace then makes him (his nose being close to the ground) the less likely to overrun it; and the faster he pursues the less ground must he disturb, for the shorter will be the chase.

119. Retrievers are generally taught to rush in, the instant a bird falls. This plan, like most other things, has its advocates and its opponents. I confess to being one of the latter, for I cannot believe that in the long run it is the best way to fill the bag. I think it certain that more game is lost by birds being flushed while the guns are unloaded,* than could be lost from the scent cooling during the short period the dog remains at the "down charge." Unquestionably some retrievers have

* This reasoning obviously does not apply to the retrievers employed in those battues where rapid slaughter is "the order of the day,"—where the sportsmen do not condescend to charge their own guns, but are constantly supplied with relays of loaded arms.

so good a nose, that the delay would not lead to their missing any wounded game, however slightly struck (123); and the delay has this great advantage, that it helps to keep the retriever under proper subjection, and diminishes his anxiety to rush to every part of the line where a gun may be fired, instead of remaining quietly at his master's heels until signaled to take up the scent. Morever, a retriever, by neglecting the "down charge," sets an example to the pointers or setters who may be his companions, which it is always more or less difficult to prevent the dogs, if young, from following. But I once shot over a retriever which I could hardly wish not to have "run on shot." On a bird being hit he started off with the greatest impetuosity, kept his eye immoveably fixed on its flight, and possessed such speed, that a winged bird scarcely touched the ground ere it was pinned. He would, too, often seize a slightly injured hare before it had acquired its best pace. The pursuit so soon terminated, that possibly less game escaped being fired at, than if the retriever had not stirred until the guns were reloaded. On a miss he was never allowed—indeed appeared little inclined—to quit "heel." Of course a trainer's trouble is decreased by not breaking to the "down charge," which may induce some to recommend the plan; though it is to be observed, that this class of dogs is more easily than any other perfected in it, because the breaker nearly always possesses the power of treading upon or seizing the checkcord the instant a bird is sprung.

120. The nature of your shooting will much influence you in deciding which of the two methods to adopt; but should you select the one which the generality of good sportsmen consider to be most according to rule, and to possess the greatest beauty, viz., the "down

charge," rather lose any bird, however valuable, so long as your retriever remains young, than put him on the "foot" a second before you have reloaded. Undoubtedly it ought to be taught to every dog broken for sale, as the purchaser can always dispense with it should he judge it unnecessary:—it can soon be untaught. It is clear that not "quitting heel" until ordered, is tantamount to the regular "down charge," but I think the last is the easiest to enforce constantly. It is the more decided step.

121. Mr. K——g (mentioned in 231) had a famous retriever whose build, close curly hair, and aquatic propensities, showed his close affinity to the water spaniel, though doubtless there was some strain of the Landsman. He retrieved with singular zeal and pertinacity. Indeed his superiority over all competitors in his neighbourhood, was so generally admitted, that his master was hardly ever asked to shoot at any place, without a special invitation being sent to "Ben." When beating a cover, there was a constant call for "Ben." No merely winged pheasant fell to the ground, and no hare went off wounded but there was heard, "Ben, Ben." On one occasion, when K——g was posted at the extremity of the line, the dog was called away so often that his master got annoyed, and declared that the animal should attend to no one but himself. Soon there was a double shot, and, of course, the usual vociferations for "Ben," but he was ordered to keep close. Louder and louder were the cries for "Ben," but all in vain,—he obediently followed only his master's orders. At length when the cover was beaten through, K——g inquired into the cause of the hubbub. Young B——k told him, in no kind humour, that his churlishness in retaining the dog had lost them a fine hare. "If," said K——g, "you are certain you wounded it, and can put me on the exact spot where it was when you fired, I will bet you £5 that 'Ben' shall find her." B——k observed that he knew perfectly the precise place, having carefully marked it with a stick, but added, that he much doubted the possibility of the dog's picking up the scent, as more than half an hour had since elapsed. K——g, however, stuck to his offer. They went back and found some pile, which proved that the hare had been struck. The dog was put on the trail. He at once took it, but was so long away, (perhaps twenty minutes,) that they thought it best to search for him. They found him almost immediately, lying down with the hare alongside of him. His tongue was hanging out of his mouth, and he showed other symptoms of great distress. Evidently he had brought the hare from a considerable distance.

122. "Ben" had numerous excellent qualities, but his greatest admirers, and few dogs had so many, were obliged to admit, that he was of a quarrelsome, pugnacious disposition. It unluckily happened that he had taken a great dislike to a large cubbish young retriever belonging to the aforesaid Mr. B——k, who often shot with K——g; and I am sorry to say none of "Ben's" prejudices were removed by the kindly fellowship and good feeling usually engendered by association in field-sports. The day's work generally commenced by "Ben's" making a rush at his big awkward companion, and overturning him. After this feat, upon which he evidently greatly plumed himself, he would proceed to business. It happened that one of the sportsmen once knocked over a pheasant which fell outside the hedge surrounding the copse they were beating. It proved to be a runner; "Ben," however, soon got hold of it, and was carrying it to his master in the cover, when up came the other dog wishing to assist. "Ben's" anger was roused,—he was anxious to punish such intrusive interference—but how to manage it was the question, for if he put down the winged bird it would run into the wood, where there might be much trouble in recovering it. Quick as thought, off ran "Ben" to the middle of the large ploughed field,—there he dropped the bird,—then dashed at his lumbering rival, quickly gave him a thrashing, and afterwards started in pursuit of the pheasant, which he managed to overtake before it regained the copse. If that was not reflection it was something very like it.

123. One more anecdote of poor "Ben." I say "poor," because he died prematurely from a swelling under the throat which might, in all probability, have been cured, had a long seton been run through it, or rather under the adjacent skin,—a mode of treatment attended with the happiest results in the case of another dog attacked in a similar manner in the same kennel. "Ben" and an old setter were K——g's only canine attendants when he was once pheasant shooting with a friend on some steep banks. K——g was at the bottom, his friend on the top. A cock pheasant was sprung and winged by the latter. The bird not being immediately found, there was the usual cry for "Ben." "Go along," said K——g. Away went the dog, who soon took up the scent and dashed off, but had not gone many yards before he started a hare; K——g had soon an opening to fire, and wounded it. "Ben" pursued it, urged on by his master, who felt sure the dog would be able to retrieve the pheasant afterwards. The hare was viewed scrambling up the bank. "Ben" soon appeared in sight and caught it. K——g's friend much abused poor "Ben" for quitting one scent for another. "Do not put yourself out of humour," said K——g; "you don't know the dog,—wait till he comes back, and if he does not then get the bird, blame me." Having allowed "Ben" a little breathing time, K——g took him to the place where the bird fell. The dog quickly hit off the scent. K——g, now perfectly satisfied that all was right, made his friend sit down. In little more than a quarter of an hour "Ben" came back with the bird

alive in his mouth, it having no other wound that could be perceived than on the pinion of one wing.

124. With such a nose as "Ben's" could there have been any harm in his being taught to "down charge," and might there not have been much good (119)? You see that owing to his having put up the hare while K——g's friend was loading, it might have escaped, had it, as is usually the case, at once taken to the hills.

125. Large retrievers are less apt to mouth their game than small ones : but very heavy dogs are not desirable, for they soon tire. And yet a certain medium is necessary, for they ought to have sufficient strength to carry a hare with ease through a thicket, when balanced in their jaws, and be able to jump a fence with her. They should run mute. And they should be thick coated : unless they are so,—I do not say long coated,—they cannot be expected to dash into close cover, or plunge into water after a duck or snipe when the thermometer is near zero.

126. From education there are good retrievers of many breeds, but it is usually allowed that, as a general rule, the best land retrievers are bred from a cross between the setter and the Newfoundland,—or the strong spaniel and the Newfoundland. I do not mean the heavy Labrador, whose weight and bulk is valued because it adds to his power of draught, nor the Newfoundland, increased in size at Halifax and St. John's to suit the taste of the English purchaser,—but the far slighter dog reared by the settlers on the coast,—a dog that is quite as fond of water as of land, and which in almost the severest part of a North American winter will remain on the edge of a rock for hours together, watching intently for anything the passing waves may carry near him. Such a dog is highly prized. Without his aid the farmer would secure but few of the many wild ducks he shoots at certain seasons of the year. The patience with which he waits for a shot on the top of a high cliff (until the numerous flock sail leisurely underneath) would be fruitless, did not his noble dog fearlessly plunge in from the greatest height, and successfully bring the slain to shore.

127. Probably a cross from the heavy, large-headed setter, who, though so wanting in pace, has an exquisite nose ; and the true Newfoundland, makes the best retriever. Nose is the first desideratum. A breaker may doubt which of his pointers or setters possesses the greatest olfactory powers, but a short trial tells him which of his retrievers has the finest nose.

128. Making a first-rate retriever is a work of time, but his being *thoroughly* grounded in the required initiatory lessons facilitates matters surprisingly. Indeed after having been taught the "drop" (23, 25, 26) —to "fetch" (107 to 109)—and "seek dead" in the precise direction he is ordered (XI. of 141), almost any kind of dog can be made to retrieve. The better his nose is, the better of course he will retrieve. Sagacity, good temper, quickness of comprehension, a teachable disposition, and all cultivated qualities, are almost as visibly transmitted to offspring as shape and action; therefore the stronger a dog's hereditary instincts lead him to retrieve, the less will be the instructor's trouble; and the more obedient he is made to the signals of the hand, the more readily will he be put upon a scent. Dogs that are by nature quick rangers do not take instinctively to retrieving. They have not naturally sufficient patience to work out a feeble scent. They are apt to overrun it. A really good retriever will pursue a wounded bird or hare as accurately as a bloodhound will a deer or man; and if he is put on a false scent, I mean a scent of uninjured flick or feather, he will not follow it beyond a few steps:—experience will have shown him the inutility of so doing. (545.)

129. Avail yourself of the first opportunity to make a young retriever lift a woodcock, lest in after life, from its novel scent, he decline touching it, as many dogs have done to the great annoyance of their masters. Ditto, with the delicate landrail.

130. The directions given about "fetching," led me to talk of retrievers; and having touched upon the subject, I thought it right not to quit it, until I had offered the best advice in my power. I have but one more recommendation to add before I return to your

setter (or pointer) pup: carefully guard a young retriever (indeed any dog bred for the gun) from being ever allowed to join in a rat-hunt. Rat-hunting would tend to destroy his tenderness of mouth, nay possibly make him mangle his game. But this is not all. It has often gradually led good dogs to decline lifting hares or rabbits, apparently regarding them more in the light of vermin than of game. Some dogs, however, that are not bad retrievers, are capital ratters, but they are exceptions to the general rule. Indeed, you should never permit your dog to retrieve any kind of ground or winged vermin. If the creature were only wounded it might turn upon him. He in self-defence would give it a grip, and he might thus be led to follow the practice on less pardonable occasions. Remember, that a winged bittern or heron might peck out his eye.

CHAPTER V.

INITIATORY LESSONS OUT OF DOORS.—TRICKS.

131. Lessons in Country Walks.—132. "Instruction in quartering;" hunted where least likely to find Game; taught while young. In note, Bitch shot over when seven months old. -133. If unreasonably long before taking to hunting, the remedy.—134. Utility of Initiatory Lessons; taught without punishing.— 135. Self-confidence of timid Dogs increased.—136. The more Dogs learn, the more readily they learn.—137. Two superior Dogs better than half-a-dozen of the ordinary sort; Action of Dogs; their Feet; Loins; dash of Foxhound gives endurance; cross with Bull hunts with nose too low; Reliefs desirable; best Dog reserved for evening.—138. Immense sums spent in shooting, yet begrudged for superior Dogs.—139. Memorandum, never to ride through gate with gun athwart-ship; instance of Dog's behaving admirably the first day shown Game. —140. Proves the value of Initiatory Lessons.—141. Summary of knowledge imparted by them.—142. Why to signal with *right* Hand.—143. Obedience of Shepherd's Dogs to Signals.—144. *One* Word only of command; dogs attend to the general *Sound*, not to the several *Words*.—145. Names of Dogs not to end in "O;" to be easily called; to be dissimilar.—146. "Drop" better word of command than "Down;" use words of command least likely to be employed by others; when purchasing a Dog, ascertain what words he is accustomed to.— 147 to 149. Ladies have no control over Dogs; the reason.—150. They possess patience and temper: could teach any Tricks; Dogs how taught to fag at Cricket.—151. Newfoundland carrying off lady's Parasol for a Bun.—152. He was a Physiognomist.—153. Method of teaching "carrying," greatly differs from method of teaching "fetching."—154. Tricks exhibited with effect.—155 to 157. Instanced at Tonbridge Wells.—158, 159. Instanced at Gibraltar; Game of Draughts.—160, 161. Elephant shown off.—162. Bewilderment of Keeper of Menagerie.—163. Ladies' Pets too pampered; Shepherd's Collies.—164. Kindness without petting.—165, 166. Instance of bad Habit cured by perseverance. Ladies breaking in Dogs for the gun. In note, Whale fishing at Bermuda.— 167. Dog's Affections; always gained by first attentions; win his love, that he may exert himself to please.—Dog sleeping on poacher's clothes.—169. Esquimaux Dogs; Esquimaux Women.

131. As I before observed, you can practise most of the initiatory lessons in your country walks. Always put something alluring in your pocket to reward your pupil for prompt obedience. Do not take him out unnecessarily in bad weather. On no account let him amuse himself by scraping acquaintance with every idle cur he meets on the way; nor permit him to gambol

about the lanes. Let him understand by your manner that there is business in hand. Never let him enter a

INCLINED TO 'RAT.'

field before you. *Always keep him at your heels, until you give him the order to be off.* You will find him disposed to presume and encroach. According to the old adage, " Give him an inch, and he will take an ell." He will be endeavouring to lead rather than to follow, and, should he fancy himself unobserved, he will most perseveringly steal inch upon inch in advance. Be ever on the watch, ready to check the *beginning* of every act of disobedience. Implicit obedience in trifles will insure it in things of more importance—but see par. 345.

132. For some time, but the period is uncertain,— say from his being eight months old until double that

age,*—he will merely gallop and frisk about, and probably will take diligently to persecuting butterflies. Let him choose what he likes. Don't think that he will prize small beer, when he can get champagne. He will leave off noticing inferior articles as he becomes conversant with the taste of game. It is now your main object to get him to hunt; no matter what, so that he is not perpetually running to "heel." And the more timid he is, the more you must let him chase, and amuse himself as his fancy dictates. When you see that he is really occupying himself with more serious hunting, *eagerly* searching for small birds, especially larks, you must begin instructing him how to quarter his ground to the greatest advantage, *under your constant direction*. Should any one join you, or anything occur likely to prevent your giving him your strictest attention, on no account permit him to range,—keep him to "heel" until you are quite prepared to watch and control all his movements. Hunt him where he is least likely to find game, for he will take to quartering his ground far more regularly, under your guidance, where his attention is least distracted by any scent. The taint of partridge would be almost sure to make him deviate from the true line on which you are anxious he should work. Labour now diligently, if possible daily, though not for many hours a day; for be assured, a good method of ranging can only be implanted when he is young: but be discreet, if he be naturally timid, you may make him afraid to leave your heel—the worst of faults.

133. Should your pup be so long before taking to

---

* I once had a pointer pup whose dam was broken in (after a fashion) and regularly shot to when seven months old. Without injury to her constitution, she could not have been hunted for more than an hour or two at a time. She ought not to have been taken to the field for *regular* use until fully a year old.

hunting that your patience becomes exhausted, let an old dog accompany you a few times. When *he* finds birds, gradually bring the young one upon them from leeward, and let him spring them. Encourage him to sniff the ground they have quitted, and allow him to run riot on the haunt. After that enjoyment, the example of the old dog will most likely soon make him range, and employ his nose in seeking a repetition of what has afforded him such unexpected delight. If it does not, and the old dog is steady and good-humoured enough to bear the annoyance cheerfully, couple the young one to him. Before this he should have learned to work kindly in couples (48). But I am getting on too fast, and swerving from the track I had marked for myself. By-and-by I will tell you how I think you should instruct your youngster to quarter his ground to the best advantage. (173, &c.)

134. Common sense shows that you ought not to correct your dog for disobedience, unless you are certain that he knows his fault. Now you will see that the initiatory lessons I recommend, must give him that knowledge, for they explain to him the meaning of almost all the signs and words of command you will have to employ when shooting. That knowledge, too, is imparted by a system of rewards, not punishments. Your object is not to break his spirit, but his self-will. With his obedience you gain his affection. The greatest hardship admissible, in this early stage of his education, is a strong jerk of the checkcord, and a sound rating, given, *when necessary*, in the loudest tone and sternest manner; and it is singular how soon he will discriminate between the reproving term "bad" (to which he will sensitively attach a feeling of shame), and the encouraging word "good,"—expressions that will here-

after have a powerful influence over him, especially if he be of a gentle, timid disposition.

135. In educating such a dog,—and there are many of the kind, likely to turn out well, if they are judiciously managed, often possessing noses so exquisite (perhaps I ought to say cautious), as nearly to make up for their general want of constitution and powers of endurance :— it is satisfactory to think that all these lessons can be inculcated without in the slightest degree depressing his spirit. On the contrary, increasing observation and intelligence will gradually banish his shyness and distrust of his own powers; for he will be sensible that he is becoming more and more capable of comprehending your wishes, and therefore less likely to err and be punished (347).

136. I fear you may imagine that I am attributing too much reasoning power to him. You would not think so if you had broken in two or three dogs. What makes dog-teaching, if not very attractive, at least not laborious, is the fact that the more you impart to a dog, the more readily will he gain further knowledge. After teaching a poodle or a terrier a few tricks, you will be surprised to see with what increasing facility he will acquire each successive accomplishment. It is this circumstance which, I think, should induce you not to regard as chimerical the perfection of which I purpose to speak by-and-by, under the head of "refinements in breaking." Indeed I only adopt this distinction in deference to what I cannot but consider popular prejudice; for I well know many will regard such accomplishments as altogether superfluous. It is sad to think that an art which might easily be made much more perfect, is allowed, almost by universal sufferance, to stop short just at the point where excellence is within grasp.

137. Far more dogs would be *well-broken*, if men would but keep half the number they usually possess. *The owner of many dogs cannot shoot often enough over them to give them great experience.*

Is it that some youngsters are fond of the *éclat* of a large kennel? That can hardly be, or ought not to be ; for clearly it would be more sportsmanlike to pride themselves upon the rare qualities of a few highly-trained animals. A lover of the trigger might be excused an occasional boast, if made with an approach to truth, that he shot over the best-broken dogs in the county. I say seriously, that if I had a considerable bet upon the quantity of game that I was to kill in a season, I had much rather possess two perfectly educated dogs than half-a-dozen commonly called broken ;—and even if I gave fifty or sixty guineas for the brace, it would be more economical than to purchase twice as many of the everyday sort ; for, to say nothing of the tax-gatherer, consider what would be the saving at the end of a very few years between the keep of *two*, and of four or five dogs. I suspect the difference would soon repay the large price paid for the highly-educated favourites. Oh ! yes. I anticipate what you would say ; but, keen sportsman as I am, I own I have not time or inclination to shoot oftener than three or four out of the six working-days of the week,—and I suspect not many men have, except just at the beginning of a season. Moreover, in reference to what I fancy are your thoughts respecting the insufficiency of two, I must premise that they are to be good-hearted dogs,—good feeders after work,—probably of the sort whose exuberant animal spirits, untiring energies, and rapture at inhaling the exciting perfume of game, have led them to run riot in many a lawless chase ; who have consequently used up more than their fair share of the breaker's checkcord, and consumed an undue portion of his time. They must not be those whose constitutions have been injured in their growth by excessive work ; for dogs vary as much as horses in the quantity of labour they are able to perform, both from diversity of natural capabilities, and from the greater or less care bestowed upon them while progressing towards maturity. The Esquimaux, who from anxious observation must be a competent judge,—his very existence depending upon the powers and endurance of his dogs,—not only occasionally crosses them with the wolf (the progeny is prolific) to increase their strength and hardiness,—I do not say sagacity,—but he is so impressed with the necessity of not overtasking them until they have attained their full stamina and vigour, that although he breaks them into harness before they are quite a twelvemonth old, when their immediate services would be convenient, he yet abstains from putting them to severe labour until they are nearly three years of age. My supposed dogs must, too, have as united a gallop as a good hunter, and have small, round, hard feet ; for this I hold to be a more certain test of endurance in the field, than any other point

G

that you can name. Rest assured, that the worst loined dogs with good feet * are capable of more fatigue in stubble or heather, than the most muscular and best loined, with fleshy "understandings." The most enduring pointers I have ever seen hunted, had more or less of the strain of the fox-hound; but doubtless they were proportionately hard to break, for their hereditary bias on one side of the house must have given them an inclination to chase and carry their heads low. I have shot over a cross with the bull-dog. The animal showed great courage, perseverance, and nose, but he hunted with his head so near the ground, that he hit off no game unless he came upon its run. The strongest heather could not have cured such a sad carriage. It would be quite unreasonable to expect that dogs so bred (from either fox-hound or bull-dog), would have acted like Mr. M——t's, (see 280) the first day they were shown game. Remember also that I do not expect to lose any shots from the birds being scared by my being forced to call or whistle to the dogs, and that I confidently hope to shoot more coolly and collectedly, from not being worried and annoyed by their misconduct; I allow, however, that in any open country more than two dogs are desirable; and I especially admit, that whenever I might have the good luck to get away to the moors, I should be unwilling to start with no more than a brace; but even in this case, as I should hope for better society than my own, have I not a right to calculate upon the probable contingent to be brought by my friend? and if his turned out superior to mine, we should always reserve his for our evening's beat, which ought to be the best feeding ground, and towards which it would be our endeavour throughout the day to drive the birds; for, unlike the partridge, the later it is, *early in the season*, the better grouse lie. Many dogs are desirable, not that they may be hunted together, but that they may be hunted in reliefs. But some possess so much power and bottom, that their owners need seldom think about reliefs in partridge-shooting.

138. In enlarging a kennel, it ought always to be remembered, that the companionship of one disorderly cur nominally cheap, but in reality dear, soon leads astray the better disposed. Men who spare no expense in preserving their grounds, in rearing and feeding birds, &c. will often be found to begrudge a few extra pounds in the purchase of a dog, however good. This appears odd, but it is too true. If they would but sum up the rent they pay for the right of shooting, (or what is the same thing, its value, if they choose to let it), the wages of men, the cost of breeding game, taxes, and all

---

* I often shoot over a setter bitch (belonging to one of my relations) that has capital feet, but is very defective across the loins. She is extremely fast, and a brilliant performer for half a day; but she then shuts up completely. A little rest, however, soon brings her round for another half day's brilliant work. Unless a dog is particularly light in body, bad feet quickly scald upon heath or stubble, and they are longer getting round, than is a bad loined dog in recovering from a day's fatigue.

BROACHING A BARREL.

"The extremities of the gun caught the side-posts."—Par. 139.

other attendant expenses, they would find that they wreck themselves at last for *comparatively* a trifle.

139. I am, however, wandering from our immediate subject. Let us return to the lecture, and consider how much knowledge your pupil will have acquired by these preliminary instructions. We shall find that, with the exception of a systematically confirmed range, really little remains to be learned, save what his almost unaided instinct will tell him.

I will give you an instance of what I mean in the conduct of a young pointer I saw shot over the first day he was ever shown game. You know that in Ireland grouse-shooting does not commence before the 20th of August,—a date far more judicious than ours. I well remember that day at Clonmel in the year 1828. Long before any glimmering of light, one of our party had fractured the stock of a favourite double barrel, by carelessly letting it hang across his body at the moment a skittish cob he was riding rushed through a narrow gateway. The extremities of the gun caught the side-posts, and if it had not given way, he must have parted company with his nag. I believe we each made a memorandum, never whilst riding through a gate to let our guns get athwart-ship. The morning turned out so dreadfully wet that, after remaining for hours in a hovel at the foot of the Galtee Mountains, we were forced to return home. The following day we made a fresh start. Being sadly in want of dogs, we took out a young pointer who had never seen a bird, but was tolerably *au fait* in the initiatory lessons which I have described. In a short time he began to hunt,—made several points in the course of the day,—and though *every* thing was strange to him, (for it was the first time he had been associated in the field with other dogs,—nay, almost the first time of his being hunted at all,) yet, from his comprehension of the several orders that he received, and perfect obedience, he acquitted himself so creditably, that he was allowed, not only to be one of the best, but nearly the very best *broken* dog of the party. Indeed, the sportsmen who accompanied the owner (for three guns shot together—a mal-arrangement attributable to accidental circumstances, not choice) could hardly be persuaded that the dog had not been shot over the latter end of the preceding season.

140. I name this instance, and I can vouch for its truth, not as an example to be followed, for it was most injudicious to have so soon taken out the youngster with companions, but to prove to you how much you can effect by initiatory instruction; indeed, afterwards,

you will have little else to do than teach and confirm your dog in a judicious range,—his own sagacity and increasing experience will be his principal guides,—for, consider how much you will have taught him.

141. He will know—

I. That he is to pay attention to his whistle,—the whistle that you design always to use to him. I mean that, when he hears *one* low blast on his whistle he is to look to you for orders, but not necessarily run towards you, unless he is out of sight, or you continue whistling (19).

II. That "Toho," or the right arm raised nearly perpendicularly, means that he is to stand still (19 to 22).

III. That "Drop," or the left arm raised nearly perpendicularly, or the report of a gun, means that he is to crouch down with his head close to the ground, between his feet, however far off he may be ranging. Greater relaxation in the position may be permitted after he has been a little time shot over (23 to 27).

IV. That "On," (the short word for "hie-on",) or the forward underhand swing of the right hand, signifies that he is to advance in a forward direction (the direction in which you are waving). This signal is very useful. It implies that you want the dog to hunt ahead of you. You employ it also when you are alongside of him at his point, and are desirous of urging him to follow up the running bird or birds, and press to a rise. If he push on too eagerly, you restrain him by slightly raising the right hand—XII. of this paragraph (19 to 22).

V. That a wave of the right arm and hand (the arm

being fully extended and well to the right) from left to right, means that he is to hunt to the right. Some men wave the left hand across the body from left to right, as a direction to the dog to hunt to the right; but that signal is not so apparent at a distance as the one I have described (36).

VI. That a wave of the left arm from right to left (the arm being fully extended and well to the left), means that he is to hunt to the left (36).

VII. That the "Beckon," the wave of the right hand towards you, indicates that he is to hunt towards you (37). See also 71.

VIII. That the word "Heel," or a wave of the right hand to the rear (the reverse of the underhand cricket-bowler's swing), implies that he is to give up hunting, and go directly close to your heels (44).

IX. That "Fence" means that he is not to leave the place where you are. After being so checked a few times when he is endeavouring to quit the field, he will understand the word to be an order not to "break fence" (46, 47).

X. That "Find," or "Seek," means that he is to search for something which he will have great gratification in discovering. When he is in the field he will quickly understand this to be game (34, 35).

XI. That "Dead" (which it would be well to accompany with the signal to "Heel") means that there is something not far off, which he would have great satisfaction in finding. On hearing it, he will come to you, and await your signals instructing him in what direction he is to hunt for it. When, by signals, you have put him as near as you can upon the spot where you think the bird has fallen, you will say, "Find;" for, until you say that word, he ought to be more occupied in attending to your signals than in searching for the bird. . When you have shot a good many birds to him, if he is within sight, in order to work more silently, omit saying "Dead," only signal to him to go to "Heel" (19, 34, 35, 44).

XII. That "Care" means that he is near that for which he is hunting. This word, used with the right hand slightly raised (the signal for the "Toho," only not exhibited nearly so energetically), will soon make him comprehend that game is near him, and that he is therefore to hunt cautiously. You will use it when your young dog is racing too fast among turnips or potatoes (39).

XIII. That "Up" means that he is to sniff with his nose high in the air for that of which he is in search (41).

XIV. That "Away" (or "Gone," or "Flown") is an indication that the thing for which he was hunting, and of which he smells the taint, is no longer there. This word is not to be used in the field until your young dog has gained some experience (45).

XV. That "Ware" (pronounced "War") is a general order to desist from whatever he may be doing. "No" is perhaps a better word: it can be pronounced more distinctly and energetically. If the command is occasionally accompanied with the cracking of your whip, its meaning will soon be understood (47).

XVI. He will also know the distinction between the chiding term "Bad" and the encouraging word

"Good;" and, moreover, be sensible, from your look and manner, whether you are pleased or angry with him. Dogs, like children, are physiognomists (40, end of 134).

142. You will perceive that you are advised to use the right hand more than the left. This is only because the left hand is so generally employed in carrying the gun.

<small>143. By often and uniformly employing the signals I have named, you will find it more easy to place your pupil, and make him hunt *exactly* where you wish, than you may at first suppose. In an open country the movements of sheep are entirely controlled by dogs; and if you never have had the opportunity of observing it, you would be no less surprised than interested at witnessing with what accuracy a shepherd, standing on a hill side, can, by the motions of his hand and arm, direct his dog to distant points in the valley below. If you could see it, you would be satisfied it was not by harsh means that he obtained such willing, cheerful obedience. His signals to the right, left, and inwards, are very similar to those just described. He, however, instructs his dog to go further ahead, by using his hand and arm as in the action of throwing, but keeping an open palm towards the animal (the arm raised high): a signal undeniably more visible at a distance than the one named in IV. of 141, though not generally so well suited to the sportsman.</small>

144. You will also observe, that when the voice is employed (and this should be done only when the dog will not obey your signals), I have recommended you to make use of but *one* word. Why should you say, "Come to heel," "Ware breaking fence," "Have a care?" If you speak in sentences, you may at times unconsciously vary the words of the sentence, or the emphasis on any word; and as it is only by the sound that you should expect a dog to be guided, the more defined and distinct in sound the several commands are, the better.

145. This consideration leads to the remark that, as, by nearly universal consent, "Toho" is the word employed to tell a dog to point, the old rule is clearly a judicious one, never to call him "Ponto," "Sancho," or

90 "DROP" BETTER THAN "DOWN." [CH. V.

by any name ending in "o." Always, too, choose one that can be hallooed in a sharp, loud, high key. You will find the advantage of this whenever you lose your dog, and happen not to have a whistle. Observe, also, if you have several dogs, to let their names be dissimilar in sound.

146. I have suggested your employing the word "Drop," instead of the usual word "Down," because it is less likely to be uttered by any one on whom the dog might jump or fawn; for, on principle, I strongly object to any order being given which is not strictly enforced. It begets in a dog, as much as in the nobler animal who walks on two legs, habits of inattention to words of command, and ultimately makes greater severity neces-

DEAF TO THE VOICE OF PERSUASION.—Par. 148.

sary. If I felt certain I should never wish to part with a dog I was instructing, I should carry this principle so far as to frame a novel vocabulary, and never use any word I thought he would be likely to hear from others, By the bye, whenever you purchase a dog, it would be advisable to ascertain what words of command, and what signals he has been accustomed to.

147. The fair sex, though possessing unbounded and most *proper* influence over us, notoriously have but little control over their canine favourites. This, however, solely arises from their seldom enforcing obedience to the orders which they give them.

148. If a lady takes a dog out for a walk, she keeps constantly calling to it, lest it should go astray and be lost. The result is, that ere long, the dog pays not the slightest attention to her, his own sagacity telling him that he need not trouble himself to watch her, as she will be sure to look after him. But she can plead a charming authority for her weakness,—Charles Lamb—who felt obliged to follow wherever "Dash" chose to lead; for "Dash" soon found out that he might take what liberties he pleased with "Elia."

149. There is also a varying in the manner, tone of voice, and words of command, which generally prevents the success of ladies in teaching a four-footed pet any tricks beyond the art of begging.

A SOLICITOR.

This feat they accomplish because they cannot well deviate from the beaten path. They naturally hold the animal in a proper position while they say, "Beg; beg, sir, beg;" and do not give him the reward until he has obeyed orders more or less satisfactorily.

150. Honesty compels us to give them credit for more temper and patience than fall to the lot of the sterner sex; and if they would but pursue one steady, uniform, consistent plan, they might (sitting in a begging attitude not being naturally an agreeable

position for a dog) quite as easily teach him to dance,—hold a pipe in his mouth,—stand up in a corner,—give the right or left paw,—shut the door,—pull the bell rope,—leap over a parasol,—or drag forth his napkin, and spread it as a table-cloth at dinner-time,* &c.; and, by following the method elsewhere explained (96, 107, 109,) seldom lose anything in their walks, as their faithful companion would almost invariably be on the alert to pick up and carry to them whatever they might drop. It is in this manner that dogs are sometimes made very useful assistants at cricket. A golf-ball maker at St. Andrew's, A——n R——n, employs his dog yet more usefully—at least more profitably. He has taught the animal to search the links by himself for balls, and to take home all he finds. Until the introduction of the universally applied gutta percha, the price of golf-balls was two shillings each. It may, therefore, be easily imagined that the diligent little fellow paid liberally for his board and lodging. But the trick of carrying has been made as serviceable to the dog as to his master.

151. A cousin of one of my brother officers, Colonel A——n, was taking a walk in the year '49, at Tonbridge Wells, when a strange Newfoundland made a snatch at the parasol she held loosely in her hand, and quietly carried it off. His jaunty air and wagging tail plainly told, as he marched along, that he was much pleased at his feat. The lady civilly requested him to restore it. This he declined, but in so gracious a manner, that she essayed, though ineffectually, to drag it from him. She therefore laughingly, albeit unwillingly, was constrained to follow her property rather than abandon it altogether. The dog kept ahead, constantly looking round to see if she followed, and was evidently greatly pleased at perceiving that she continued to favour him with her company. At length, he stepped into a confectioner's, where the lady renewed her attempts to obtain possession of her property; but as the Newfoundland would not resign it, she applied to the shopman for assistance, who said that it was an old trick of the dog's to get a bun; that if she would give him one, he would immediately return the stolen goods. She cheerfully did so, and the dog as willingly made the exchange.

152. I'll be bound the intelligent animal was no mean observer of countenances, and that he had satisfied himself, by a previous scrutiny, as to the probability of his delinquencies being forgiven.

153. "Carrying" is a pretty—occasionally, as we see, a useful—trick, but it does not further any sporting object. "Carrying" and "fetching" are essentially

---

* A trick that historical research probably would show to have been devised in a conclave of housemaids, and which was constantly performed by one of my oldest acquaintances, "Little-brush," a worthy son of the "Dearest-of-men," as he used to be called by his fond mistress, who, I need not say, had no children of her own on whom to lavish her caresses.

different. The object chiefly sought in the latter is to make the dog deliver *expeditiously* (107),—in the former, to make him carry *perseveringly* for miles and miles. To inculcate carrying, always make him suppose that you greatly regard what is confided to his charge. Many a good carrier is spoiled by children picking up any stick and giving it to him. He has the sense to know that it is valueless, and when he is tired of the fun, he drops it *unrebuked*, and, after a time, is supplied with another. If you practise a pup in carrying a stick, show more discretion than to let it be so long that it must jar against his teeth by trailing on the ground, or hitting the walls.

154. Being on the subject of tricks, as several ladies have done me the unexpected but highly appreciated honour of reading what I have said respecting their four-footed attendants, I think it as well to observe, should they be tempted to teach a favourite any accomplishments, that these should be practised occasionally, or they may be forgotten, (all the sooner, like more serious studies, the more easily they were acquired;) and that the exhibition of them might be made much more effective and striking by a little exercise, on the ladies' part, of the address and tact with which Dame Nature has so liberally endowed them.

155. Quite a sensation was created many years ago, at Tonbridge Wells, by the Hon. C. D——s, who possessed a dog which had been taught by a former master, for very unlawful purposes, to fetch, when ordered, any article to which his owner had slily directed the animal's attention.

156. The gentleman was walking up and down the crowded Pantiles, listening to the public band, and playing the agreeable to a titled lady, whom he subsequently married; when, bowing to some passing acquaintance, he casually observed, "How badly my hat has been brushed!" at the same time giving the private signal to the dog, who instantly ran off to one of the adjacent toy-shops, and brought away the hat-brush which his master had pointed out to him about a quarter of an hour before.

157. As Mr. D——s kept his own counsel, the lady and many of their friends, as well as the pursuing shopman, fancied the dog had sufficient intelligence to understand what had been said, and had, from his own sagacity, volunteered fetching what he conceived was required.

158. The barrack-rooms at Gibraltar used not to be furnished with bells. An officer of the Artillery, quartered on the Rock

while I was there, and, by the bye, so good a player at draughts, that he used to aver—and his unusual skill seemed to prove the correctness of the assertion—that, if he had the first move, he could win to a certainty, was accustomed to summon his servant by sending his dog for him. On getting the signal, away the Maltese poodle would go, not much impeded by closed doors in that hot climate, and, by a bark, inform the man that he was wanted.

159. The daily routine of a quiet bachelor's life is so unvaried in those barracks, that the servant could generally guess what was required; and visitors were often surprised at hearing the officer (Major F——e) say to his dog, " Tell John to bring my sword and cap," or " the breakfast," &c. and still more surprised at seeing that such orders were punctually obeyed.

160. But for exhibiting tricks with effect doubtless my old warm-hearted friend K——g, (elsewhere mentioned 450,) bears off the palm. He brought two young elephants to England from Ceylon; one he secured when it was a mere baby, and would not quit the side of its dam after he had shot her. The other was about seven feet high. He had taught them several tricks before they embarked, and during the long voyage home, passed on deck, they had learned many others from the sailors, and, when needed, would usefully help in giving " a long pull,—a strong pull,—and a pull all together."

161. General B——g having spoken to the Duchess of Y——k about the little animals, she happened to say she would like to possess the smallest; of course K——g was too gallant a man not to send it at once to Oatlands. George the Fourth heard of the other; and on some of his staff mentioning that it would be acceptable to His Majesty, it went to the Pavilion at Brighton. It was kept there until they were tired of it, when it was transferred to the Tower. Hearing of its being there, K——g one morning went into the menagerie. An officer of the Guards, on duty at the Tower, was at the moment seeing the animals with a party of ladies; K——g was in a hurry, and inquired where the elephant was, saying he had come expressly to have a look at him and nothing else. The officer very good-humouredly observed that it mattered not what beasts they saw first, so the party adjourned to the elephant. K——g urged the keeper to go into the den to show him off, but the man said the animal had so recently arrived there that he was afraid. K——g offered to go in. The man refused leave, stating it was more than his situation was worth to permit it. K——g pressed to be allowed. The officer warmly urged the keeper to comply, " as the gentleman felt so confident," and the keeper wavering, K——g, without saying another word, squeezed himself through the massive oak bars, went up boldly to the elephant, put his hand on his shoulder as he used to do in old days; the sagacious brute at once obeyed the signal and lay down, got up again when desired, salaamed to the ladies, held a foot out for K——g to stand on, then raised it up to aid K——g in getting on his back, and afterwards lay down to enable his old master to

dismount conveniently. K——g then tickled him to make him kick, which the awkward looking beast did in a very laughable manner, and the laugh of the spectators was not diminished by his squeezing K——g so close into a corner, that he could only escape by slipping under the creature's belly. K——g finished the exhibition by making him turn round, and again salaam the company.

162. I will not swear that K——g, who has much quiet humour, did not propose going into any other den and show off all the lions and tigers in a similar manner, but he found, of course unexpectedly, on looking at his watch, that he was obliged to hurry off instantly. The delighted and bewildered keeper entreated him to reveal the secret by which such marvellous feats were performed. K——g promised to do so on his return to London; and he would have kept his word, had not the poor elephant soon afterwards died in cutting his tusks. So the man to this day, for all I know to the contrary, thinks my friend little less than a necromancer.

163. It is to be observed that ladies' dogs are generally so pampered and overfed that a common reward does not stimulate them to exertion in the same degree it does dogs less favoured. I should

REPLETE WITH GOOD THINGS.

speak more correctly if I said less *fed*; for I am ungallant enough to fancy, that an *unpacked* canine jury would consider the good health, high spirits, and keen appetite of the latter, a fair set-off against the delicacies and caresses bestowed by the prettiest and most indulgent of mistresses. Though the collie is the shepherd's constant companion, the shepherd well knows that always petting the dog would spoil him. Sir J——s M——e, a Highlander, observed to his gamekeeper, that he never saw the shepherds coaxing and caressing their collies. "True," the man replied, "but you never saw one strike his dog; he is always kind to them." Hear this, ye ladies, who would be right glad that your pretty pets were a hundred times more obedient than you find them.

164. There are few animals whose confidence, if not attachment, may not be gained by constant kindness without petting. One summer's morning I walked from Ross to breakfast with Mr. C——s at his picturesque old-fashioned house, built near a small tributary to the Wye. I was specially invited to see some tame trout, whose timidity Mr. C——s had overcome by feeding them regularly every day. Until he made his appearance near the waters, not a fish was visible; and it was very interesting to watch the perfect confidence they evinced, I might add pleasure, whenever he approached the banks. He said he felt sure he could get them to feed out of his hands, if he chose to devote sufficient time to them. There was one fine fellow for whom all the rest most respectfully made way. He weighed close upon 5 lbs. This was proved; for a party, whose name I dare not mention, secretly caught the animal in order to weigh it, and though he immediately replaced it in the water perfectly uninjured, yet its old distrust was so much re-awakened that it hid itself for four or five months. Mr. C——s naturally thought that it had been captured by some poacher, and had met with the same unlucky fate as a former favourite, of still larger dimensions, which a newly-hired cook had contrived to secure whilst it was basking in the shallows; and had served up at dinner time, in the full expectation of receiving much commendation for her piscatory skill.

165. Judicious perseverance,—in other words, consistency,—will not only teach accomplishments, but correct bad manners. The oldest friend I possess used to allow a favourite dog to sleep in his bed-room. The animal, though he had a very short, clean coat, was always more or less annoyed by those nimblest of tormentors * to

---

* It is astonishing what myriads of fleas are bred in the sand in many hot countries. When walking along some of the roads during the spring, numbers of the little creatures will pay you the compliment of attaching themselves to your dress and person. At Bermuda they so regularly make their appearance with the whales, that the Niggers think there must be some intimate, however mysterious, connexion between the two. In India the natives expel the intruders from their houses by strewing fresh saffron leaves about the rooms; and a decoction from these said leaves, applied liberally to a dog's coat, rids him of the unwelcome visitors, however numerous. I have read that the same good effect will be produced

be found in most countries, particularly in warm ones; and there being no carpet in the room, his scratching at night, as you may well imagine, made a loud, disagreeable thumping against the boards, which *invariably* awoke my friend (a very light sleeper), and he as *invariably* scolded the dog. This undeviating consistency made the dog at length entirely relinquish the obnoxious practice, until his master was fairly awake, or at least had begun to stretch and yawn.

166. Now, I want you to observe, that had the noise but only *occasionally* awakened my friend, however much he might then have scolded, the dog would not have given up the habit; he would constantly have entertained the hope that he might endeavour to remove his tiny persecutors unreproved, and the temptation would have outweighed the risk. It would have been inconsistent to have frequently but not always checked him. I know a lady, possessing great perseverance and temper, who has taught even cats many tricks—nay, since the last edition of this book was printed I have heard of several ladies having most successfully educated dogs for the field. A very pleasant girl, Miss G——h, almost a stranger to me, who sat next to me at a large dinner-party about a year ago, asked me in the course of conversation whether I was related to the author of "Dog-Breaking,"—and then greatly gratified me by saying that her sister had broken in several Pointers for her brother, a M.F.H. She spoke of one particular 1st of September, when her sister was rather nervous as a well-known keen sportsman had been invited to shoot, and a young well-bred dog, solely tutored by herself, was to bear his first shot—but at dinner-time she was amply recompensed for all the trouble she had taken by having the delight of learning that her pupil had performed admirably, and had understood and been attentive to every signal. I asked how it was that

if his hair be well wetted with a solution of the gum of the sloe-tree in water. Fourteen grains of the gum to one quart of water.

The capture of the whale, by the bye, at Bermuda, affords sport as exciting as it is profitable. The fish are struck within sight of the Islands, and as the water is shoal, owing to sandbanks, a short line is employed. By this line the stricken animal tows the harpooner's boat along with fearful rapidity, an immense wave curling far above the high bow. The flesh of the young whale is excellent,—very like veal,—and with the black population the whaling season is one of great feasting and enjoyment. By a colonial law no charge can be made for the flesh of the fish. Every comer has a right to carry off as much of the meat as he may require, *but no blubber*. On a whale being killed, a well-known signal, hoisted at the several look-out posts, quickly informs the coloured inhabitants of the successful seizure, and whether it has been effected at the north or south side. Numerous claimants then hurry off, on foot or in boat, to secure a sufficiency for several days' consumption, of a food they prize far more than beef or mutton. What is not immediately used is cut into strips, and dried in the sun.

H

the youngster was not alarmed at the report of the gun. She replied that it was doubtless attributable to his perfect confidence that he should not be hurt, as he had never undergone any punishing during the whole course of his training.

167. Ladies' pets are a proof that dogs can, as easily as children, be effectually spoiled by injudicious kindness; but canine nature contrasts with infant nature in this, that no petting or spoiling will withdraw a dog's affection from the individual to whom he first becomes attached in a new home, provided that person continues but decently civil to him. And be this a caution to you. If ever you have a stranger to instruct, let no one but yourself associate with or feed him for many days after his arrival. You may then feel assured of afterwards possessing his unrivalled affections, especially if to you alone he is to be grateful for his enjoyment in the field; and you must win his affection, or he will not strive to his utmost to assist you.

168. A well-known poaching character,—though ostensibly, and by *profession*, a dog-breaker,—was remarkable for the fondness immediately evinced for him by all dogs placed under his care. He was not particular about his dress; and it at length transpired that it was his custom to make up a bed, for all new comers, in his room, of the clothes he had just taken off. This so habituated the dogs to the scent of his person, by night as well as by day, that they became unwilling to quit it, especially as the man was naturally good-tempered, and always treated them with great kindness.

169. Captain Parry relates of the Esquimaux dogs, that they are far more attached,—from kindnesses received in youth,—to the women, than to the men; and that, consequently, the latter, in all cases of difficulty, are obliged to apply to their wives to catch the almost woolly animals, and coax them to draw unusually heavy loads. The beloved voice of the women will control and animate the dogs to exertion, at a time when the words of the men would be powerless, and their blows only produce irritation or obstinacy.

CHAPTER VI.

FIRST LESSON IN SEPTEMBER COMMENCED. RANGING.

170. Regular Breakers make Dogs "point" paired birds in Spring; tends to blinking.—171. Better not to see Game until shot over; taken out alone on a fine day in September.—172. Perpetually whistling to animate dogs, injudicious.—173. Beat largest Fields, and where least likely to find Game.—174. Commence from leeward; Scent bad in a calm or gale; observations on Scent; it differently affects Pointers and Setters; see Note.—175 to 179. Instructions in "ranging."—180. Kept from hedge; Range greater on moors than stubble.—181. Distance between Parallels dependent on tenderness of nose.—182. A point at Partridge a hundred yards off.—183. At Grouse a hundred and fifty yards off; Mr. L——g's opinion of distance at which Dogs wind birds.—184. If the Dog is to hunt with another, the Parallels to be further apart.—185. No interruption when winding birds, yet not allowed to puzzle; Nose to gain experience.—186. Birds lie well to Dog that "winds," not "foots" them.—187. White Dogs most visible to *birds* and to *you;* a disadvantage and advantage; white Feet often not good; feet of Setters better than of Pointers.—188. Inattentive to Whistle, made to "drop," &c.; when rating or punishing, the disregarded order or signal to be often repeated; Whip to crack loudly.—189. The attainment of a scientific Range difficult, but of surpassing value; the best ranger must in the end find most game.

170. A KEEPER nearly always breaks in his young dogs to point, (or "set" as some term it) if their ages permit it, on favourable days in Spring, when the partridges have paired.* He gets plenty of points, and the birds lie well. But I cannot believe it is the best way to attain great excellence, though the plan has many followers : it does not cultivate the intelligence of his pupils, nor enlarge their ideas by making them sensible of the object for which such pains are taken in hunting them. Moreover, their natural ardour (a feeling that it should be his aim rather to increase than weaken) is more or less damped by having often to stand at

* In ordinary seasons immediately after St. Valentine's Day, —before the birds have made their nests.

H 2

game, before they can be rewarded for their exertions by having it killed to them,—it prevents, rather than imparts, the zeal and perseverance for which Irish dogs are so remarkable (565). Particularly ought a breaker, whose pupil is of a nervous temperament, or of too gentle a disposition, to consider well that the want of all recompence for finding paired birds, must make a timid dog far more likely to become a "blinker," when he is checked for not pointing them, than when he is checked for not pointing birds, which his own impetuosity alone deprives him of every chance of rapturously "touseling." (See also end of 280.) The very fact that "the birds lie well" frequently leads to mischief; for, if the instructor be not very watchful, there is a fear that his youngsters may succeed in getting too close to their game before he forces them to come to a stanch point. A keeper, however, has but little choice, (and it is not a bad time to teach the back,) if his master insist upon shooting over the animals the first day of the season, and expect to find them what some call "perfectly broken in." But I trust some few of my readers may have nobler ends in view, and that they will cheerfully sacrifice a little of their shooting the first week of the season, to ensure super-excellence in their pupils at its close. Remember, I do not object to spring drilling, (vide 131) but to much spring pointing.

171. I will suppose your youngster to have been well grounded in his initiatory lessons, and that you take him out when the crops are nearly off the ground (by which time there will be few squeakers) on a fine cool day in September, (alas! that it cannot be an August day on the moors,) to show him birds for the first time. As he is assumed to be highly bred, you may start in

the confident expectation of killing partridges over him, especially if he be a pointer. Have his nose moist and healthy. Take him out when the birds are on the feed, and of an afternoon in preference to the morning, (unless from an unusually dry season there be but little scent,) that he may not be attracted by the taint of hares or rabbits. Take him out alone, if he evince any disposition to hunt, which, at the age we will presume him to have attained this season, we must assume that he will do, and with great zeal. Be much guided by his temper and character. Should he possess great courage and dash, you cannot begin too soon to make him point. You should always check a wild dog in racing after pigeons and small birds on their rising; whereas you should encourage a timid dog (one who clings to "heel") in such a fruitless but exciting chase. The measures to be pursued with such an animal are fully detailed in 132, 133.

172. I may as well caution you against adopting the foolish practice of attempting to cheer on your dog with a constant low whistle, under the mistaken idea that it will animate him to increased zeal in hunting. From perpetually hearing the monotonous sound, it would prove as little of an incentive to exertion as a continued chirrup to a horse; and yet if habituated to it, your dog would greatly miss it whenever hunted by a stranger. Not unregarded, however, would it be by the birds, to whom on a calm day it would act as a very salutary warning.

173. Though you have not moors, fortunately we can suppose your fields to be of a good size. Avoid all which have been recently manured. Select those that are large, and in which you are the least likely to find birds until his spirits are somewhat sobered, and he

begins partly to comprehend your instructions respecting his range. There is no reason why he should not have been taken out a few days before this, *not to show him birds,* but to have commenced teaching him how to traverse his ground. Indeed, if we had supposed him of a sufficient age (132), he might by this time be somewhat advanced towards a systematic beat. It is seeing many birds early that is to be deprecated, not his being taught how to range.

174. *Be careful to enter every field at the leeward* side (about the middle), that he may have the wind to work against.* Choose a day when there is a breeze, but not a boisterous one. In a calm, the scent is stationary, and can hardly be found unless accidentally. In a gale it is scattered to the four quarters.† You

---

* "Leeward"—a nautical phrase —here meaning the side towards which the wind blows *from* the field. If you entered elsewhere, the dog while ranging would be tempted, from the natural bearing of his nose towards the wind, to come back upon you, making his first turn inwards instead of outwards.

† But, independently of these obvious reasons, scent is affected by causes into the nature of which none of us can penetrate. There is a contrariety in it that ever has puzzled, and apparently ever will puzzle, the most observant sportsman (whether a lover of the chase or gun), and therefore, in ignorance of the doubtless immutable, though to us inexplicable, laws by which it is regulated, we are contented to call it "capricious." Immediately before heavy rain there frequently is none. It is undeniable that moisture will at one time destroy it,—at another bring it. That on certain days— in slight frost, for instance,— setters will recognise it better than pointers, and, on the other hand, that the nose of the latter will prove far superior after a long continuance of dry weather, and this even when the setter has been furnished with abundance of water, —which circumstance pleads in favour of hunting pointers and setters together. The argument against it, is the usual inequality of their pace, and, to the eye of some sportsmen, the want of harmony in their appearance. Should not this uncertainty respecting the recognition of scent teach us not to continue hunting a good dog who is frequently making mistakes, but rather to keep him at "heel" for an hour or two? He will consider it a kind of punishment, and be doubly careful when next enlarged. Moreover, he may be slightly feverish from overwork, or he may have come in contact with some impurity,—in either of which cases his nose would be temporarily out of order.

want not an undirected ramble, but a judicious traversing beat under your own guidance, which shall leave no ground unexplored, and yet have none twice explored.

175. Suppose the form of the field, as is usually the case, to approach a parallelogram or square, and that the wind blows in any direction but diagonally across it. On entering at the leeward side send the dog from you by a wave of your hand or the word "On." You wish him, while you are advancing up the middle of it, to cross you at right-angles, say from right to left,—then to run up-wind for a little, parallel to your own direction, and afterwards to recross in front of you from left to right, and so on until the whole field is regularly hunted. To effect this, notwithstanding your previous preparatory lessons, you will have to show him the way, as it were (setting him an example in your own person), by running a few steps in the direction you wish him to go (say to the right), cheering him on to take the lead. As he gets near the extremity of his beat, when he does not observe you, you can steal a small advance in the true direction of your own beat, which is directly up the middle of the field, meeting the wind. If perceiving your advance he turns towards you, face him,— wave your right hand to him, and while he sees you, run on a few paces in his direction (that is *parallel* to his true direction). As he approaches the hedge (the one on your right hand, but be careful that he does not get close to it, lest, from often finding game there, he ultimately become a potterer and regular hedge-hunter) face towards him, and on catching his eye, wave your left arm. If you cannot succeed in catching his eye, you must give one low whistle,—the less you habituate yourself to use the whistle, the less you

will alarm the birds,—study to do all, as far as is practicable, by signals. You wish your wave of the left arm to make the dog turn to the left (his head to the wind), and that he should run parallel to the side of the hedge for some yards (say from thirty to forty) before he makes his second turn to the left to cross the field; but you must expect him to turn too directly towards you on your first signal to turn. Should he by any rare chance have made the turn (the first one) correctly, and thus be hunting up-wind, on no account interrupt him by making any signals until he has run up the distance you wish, (the aforesaid thirty or forty yards,)—then again catch his eye, and, as before (not now, however, faced towards him and the hedge, but faced towards your true direction), by a wave of the left arm endeavour to make him turn to the left (across the wind). If, contrary to what you have a right to suppose, he will not turn towards you on your giving a whistle and wave of your hand, stand still, and continue whistling—eventually he will obey. But you must not indulge in the faintest hope that all I have described will be done correctly; be satisfied at first with an approach towards accuracy; you will daily find an improvement, if you persevere steadily. When you see that there is but little chance of his turning the way you want, at once use the signal more consonant to his views, for it should be your constant endeavour to make him fancy that he is always ranging according to the directions of your hands. Be particular in attending to this hint.

176. His past tuition (38) most probably will have accustomed him to watch your eye for directions, therefore it is not likely, even should he have made a wrong turn near the hedge (a turn down-wind instead of up-

wind, which would wholly have prevented the required advance parallel to the hedge), that he will cross in rear of you. Should he, however, do so, retreat a few steps, (or face about if he is far in the rear,) in order to impress him with the feeling that all his work must be performed under your eye. Animate him with an encouraging word as he passes. When he gets near the hedge to the left, endeavour, by signals (agreeably to the method just explained (175), to make him turn to the (his) right, his head to the wind, and run up alongside of it for the thirty to forty yards, if you can manage it, before he begins to recross the field, by making a second turn to the right. If you could get him to do this, he would cross well in advance of you.

177. Though most likely his turn (the first—the turn up-wind) will be too abrupt (too much of an acute angle instead of the required right angle), and that consequently, in order to get ahead of you, he will have to traverse the field diagonally, yet after a few trials it is probable he will do so, rather than not get in front of you. This would be better than the former attempt (not obliging you to face about),—express your approval, and the next turn near the hedge may be made with a bolder sweep. Remember your aim is, that no part be unhunted, and that none once commanded by his nose be again hunted. He ought to cross, say thirty yards in front of you, but *much* will depend upon his nose.

178. Nearly on every occasion of catching his eye, except when he is running up-wind parallel to the hedge, give him some kind of signal. This will more and more confirm him in the habit of looking to you, from time to time, for orders, and thus aid in insuring his constant obedience. After a while, judging by the way in which your face is turned, he will know in what direction you

purpose advancing, and will guide his own movements accordingly. Should he, as most probably he will for some time, turn too sharply towards you when getting near the hedge, I mean at too acute an angle, incline or rather face towards him. This, coupled with the natural wish to range unrestrained, will make him hunt longer parallel to the hedge, before he makes his second turn towards you.

179. You may at first strive to correct your dog's turning too abruptly inwards (the first turn), by pushing on in your own person further ahead on your own beat; but when he has acquired if merely the slightest idea of a correct range, be most careful not to get in advance of the ground he is to hunt. Your doing so might habituate him to cross the field diagonally (thereby leaving much of the sides of the fields unhunted), in order to get ahead of you; and, moreover, *you* might spring birds which you are anxious *he* should find. Should he, on the other hand, be inclined to work too far upward before making his turn to cross the field, hang back in your own person.

180. Though you may be in an unenclosed country, let him range at first from no more than from seventy to eighty yards on each side of you. You can gradually extend these lateral beats as he becomes conversant with his business—indeed, at the commencement, rather diminish than increase the distances just named, both for the length of the parallels and the space between them. Do not allow the alluring title "a fine wide ranger" to tempt you to let him out of leading-strings. If he be once permitted to imagine that he has a discretionary power respecting the best places to hunt, and the direction and length of his beats, you will find it extremely difficult to get him again well in hand. On

the moors his range must be far greater than on the stubbles, but still the rudiments must be taught on this contracted scale, or you will never get him to look to you for orders. Do *you* keep entire control over his beats; let *him* have almost the sole management of his drawing upon birds, provided he does not puzzle, or run riot too long over an old haunt. Give him time, and after a little experience his nose will tell him more surely than your judgment can, whether he is working on the "toe" or "heel" of birds, and, whether he diverges from or approaches the strongest and most recent haunt,—do not flurry or hurry him, and he will soon acquire that knowledge.

181. As the powers of scent vary greatly in different dogs, the depth of their turns (or parallels) ought to vary also, and it will be hereafter for you to judge what distance between the parallels it is most advantageous for your youngster ultimately to adopt in his general hunting. The deeper his turns are, of course, the more ground you will beat within a specified time. What you have to guard against is the possibility of their being so wide that birds may be passed by unnoticed. I should not like to name the distance within which good *cautious* dogs that carry their heads high, will wind game on a favourable day.

182. I was partridge shooting the season before last with an intimate friend. The air was soft and there was a good breeze. We came upon a large turnip-field, deeply trenched on account of its damp situation. A white setter, that habitually carried a lofty head, drew for awhile, and then came to a point. We got up to her. She led us across some ridges, when her companion, a jealous dog (a pointer), which had at first backed correctly, most improperly pushed on in front, but, not being able to acknowledge the scent, went off, clearly imagining the bitch was in error. She, however, held on, and in beautiful style brought us direct to a covey. My friend and I agreed that she must have been but little, if at all, less than one hundred yards off when she first winded the birds; and it was clear to us that they could not have been running, for the

breeze came directly across the furrows, and she had led us in the wind's eye. We thought the point the more remarkable, as it is generally supposed that the strong smell of turnips diminishes a dog's power of scenting birds.

183. R——t T——n, a gamekeeper, once assured me he had seen a point at grouse which were at the least one hundred and fifty yards off. The dogs were on the edge of a valley—the pack on a little hillock from which direction the wind blew—an intervening wall near the top of the hillock separated them from the dogs; and as intermediately there was no heather, the man was satisfied that the birds had not run over the ground. When I was talking one day to Mr. L——g, the well-known gunmaker in the Haymarket, about the qualities of dogs' noses,—and from his long experience he ought to be a judge of such matters,—he told me, before I had said a word respecting distances, that he thought he had seen more than once a dog point at one hundred and fifty yards from his game.

184. If you design your pupil, when broken in, to hunt with a companion, and wish both the dogs, as is usual, to cross you, you will, of course, habituate him to make his sweeps (the space between the parallels) wider than if you had intended him to hunt without any one to share his labours.

185. I need hardly warn you to be careful not to interrupt him whenever he appears to be winding birds. However good his nose may be by nature, it will not gain experience and discrimination, unless you give him a certain time to determine for himself whether he has really touched upon a faint scent of birds, and whether they are in his front or rear, or gone away altogether. Like every other faculty, his sense of smell will improve the more it is exercised. But on the other hand, as I observed before, do not let him continue puzzling with his nose close to the ground,—urge him on,—make him increase his pace,—force him to search elsewhere, and he will gradually elevate his head, and catching the scent of other particles, will follow up these with a nose borne aloft, unless he is a brute not worth a twentieth part of the pains which you think of bestowing upon him; for,

186. Besides the greatly decreased chance of finding them, birds that to a certainty would become uneasy, and make off if pursued by a dog tracking them, will often lie well to one who finds them by the wind. They are then not aware that they are discovered, and the dog, from the information his nose gives him, can approach them either boldly or with great wariness, according as he perceives them to be more or less shy.

187. It is rather foreign to our immediate subject, but I will here observe, that it is generally thought white dogs cannot approach shy birds * as closely as dogs of a dark colour can (93) ; but there is a set-off to this supposed disadvantage in *your* being able to distinguish the light ones more readily at a distance,—a matter of some moment on heather. If you have not your eye on a steady brown setter at the moment he drops on grouse, you may spend half an hour most vexatiously in searching for him. When you expect to find the birds wild, should your kennel allow you the choice, you ought to take out out those of a sombre hue. Light coloured dogs have not generally such well-shaped feet as their darker brethren. It is curious that white feet in dogs as well as in horses should often be objectionable. As a rule, setters have harder, tougher feet than pointers. This is very apparent in a flinty country or in frosty weather, and is partly attributable to their being better defended with hair round the ball, and between the toes.

188. If, being unable to catch the dog's eye, you are forced to use the whistle frequently, and he continues inattentive to it, notwithstanding his previous tuition, stand still,—make him lie down (by the word "drop," if he will not obey your raised left arm)—go up to him,— take hold of his collar, and rate him, saying, "Bad, bad," cracking your whip over him (let the whip be one that will crack loudly, not for present purposes, but that, when occasion requires, he may hear it at a distance) and whistling softly. This will show him (should you beat him, you would confuse his ideas) that he is chidden for not paying attention to the whistle. Indeed,

---

* There are sportsmen who aver that a setter's "falling" instead of standing is advantageous, as it does not so much alarm the birds.

whenever you have occasion to scold or punish him, make it a constant rule, while you rate him, to repeat many times the word of command, or the signal which he has neglected to obey. There is no other way by which you will make him understand you *quickly*.

189. You must expect that your young dog will for some time make sad mistakes in his range;—but be not discouraged. Doubtless there is no one thing,—I was going to say, that there are no dozen things,—in the whole art of dog-breaking, which are so difficult to attain, or which exact so much labour, as a high, well-confirmed, systematic range. Nature will not assist you:—you must do it all yourself; but in recompense there is nothing so advantageous when it is at length acquired. It will abundantly repay months of persevering exertion. It constitutes the grand criterion of true excellence. Its attainment makes a dog of inferior nose and action far superior to one of much greater natural qualifications who may be tomfooling about, galloping backwards and forwards sometimes over identically the same ground, quite uselessly exerting his travelling powers; now and then, indeed, arrested by the suspicion of a haunt, which he is not experienced enough, or sufficiently taught, to turn to good account,— and occasionally brought to a stiff point on birds accidentally found right under his nose. It is undeniable, *cæteris paribus*, that the dog who hunts his ground most according to rule must in the end find most game.

CHAPTER VII.

FIRST LESSONS IN SEPTEMBER CONTINUED. CAUTION.—NATURE'S MYSTERIOUS INFLUENCES.

190. Dog to be hunted alone.—191. Many Breakers exactly reverse this; it expedites an inferior education, but retards a superior.—192. Turnips, Potatoes, &c., avoided. Range of Dogs broken on moors most true.—193. In Turnips, &c., young Dogs get too close to birds.—194. *Cautious* Dogs may with advantage be as fast as wild ones; the two contrasted; in Note, injudiciousness of teaching a Puppy to "point" Chickens.—195. Instance of a Dog's running to "heel," but not "blinking," on finding himself close to birds.—196. A Dog's Nose cannot be improved, but his *caution* can, which is nearly tantamount; how effected. —197. How to make fast Dogs cautious.—198. The cause why wild Dogs ultimately turn out best.—199. Dog tumbling over and pointing on his Back.— 200. Dog pointing on top of high-log Fence at quail in tree; in Note, Militia Regiment that sought safety by taking to Trees.—201. The day's Beat commenced from leeward.—202. Wondrous Dogs, which find Game without hunting, —203. Colonel T——y's opinion.—204 to 209. His dog "Grouse," that walked up direct to her Game.—210. "Grouse's" portrait.—211 to 213. Probable solution of "Grouse's" feat; in Note, why high nose finds most game.—214. Reason why Dogs should be instructed separately, and allowed Time to work out a Scent; young dogs generally too much hurried.—215. Mysterious Influences.—216. Retriever that runs direct to hidden object.—217. Not done by nose.—218. Newfoundland that always swam back to his own Ship.—219. Another that did the same.—220. Now belongs to the Duke of N——k.—221. Cats and Dogs carried off in baskets, finding their way back; Nature's Mysteries inexplicable. In Note, instance of extraordinary memory in a Horse.

190. If it is your fixed determination to confirm your dog in the truly-killing range described in the last Chapter, do not associate him for months in the field with another dog, however highly broken. It would be far better to devote but two hours per diem to your pupil exclusively, than to hunt him the whole day with a companion.

191. Many breakers do exactly the reverse of this. They take out an old steady ranger, with the intention that he shall lead the young dog, and that the latter, from imitation and habit, shall learn how to quarter his

ground. But what he gains by imitation will so little improve his intellects, that, when thrown upon his own resources, he will prove a miserable finder. On a hot, dry day he will not be able to make out a feather, nor on any day to "foot" a delicate scent. I grant that the plan expedites matters, and attains the end which *most* professional trainers seek; but it will not give a dog self-confidence and independence, it will not impart to him an inquiring nose, and make him rely on its sensitiveness to discover game, rather than to his quickness of eye to detect when his friend touches upon a haunt; nor will it instruct him to look from time to time towards the gun for directions. It may teach him a range, but not to hunt where he is ordered; nor will it habituate him to vary the breadth of the parallels on which he works, according as his master may judge it to be a good or bad scenting day.

192. To establish the rare, noble beat I am recommending,—one not hereafter to be deranged by the temptation of a furrow in turnips or potatoes,—you must have the philosophy not to hunt your dog in them until he is accustomed in his range to be guided entirely by the wind and your signals, and is in no way influenced by the nature of the ground. Even then it would be better not to beat narrow strips across which it would be impossible for him to make his regular casts. Avoid, too, for some time, if you can, all small fields (which will only contract his range), and all fields with trenches or furrows, for he will but too naturally follow them instead of paying attention to his true beat. Have you never, in low lands, seen a young dog running down a potato or turnip trench, out of which his master, after much labour, had no sooner extracted him than he dropped into the adjacent one? It is the

absence of artificial tracks which makes the range of nearly all dogs *well* broken on the moors so much truer than that of dogs hunted on cultivated lands.

193. Moreover, in turnips, potatoes, clover, and the like thick shelter, birds will generally permit a dog to approach so closely, that if he is much accustomed to hunt such places, he will be sure to acquire the evil habit of pressing too near his game when finding on the stubbles (instead of being startled as it were into an instantaneous stop the moment he first winds game), and thus raise many a bird out of gun-shot that a *cautious* dog,—one who slackens his pace the instant he judges that he is beating a likely spot,—would not have alarmed.

194. "A *cautious* dog"! Can there well be a more flattering epithet?* Such a dog can hardly travel too fast † in a tolerably open country, where there is not a superabundance of game, *if* he really hunt with an inquiring nose;—but to his master what an all-important "if" is this! It marks the difference between the sagacious, wary, patient, yet diligent animal, whose every sense and every faculty is absorbed in his endeavour to make out birds, not for himself but for the gun, and the wild harum-scarum who blunders up three-fourths of the birds he finds. No! not *finds*, but frightens,—for he is not aware of their presence until they are on the wing, and seldom points unless he gets some heedless bird right under his nose, when an ignoramus, in admi-

---

* Provided always he be not perpetually pointing, as occasionally will happen—and is the more likely to happen if he has been injudiciously taught as a puppy to set chickens, and has thereby acquired the evil habit of "standing by eye;" which, however, may have made him a first-rate hand at pointing crows.

† With the understanding that the pace does not make him "shut up" before the day is over.

ration of the beauty of the dog's sudden attitude, will often forget the mischief which he has done.

195. Nature gives this caution to some dogs at an early age. A clergyman of my acquaintance, Mr. G. M——t, a keen sportsman in his younger days, told me that when he was partridge-shooting once in Essex, a favourite pointer of his, that was ranging at a rapid pace alongside a thick hedge, coming suddenly upon an opening where there should have been a gate, instantly wheeled round and ran to heel, and then commenced carefully advancing with a stiffened stern towards the gap; and so led his master up to five birds which were lying close to it, but on the further side. Evidently the *cautious* dog,—for he was no blinker,—on so unexpectedly finding himself in such close vicinity to the covey, must have fancied that his presence would alarm them, however motionless he might remain.

196. Though you cannot improve a dog's nose, you can do what is really tantamount to it—you can increase his caution. By watching for the slightest token of his feathering, and then calling out "Toho," or making the signal, you will gradually teach him to look out for the faintest indication of a scent, and *point the instant he winds it*, instead of heedlessly hunting on until he meets a more exciting effluvia. (See 259 to 261, also 329.) If from a want of animation in his manner you are not able to judge of the moment when he first winds game, and therefore are unable to call out "Toho" until he gets close to birds, quietly pull him back from his point "dead to leeward" for some paces, and there make him resume his point. Perseverance in this plan will ultimately effect your wishes, unless his nose be radically wrong. A dog's pointing too near his game more frequently arises from want of caution,—in other words, from want of good instruction,—than from a defective nose.

197. Slow dogs readily acquire this caution; but fast dogs cannot be taught it without great labour. You have to show them the necessity of diminishing their

pace, that their noses may have fair play. If you have such a pupil to instruct, when you get near birds you have marked down, signal to him to come to "heel." *Whisper* to him "Care," and let him see by your light, slow tread your anxiety not to alarm the game. If he has never shown any symptoms of blinking, you may, a few times, thus spring the birds yourself while you keep him close to you. On the next occasion of marking down birds, or coming to a very likely spot, bring him into "heel," and after an impressive injunction to take "care," give him two or three very limited casts to the right or left, and let *him* find the game while you instruct him as described in 329. As there will be no fear of such a dog making false points, take him often to the fields where he has most frequently met birds. The expectation of again coming on them, and the recollection of the lectures he there received, will be likely to make him cautious on entering it. I remember a particular spot in a certain field that early in the season constantly held birds. A young dog I then possessed never approached it afterwards without drawing upon it most carefully, though he had not found there for months. At first I had some difficulty in preventing the "draw" from becoming a "point."

198. I have elsewhere observed that fast dogs, which give most trouble in breaking, usually turn out best. Now if you think for a moment you will see the reason plainly. A young dog does not ultimately become first-rate because he is wild and headstrong, and regardless of orders, but because his speed and disobedience arise from his great energies,—from his fondness for the sport; from his longing to inhale the exhilarating scent and pursue the flying game. It is the possession of these qualities that makes him, in his anxious state of

excitement, blind to your signals and deaf to your calls. These obviously are qualities that, *under good management*,* lead to great excellence and superiority,—that make one dog do the work of two. But they are not qualities sought for by an idle or incompetent breaker. He would prefer the kind of dog mentioned in 280, and boast much of the ability he had displayed in training him. These valuable qualities in the fast dog, must, however, be accompanied by a searching nose. It is not enough that a dog be always apparently hunting, that is to say, always on the gallop—his nose should always be hunting. When this is the case (and you may be pretty certain it is if, as he crosses the breeze, his nose has intuitively a bearing to windward), you need not fear that he will travel too fast, or not repay you ultimately for the great extra trouble caused by his high spirits and ardour for the sport.

199. The Rev. Mr. M——t (spoken of in 195) had one of these valuable, fast, but cautious dogs. The dog, in leaping over a stile that led from an orchard and crowned a steep bank, accidentally tumbled head over heels. He rolled to the bottom of the bank, and there remained motionless on his back. Mr. M——t went up in great distress, fancying his favourite must have been seriously injured. However, on his approaching the dog, up sprung some partridges, which, it appears, the *careful* animal must have winded, and fearing to disturb, would not move a muscle of his body, for happily he was in no way hurt by the fall.

200. I was shooting in the upper provinces of Canada over a young dog, who suddenly checked himself and came to a stiff " set " on the top of a high zigzag log fence. I could not believe that he was cunning enough to do this for the purpose of deceiving me, because I was rating him for quitting the field before me ; and yet why should he be pointing in mid-air as rigidly as if carved in stone ? On my going up the enigma was solved, by a bevy of quail flying out of a neighbouring tree.† It is said they often take to them

---

* The more resolute a dog is, the more pains should be taken, before he is shown game, to perfect him in the instant " drop " (26), however far off he may be ranging.

† The mention of quails taking to trees recalls to my recollection a novel light infantry manœuvre (for the exact particulars of which I will not, however, positively pledge myself,) that was con-

"He rolled to the bottom of the bank, and there lay motionless on his back."
Par. 199

in America: but this was the only instance I ever saw. But we will now hark back to your pup, which, for your sake, I wish may turn out as cautious a dog.

201. You have been recommended invariably to enter every field by the leeward side. This you can generally accomplish with ease, if you commence your day's beat to leeward. Should circumstances oblige you to enter a field on the windward side, make it a rule, as long as your dog continues a youngster, to call him to "heel," and walk down the field with him until you get to the opposite side (the leeward),—then hunt him regularly up to windward.

202. I have read wondrous accounts of dogs, who, without giving themselves the trouble of quartering ceived with such admirable rapidity by the commanding officer on an occasion of great emergency, and executed with such wonderful celerity by the troops under him, that I hope my professional partialities will be allowed to excuse my describing it.

Bermuda, "the blest little island," as the fascinating Tommy Moore styles her, although now well supplied with all the necessaries of life, especially since the improvements in husbandry, introduced by its late excellent governor, Colonel R——d (now Sir William), was formerly but little better provided with fresh meat than a man-of-war victualled for a six months' cruise. At the time I allude to there were but few cows, and only one bull on the islands; and what made matters more disagreeable, it had been slanderously reported of the strange beast that "he was an awfully vicious animal." It is certain that he bellowed fearfully. The inhabitants (who have always been highly esteemed by those who know them) though they were not at that period as well fed with the roast beef of old England as when I was recently quartered among them, were, notwithstanding, a right loyal set, and prided themselves greatly upon their efficient militia. On a hot day,—as are most of their days,— when these good soldiers were at drill under their esteemed commander—let us say, Col. O——e, —a breathless messenger ran up to him as he was mounted on his grey charger in front of the steady line, and uttered some mysterious words. The gallant colonel's countenance assumed a look of deep anxiety,—for an instant his cheek blanched,—his lip quivered :— but quickly rallying, he abandoned his horse, and with infinite presence of mind, gave in unfaltering accents the order, "Gentlemen, *tree* yourselves,—Moll Burgess's Bull is loose." Precept and example were here happily combined, and the able commander was among the first to find safety in the topmost branches of a neighbouring cedar. Military annals record no instance of more prompt, zealous obedience.

their ground, would walk straight up to the birds if there were any in the field. It has never been my luck, I do not say to have possessed such marvellous animals, but even to have been favoured with a sight of them. I therefore am inclined to think that, let your means be what they may, you would find it better not to advertise for creatures undoubtedly most rare, but to act upon the common belief that, as the scent of birds, more or less, impregnates the air, no dog, let his nose be ever so fine, can, except accidentally, wind game unless he seek for the taint in the air,—and that the dog who regularly crosses the wind must have a better chance of finding it, than he who only works up wind,—and that down wind he can have little other chance than by "roading."

203. Thus had I written, for such was my opinion, but Colonel T——y, mentioned in 99, having seen the preceding paragraph, in the first edition, spoke to me on the subject, and, as he thinks such a dog occasionally may be found, and gave good reasons for so believing, I begged him to commit the singular facts to paper; for I felt it a kind of duty to give my readers the most accurate information in my power on a matter of such interest. He writes:—

204. "I should like to show you the portrait of a favourite old pointer of mine, who certainly had the gift of walking up straight to her birds without, apparently, taking the trouble of looking for them, and about which I see you are naturally somewhat sceptical It was in this wise:—

205. "I had gone down into Wales, with my Norfolk pointers, in order to commit great slaughter upon some packs of grouse frequenting the moors belonging to my brother-in-law; my dogs, I think, were fair average ones, but the three did not find so many birds, I was going to say, in a week as old 'Grouse' (the pointer alluded to) did in a day. She had been, previous to my arrival, a sort of hanger-on about the stables,—gaining a scanty subsistence by foraging near the house,—until she was four years old, without ever having been taken to the adjoining moor, at least, in a regular way.

206. "One morning as I was riding up to the moor she followed me; happening to cast my eyes to the right I saw her pointing very steadily in a batch of heather not far from a young plantation. I rode up, and a pack of grouse rose within twenty yards. This induced me to pay more attention to my four-footed companion;

SAFELY MOORED 'STEM' AND 'STERN.'
Page 119, Note.

and the result was, that in a week's time the Norfolk pointers were shut up in the kennel, and the neglected 'Grouse' became my constant associate. A more eccentric animal, however, cannot well be conceived. She hunted just what ground she liked—paid no attention whatever to call or whistle—would have broken the hearts of a dozen Norfolk keepers, by the desperate manner in which she set all rules for quartering at defiance,—but she found game with wonderful quickness, and in an extraordinary manner. She seemed, in fact, to have the power of going direct to where birds lay, without taking the preliminary trouble of searching for them; and, when the packs of grouse were wild, I have seen her constantly leave her point, make a wide circuit, and come up in such direction as to get them between herself and me.

"She was, in every way, a most singular creature. No one did she regard as her master:—no one would she obey. She showed as little pleasure when birds fell, as disappointment when they flew away; but continued her odd, eccentric movements until she became tired or birds scarce, and then quietly trotted home, totally regardless of my softest blandishments or my fiercest execrations.

208. "She was beautifully-shaped, with round well-formed feet, her forehead prominent, and her nostrils expanded more, I think, than I ever saw in any dog.

209. "I bred from her, but her offspring were not worth their salt, although their father was a good dog, and had seen some service in Norfolk turnips."

210. As a horse-dealer once said to me, "I'd ride many a mile, and pay my own pikes," to see such an animal; but, "Grouse," being, unhappily, no longer in the land of the living, I was forced to content myself with merely looking at her portrait. This, however, afforded me much pleasure; I therefore obtained the owner's permission to have it engraved. He says that she always much arched her loins when at a point close to game, and that the artist has most happily hit off her attitude. She is the darker dog of the two, and stands, as soldiers say, on the "*proper* left." Her companion, "Juno," was far from a bad bitch.

211. Might not this singular feat of " Grouse's " be thus explained?—

212. The longer the time that has elapsed since the emission of particles of scent, the more feeble is that scent, on account of the greater dispersion of the said particles; but, from the greater space* they then occupy, a dog would necessarily have a greater chance of meeting some of them, though, possibly, his nose might not be fine enough to detect them.

213. Now, my idea is, that " Grouse's " exquisite sense of smell made her often imagine the possible vicinity of game from the very

---

* This dispersion of scent in the atmosphere explains why a dog who carries his head high finds more game than a dog who hunts with his nose near the ground.

faintest indications,—that her sagacity led her not to abandon hastily such tokens, however feeble, but rather to seek patiently for a confirmation or disproval of her surmises,—that these fancies of hers often ending in disappointment, her manner did not exhibit any excitement that could have induced a spectator to guess what was passing in her mind,—that he, therefore, noticed nothing unusual until after the removal of her hesitation and doubts, when he observed her walking calmly direct up to her birds,—and that he thus was led to regard as an unexplained faculty what really ought to have been considered as simply an evidence of extreme sensitiveness of nose combined with marvellous caution,—a caution it is the great aim of good breaking to inculcate. If I am right in my theory, extraordinary "finder" as "Grouse" was, she would have been yet more successful had she been taught to range properly.

" Stiff by the tainted gale with open nose,
Outstretched and finely sensible."—THOMSON'S SEASONS.

Par. 210.

214. It is heedlessness,—the exact opposite of this extreme caution,—that makes young dogs so often disregard and overrun a slight scent; and since they are

A DOG-FISH.—Par. 218.

more inclined to commit this error from the rivalry of companionship, an additional argument is presented in favour of breaking them separately, and giving them their own time, quietly and methodically, to work out a scent, *provided the nose be carried high*. I am satisfied most of us hurry young dogs too much. Observe the result of patience and care, as exhibited in the person of the old Dropper, noticed in 228.

215. But, doubtless, there are mysterious influences and instincts of which the wisest of us know but little.

216. An old brother-officer of mine, the Hon. F. C——h, has a very handsome black retriever that possesses the extraordinary gift of being able to run direct to any game, or even glove, you may leave behind you, however tortuous may be your subsequent path. C——h told me that he has, in the presence of keepers, frequently dropped a rabbit within sight of the dog, and then walked in a circle, or rather semicircle, to the other side of a low hill—a distance, possibly, of nearly a mile—before he desired the dog to fetch it; yet, on receiving the order, the animal invariably set off in an undeviating line straight to the rabbit, unless his attention had been drawn away by playing with other dogs—a license C——h sometimes designedly allowed. The retriever would then shuffle about a little before he went off, but when he started it would be in as direct a line to the object as usual.

217. No one could explain by what sense or faculty he performed this feat. It appears not to have been by the aid of his olfactory powers, for C——h (who is a keen sportsman, and capital shot, by the bye) would often purposely manage that the dog, when he was desired to "fetch" the object, should be immediately to windward of it ; and in the most unfavourable position, therefore, for deriving any advantage from the exercise of his nasal organs.

218. Capt. G——g, R.N. mentioned to me, that a ship, in which he had served many years ago in the Mediterranean, seldom entered a port that the large Newfoundland belonging to her did not jump overboard the instant the anchor was dropped, swim ashore, and return, after an hour or two's lark, direct to his own ship, though she might be riding in a crowd of vessels. He would then bark, anxiously, until the bight of a rope was hove to him. Into this he would contrive to get his fore legs, and, on his seizing it firmly with his teeth, the sailors, who were much attached to him, would hoist him on board.

219. Mr. W——b, of S——a, had a young Newfoundland that from very puppyhood took fearlessly to water, but acquired as he grew up such wandering propensities on land, that his master determined to part with him, and accordingly made him a present to his

friend Lieut. P——d, R.N. then in command of H.M. Cutter "Cameleon." "Triton," however, was so attached to his old roving habits, that whenever the cutter went into port he would invariably swim ashore of his own accord, and remain away for several days, always managing, however, to return on board before the anchor was weighed. Such, too, was his intelligence that he never seemed puzzled how to pick out his own vessel from amidst forty or fifty others. Indeed, Lieut. P——d, (he lately commanded the "Vulcan,") to whom the question, at my request, was expressly put, believes, (and he has courteously permitted me to quote his name and words,) that, on one occasion, " Triton " contrived to find his own vessel from among nearly a hundred that were riding at anchor in Poole harbour. The dog's being ever so well acquainted with the interior of the craft does not explain why he should be familiar with her external appearance. Did he judge most by the hull or the rigging?

220. The Duke of N——k so much admired the magnificent style in which " Triton " would spring into the strongest sea, that Lieut. P——d gave the fine animal to his Grace, who, for all I know to the contrary, still possesses him.

221. Who can account for the mode in which a dog or cat, carried a long journey from home, in a covered basket, instinctively, finds its way back?—yet, numerous are the well authenticated instances of such occurrences.* But, enough of this,—fortunately I have not undertaken to attempt an elucidation of any of Nature's many mysteries, but simply to show how some of the faculties she has bestowed upon the canine race may easily be made conducive to our amusements.

---

* When quartered, years ago, in County Wexford, I used frequently to see a fine strong-knit, well-built horse, who could never see me—for he was stone-blind; yet, odd to say, all his progeny had capital eyes.[1] He had rather a queer temper, as his name, "Restless," partly implied. During the spring he was led about the country, and what is very surprising, there was always a fight to get him past the lane or gate leading to any farmhouse where his services had ever before been required. As it is certain that he was *perfectly* blind, no faculty we can believe him to be possessed of, unless it be memory, will explain how, at such long intervals, he could recognise the many different places so accurately; and if it be attributable to memory, that of the Senior Wrangler of Cambridge's best year can in no way be compared with it.

[1] This is the more singular, as, from unexplained causes, diseases of that organ are but too common in Ireland. One veterinary surgeon attributed it to the dampness of the climate. His young English horses suffered while at Cork as much as his Irish ones.

CHAPTER VIII.

FIRST LESSON IN SEPTEMBER CONTINUED. CUNNING OF AGE.—
RANGE OF FROM TWO TO SIX DOGS.

222. Your dog not to "break fence;" how taught; birds often sprung while you are scrambling over hedge.—223. Turning one's back upon a dog to bring him away; stooping down, &c. to make him hunt close.—224. Dog, when fatigued, not to be hunted; leads to false points.—225. Sent home, brushed, and allowed a warm berth; not to follow all day at "heel."—226. Instance of longevity and vigour flapper shooting.—227. Value of good old dogs.—228. Exemplified in an old dropper on the moors.—229. Young dogs get thrown out; cunning of old birds exemplified in a Grouse.—230. Annual "fall" of underwood in Kent.—231 Mr. K——g, good fisherman; in Note, anecdote of voracity of pike. Wheatley's "Rod and Line."—232. Extraordinary chase after a wounded pheasant.—233 Singular appearance of the pheasant on its capture.—234. Description of the Spaniel "Dash."—235. Evil of "fetching," not having been taught in youth exemplified.—236. Another instance of the cunning of an old Pheasant. In Note, how to choose and tell age of Pheasants.—237. The last Duke of Gordon his black setters; his shooting over *old* dogs.—238 to 240.—Beat of two dogs how regulated.—241. Whatever number be hunted, all should look to the gun for orders; Mr. Herbert's opinion in his "Field Sports in United States."— 242, 243. Beat of three dogs.—244. Of four dogs.—245 to 247. Of five or six dogs.—248. Great precision impracticable, but the necessity of a system maintained; System particularly essential where game is scarce; dogs to be brigaded not employed as a pack.—249. When each keeper hunts a brace.—250. Major B——d's highly broken pointers.—251, 252. His making six alternately "road;' their running riot when ordered.—253. Not a good shot, which shows excellence in shooting not to be essential in a breaker.—254. A brigade of fine rangers worth from fifty to sixty guineas a brace.—255. Bad rangers afford some sport where game is plentiful; Captain R——s' dogs on Quail.—256. Fastest walkers do not necessarily beat most country.—257. Nor do always the fastest dogs.— 258. How slow dogs may hunt more ground than faster.

222. Of course, you will not let your pupil "break fence," or get out of your sight. If he be a small, active pointer or setter he may be out of sight before you are aware of it. Be on the watch to whistle or call out "Fence," the instant you perceive that he is thinking of quitting the field. Do not wait until he is over; check him by anticipating his intentions. Should he, unperceived, or in defiance of your orders, get into a field

K

before you, call him back (by the same opening, if practicable, through which he passed, the more clearly to show him his folly); and do not proceed further until he has obeyed you. A steady adherence to this rule will soon convince him of the inutility of not exercising more patience, or at least forbearance; then signal to him "away" in the direction *you* choose, not in the direction *he* chooses. It is essential that you should be the first over every fence. In the scramble, birds, at which you ought to have a shot, are frequently sprung. If he is not obedient to your orders make him "drop," and rate him as described in 188.

223. A dog from his own observation so much feels, —and in a greater or less degree, according to his education,—the necessity of watching in what direction you are walking, that if he is habituated to work under your eye,—I mean, is never allowed to hunt behind you,—by turning your back upon him when he is paying no attention to your signals, you will often be able to bring him away from a spot where he is ranging (perhaps down wind) against your wishes, at a time when you are afraid to whistle, lest you should alarm the birds. Waving your hand backwards and forwards near the ground, and stooping low while walking slowly about, as if in search of something, will often attract the attention of an ill-taught self-willed dog; and his anxiety to participate in the find, and share the sport which he imagines you expect, will frequently induce him to run up, and hunt alongside of you for any close lying bird.

224. Never be induced to hunt your young dog, (nor indeed, any dog), when he is tired. If you do, you will give him a slovenly carriage and habits, and lessen his zeal for the sport. In order to come in for a sniff, at

"Small, active Pointer."—Par. 222.

a time when he is too fatigued to search for it himself, he will crawl after his companion, watching for any indication of his finding. As they become wearied you will have a difficulty in keeping your old well-broken dogs separate—much more young ones, however independently they may have ranged when fresh. You may also, to a certainty, expect false points; but what is of far more consequence, by frequently overtasking your young dog, you will as effectually waste his constitution as you would your horse's by premature work.

225. If he is very young when first entered, two or three hours' work at a time will be sufficient. When he is tired, or rather before he is tired, send him home with the man who brings you a relief. Do not fancy your dog will be getting a rest if he be allowed to follow at your heels for the remainder of the day, coupled to a companion. His fretting at not being allowed to share in the sport he sees, will take nearly as much out of him as if you permitted him to hunt. If you can persuade John always to rub him down, and brush and dry him—nay even to let him enjoy an hour's basking in front of the fire—before he shuts him up in the kennel, you will add years to his existence; and remember that one old experienced dog, whose constitution is uninjured, is worth two young ones.

226. A gentleman in Eyrecourt, County Galway, gave me, as a valuable present, a black setter thirteen years of age. And most valuable was the setter to my friend, who had carefully reared him from a puppy, and had him well under command; but with me he was so *wild*,—I make use of the term most advisedly,—that he did me more harm than good the only season I shot over him. He was stolen from me, and his teeth were so sound, and he bore so little the appearance of age, that I have no doubt he was sold as a tolerably young dog. He was the best specimen I ever saw of the vigour that may be retained for old age by judicious treatment in youth. The excellence of his constitution was the more remarkable, from the fact of his having always been extremely fond of the water. Few dogs could equal him for flapper shooting, that vilest

of sports, if followed before the unfortunate birds get strong on the wing—as unprofitable, too, for the table, as unsatisfactory to the real sportsman. Sir J——s M——e, of Perthshire, told me that he had shot grouse over an Oxfordshire pointer bitch (the best he ever possessed and the founder of his kennel-stock) until she was eighteen years of age, when she could do no more than crawl up the side of a hill, occasionally, to gain time, making false points. Once, however, on the top, she would work merrily downwards,—no false points then.

227. But canine veterans, of however invalided a constitution, if they have been really first-rate in their youth, are not always to be despised. Occasionally you may come across one who will, from his past experience and superior nose, prove a more valuable auxiliary in the field, than many a campaigner of greater activity and vigour.

228. Many years ago I went from the south of England for some grouse shooting in Scotland. When arranging with my companion (Captain S——s, a connexion of the kind-hearted old warrior, whose crowning victory was Goojerat,) what dogs should accompany us, he remarked, that it would be useless to take his old Dropper (one far more resembling a pointer than a setter), as he was too aged to undergo any work. I observed, that he could do us no harm if he did us no good; and, as he had been an admirable animal, I advised his being taken. Off he went to the North; and frequently did we afterwards congratulate ourselves upon this decision, for the old fellow, apparently grateful for the compliment seemed to feel that he ought to make us some return, and that the less ground he could traverse with his legs the more he was bound to traverse with his nose. The result was, that while he was slowly pottering about, (the season being unusually hot and dry, there was but little scent) he was constantly finding us birds which his more flashy companions had passed over; and before we left Scotland we agreed that none of our dogs had procured us so many shots as the slow, careful old gentleman.

229. Old birds become very cunning; they are quite sensible of the danger they incur by rising, and to escape from the dog, and puzzle him, have as many wiles and twists as a hunted hare. It may be that as old age advances, their decreasing bodily powers warn them to add to their security by the exercise of their wits. It is often remarked, that if ever we kill any of their natural enemies, whether winged or four-footed, we are sure to find them in fair condition. This condition makes it obvious, that they must have gained with years the experience which enables them to obtain a good livelihood by craft, at a time of life when their failing strength would prevent their procuring a single meal by a direct pursuit.*
If then we argue from analogy, we shall think it almost impossible

---

* Indeed, through a merciful dispensation, it seems to be ordained, that no animal (in the general course of nature) shall die a lingering, painful death from starvation, but shall serve for the nourishment of others before his body becomes attenuated from want.

for any unpractised dog, however highly bred, to procure us so many shots as one who has been hunted for several seasons. And such is really the case. A young dog will not keep to the trail of an old bird for more than about forty yards; after that he will give it up altogether, or rush in. It is when he is "roading" one of these knowing aged patriarchs, that you become aware of the great value of experience in a dog. You may have seen a young one bewildered in the devious intricacies of the broken hags, sought as a refuge by an old cock-grouse, and have probably imagined that the youngster had only been following a recent haunt, and that the game was gone. Not so, the dog was right at first. He "footed" it out admirably until he came to the dark bush, which you must have wondered to see growing in such a situation; there the sly bird doubled, then turned short to the right for nearly a hundred yards before it resumed its course down wind. A dog more up to his work would have again hit off the scent, and an old stager, probably, never have lost it.

230. In order to be generally understood, I will preface the following anecdote by mentioning that in the large Kentish woods, where the annual falls of underwood take place to the extent of forty or fifty acres, it is usual to drain the land by digging watercourses, or as they are commonly called, Grips. The first year's growth of the underwood is called yearling Fall (or Spring); the second, two-year old Fall (or Spring); and so on.

231. Mr. K——g, a good sportsman, and so successful an angler,* that he is familiarly called by his friends "the King-fisher," to distinguish him from others who bear his name, was pheasant shooting in the winter of 1848-9, in two-year old springs, where, with all

---

* Numerous accounts have been given of the voracity of the pike. K——g told me of a very remarkable instance, and one which clearly shows that fish do not always suffer so much torture when hooked as many suppose. He was spinning a gudgeon for pike in the river Stour, near Chilham, having bent on four large hooks, back to back, and a large lip-hook. He was run at by a pike, which he struck, but the line unfortunately breaking, the fish carried off fully four yards of it, together with half a yard of gimp, two large swivels, and a lead. K——g put on fresh tackle and bait. At the very first cast he was run at again, and succeeded in landing the fish, which weighed 12 lbs. To K——g's great surprise, he observed the lost line, swivel, and lead hanging out of its mouth, while,—apparently not much to the animal's discomfort,—the bait and hooks quietly reposed in its interior. On turning the gullet inside out, K——g found the bait so uninjured that he again fastened it to his line along with the recovered tackle, and actually caught another pike weighing 4 lbs., and a perch of 2½ lbs., with the very gudgeon that had been in the stomach of the large pike for nearly a quarter of an hour.

Those who are fond of trolling for trout would not find their time thrown away in reading Wheatley's *novel hints* on all kinds of spinning baits. His "Rod and Line" is an excellent little book.

acknowledged partiality for Kent, it must be admitted that birds are not so plentiful as in certain preserves in Norfolk, though probably foxes are fully as numerous. It has been remarked, by the bye, that where foxes abound, old pheasants are very cunning; doubtless from having been often put to their shifts to escape from their wily adversaries.

232. K——g sprung a splendid cock-pheasant, which, although a long way off, he shot at and dropped. Judging from the manner in which it fell that it was a runner, and well knowing the racing propensities of the old cocks, he hastened to the spot where it tumbled, and, giving his gun to the marker, prepared for a sharp burst, though he little expected the extraordinary chase that was to follow. He found, as he had anticipated, some breast feathers, but no bird. After fruitlessly trying in every direction, for nearly a quarter of an hour, to put "Dash" on the scent, K——g's eyes rested on one of the grips just spoken of: it ran close to where the bird had fallen, and the thought struck him that possibly the cunning creature might have taken refuge in it, and thus have thrown out the spaniel. K——g got into it, and though finding fully six inches of water, he persevered in following it. It brought him to a high wood about one hundred yards off, and towards which the pheasant had been flying when shot at, but "Dash" could not obtain the least scent of the bird. As a last resource, K——g then returned to the spot where he had left the marker with his gun, being determined to try the grip in the opposite direction, notwithstanding its leading exactly contrary to the point for which the bird had been making. He did so, and by calling energetically to "Dash," he endeavoured to make the dog believe that at length the bird was in view. The plan succeeded. "Dash," who had become slack from disappointment, hunted with renewed animation, and, after pursuing the grip for some time, took the scent full cry across the springs until he came to an old waggon-road, along which he went at speed. Feeling assured that all was now right, K——g gladly moderated his pace, for he was much out of breath. When at length he overtook "Dash," instead of seeing him in possession of the bird, he only found him completely at fault, trying up and down the well-indented wheel-ruts. On the other side of the road there was another grip. Into it K——g jumped, followed the plan he had before adopted, and with like success; for on running up the grip for about sixty yards, the spaniel again hit off the scent, and after taking it away at a right angle (so far that K——g could only now and then catch a faint tingle of the bell), brought it back to the same grip, but some 200 yards higher, where he suddenly threw up." For the fourth time in went K——g. "Dash" now seemed thoroughly to understand matters, and kept trying both sides of the grip for the scent. At length he found it, and went full cry across a yearling fall, which was everywhere very bare, except here and there an occasional patch of high strong grass. At one of these K——g found him again at fault. The dog seemed quite done; but still it was evident, from his excited manner, that

"Short-legged, strong-loined, Sussex Spaniel."—Par. 236.

he thought the pheasant was not far distant. After a time he began scratching at the long grass. K——g went up, and, on putting the stalks aside, fancied he perceived the end of some tail feathers. He thrust in his arm, and ultimately succeeded in dragging forth the well-hunted bird, quite alive, out of the deep wheel-track in which it had buried itself. The coarse grass had grown so closely over the rut, that the bird had been able to creep in for three or four yards.

233. A more miserable appearance than the poor creature presented, cannot easily be conceived. Its feathers were so completely sopped, and stuck so close to its body, that it looked a mere skeleton; and yet it was a noble bird, measuring three feet and an inch from the tip of its bill to the extremity of its tail, and weighed 3 lbs. 6 oz.

234. As "Dash" plays so conspicuous a part in the foregoing history, it appears right that a few words should be given to describe him. He is a low, strong-limbed, broad-backed nearly thoroughbred Sussex spaniel, with an extremely intelligent-looking head, but a sadly mean stern. His colour is black. K——g generally hunts him with a bell, especially where the underwood is thick. If he is sharply called to when he is on game he will slacken his pace, look round for his master, and not "road" keenly until the gun approaches him; he will then rush in with a bark to flush, though at other times hunting mute. The intelligent animal seems, however, perfectly to know when the cover is too high or strong for K——g to follow, for he then invariably runs full cry from first touching on a scent. He never deceives the sportsman, for he never gives one of his eloquent looks unless he is certain of being on game; and his nose is so good, and he hunts so true, that he invariably "pushes" his pheasant, however much it may turn or double.

235. He is also undeniable at "seeking dead," but unluckily was not taught as a youngster to fetch. Much time is, therefore, often lost in finding him after he has been sent for a winged bird; but when he is at length discovered it is sure to be with him.

236. I was told of a farmer in Kent—one of her fine yeomen, of whom England has such cause to feel proud, (pity that in some other counties the class is not as distinctly preserved!)—who was shooting with an old short-legged, strong-loined, Sussex spaniel. The dog, after "roading" a pheasant along many a tortuous path, led the farmer to the edge of a shallow brook, up the middle of which, far away to his right, he was lucky enough to see the animal running, obviously with the design of throwing out the dog. A light pair of heels soon brought the sportsman within shot, and enabled him to bag the heaviest and richest feathered bird he had ever seen. The sharp long spurs* showed it to be at least five years of age, and its

---

* There are poulterers who would pare such a spur to diminish the appearance of age. The shorter and blunter the spur, and the smoother the leg, the younger is the bird. Dr. Kitchener, who appears not to have had much luck in stumbling upon well-fed

sagacity would probably have borne it triumphantly through another campaign or two, had not the farmer's quick eye detected its adroit manœuvre,—one that forcibly calls to mind Cooper's descriptions of the stratagems employed by the North American Indians to baffle pursuit by leaving no indication of their trail.

237. Must there not be experience on the part of dogs to contend successfully with such wiliness as this? So much was the last Duke of Gordon convinced of its necessity,—and he is well known to have been a capital sportsman, and to have paid great attention to his fine breed of black setters,—that he would never allow one of them to accompany him to the moors that had not been shot over five or six seasons—and "small blame" to his Grace "for that same," as he had a choice from all ages. But it must be acknowledged, that however excellent* in many respects,—and when in the hands of the breaker their indomitable energies would cause the bunch of heather, fastened to the end of their checkcords, to dance merrily over the mountains from morning until night-fall,—most of them were a wild set in their youth, and required constant work to keep them in order. Every experienced sportsman in the Highlands is aware that young dogs will romp (for it cannot be termed hunting), with their noses here, there, and everywhere, obtaining but few points over ground on which knowing old dogs will immediately afterwards keep the gun-barrels at an exhilarating temperature.

238. When you hunt a brace of dogs, to speak theoretically, they should traverse a field in opposite directions, but along parallel lines, and the distance between the lines should be regulated by you according as it is a good or a bad scenting day, and according to the excellence of the dogs' noses. Mathematical accuracy is, of course, never to be attained, but the closer you approach to it the better.

pheasants, avers that they have not the flavour of barn-door fowls if they are cooked before they drop from the single tail feather by which, he says, they should be hung up in the larder; or, rather, he advises that two pheasants should be suspended by *one* feather until both fall. Birds of full, beautiful plumage gratify the eye more than the palate. It is an indication of age in *all sorts* of birds. The hens are the tenderest. On the body of birds, immediately under the wing, there is what keepers often call, "the condition vein." The more fat and yellow that appears, the higher is the condition of the animal. Blow aside the feathers of a snipe; and if the flesh is nearly black the bird wants condition,—it should be white.

* On the 7th of July, 1836, his kennel was put up to auction, when three of his setters fetched, severally, seventy-two, sixty, and fifty-six guineas. Two puppies brought fifteen guineas each, — and two of his retrievers, "Bess" and "Diver," forty-six and forty-two guineas.

"Duke of Gordon's fine breed of Black Setters."—Par. 237.

239. You should attempt it (on entering the field to *leeward*, as before directed) by making one dog go straight a-head of you to the distance which you wish the parallel lines to be apart from each other, before you cast him off (say) to the right; then cast off his companion to the left. If the dogs are nearly equal in pace, the one a-head, so long as he does not fancy he winds game, should continue to work on a parallel more advanced than the other.

240. Should you not like to relinquish, for the sake of this formal precision, the chance of a find in the neglected right-hand corner of the field, cast off one dog to the right, the other to the left on entering it, and make the one that soonest approaches his hedge take the widest sweep (turn), and so be placed in the *advanced* parallel.

241. With regard to hunting more than a brace— when your difficulties wonderfully multiply—your own judgment must determine in what manner to direct their travelling powers to the greatest advantage. Much will depend upon the different speed of the dogs; the number you choose, from whim or otherwise, to hunt; the kind of country you beat; and the quantity and sort of game you expect to find. It is, however, certain you must wish that each dog be observant of the direction in which your face is turned, in order that he may guide his own movements by yours;—that he from time to time look towards you to see if you have any commands;—and that he be ever anxious to obey them.

Herbert writes as follows, in his work on shooting in the United States :* his words ought to have influence, for manifestly he is a good sportsman ; but I own I cannot quite agree with him as to

---

* Entitled, " Field Sports in the United States and British Provinces, by Frank Forester."

the *facility* with which a range can be taught : " It is wonderful how easily dogs which are always shot over by the same man—he being one who knows his business—will learn to cross and re-quarter their ground, turning to the slightest whistle, and following the least gesture of the hand. I have seen old dogs turn their heads to catch their master's eye, if they thought the whistle too long deferred ; and I lately lost an old Irish setter, which had been stone deaf for his last two seasons, but which I found no more difficulty in turning than any other dog, so accurately did he know when to look for the signal."

242. To beat your ground *systematically* with three dogs you should strive to make them cross and re-cross you, each on a different parallel, as just described for two dogs ; but each dog must make a proportionately bolder sweep (turn) ; or,

243. If you have plenty of space, you can make one dog take a distinct beat to the right, another a separate beat to the left, and direct the third (which ought to be the dog least confirmed in his range) to traverse the central part,—and so be the only one that shall cross and recross you. If one of your dogs is a slow potterer, and you prefer this method to the one named in 242, give him the middle beat, and let his faster companions take the flanks. In our small English fields you have not space enough, but on our moors, and in many parts of the Continent, it cannot be want of room that will prevent your accomplishing it. To do this well, however, and not interfere with each other's ground, how magnificently must your dogs be broken! In directing their movements, the assistance that would be given you by each dog's acknowledging his own particular whistle, and no other (505), is very apparent.

244. It is difficult enough to make three dogs traverse across you on tolerably distinct parallels, and at a judicious distance between the parallels ; you will find it hopeless to attempt it with more than three ; and one can hardly imagine a case in which it would be advan-

tageous to uncouple a greater number of good rangers. If, however, the scarcity of game, and the extensiveness of your beat, or any peculiar fancy, induce you habitually to use four dogs, hunt one brace to the right, the other to the left; and, so far as you can, let those which *form a brace be of equal speed.** Your task will be facilitated by your always keeping the same brace to one flank,—I mean, by making one brace constantly hunt to your right hand; the other brace to your left. The same reasoning holds with regard to assigning to each dog a particular side when hunting three, according to the mode described in last paragraph. It should, however, be borne in mind, that constantly hunting a dog in this manner on one and the same flank, tends to make him range very disagreeably whenever employed single-handed.

245. If you hunt five dogs, four of them ought to work by braces to the right and left, and the fifth (the dog whose rate of speed most varies from the others) should have a narrow beat assigned him directly in advance of you.

246. If three brace are to be used, let the third brace hunt the central ground, as recommended for the fifth dog,—or they could be worked in leashes, one on the right of the gun, the other on the left.

247. These are the correct *theoretical* rules, and the more closely you observe them, the more truly and killingly will your ground be hunted.

248. Probably you will think that such niceties are utterly impracticable. They must be impracticable, if you look for mathematical precision; but if you are determined to hunt many dogs and hope to shoot over more than a mere rabble, you should work upon *system*. If you

---

* A rule to be followed whenever you employ relays of braces.

do not, what can you expect but an unorganized mob?—an undrilled set, perpetually running over each other's ground,—now scampering in this part, now crowded in that,—a few likely spots being hunted by all (especially if they are old dogs), the rest of the field by none of them; and to control whose unprofitable wanderings, why not employ a regular huntsman and a well-mounted whip? Doubtless it would be absurd to hope for perfect accuracy in so difficult a matter as a systematic range in a brigade of dogs; but that you may approach correctness, take a true standard of excellence. If you do not keep perfection in view, you will never attain to more than mediocrity. I earnestly hope, however, that it cannot be your wish to take out a host of dogs,—but should you have such a singular hobby, pray let them be regularly brigaded, and not employed as a pack. In my opinion, under no circumstances can more than relays of leashes be desirable; but I should be sorry in such matters to dispute any man's right to please himself; I only wish him, whatever he does, to strive to do it correctly.

249. Some men who shoot on a grand scale make their keepers hunt each a distinct brace of dogs,—the gun going up to whatever dog points. It is the most killing plan to adopt; but that is not the matter we were considering. The question was, what method a man ought to pursue who had a fancy to himself hunt many dogs at a time.

250. The late Major B——d, of B——d, in Lancashire, had this fancy. The moors over which he shot were by no means well stocked with game; but the wonderful control he obtained over his pointers showed, in the strongest manner, the high grade of education that can be imparted to dogs by gentle and judicious treatment.

251. He was accustomed to hunt three brace at a time. Each dog when he was ranging would take up his separate ground, with-

out interfering with that of his companions. The Major's raising his arm was the signal for all to drop.

252. If one of the dogs was pointing, the Major would go up perhaps to the dog furthest off, and make him approach the dog that was standing; and in October (when grouse run much) he has thus brought all six dogs in a line, one following the other, and made each in succession take the lead, and "foot" the birds for a short distance. The same dogs, on the same day, at a given signal, would run riot; scamper over the moor; chase hares, sheep, or anything they came across; and at the well-known signal again would drop, and, as if by magic, resume their perfect obedience.

253. Major B——d was quite one of the old school; used flint and steel; and looked with ineffable contempt at the detonators of the youngsters. He was not remarkable for being a good shot, capital sportsman as he undoubtedly was in the highest sense of the word, showing the truth of what was said in the fifth paragraph, that excellence in shooting, though of course advantageous, is not a necessary qualification in a breaker.

254. If a professional breaker could show you a brigade of dogs well trained to quarter their ground systematically, and should ask from fifty to sixty guineas* a brace for them, you ought not to be surprised. What an extent of country they could sweep over in an hour and not leave a bird behind! And consider what time and labour must have been spent in inculcating so noble a range. He would have been far better paid, if he had received less than half the money as soon as they "pointed steadily," both at the living and the dead; "down charged;" "backed;" and were broken from "chasing hare," or noticing rabbits.

255. The great advantage of fine rangers is not much considered where game is abundant. A friend of mine, a capital shot (though far inferior to his namesake, Captain R——s of sporting celebrity), with whom I have enjoyed some pleasant quail shooting in America, used constantly to hunt a leash of pointers, "Jem," "Beau," and "Fag,"—the last a regular misnomer, for the dog was incorrigibly idle. It was curious to watch how pertinaciously, like sheep, they herded together,—seldom did one wind a bird that would not have been found a few seconds afterwards by the others. R——s, long before I knew him, had relinquished all attempts at making them beat separately—indeed, I am not positive that he was fully sensible

---

* That price was named in the Table of Contents of the first edition.

of its utility. As they all "backed" promptly—instantly "down-charged," and had not a shade of jealousy, they did little harm; and sometimes on a broiling day "Beau," who generally took the lead, was not the first to come on a dead bird. Where game is plentiful, as bad rangers as the trio belonging to my old friend, will afford you sport; but it is certain that they will pass by many birds, unless you undergo the fatigue of walking over most of the ground yourself, and it is clear if you do, that you will not be able to hunt half as many acres in a day, as you could if you kept to your general central direction while the dogs hunted according to rule. Few Frenchmen agree with us respecting a fine range. They make their pointers and setters hunt almost as close as spaniels. They prefer bitches to dogs, saying that they are more affectionate ("plus fidèles"), and therefore range nearer. In England, in old days, when our dogs were far heavier and slower than they are now, and, in consequence, could not run over so much ground, they were taught to traverse little more than from thirty to sixty yards on each side of the gun.

256. Some men fancy that the faster they walk, the more country they hunt. This is far from being always the case. Dogs travel at one rate, whether you walk fast or slow, and the distance between the parallels on which they work, (being determined by the fineness of their noses, and the goodness of the scent,) ought not to be affected by your pace. Suppose, therefore, that you shoot in an unenclosed country, whether you walk quickly, or merely crawl along, the only difference in the beat of your dogs *ought* to be that, in the latter case, they range further to the right and left. You thus make up in your *breadth* what you lose in your *length* of beat.

257. Nor do the fastest dogs, however well they may be broken, always truly hunt the most ground. The slower dogs have frequently finer olfactory nerves than their fleeter rivals,—therefore the parallels on which the former work, may correctly be much wider apart than the parallels of the latter. The finer nose in this manner commands so much more ground, that it beats the quicker heels out and out.

258. You will see, then, how judicious it is to show forbearance and give encouragement to the timid, but high-bred class* of dogs described in 116; for it is obvious that, though they may travel slower, yet they may really hunt *properly*, within a specified time, many more acres of ground than their hardier and faster competitors: and it is certain that they will not so much alarm the birds. Dogs that are most active with their heels are generally least busy with their noses.

* It is admitted, however, that they are often difficult animals to manage; for the *least* hastiness on the part of the instructor may create a distrust that he will find it very hard to remove.

CHAPTER IX.

FIRST LESSON IN SEPTEMBER CONTINUED. "POINT" NOT RELINQUISHED FOR "DOWN CHARGE."

259. Affection makes Dog anxious to please—when he rushes in to be dragged back.—260. Rule pressed.—261. Reason for Rule—Experience anticipated.—262. To "stand" far off—Pointer procuring shots at black game, but raising Grouse.—263. Patience enjoined—Not to part as enemies.—264. The first good point—Remain yourself stationary.—265. "Heading" Dog—Your circle to be wide. The first bird killed.—266. Finding dead bird, it being to Leeward.—267. Pointing it—Blinking it—The cause.—268. Woodcock lost from Dog not "pointing dead."—269. Bird killed, the Dog to go to "heel."—270. Supposed objection.—271. Answered.—272. Temptation to run after fallen bird greater than to run to "heel."—273. Dog pointing one bird, and after "down charge" springing the others. The cause.—274. The preventive. Dog never to discontinue his point in order to "down charge." How taught.—275. Its advantages exemplified.—276. Decide whether Dog goes direct to bird, or first to you.—277. Dog which performed well. Snipe shooting on banks of Richlieu.—278. Coolness recommended. Inconsistency deprecated.

259. To proceed, however, with our imaginary September day's work. I will suppose that your young dog has got upon birds, and that from his boldness and keenness in hunting you need not let him run riot on a haunt, as you were recommended (in 132), when you wished to give courage and animation to a timid dog. You must expect that his eagerness and delight will make him run in and flush them, even though you should have called out "Toho" when first you perceived his stern begin feathering, and thence judged that his olfactory nerves were rejoicing in the luxurious taint of game. Hollo out "Drop" most energetically. If he does not immediately lie down, crack your whip loudly to command greater attention. When you have succeeded in making him lie down, approach him quietly;

be not angry with him, but yet be stern in manner. Grasping the skin of his neck, or what is better, putting your hand within his collar (for he ought to wear a light one), quietly drag him to the precise spot where you think he was *first* aware of the scent of the birds. There make him stand, (if stand he will, instead of timidly crouching), with his head directed towards the place from which the birds took wing, and by frequently repeating the word "Toho," endeavour to make him understand that he ought to have pointed at that identical spot. Do not confuse him by even threatening to beat him. The chances are twenty to one that he is anxious to please you, but does not yet know what you wish. I assume also that he is attached to you, and his affection, from constantly inducing him to exert himself to give satisfaction, will greatly develop his observation and intelligence.

260. Consider it a golden rule never to be departed from (for I must again impress upon you a matter of such importance), invariably to drag a dog who has put up birds incautiously, or wilfully drawn too near them, and so sprung them (or, what is quite as bad,—though young sportsmen will not sufficiently think of it,— *endangered* their rising out of shot), to the exact spot at which you judge he ought to have pointed at first, and awaited your instructions.

261. Think for one moment what could be the use of chiding (or beating, as I have seen some * * * * * do) the poor animal at the spot where he flushed the birds. You are not displeased with him (or ought not to be) because the birds took wing,—for if they had remained stationary until he was within a yard of them, his fault would have been the same : nor are you angry with him because he did not catch them (which interpretation he

might, as naturally as any other, put upon your rating him at the spot where he flushed them),—you are displeased with him for *not having pointed* at them steadily the moment he became sensible of their presence. This is what you wish him to understand, and this you can only teach him by dragging him, as has been so often said, to the spot at which he ought to have "toho-ed" them. Your object is to give the young dog by instruction, the caution that most old dogs have acquired by experience. Doubtless experience would in time convince him of the necessity of this caution; but you wish to *save* time,—to anticipate that experience; and by a judicious education impart to him knowledge which it would take him years to acquire otherwise. What a dog gains by experience is not what you teach him, but what he teaches himself.

262. Many carelessly-taught dogs will on first recognising a scent make a momentary point, and then slowly crawl on until they get within a few yards of the game, —if it be sufficiently complaisant to allow of such a near approach,—and there "set" as steady as a rock by the hour together. Supposing, however, that the birds are in an unfriendly distant mood, and not willing to remain on these neighbourly terms, "your game is up," both literally and metaphorically,—you have no chance of getting a shot. This is a common fault among dogs hastily broken in the spring.

<small>I speak feelingly on the subject from a still unpleasant recollection of my extreme vexation on a certain 20th of August,* when shooting over a young pointer-bitch of excellent natural capabilities, but who had been injudiciously allowed, during her tuition in the spring, to stand too close to her birds. She was a quick ranger,— carried a high diligent nose,— had much endurance, and procured me several shots at young black game, but not one, if I remember</small>

---

* The first day for killing black-cock.

right, at grouse. I was always aware when she first found, for her attitudes were fine and marked, but, in defiance of all my signals, and occasional calls, she would persist in creeping nearer, a proximity the grouse would not endure. As a violent jerk would not have been necessary, often did I wish that day, whenever she approached a likely spot, that it was in my power to attach to her collar a stiff thin checkcord about 100 yards long,*—such a one as would have been handed to me at a fishing-tackle shop on my asking for a strong hemp salmon line,—the kind used in former days after being soaked for weeks in oil,—now, however, considered heavy and unmanageable. A mild spiked collar applied as described in 302 to 304, would, I think, have noiselessly reclaimed her, without injuring my shooting.

263. But to resume our supposed lesson. You must not be in a hurry—keep your dog for some time—for a long time, where he should have pointed. You may even sit down alongside him. Be patient; you have not come out so much to shoot, as to break in your dog. When at length you give him the wave of the hand to hie him on to hunt, you must not part as enemies, though I do not say he is to be caressed. He has committed a fault, and he is to be made sensible of it by your altered manner.

264. Suppose that, after two or three such errors, all treated in the way described, he makes a satisfactory point. Hold up your right hand, and the moment you catch his eye, remain quite stationary, still keeping your arm up. Dogs, as has been already observed, are very imitative; and your standing stock still will, more than anything else, induce him to be patient and immovable at his point. After a time (say five minutes if, from the hour of the day and the dog's manner, you are convinced that the birds are not stirring), endeavour to get up to him so quietly as not to excite him to move. Whenever you observe him inclined to advance,—of which his

---

* If painted white it will be the more readily seen and *trodden* on, —a *step* advisable preparatory to seizing it, or an ungloved hand may suffer should the dog be ranging rapidly.

lifting a foot or even raising a shoulder, or the agitation of his stern will be an indication,—stop for some seconds, and when by your raised hand you have awed him into steadiness, again creep on. Make your approaches within his sight, so that he may be intimidated by your eye and hand. If you succeed in getting near him without unsettling him, actually stay by him, as firm as a statue, for a quarter of an hour by one of Barwise's best chronometers. Let your manner, which he will observe, show great earnestness. Never mind the loss of time. You are giving the dog a famous lesson, and the birds are kindly aiding you by lying beautifully and not shifting their ground.*

265. Now attempt a grand *coup*, in which if you are successful, you may almost consider your dog made staunch for ever. Keeping your eye on him, and your hand up (of course the right one), make a circuit, so that the birds shall be between him and you. Be certain that your circle is sufficiently wide,—if it is not, the birds may get up behind you, and so perplex him, that at his next find he will feel doubtful how to act. Fire at no skirter, or chance shot. Reserve yourself for the bird or birds at which he points; a caution more necessary on the moors than on the stubbles, as grouse spread while feeding. When you have well headed him, walk towards him and spring the birds. Use straight shooting-powder. Take a cool aim well forward, and knock down one. Do not flurry the dog by firing more than a single barrel, or confuse him by killing more than *one* bird. If you have been able to accomplish all this without his stirring (though, to effect it, you may have been obliged to use your voice), you have every

* Should they (unluckily for the lesson) run, you must endeavour to manage as detailed in 285.

right to hope, from his previous education, that he will readily "down-charge" on hearing the report of your gun. Do not hurry your loading:—indeed, be unnecessarily long, with the view of making him at all such times patient and steady. If, in spite of all your calls and signals, he gives chase to the sprung birds, make him "drop,"—instantly if possible,—and proceed much as described in 259, dragging him back to the place where he should have "down-charged."

266. When you have loaded, say, "Dead,"* in a low voice, and signalling to "heel" make him come up to you, yourself keeping still. By signs (XI. of 141) place him as near as you can, *but to leeward* of the dead bird. Then, and not till then, say, "Find;" give him no other assistance. Let him have plenty of time to make out the bird. It is not to be find and *grip*, but find and *point*,† therefore the moment you perceive he is aware that it is before him, make him (by word of command) "toho:"—go up to him, stay for a while alongside him, then make a small circuit to head him, and have the bird between you and him; approach him. If he attempt to dash in, thunder out "No," and greet him with at least the sound of the whip: slowly pick up the dead bird; call the dog to you; show him the bird; but on no account throw it to him, lest he snatch at it; lay it on the ground, encourage him to sniff it; let him (for reason why see 313) turn it over with his nose,— teeth closed,—say to him, "Dead, dead;" caress him;

* As he acquires experience he will wish to rise the moment he observes that your loading is completed. Do not allow him to move, however correctly he may have judged the time. Let his rising be always in obedience to signal or word. You may occasionally make a mistake in charging, or your friend may not load as expeditiously as yourself.

† Never being allowed to grip conduces so much to making him tender-mouthed, that, should he hereafter be permitted to lift his game, it is probable he will deliver it up perfectly uninjured.

sit down; smooth the feathers of the bird; let him perceive that you attach much value to it; and after a while loop it on the game bag, allowing him all the time to see what you are doing. After that, make much of him for full five minutes: indeed with some dogs it would be advisable to give a palatable reward, but be not invariably very prodigal of these allurements; you may have a pupil whose attention they might engross more than they ought. Then walk about a little time with him at your heels. All this delay and caressing will serve to show him that the first tragedy is concluded, and has been satisfactorily performed. You may now hie him on to hunt for more birds.

267. Pray mind what is said about making your youngster point the dead bird staunchly, the moment you perceive that he first scents it. Should he be allowed to approach so near as to be able to touch it (instead of being made to point the instant he finds), the chances are, that, if hard-mouthed he will give it a crunch, if tender-mouthed a fumbling of the feathers; and either proceeding satisfying him, that he will quit it, and not further aid you in a search. As "pointing" is only a natural pause (prolonged by art) to determine exactly where the game is lying, preparatory to rushing forward to seize, it would be unreasonable to expect him willingly to make a second point at game he has not only found but mouthed:—the evil, however, does not rest here. There is such a disagreeable thing as blinking a dead bird, no less than blinking a sound one. For mouthing the bird you may possibly beat the dog, or for nosing it and not pointing you may rate him harshly, either of which, if he be not of a bold disposition, may lead, on the next occasion, to his slinking off after merely obtaining a sniff. You ought, in fact, to watch

LARGE HEAVY POINTER.

as carefully for your pupil's first "feathering" upon the dead bird, as you did (259) upon his first coming upon the covey. You see, then, that your teaching him to "point dead" is absolutely indispensable; unless, indeed, you constantly shoot with a retriever. Pointing at a live bird or at a dead one, should only differ in this, that in the latter case the dog makes a nearer point. *Begin* correctly, and you will not have any difficulty; but you may expect the greatest, if you let your dog go up to one or two birds and mouth them, before you commence making him point them. The following season, should you then permit him to lift his game (538), it will be time enough to dispense with his "pointing dead." I dwell upon this subject because many excellent dogs, from not having been properly taught to "point dead," often fail in securing the produce of a successful shot, while, on the contrary, with judiciously educated dogs it rarely happens that any of the slain or wounded are left on the field. Moreover, the protracted search and failure (as an instance see 314) occasions a lamentable loss of time. Were a sportsman who shoots over dogs not well broken to "point dead" (or retrieve) to calculate accurately, watch in hand, he would, I think, be surprised to find how many of his best shooting hours are wasted in unprofitable searching for birds, of the certainty of whose untimely fate his dogs had probably long before fully convinced themselves.

268. I was shooting some seasons back where woodcocks, being scarce, are considered great prizes. If one is sprung, the pheasants are immediately neglected, and every exertion is made to secure the rara avis. We flushed one; at length it was killed; it fell in thick cover,—was found by a setter (a feather or two in his mouth betraying him); but as the dog had not been properly taught to "point dead," we were obliged to leave the bird behind, after spending nearly half an hour in a fruitless search.

269. As to the word "Dead," whether you choose to

continue using it immediately after loading, or, as I have recommended (XI. of 141), *after a time* omit it, and merely let the signal to "heel" intimate that you have killed, always make your dog go to you before you allow him to seek for the fallen bird.

270. Some may say, "As a dog generally sees a bird fall, what is the use of calling him to you before you let him seek?—and even if he does not see the bird, why should any time be lost? Why should not you and he go as direct to it as you can?"

271. Provided you have no wish that the "finder" (see 541), rather than any of his companions, should be allowed the privilege of "seeking dead," I must admit that in the cultivated lands of England, when a dog "sees a bird fall," he might in nine cases out of ten go direct to it without inconvenience. Even here, however, there are occasions when intervening obstacles may prevent your observing what the dog is about; and in cover, so far from being able to give him any assistance by signaling, you may be ignorant whether or not he has seen the bird knocked over, or is even aware of the general direction in which he ought to seek. But in the oft-occurring cases in which "he does not see the bird fall," it is obvious (particularly when he happens to be at the extremity of his beat), that you will far more quickly place him where you wish, if you make him, at first, run up to you, and then advance from you, straight to the bird, by your forward signal (277). These good results at least will follow, if you remain stationary, and make him join you. You do not lose sight of the spot where you marked that the bird or birds fell. The foil is not interfered with by your walking over the ground (a matter of much importance, especially on bad-scenting days). The dog, if habituated to "seek"

without your companionship, will readily hunt morasses and ravines, where you might find it difficult to accompany him. He will feel the less free to follow his own vagaries; and this consciousness of subjection will dispose him to pay more watchful attention to your signals. He will the more patiently wait at the "down charge;" and when you are reloaded, will not be so tempted to dash recklessly after the bird, regardless whether or not he raises others on the way. If he is dragging a cord, you can the more easily take hold of its end, in order to check him, and make him point when he first winds the dead bird,—and should you be shooting over several dogs, by none of them being permitted to run direct to the fallen bird, they will the less unwillingly allow you to select the one who is to approach close to you before "seeking dead."

272. The opponents of this method argue, that the practice may give the dog the bad habit of running immediately after the "down charge" to the gun, instead of recommencing to hunt; particularly if he is shot over by a first-rate performer. Granted; but is not the temptation to bolt off in search of a dead bird still stronger? To check the former evil, endeavour to make the coming to "heel" an act of obedience rather than a voluntary act, by never failing, as soon as you are reloaded, to give the customary signal (VIII. of 141) when you have killed, or the signal to "hie on" should you have missed.

273. Moreover, you will sometimes meet with a dog who, when a bird has been fired at, though it be the first and only one sprung of a large covey, commences "seeking dead" immediately after the "down charge," apparently considering that his first duty. This sad, sad fault—for it frequently leads to his raising the

other birds out of shot—is generally attributable to the dog's having been allowed to rush at the fallen bird, instead of being accustomed to the restraint of having first to run up to the gun.

274. To prevent your pupil from ever behaving so badly, often adopt the plan of not "seeking dead" immediately after loading, especially if the birds are lying well. Mark accurately the spot where your victim lies, and closely hunt for others, endeavouring to instil great caution into the dog, much in the manner (being guided by his disposition and character) described in 196, 197, and 329. As long as any of the covey remain unsprung, you ought not to pick up one dead bird, though you should have a dozen on the ground. Your dog ought not even to "down charge" after you have fired, if he is fully aware that more birds are before him. To impart to him the knowledge that, *however important is the "down charge," his continuing at his point is still more so*, you may, when the birds are lying well and he is at a fixed point, make your attendant discharge a gun at a little distance while you remain near the dog, encouraging him to maintain his "toho." If you have no attendant, and the birds lie like stones, fire off a barrel yourself while the dog is steadily pointing.* He will fancy you see birds which he has not noticed, and, unless properly tutored and praised by you, will be desirous to quit those he has found, to search for the bird he conceives you have shot.

275. It is a fine display of intelligence in the dog, and of judicious training in the breaker (may it be your desert and reward ere long to witness it in your pupil), when a pointer (or setter) in goodly turnips or strong potatoes draws upon birds which obligingly rise one

* Oftener practicable on heather than on stubble.

after the other, while by continuing his eloquent attitude he assures you that some still remain unsprung, to which he is prepared to lead you, if you will but attend to them and him, and, instead of pot-hunting after those you have killed, wait until his discriminating nose informs him that having no more strangers to introduce, he is at liberty to assist you in your search.

276. To revert, however, to the point particularly under discussion, viz., whether you prefer that your dog go direct to the fallen bird, or (as I strongly recommend) that he first join you, pray be consistent ; exact which you will, but always exact the same, if you are anxious to obtain cheerful unhesitating obedience.

277. I have seen the advantage of the latter method very strikingly exemplified in America, in parts of which there is capital snipe-shooting. In the high grass and rushes on the banks of the Richelieu, many a bird have I seen flushed and shot at, of which the liver and white pointer, ranging at a little distance, has known nothing. As he was well broken in, he, of course, dropped instantly, on hearing the report of the gun. If the bird had fallen, his master, after reloading, used invariably to say "Dead,"* in a low tone of voice, on which the dog would *go up to him;* and then his master, without stirring from the spot where he had fired, directed him by signals to the place where the bird fell, to reach which the dog often had to swim the stream. His master then said "Find." At that word, and not before it, his intelligent four-footed companion commenced searching for the bird, nor did he ever fail to find and bring ; and so delicate was his mouth that I have often seen him deliver up a bird perfectly alive, without having deranged a feather, though, very probably, he had swam with it across one of the many creeks which intersect that part of the country. If the shot was a miss, his master's silence after reloading, and a wave of his arm to continue hunting (or the command to "Hie on," if the dog was hidden by the rushes—perhaps a low whistle would have been better), fully informed his companion of the disappointment. He was quite as good on the large quail, and small wood-cock found in Canada, which latter makes a ringing noise on rising, not unlike the sound of a distant

---

* In order to work in silence, I advised (XI. of 141) that the signal to "heel," whenever the dog could observe it, should supersede the word "dead." It might be necessary to sing out with a boatswain's voice should the dog be far off.

soft bell ; but reminiscences of that capital old dog are leading me away from your young one.

278. For some days you cannot shoot to your pupil too steadily and quietly—I had well-nigh said too slowly. By being cool, calm, and collected yourself, you will make him so. I am most unwilling to think that you will be too severe, but I confess I have my misgivings lest you should occasionally overlook some slight faults in the elation of a successful right and left. Filling the game-bag must be quite secondary to education. Never hesitate to give up any bird if its acquisition interfere with a lesson. Let all that you secure be done according to rule, and in a sportsman-like manner.

CHAPTER X.

FIRST LESSON IN SEPTEMBER CONTINUED. ASSISTANT.—VERMIN.

279. Some Dogs will not point readily—Breeding in and in, error of.—280. Instance of two young, *untaught*, highly-bred Pointers, behaving well first day shown Game—Dogs more inclined to point at first than afterwards.—281. Checkcord employed—spike attached to it.—282. With wild dog assistant useful—Signals to.—283. How particularly useful with a badly broken Dog—Range of Stoat—Traps better than Guns. In Note, Hen-harrier feeding her young—Decoy Owl for Winged-Vermin—Keeper to possess Dog that hunts Vermin—Account of a capital Bull-Terrier—Destructiveness of Stoats. (See Appendix).—284. Shy birds, how intercepted between Guns and dog. Cheeta driven near Antelopes by cart circling and never stopping. In Note, Cheeta always selects the Buck. Cheeta how trained.—285. "Heading" Dog at his point—not practised too often—Dog to acquire a knowledge of his distance from Game.—286. Beautiful instance of Pointer correcting his Distance.—287. Constantly "Heading" Dog may make him too immoveable.—288. A fault often caused by over-punishment. —289. Mr. C——t's Bitch, which persisted 'three times in taking up the same point.—290 to 292. Instance of fine "roading" in a young Dog.—293. False points caused by over-punishment—Self-confidence and experience only cures for over-caution.—294. Dog's manner shows position of birds.—295. Curiously instanced in a Dog of Lord M——d's.—296. Also shows species of Game—Pointer on Rabbits.—297. Young Dog drawing upon his first Blackcock.—298. Terrier pointing four kinds of game, and each in a different attitude.

279. IT is proper you should be warned that you must not always expect a dog will "toho" the first day as readily as I have described, though most will, and some (especially pointers) even more quickly, if they have been previously well-drilled, and have been bred for several generations from parents of pure blood.

I do not say bred in and in. Breeding in and in, to a certainty, would enfeeble their intellects as surely as their constitutions. In this way has many a kennel been deprived of the energy and endurance so essential in a sportsman's dog.

280. The late Lord Harris gave Mr. M——t (mentioned in 195), then residing in Essex, two young, very highly bred pointer pups, a brother and sister. Mr. M——t, after some months, carried them into Kent, and, without their having had the least preliminary instruction, or ever having seen a bird, took them out partridge-

shooting. He had no older dog to set them a good example, and as they were wholly unbroken, he feared they would bolt for home the moment he squibbed off his gun; but, though they seemed much astonished and extremely nervous at the report, great caressing and encouragement induced them to remain. After awhile the dog went forward, and sniffed about,—then he began to hunt,—at length he did so very assiduously; but his sister not so keenly, for she did little more than follow in his wake. Generally it is otherwise, bitches being usually the earliest in the field. At length the dog came to a stiff point at the edge of some turnips. The bitch perceived him and timidly backed. Mr. M——t hastened up—birds arose—one fell, fortunately killed outright—the dog dashed at it, and, tremulous with a world of new and pleasurable emotions, nosed and fumbled it about in a very excited manner, but did not attempt to gripe it. Mr. M——t, lest he should damp the youngster's ardour, refrained from rating, or even speaking to him, but left him entirely to himself. After a time, singular to say,—for he had not been taught as a puppy to "fetch,"—he lifted the partridge, and carried it to his master,—a practice he was afterwards allowed to pursue. Is it not clear that, if he had been well instructed in the initiatory lessons, Mr. M——t would have found him perfectly made with the exception of having no systematic range? He turned out extremely well, and constantly showed himself superior to his sister, who always wanted mettle.

As in the present instance, it often occurs that a dog is less inclined to dash in at first than when he is more acquainted with birds. He is suddenly arrested by the novelty of the scent, and it is not until he is fully assured from what it proceeds that he longs to rush forward and give chase. In autumnal breaking the dog gets his bird—it is killed for him—he is satisfied—and therefore he has not the same temptation to rush in as when he is shown birds in the spring.

281. If you find your dog, from excess of delight and exuberance of spirits, less under general command than from his initiatory education you had expected, and that he will not "toho" steadily at the exact spot at which you order him, at once attach a checkcord to his collar. It will diminish his pace, and make him more cautious and obedient. The moment you next see him begin to feather, get up quickly, *but without running*, to the end

of the cord, and check him with a sudden jerk if you are satisfied that game is before him and that he ought to be pointing. If from his attitude and manner you are *positive* that there is game, drive a spike (or peg) into the ground, and tie the cord to it. I only hope the birds will remain stationary. If they do, you can give him a capital lesson by remaining patiently alongside of him, and then heading him and the birds in the manner before described (264, 265).

282. As a general rule, an attendant or any companion cannot be recommended, because he would be likely to distract a young dog's attention (10); but an intelligent fellow who would readily obey your signals, and not presume to speak, would, doubtless, with a very wild dog, be an advantageous substitute for the spike. You could then employ a longer and slighter cord than usual, and, on the man's getting hold of the end of it, be at once free to head and awe the dog. Whenever you had occasion to stand still, the man would, of course, be as immoveable as yourself.

Your signals to him might be :—
The gun held up,—" Get near the dog."
Your fist clenched,—" Seize the rope."
Your fist shaken,—" Jerk the cord."
Your hand spread open,—" Let go the cord."
Or any signs you pleased, so that you understood each other without the necessity of speaking.

283. Should it ever be your misfortune to have to correct in a dog evil habits caused by past mismanagement, such an attendant, if an active, observant fellow, could give you valuable assistance, for he sometimes would be able to seize the cord immediately the dog began "feathering," and generally would have hold of it before you could have occasion to fire. But the fault

most difficult to cure in an old dog is a bad habit of ranging. If, as a youngster, he has been permitted to beat as his fancy dictated, and *has not been instructed in looking to the gun for orders,* you will have great, very great difficulty in reclaiming him. Probably he will have adopted a habit of running for a considerable distance up wind, his experience having shown him that it is one way of finding birds, but not having taught him that to seek for them by crossing the wind would be a better method.

Curiously enough, nature has given this systematic range to the stoat,* though, happily for the poor rabbits, it cannot carry a high nose, and therefore the parallels on which it hunts are necessarily not far apart. This interesting proceeding is occasionally witnessed by those keepers who injudiciously prefer their game-disturbing guns to their vermin-destroying traps.†

284. The great advantage of teaching a dog to point the instant he is sensible of the presence of birds (260), and of not creeping a foot further until he is directed by you, is particularly apparent when birds are wild. While he remains steady, the direction of his nose will lead you to give a tolerable guess as to their "whereabouts," and you and your companion can keep quite wide of the dog (one on each side), and so approach the birds from both flanks. They, meanwhile, finding themselves thus intercepted in three directions, will probably lie so close as to afford a fair shot to, at least, one gun, for they will not fail to see the dog and be awed by his presence. Raise your feet well off the ground to avoid making a noise. Walk quickly, but with no unnecessary flourish of arms or gun. They may fancy that you intend to pass by them :—a slow cautious step often raises their suspicions. (Most sportsmen in the Highlands prefer a low cap, or a wide-awake, to a hat; one of the motives for this choice being that the wearer is less conspicuous,—not appearing so tall. It is because he will not appear so tall that he thinks he can get nearer to a pack by approaching the birds up hill, rather than by coming down upon them from a height. Many an old sportsman crouches when approaching wild birds.) As soon as you and your friend are in good positions, you can motion to the dog to advance and flush the birds. You should on no account halt on the

---

* Which becomes white in a severe winter,—a regular ermine; the only one of the weazel-tribe that does so in England.

† This note on the subject of trapping, and keeper's vermin-dogs, &c., is so long that the printer has placed it in an Appendix.

way, for the moment you stop they will fancy they are perceived, and take wing. It is by driving round and round, constantly contracting the circle, and *never stopping*, that the bullock-cart, carrying the trained cheeta, is often brought within 100 yards of the herd of antelopes, amidst which is unsuspiciously browsing the doomed dark buck.* Driven directly towards the herd, the cart could not ap-

---

* The cheeta invariably selects the buck, passing by the nearer does and fawns. I never saw but one instance to the contrary. On that occasion the cheeta endeavoured to secure what appeared to be his easiest victim—a young fawn; but the little creature twisted and doubled so rapidly, that it escaped perfectly uninjured. The turbaned keeper, greatly surprised, begged the spectators to remain at a respectful distance while he proceeded to secure the panting, baffled animal. The caution was not unnecessary; for the disappointed beast, though usually very tractable, struck at the man's arm and tore it. On examination a large thorn was found in one of the animal's fore paws, which fully explained the cause of his not *bounding* after the lord of the herd, when he had, in cat-like manner, stealthily crawled as near as any intervening bushes would afford concealment. This preliminary part of the affair is at times very tedious; the rest is quickly settled: for the wondrous springs of the cheeta (whose form then so apparently dilates,[1] that the observer, if a novice, starts in the belief that he suddenly sees a royal tiger) soon exhaust him, which accounts for his always creeping as near as possible before openly commencing his attack.

The education of the cheeta is no less progressive than that of the dog; and whatever patience the latter may require from his instructor, the former demands far greater; not so much from want of docility, as from the nearly total absence of all the feelings of attachment so conspicuous in the canine race. The cubs when they are very young are stolen from the rocky fastnesses where they are usually bred. They are immediately hooded, and allowed no other exercise than what they can take when they are led about by their keeper. While he is feeding them, he invariably shouts in a peculiar key. In a month or so their eager looks, animated gestures, and possibly cheerful purring, testify that they comprehend its import as fully as a hungry young ensign does "the roast beef of old England." They are then slightly chained, each to a separate bandy (bullock-cart), and habituated to its motion. They are always fed during the drive. They thus learn to expect a good meal in the course of their airing. After a time the keeper, instead of feeding a promising pupil while he is a prisoner, goes to a little distance from the bandy and utters the singular cries now so joyfully heard, upon which—an attendant slipping off the chain and hood— the liberated cheeta runs to his trainer to be fed. By degrees this is done at increased distances. He is always conducted back to the carriage by the keeper's dragging at the lump of meat of which the

---

[1] A dealer often says in praise of a small horse,—and great praise it is—"You may fancy him a little one now, but wait till you see him move, and then you'll think him a big one."

proach within thrice that distance. In Yorkshire, very late in the season, when the grouse are so scared that they will not allow a dog or man to get near them, it often happens that a good bag is made by the gun keeping just a-head of a cart and horse. Here, however, no circuit is made. The birds are found by chance. The only dog employed is the retriever, kept in the cart until he is required to fetch.

285. You must not, however, too often try to work round and head your pupil when he is pointing. Judgment is required to know when to do it with advantage. If the birds were running, you would completely throw him out, and greatly puzzle and discourage him, for they probably would then rise out of shot, behind you, if they were feeding up wind,—behind him, if they were feeding down wind.* Far more frequently make him work out the scent by his own sagacity and nose, and lead you up to the birds, every moment bristling more and more, at a pace † entirely controlled and regulated by your signals. These being given with your right

animal retains a firm hold. The next step is for the man again to commence feeding *near* the cart, but without making any noise,— the removal of the hood being the only thing that tells the spotted beast to look about him for his dinner. The last step is the substitution of a kid or wounded antelope, for the keeper with his provision basket, when it rarely happens that nature's strong instinct does not make the cheeta seize with eagerness the proffered prey. His education is now completed; but for many months he is never unhooded at a herd unless the driver has managed to get the cart within a very favouring distance.

The cheeta knocks over the buck with a blow of his paw on the hind-quarters, given so rapidly that the eye cannot follow the motion, and then grasps him firmly by the throat; nor will he quit hold of the wind-pipe as long as the prostrate animal can make the slightest struggle for breath. This affords the keeper ample time to cut off a limb, which he thrusts against the cheeta's nose, and as soon as the still quivering dainty tempts him to grasp it, he is again led off to his cart. He is then further rewarded with a drink of warm blood taken from the inside of the antelope, and the scene concludes by the carcass being strapped under the bandy.

* Many think that grouse feed more down wind than partridges.

† A pace that keeps the sportsman at a brisk walk is obviously the best. It is very annoying to be unable, by any quiet encouragement, to get a dog to "road" as rapidly as you wish—an annoyance often experienced with naturally timid dogs, or with those which have been overpunished.

hand will be more apparent to him if you place yourself on his left side. It is in this manner that you give him a lesson which will *hereafter* greatly aid him in recovering slightly winged birds,—in pressing to a rise the slow-winged but nimble-heeled rail,—or in minutely following the devious mazes through which an old cock pheasant, or yet more, an old cock grouse, may endeavour to mislead him. And yet this lesson should not be given before he is tolerably confirmed at his point, lest he should push too fast on the scent; and make a rush more like the dash of a cocker than the sober, convenient "road" of a setter. As his experience increases he will thus acquire the valuable knowledge of the position of his game :—he will lead you to the centre of a covey, or what is of greater consequence—as grouse spread—to the centre of a pack, (instead of allowing himself to be attracted to a flank by some truant from the main body), and thus get you a good double shot, and enable you effectually to separate the birds:—he will, moreover, become watchful, and sensible of his distance from game—a knowledge all important, and which, be it remarked, he never could gain in turnips or potatoes, or any thick cover.

286. Mr. C——s R——n, well known in Edinburgh, told me that a black and tan pointer of his (Admiral M——y's breed) gave, on one occasion, a very clever proof of his knowledge of the distance at which he ought to stand from his game. He was ranging in thick stubble. Some partridge, being slightly alarmed, rose a little above the ground, and then dropped very near the dog,—upon which the sagacious creature instantly crouched close to the ground, his head between his fore-legs, and in that constrained position *ventre-à-terre*, pushed himself backwards until he had retreated to what he conceived to be a judicious distance from the covey, when he stood up and pointed boldly.

287. There is another and yet stronger reason why you should not consider it a rule always to head your young dog at his point. You may—although at first it

seems an odd caution to give—make him too stanch. This, to be sure, signifies less with partridges than with most birds; but if you have ever seen your dog come to a fixed point, and there, in spite of all your efforts, remain provokingly immoveable—plainly telling you of the vicinity of birds, but that you must find them out for yourself—your admiration of his steadiness has, I think, by no means reconciled you to the embarrassing position in which it has placed you. I have often witnessed this vexatious display of stanchness, although the owner cheered on the dog in a tone loud enough to alarm birds two fields off.

288. A keeper will sometimes praise his dog for such stanchness ; but it is a great fault, induced probably by over-severity for former rashness,—and the more difficult to be cured, if the animal is a setter, from the crouching position which he often naturally assumes when pointing.

289. A friend of mine was told by Mr. C——t (to whom those interested in the prosperity of the Edinburgh Zoological Gardens ought to feel much indebted), that a little pointer bitch of his came, on a hot, dry, bad scenting day, to a fixed point. He could not persuade her to move, nor could he or his friend spring any game ; and two not bad-nosed dogs that were hunting with her would not acknowledge the scent, even when they were brought close to the bitch. As she would neither advance nor retire, he actually had her carried off in a boy's arms. When she was put down, away she ran and resumed her point. After another ineffectual attempt to raise birds, again she was borne off, but only to take up for a *third* time her point. At length, after a yet closer search—in which, however, she still refused to join,—a young blackcock was perceived closely buried under a thick piece of heather. The very excellence of the bitch's nose, and her admirable perseverance, made it the more vexatious that she had not been taught the meaning of the signals to advance. One grieves that anything should have been neglected in the education of so superior a creature.

290. I advised (285) your practising your young dog in "footing" out a scent. Though it occurred many years ago, I remember as if it were but yesterday (from my annoyance at shooting so execrably, when it was peculiarly incumbent on me not to miss), my nearly making a sad mistake with a very young dog, who was following up a retreating bird most magnificently.

291. I was looking for grouse where I thought that there might be some, but was sure there could not be many. After beating for

CARRYING A POINT, AND CARRYING A POINTER.—Par. 289.

a considerable time unsuccessfully, the youngest of the dogs that were hunting made a stanch point. I got up to him;—nothing rose. I encouraged him to press on. He did so, and at a convenient pace which allowed me to keep parallel with him. He so seldom stopped, and bristled so little, that I thought he was making a fool of me. Still, as he now and then looked round sagaciously, as if to say "There really is game a-head," I did not like to tell him of my suspicions. Though my patience was sorely tried, for he led me a distance which I dare not name, I resolved to let him have his own way, and to see what would be the result, satisfied that undue precipitance on my part might effect more evil than could arise from an erroneous participation in his proceedings. At length, when my good resolutions were all but exhausted, and I was thinking of chiding the dog for his folly, we approached a bare spot, free from heather :—up sprung a noble cock-grouse, challenging splendidly.

292. I had been so perplexed, and was, I am ashamed to say, so unnerved, that, though the bird went off in a line directly from me, I missed him with both barrels ; I don't know when I was more vexed :—nothing but my bungling lost the young dog the reward he so richly deserved.

293. I recount this story, though it is little in my favour, to warn you against the too common error of fancying that a young dog is making false points if birds do not get up directly. They may have taken leg-bail, and thus have puzzled him in his inexperience. Dogs not cowed by punishment will, after a little hunting, seldom make false points, while they are unfatigued. To a certainty they will not draw upon a false point for any distance: therefore, never punish what is solely occasioned by over-caution. Your doing so would but increase the evil. Self-confidence and experience are the only cares for a fault that would be a virtue if not carried to excess. Even a good dog will occasionally make a point at larks from over-caution when birds are wild; but see the first note to 194.

294. After you have shot over a dog a short time, his manner and attitude will enable you to guess pretty accurately whether birds are really before him; whether they are far off or near; and whether or not they are on the move. Generally speaking, the higher he carries his head, and the less he stiffens his stern, the further off are the birds. If he begin to look nervous, and become fidgety, you will seldom be wrong in fancying they are on the run. But various, and at times most curious, are the methods that dogs will adopt, *apparently* with the wish to show you where the birds are, and *certainly* with the desire to get you a shot.

295. A pointer, belonging at the present moment to a nobleman in Perthshire, Lord M——d, (from whose lips my informant heard the strange story), has quite a novel mode of telling that birds are on the move. While they continue quiet, he points them in the usual manner, with his head towards them, but so soon as they begin to walk off, he directly faces about, very disrespectfully presenting his stern to them,—whether to express contempt for their want of courtesy, or to warn his lordship to look out for a long shot, I will leave you to decide.* I particularly inquired if he did this indifferently,

---

* "Suwarrow's" manœuvre (530) clearly shows the true reason.

whether the birds were running up or down wind. This my informant could not positively tell. All he knew was that his lordship had said, in a general way, that the singularly mannered animal invariably repeated this eccentric proceeding whenever the birds moved.

296. Not only will a dog's manner often show you whether or not birds are on the move, but his carriage, when you are accustomed to him, will frequently tell you what species of game is before him. I know an old pointer that is capital in light cover. His owner shoots rabbits over him, and whenever the dog finds one, though he points steadily, his tail vibrates as regularly as a pendulum.

297. Years ago, when I was shooting in the North, I was crossing some land which the encroachments of husbandry had converted from wild heather to profitable sheep-walks; suddenly a young dog that was with me came to a more rigid point than I had ever seen him make—every muscle appeared distended—I was puzzled—I felt satisfied that he had winded something very unusual, but what to expect I could not imagine, for there seemed not cover for a tomtit. When I got up to him he was so nervously anxious that I had some difficulty in making him advance, but at length he slowly brought me towards a small bush, to which he nailed his nose. Further he would not proceed. I kicked the bush; when, to my great gratification, up gradually rose a young blackcock, which went off to killing distance with a flight not more rapid than that of the florikin. It was the first black game that the dog had ever seen. It was also the first that I had ever seen on the wing, and this may account for all the attendant circumstances being so strongly impressed upon my memory.

298. Colonel C——n, on the staff of the Duke of C——e, told me that about ten years ago he heard a gentleman, then living on the Mall at Birr, make a bet of a pony (he offered to wager a much larger sum) that his terrier bitch would point all the kinds of game found in the neighbouring bog—and further, that before it was sprung he would name what description of game the dog was pointing. The gentleman won his bet handsomely, though they found snipe, woodcock, grouse, hare, and something else,—as well as Colonel C——n now remembers,—a duck. It was soon evident to the spectators, that the attitude of the clever animal—short-eared, with a considerable cross of the bull-dog—varied according to the nature of the game she came across. To an English ear shooting on a bog does not sound very attractive,—but though the walking is generally difficult, the sport is often interesting, from the variety of game the sportsman frequently meets with.

CHAPTER XI.

FIRST LESSON IN SEPTEMBER CONCLUDED. BAR.—LEG STRAP.— SPIKE COLLAR.

299. Bar cure for too high spirits. A leg strapped up. Why these remedies are better than starvation and excessive work.—300. The regular Spike Collar described. French Spike Collar.—301. One less objectionable.—302 to 305. How, in extreme cases, the Spike collar might be employed.—306. Dog springing Birds without noticing them; how to be treated.—307. The first Birds fired at to be killed outright; the Search for winged Birds, Dog being to leeward.—308. Had the Dog seized. Firing at running Bird.—309. The Search for winged Bird, Dog being to windward.—310. "Lifting" a Dog, when recommended. "Footing" a scent. In Note, speed of Red-legged Partridge.—311. Evil of a Young Sportsman always thinking his birds killed outright; often calls away Dog improperly.—312. Loss of dead bird discouraging to Dog.—313. Perseverance in Seeking, how fostered.—314. "Nosing" Bird allowed.—315. Its advantage instanced in Sir W——m F——n's dogs.—316. Error of picking up winged bird before Loading. In Notes, ingenious Argument in its favour; Bird picked up in the Evening; rejoins Covey.—317. If winged bird be a fast runner, and out of shot.—318. Dog that was devoted to "seeking dead," would retrieve Snipe she would not point; probable cause of her fondness for retrieving.—319. Dog which kept his paw on winged bird; how taught. "Beppo" in Africa.—320. Blenheim, which hated Water, yet would always retrieve Wild Fowl.—321. If dog rushes forward yet yields to menaces and stops.—322. If he seizes the dead bird; if he has torn it.—323. How to administer Punishment.—324. Part good friends. Your own temper not to be ruffled.—325. He is no Breaker who cannot always get hold of Dog.—326. Be certain of Dog's guilt before punishing.—327. Dog's Ears not to be pulled violently.—328. To "drop" whenever Bird or Hare rises.— 329. Lesson in Turnips. — 330. Real Lesson in "Gone" or "Flown" given *after* dog has had some experience; reason why.

299. AFTER a few trials you will, I hope, be able to dispense with the peg recommended in 281, and soon after with the checkcord also. But if your dog possesses unusually high spirits, or if he travels over the ground at a pace which obviously precludes his making a proper use of his nose, it may be advisable to fasten to his collar a bar, something like a diminutive splinter-bar, that it may, by occasional knocking against his shins, feelingly admonish him to lessen his stride. If he gets

it between his legs and thus finds it no annoyance, attach it to both sides of his collar from points near the extremities. One of his forelegs might occasionally be passed through the collar; but this plan is not so good as the other; nor as the strap on the hind leg (60). These means (to be discarded, however, as soon as obedience is established) are far better than the *temporary* ascendancy which some breakers establish by low diet and excessive work, which would only weaken his spirits and his bodily powers, without eradicating his self-will, or improving his intellects. You want to force him, when he is in the highest health and vigour, to learn by experience the advantage of letting his nose dwell longer on a feeble scent.

300. I have made no mention of the spiked collar, because it is a brutal instrument, which none but the most ignorant or unthinking would employ. It is a leather collar into which nails, much longer than the thickness of the collar have been driven, with their points projecting inwards. The French spike-collar is nearly as severe. It is formed of a series of wooden balls,—larger than marbles,—linked (about two and a half inches apart) into a chain by stiff wires bent into the form of hooks. The sharp pointed hooks punish cruelly when the checkcord is jerked.

301. We have, however, a more modern description of collar, which is far less inhuman than either of those I have mentioned, but still I cannot recommend its adoption, unless in extreme cases; for though not so severely, it, likewise, punishes the unfortunate dog, more or less, by the strain of the checkcord he drags along the ground: and it ought to be the great object of a good breaker as little as is possible to fret or worry his pupil, that all his ideas may be engaged in an anxious wish to wind birds

On a leather strap, which has a ring at one end, four wooden balls (of about two inches diameter) are threaded like beads, at intervals from each other and the ring, say, of two inches (the exact distance being dependent on the size of the dog's throat). Into each of the balls sundry short thickish pieces of wire are driven, leaving about one-sixth of an inch beyond the surface. The other end of the strap (to which the checkcord is attached) is passed through the ring. This ring being of somewhat less diameter than the balls, it is clear, however severely the breaker may pull, he cannot compress the dog's throat beyond a certain point. The effect of the short spikes is rather to crumple than penetrate the skin.

302. I have long been sensible of the aid a spiked collar would afford in reclaiming headstrong, badly educated dogs, if it could be used at the moment—and only at the precise moment—when punishment was required; but not until lately did it strike me how the collar could be carried so that the attached cord should not constantly bear upon it, and thereby worry, if not pain the dog. And had I again to deal with an old offender, who incorrigibly crept in after pointing, or obstinately "rushed into dead," I should feel much disposed to employ a slightly spiked collar in the following manner.

303. That the mere carrying the collar might not annoy the dog, I would extract or flatten the nails fixed on the *top* of the collar, on the part, I mean, that would lie on the animal's neck. This collar I would place on his neck, in front of his common light collar. I would then firmly fasten the checkcord, in the usual way, to the spiked collar; but, to prevent any annoyance from dragging the checkcord, at about five or six inches from the fastening just made I would attach it to the com-

mon collar, with very slight twine—twine so slight that, although it would not give way to the usual drag of the checkcord, however long, yet it would readily break on my having to pull strongly against the wilful rush of an obstinate dog, when, of course, the spikes would punish him, as the strain would then be borne by the spiked collar alone.

304. Guided by circumstances, I would afterwards either remove the spiked collar, or, if I conceived another bout necessary, refasten the checkcord to the common collar with some of the thin twine, leaving, as before, five or six inches of the checkcord loose between the two collars.

305. If you should ever consider yourself forced to employ a spiked collar, do not thoughtlessly imagine that the same collar will suit all dogs. The spikes for a thin-coated pointer ought to be shorter than for a coarse-haired setter! You can easily construct one to punish with any degree of severity you please. Take a common leather collar; lay its inner surface flat on a soft deal board : through the leather drive with a hammer any number of tacks or flat-headed nails : then get a cobbler to sew on another strap of leather at the back of the nails, so as to retain them firmly in position.

306. I have supposed that your dog has *scented* the birds before they rose, but if he spring them without having previously noticed them (as in some rare cases happens even to well-bred dogs) you *must* bring him back to the spot at which you feel assured that he ought to have been sensible of their presence, and *there* make him "Toho." Afterwards endeavour to make him aware of the haunt by encouraging him to sniff at the ground that the birds have just left. The next time watch very carefully for the *slightest* indication of his feathering

and then instantly call out "Toho." After a few times he will, to a certainty, understand you.

307. You should kill outright the few first birds at which you fire. I would infinitely prefer that you should miss altogether, than that one of the two or three first birds should be a runner. Afterwards you have full leave to merely wing a bird; but still I should wish it not to be too nimble. This is a good trial of *your* judgment as well as the dog's. I hope he is to leeward of the bird, and that it will not catch his eye. See he touches on the haunt. Do not let him work with his nose to the ground. "Up, up," must be your encouraging words (or "On, on," according to circumstances), whilst with your right hand (IV. of 141) you are alternately urging and restraining him, so as to make him advance at a suitable pace. From his previous education, not being flurried by any undue dread of the whip, he will be enabled to give his undisturbed attention, and devote all his faculties to follow unerringly the retreating bird. But from inexperience he may wander from the haunt. On perceiving this, bring him, by signals, back to the spot where he was apparently last aware of the scent. He will again hit it off. If you view the bird ever so far ahead, on no account run. I hope you will at length observe it lie down. Head it, if possible, and strike it with your whip, if you think you will be unable to seize it with your hand. Endeavour to prevent its fluttering away;—it is too soon to subject the youngster to such a severe trial of his nerves and steadiness. Then, (having put the poor creature out of its misery, by piercing its skull, or rapping its head against your gun,) as before (266), show your dog the gratifying prize which your combined exertions have gained.

308. Should he unluckily have caught sight of the

running bird, and, in spite of all your calls, have rushed forward and seized it, you ought to have proceeded as described in 322. Clearly, however, you would not have dragged the dog back to the place where he "down charged," but merely to the spot from which he had made his unlawful rush. If the bird had been very active, it would have been far better to have fired at it a second time (while it was running), than to have incurred the risk of making your dog unsteady by a wild pursuit. Suppose that it was not winged, but rose again on your approaching it, and fluttered off,—a hard trial for the young dog,—you must, however, have made him bear it, and obey your loud command to "drop,"—you would (or should) have taken another shot, and have proceeded in exactly the same manner as if this had been your first find (265, 266).

309. As the wounded bird was to windward of the dog, the course to follow was obvious,—it was plain sailing; but the case would have varied greatly if the dog had been to windward. Had you pursued the usual plan, he must have roaded the bird by the "foot;" and the danger is, that in allowing him to do so, you may create in him the evil habit of hunting with his nose close to the ground, which is above all things to be deprecated. You have another mode—you can "lift" the dog (I suppose you know the meaning of that hunting term), and make him take a large circuit, and so head the bird, and then proceed as if it had fallen to windward.

310. The latter plan would avoid all risk of your making him a potterer, and it is, I think, to be recommended if you find him naturally inclined to hunt low. But the former method, as a lesson in "footing," must be often resorted to, that he may learn unhesitatingly to

distinguish the "heel" from the "toe," and how to push an old cock-grouse, or to flush a pheasant running through cover, or the red-legged, I was nearly saying, the everlasting-legged partridge;* and, indeed, generally, how to draw upon his birds, and with confidence lead you to a shot when they are upon the move and running down wind. (See end of 115 ; and for further directions, and for "seeking dead" with two dogs, look at 544). The heavy Spanish pointer, from his plodding perseverance and great olfactory powers, was an excellent hand at retrieving a slightly injured bird on a broiling, bad scenting day.

311. When I advised you (266) to let the dog "have plenty of time to make out the bird," I spoke from personal experience, and from a vivid recollection of errors committed in my novitiate. A young hand is too apt to imagine that every bird which falls to his gun is killed outright, and lying dead on the spot where it fell. He will, therefore, often impatiently, and most injudiciously, call away the dog who, at a little distance, may have hit-off the trail of the winged bird, and be "footing" it beautifully.

312. If in these lessons you should fail in obtaining one or two wounded birds, though it might not be a matter of any moment to yourself personally, it would be extremely vexatious on the dog's account, because, in this early stage of his education, it would tend to discourage him. The feeling which you must anxiously foster in him is this, that after the word "Find"† the search must never

---

* The speed with which one of these extremely beautiful, but in every other respect far, far inferior partridges will run, when only slightly wounded, is quite marvellous.

† The force of the word "Dead" (preceding the command "Find") —that joyous, exciting note of triumph—ought never to be lessened by being employed, as I have heard it, to stimulate a dog

be relinquished, even though he be constrained to hunt from morning till night. And it is clear that to make an abiding, valuable impression, this lesson must be inculcated on the several first occasions with unremitting, untiring diligence.

313. Persevere, therefore, for an hour, rather than give up a wounded bird. Join in the search yourself. Even if you see where it lies, do not pick it up hastily. On the contrary, leave it, but mark well the spot. Keep on the move. Hold your gun as if in expectation of a rise. Pretend to seek for the bird in every direction, even for a good half hour, if you can encourage your dog to hunt so long. If, indeed, you see him flag, and get wearied and dispirited, gradually bring him close, but to leeward of the spot where the bird lies, in order to make him "point dead," and be rewarded for all his diligence by finding it himself. Let him, also, have a good sniff at it and nose it (but let there be no biting or mouthing), before you put it into the bag. Otherwise, what return has he for the pains he has taken?

314. It is no conclusive argument against the practice of allowing him to "nose," that many first-rate dogs have never been so indulged. It is certain that they would not have been worse if they had; and many a dog, that would otherwise have been extremely slack, has been incited to hunt with eagerness from having been so rewarded. There are dogs who, from having been constantly denied all "touseling," will not even give themselves the trouble of searching for any bird which they have *seen* knocked over, much less think of pointing it. They seem satisfied with this ocular

to hunt when no bird is down; or, like the shepherd-boy's cry of "Wolf! wolf!" it will have little influence at the moment when it should most animate to unremitting exertions.

evidence of its death; for, odd to say, these very dogs will often zealously obey the order to hunt for any bird whose fall they have not noticed; but in winding it they will indulge in no more than a passing sniff,— which sniff, unless you are watchful, you may not observe, and so lose your bird. Never fail, therefore, to let your pupil ruffle the feathers* a little, while you bestow on him a caress or a kind word of approbation. You then incite to perseverance, by, even with dogs, a very abiding motive,—"self-interest;" but mind the important rule, that this "nosing" be only *when* the bird is in your possession, not *before* it is in your possession. If you wish to establish for ever a confirmed perseverance in "seeking dead," you must sacrifice *hours* (I say it seriously) rather than give up any of the first wounded birds. Be persuaded that every half hour spent in an unremitting search for *one* bird, if ultimately successful, will more benefit the young dog than your killing a *dozen* to him, should you bag them the moment you are reloaded. Of course you would not, when you are giving such a lesson in perseverance, fire at another bird, even if it sprang at your feet,—for your doing so, whether you missed or killed, would unsettle the young dog, and make him relinquish his search. Be stimulated to present exertion by the conviction that if he be not *now* well instructed, you must expect him to lose, season after season, nearly every bird only slightly disabled by a merely tipped wing.

---

* After a touseling you may have observed the dog rubbing his nose in the grass. He did right. I have lately had reason to think that when from the absence of grass a dog could not effectually wipe his nose, the fine down adhering to it has for some time interfered with the delicacy and discrimination of his olfactory organs. He got too near his birds before acknowledging them. Would you be shocked if I asked you to assist him occasionally in freeing his nostrils from the offending feathers?

315. I casually asked Mr. H——h what kind of sport he had had in Aberdeenshire with Sir W——m F——n. He replied, "The pleasantest imaginable. One day we killed forty-six brace, and bagged every feather. Indeed, F——n never loses a bird. I have actually known him, when his dogs were young, spend a full half hour in hunting for a dead bird; nothing would induce him to give up. The consequence is, that *now* he never loses one by any chance. He broke in the dogs entirely himself:—he would seldom allow his keeper to say a word to them. He was always very patient; and he is well rewarded for his trouble." Why not take the same trouble and obtain a like reward? This was *true* sport! What battue-shooting could compare with it?

316. I hope you will not say, as would most of our neighbours * on the other side of the Channel : "But if, instead of waiting to load, I had gone after the winged bird just as it fell, when first I saw it start off running, the evil you have now spoken of (312) could not have occurred, for there would have but been little risk of losing it." Probably not, but you would have almost ruined your dog; and to secure this one bird, in all likelihood you would subsequently lose a hundred.† How could you with justice blame him if, when next you killed, he rushed headlong after the bird (instead of dropping patiently to the "down charge"), and so sprung a dozen birds while you were unloaded?

317. Perhaps you will say, "You tell me to fire at a running bird, but when a winged cock-pheasant or red-legged partridge is racing off *out of shot*, how am I to get it, if I proceed in the slow, methodical manner you advise? May it not lead me an unsuccessful dance for

* In favour of such unsportsman-like haste they ingeniously argue that a continued noise after firing makes birds lie, from attracting their attention. They say that a sudden change to quiet (and a great change it must be, for a *chasseur* is always talking) alarms the birds. As an evidence of this, they adduce the well-known fact of its frequently happening that a partridge gets up the moment the guns have left the spot, though no previous noise had induced it to stir.

† Had you lost the bird from there being but little scent, it is probable you might have found it by renewing your search on your return homewards in the evening. If a runner, it would most likely have rejoined the covey.

an hour, if I do not allow the dog to start ahead and seize?" It may, (but I hope months will pass before you witness such agility); and this shows that those who do not employ a retriever, and yet are sticklers for a setter's (or pointer's) never being permitted to touch a feather, must on such occasions get into a dilemma; and, unless they are willing to lose the bird, must plead guilty to the inconsistency of being pleased—however loudly they may roar out " Toho," " ware dead,"—when they see their dog, in defiance of all such calls, disable it by a sudden grip. This plan, though frequently followed, cannot be correct. They blame the dog for doing what they really wish, and if he be too tender-mouthed to injure the bird, he keeps them at top speed, while he is alternately picking up the unfortunate creature, acting on his natural impulses,—and letting it fall on being rated. I therefore repeat, that even if you do not wish your dog constantly to retrieve (536), you would still act judiciously in teaching him as a puppy to fetch (96), for then he will give chase to the winged bird, and bring it to you *on getting the order*, instead of permitting it to escape for a fresh *burst*, or carrying it off, as I have seen done. You thus maintain discipline. The dog will do what you wish, in obedience to orders,—not in opposition to orders. The sticklers for dogs never being allowed to nose a feather, ought, unless they are willing to give up slightly winged birds, not to shrink from the difficult task of teaching their pupils to stop and retain with their paws (319).

318. The pertinacity with which some dogs will "seek dead" is really surprising. A relative of mine had an English pointer which was so devoted to hunting for "knocked-down" birds, that she was almost unequalled in "finding," though in other respects possessed of very ordinary qualifications. If she failed in soon winding the lost bird, she would of her own accord make a large circuit; and if still

unsuccessful, she would indefatigably traverse the field from leeward until some slight taint in the atmosphere intimated to her in what direction to continue the search. When he afterwards hunted her in Ireland, though he could not get her to point snipe, yet if he killed one, she would exert herself to the utmost to retrieve it. Her keenness probably in part arose from her having, as a young one, always been indulged with a good "touseling" of the game before it was picked up. She never wished to grip.

319. A gentleman who was my neighbour a few seasons ago, has a very old setter, which was also capital at "finding." "Don" used to lay his paw upon the wounded bird, which, I fancy, afforded him such gratification that he would zealously devote every faculty he possessed to secure the prize. You could not teach every dog this method of detaining a bird. If yours is one of a very docile disposition you may effect it by always placing the dead or wounded bird for a minute or two under his paw before you deposit it in the bag.

320. An officer of the Navy, Mr. W——b, of Southsea, once possessed a true Blenheim—naturally a tender breed—that, from having been injudiciously thrown into the water when young (see 104), had taken such a dislike to the element, that although she was extremely attached to her master, and always anxious to be with him, especially when he shouldered his gun, yet the moment she saw him appear with a towel in hand (feeling assured he purposed bathing), she would bolt off, and allow nothing to persuade her to accompany him. Now, great as was her abhorrence of a cold bath, yet her gratification in retrieving so far outweighed every other feeling, that for the moment it overcame her aversion to a plunge, and whenever Mr. W——b shot a duck she would dash in to bring it on shore. She would carefully deposit it at the edge of the bank, but not carry it a step further. " Rose " had secured it, and that was the extent of her wishes.

321. We have only spoken of instances 266, 307, 309, in which all has gone on smoothly, the dog most obediently dropping to shot and permitting *you* to take up the bird notwithstanding the poor creature's death-struggles. Suppose, however, and this may probably happen, that he does not restrain himself at the "down charge," but, in spite of all your calls and signals, rushes forward, yet yields to your menaces and halts in mid-career. It is well—your course is clear; you have to lug him back, and threaten, and lecture him. But should he not check himself until he sniffs the game, his stop

then becomes a "point;" and if he is of a timid disposition, or has ever evinced any disposition to blink, you dare not force him to retrace his steps, lest he should mistake your motives, and fancy himself encouraged to abandon his point. If you merely make him "down charge," you violate the axiom named in 359. In short, you are in a difficulty. It is a nice case, in which your own judgment of the dog's character can alone decide you.

322. But, if from inadequate initiatory instruction—for I will maintain that such marked rebellion can arise from no other cause—in the excitement of the moment he actually rushes in and seizes the bird, he must be punished, I am sorry to say it; but however much we may deplore it, *he must;* for he has been guilty of great disobedience, and he well knows that he has been disobedient. But the temptation was strong, perhaps too strong for canine nature,—that is to say, for canine nature not early taught obedience. The wounded bird was fluttering within sight and hearing :—it was, too, the first he had ever seen,—and this is almost his first glaring act of disobedience: be merciful, though firm. Make him "drop." Get up to him at once. Probably he will relinquish his grip of the bird; if not, make him give it up to you, but do not pull it from him : that would only increase the temptation to tear it. Lay it on the ground. Then drag him back to the spot from which he rushed; there make him lie down. Rate him. Call out "Toho."* Crack the whip over him—and, I am pained to add, make use of it—but moderately, not severely. Three or four cuts will be enough, provided

---

* "Toho," rather than "Drop,"—your object now being to make him stand at, and prevent his mouthing game; for you are satisfied that he would have "down charged" had the bird been missed.

he has not torn the bird; if he has, his chastisement must be greater. Let him now have one nibble without punishment, and soon a whole carcass will not suffice for his morning's meal. Do not strike him across the body, but lengthwise.

323. An ill-tempered dog might attempt to bite you. Prevent the possibility of his succeeding, by grasping and twisting his collar with your left hand, still keeping him at the "down." Consider coolly whether you are flagellating a thick-coated dog, or one with a skin not much coarser than your own. Pause between each cut; and that he may comprehend why he is punished, call out several times, but not loudly, "Toho—bad—toho," and crack your whip. Let your last strokes be milder and milder, until they fall in the gentlest manner—a manner more calculated to awaken reflection than give pain. When the chastisement is over, stand close in front of him, the better to awe him, and prevent his thinking of bolting. Put the whip quietly into your pocket, but still remain where you are, occasionally rating him and scolding him while you are loading; gradually, however, becoming milder in manner, that he may be sensible that, though your dissatisfaction at his conduct continues, his punishment is over (342 to 347). Indeed, if you have any fear of his becoming too timid, you may at length fondle him a little, provided that while you so re-encourage him, you continue to say "Toho—toho," most impressively—then, giving him the wind, go up together to the bird, and make him " point dead" close to it. Take it up, and let him fumble the feathers before you loop it on the bag.

324. Never let a dog whom you have been forced to chastise bolt or creep away until you order him. If he is ever allowed to move off at *his* wish, he will improve

upon the idea, and on the next occasion will far too soon anticipate *yours*. And do not send him off, until he has given some evidence of having forgiven you, and of his desire to be reconciled, by crawling towards you, for instance, or wagging his tail. On no occasion—under circumstances of ever such great provocation—be so weak or irritable (but I hope you do not need the warning) as to give him a kick or a blow when he is going off. He ought to have stood with reassured confidence alongside of you, for perhaps a minute or so, before you sanctioned his departure; and the severer his punishment the longer should have been the detention. You are always to part tolerable friends, while he feels perfectly convinced that his chastisement is over. If you do not, you may find it rather difficult to catch him when he commits another fault. It will be owing to your own injudiciousness if he ever become afraid of approaching you after making a blunder. Should he be so, sit down. He will gradually draw near you; then quietly put your hand on his collar.

325. If a man cannot readily get hold of any dog under his tuition whom he desires to rate or punish, you may be certain that he fails either in temper or judgment; perhaps in both. He may be an excellent man, but he cannot be a good dog-breaker. There are men who get quite enraged at a dog's not coming instantly to "heel" on being called. When at length the poor brute does come within reach, he gets a blow, perhaps a licking—a blow or licking, he has the sense to see he should have longer avoided had he stayed longer away. Thus the punishment increases instead of remedying the evil.

326. Never correct or even rate a dog, in the mere *belief* that he is in error; be first *convinced* of his guilt.

If you have good reason to suspect that, unseen by you, he has wilfully sprung birds, still rather give him an earnest caution than any severer rebuke. It is not easy to repair the mischief occasioned by unjust punishment. When from his sheepish look, or any other cause, you imagine that he has raised game, either through heedlessness, or from their being unusually wild, be sure to give him a short lecture, and accompany him to the haunt. A lingering bird may occasionally reward you. If his manner has led you to form an incorrect opinion, your warning can have no other effect than to increase his caution (rarely an undesirable result); and if you are right, the admonition is obviously most judicious.

327. Let me caution you against the too common error of punishing a dog by pulling his ears. It has often occasioned bad canker. Some men are of opinion that it is frequently the cause of premature deafness. When you rate him you may lay hold of an ear and shake it, but not with violence.

328. I would strongly recommend you always to make your young dog " drop " for half a minute or so, when he sees a hare; or when he hears a bird rise.* To effect this, stand still yourself. After a few seconds you can either hie him on, or, which is yet better, get close to him if you expect other birds to spring. You will thus, especially in potatoes or turnips, often obtain shots at birds which would have made off, had he continued to hunt, and early in the season be frequently enabled to bag the tail-bird of a covey. This plan will also tend to make him cautious, and prevent his getting a habit of blundering-up birds, and cunningly pretending not to have noticed their escape. It will also make him

* Of course, with the proviso that he is not pointing at another bird (274).

less inclined to chase hares and rabbits, or rush at a falling bird.

329. On approaching a piece of turnips, you may have heard, "Let us couple up all the dogs excepting Old Don;" the veteran's experience having shown him, that the only effect of his thundering through them would be to scare every bird and make it rise out of shot. *You*, on the contrary, when your pupil is well confirmed in his range, and has some knowledge of his distance from game, ought to wish the other dogs kept to "Heel" (especially when the seed has been broadcast), that by the word "Care" and the hand slightly raised, you may instil into him the necessary caution, and so, by judicious tuition, give him the benefit of your own experience. Most probably you would be obliged to employ the checkcord * which I presume to be always at hand ready for occasional use. Or you might strap your shot-belt round his throat, for it is essential that he traverse such ground slowly, and greatly contract his range, (see 197). The several cross scents he will encounter should afford him a valuable lesson in detecting the most recent, and in discriminating between the "heel and toe" of a run. Be patient,—give him time to work and consider what he is about. It is probable that he will frequently overrun the birds on their doubling back, and imagine that they are gone. Should he do so, bring him again on the spot where he appeared to lose the scent. He now rushes up the adjacent drill. "Slower, slower," signals your right arm; "go no faster than I can walk comfortably." On the other hand, the birds may lie like stones. Not until you have remained nearly a minute alongside of

---

* Lest the cord should cut the turnip-tops, it might be better to employ the elastic band spoken of in 60.

him let him urge them to rise; and make him effect this, not by a sudden dash, but by steadily pressing on the scent. Bear in mind, as before warned (193), that the confidence with which he can here creep on to a near find may lead, if he is now mismanaged, to his springing on future occasions, from want of care, many a bird at which he ought to get you a shot.

330. If you can contrive it, let your pupil have some little experience in the field before you give him a *real* lesson in "Gone" (or "Flown"). Instead of being perplexed, he will then comprehend you. Should you, therefore, during the first few days of hunting him, see birds make off, in lieu of taking him to the haunt (as many breakers erroneously do), carefully keep him from the spot. You cannot let him run riot over the reeking scent without expecting him to do the same when next he finds; and if, in compliance with your orders, he points, you are making a fool of him—there is nothing before him; and if he does not fancy you as bewildered as himself, he will imagine that the exhilarating effluvia he rejoices in is the sum total you both seek. This advice, at first sight, may appear to contradict that given in 132 and 306; but look again, and you will find that those paragraphs referred to peculiar cases. Should your young dog be loitering and sniffing at a haunt which he has *seen* birds quit, he cannot well mistake the meaning of your calling out, "Gone, gone."

O

CHAPTER XII.

SHOOTING HARES. COURAGE IMPARTED.—"BACKING" TAUGHT.

331. Shooting Hares not recommended; shooting Rabbits strongly condemned. In Note, why superior Grouse-Dog better than superior Partridge-Dog. Dog brought from strange country always hunts to disadvantage.—332. Put off killing Hares long as possible.—333. Dogs not to quit faint Scent of Birds for strong Scent of Hare.—334. Dog off after Hare; no racing after Dog; Puss gone down wind.—335. Checkcord employed. Drive in spike on "So-ho-ing" Hare.—336. Impropriety of Firing at Dog.—337. Hares scarce, visit Rabbit-warren.—338. Morning, hunt where no Hares; evening, where plentiful. Mountain-hares. In Note, how to choose, and tell age of, Hares and Rabbits.—339. Killing Hare in its form.—340. Shooting Bird on ground.—341. Dog taught to pursue *wounded* Hare.—342. Whip carried, saves punishment. Detention of Dog at crouching posture, saves whip.—343. Pointer's revenge for detention from hunting.—344. Few cuts, but severe ones.—345. Instance of timidity cured. Range imparted by giving Dog feet of Partridge. In Note, sinews of thigh dragged out.—346. Punishment, not defective Nose, causes Blinking.—347. Courage imparted to timid Dogs.—348. Dogs expect punishment for faults; vexed when Birds are not fired at.—349. Instance of Pointer's not hunting keenly until punished.—350. What Dog to select to teach yours to "Back."—351. Example has great influence.—352. Instanced in conduct of young bitch when hunted with steady dog. In Note, Mare teaching Colts to swim.—353. "Backing" old Dog.—354. "Finder" to "road" to a "rise;" his intrusive companion described.—355. To "Back" by Eye, not Nose.—356. Encourage old Dog before rating the other.—357. "Finder" not to advance, even if *passed* by other Dog.—358. The "Backer" should "down charge."—359. Dog when pointing never to "down charge;" how taught.—360. Much required in "Dove."

331. PROBABLY you may be in a part of the country where you may wish to kill hares to your dog's point. I will, therefore, speak about them, though I confess I cannot do it with much enthusiasm. Ah! my English friend, what far happier autumns we should spend could we but pass them in the Highlands! Then we should think little about those villanous hares (338). We should direct the whole *undivided* faculties of our dogs, to work out the haunt of the noble grouse.* As

---

* A superior dog on grouse more easily becomes good on partridge than a superior partridge-dog becomes good on grouse. Grouse

for rabbits, I beg we may have no further acquaintance, if you ever, even in imagination, shoot them to your young dog. Should you be betrayed into so vile a practice, you must resign all hope of establishing in him a confirmed systematic range. He will degenerate into a low potterer,—a regular hedge-hunter. In turnips he will always be thinking more of rabbits than birds. It will be soon enough to shoot the little wretches to him when he is a venerable grandfather. The youngster's noticing them (which he would be sure to do if you had ever killed one to him) might run so much, both when they are pairing, and after the first flight of the young pack, that a dog broken on them has necessarily great practice in "roading," ("roading," too, with the nose carried high to avoid strong heather—a valuable instructor), whereas the dog broken on partridge often becomes impatient, and breaks away when he first finds grouse. The former dog, moreover, will learn not to "break fence," and the necessity of moderating his pace when hunting stubbles and turnips, sooner than the latter will acquire the extensive fast beat so desirable on heather, where he can work for hours uninterrupted by hedge, ditch, or furrow ; making casts to the right and left a quarter of a mile in length. First impressions are as strong in puppyhood as in childhood ; therefore the advantage of having such ground to commence on must be obvious. There are, however, favoured spots in Perthshire, &c., where game so abounds that close rangers are as necessary as when hunting in England. Alas ! even the grouse-dog will take far too quickly to hedge-hunting and pottering when on the stubbles. It is, of course, presumed that he is broken from " chasing hare"—a task his trainer must have found difficult (though none are ever shot to him) from the few that, *comparatively* speaking, his pupil could have seen. Independently, however, of want of pace and practice in roading, it never would be fair to take a dog direct from the Lowlands to contend on the Highlands with one habituated to the latter,—and *vice versâ*, for the stranger would always be placed to great disadvantage. A *faint* scent of game which the other would instantly recognise, he would not acknowledge from being wholly unaccustomed to it. Sometimes, however, a grouse dog of a ticklish temper will not bear being constantly called to on "breaking fence." A fine, free ranging pointer, belonging to one of the brothers H——y, when brought to an enclosed county, became quite subdued and dispirited. He could not stand the rating he received for bounding over the hedges, and he evidently derived no enjoyment from the sport, though there were plenty of birds. On returning to the Highlands, he quite recovered his animation and perseverance. He added another to the many evidences that dogs are most attached to, and *at home* on, the kind of country they first hunted.

o 2

frequently lead to your mis-instructing him, by earnestly enforcing "Care" at a moment when you ought to rate him loudly with the command "Ware" (or "No"). But to our immediate subject.

332. Defer as long as possible the evil day of shooting a hare over him, that he may not get too fond (69) of such vermin—I beg pardon, I mean game—and when you do kill one, so manage that he may not see it put into the bag. On no account let him mouth it. You want him to love the pursuit of feather more than of fur, that he may never be taken off the faintest scent of birds by coming across the taint of a hare. I therefore entreat you, during his first season, if you will shoot hares, to fire only at those which you are likely to kill outright; for the taint of a wounded hare is so strong that it would probably diminish his zeal, and the sensitiveness of his nose, in searching for a winged bird.

333. The temptation is always great to quit for a strong scent of hare (which any coarse-nosed dog can follow), a feeble one of birds; therefore it is a very satisfactory test of good breaking to see a dog, when he is drawing upon birds, in no way interrupted by a hare having just crossed before him. If you aim at such excellence, and it is frequently attained in the Highlands, it is certain you must not shoot hares over your youngster.

334. I hope that he will not see a hare before you have shot a few birds over him. The first that springs up near him will test the perfection to which he has attained in his initiatory lessons. Lose not a moment. It is most essential to restrain instantaneously the naturally strong impulse of the dog to run after four-footed game. Halloo out "Drop" to the extent of your voice,—raise your hand,—crack your whip,—do all you

can to prevent his pursuing. Of course you will not move an inch. Should he commence running, thunder out "No," "no." If, in spite of everything, he bolts after the hare, you have nothing for it but patience.

THE FIRST COURSE.

It is of no use to give yourself a fit of asthma by following him. You have only half as many legs as he has,—a deficiency you would do well to keep secret from him as long as possible. Wait quietly where you are—for an hour if necessary. You have one consolation,—puss, according to her usual custom, has run down wind,—your dog has lost sight of her, and is, I see, with his nose to the ground, giving himself an admirable lesson in roading out a haunt. After a time he will come back looking rather ashamed of himself, conscious that he did wrong in disobeying, and vexed with himself from having more than a suspicion forced upon him, that he cannot run so fast as the hare. When he has nearly reached you, make him "drop." Scold him severely, saying, "Ware chase" (a command that applies to the chase of birds as well as of hares). Pull him to the place where he was when first he got a view of the hare,—make him lie down,—rate him well, —call out "No," or "Hare," or "Ware chase," or any word you choose, provided you uniformly employ the same. Smack the whip and punish him with it, but not so severely as you did when we assumed that he tore the bird (end of 322). You then flogged him for two offences : first, because he rushed in and seized the bird; secondly, because he tore it and *tasted* blood. If you had not then punished him severely, you could never have expected him to be tender-mouthed. On the next occasion he might have swallowed the bird, feathers and all.

335. Should he persist in running after hares, you must employ the checkcord. If you see the hare, at which he is pointing, in its form, drive a peg firmly into the ground, and attach the cord to it, giving him a few slack yards, so that after starting off he may be arrested with a tremendous jerk. Fasten the line to the part of the spike close to the ground, or he may pull it out.

336. I have known a dog to be arrested in a headlong chase by a shot fired at him :—an act which you will think yet more reprehensible than the previous mismanagement for which his owner apparently knew no other remedy than this hazardous severity.

337. When you are teaching your dog to refrain from chasing hares, take him, if you can, where they are plentiful. If they are scarce, and you are in the neighbourhood of a rabbit-warren, visit it occasionally of an

evening. He will there get so accustomed to see the little animals running about unpursued by either of you, that his natural anxiety to chase fur, whether it grow on the back of hare or rabbit, will be gradually diminished.

338. In Scotland there are tracts of heather where one may hunt for weeks together and not find a hare ; indeed, it is commonly observed, that hares are always scarce on those hills where grouse most abound. In other parts they are extremely numerous. Some sportsmen in the Highlands avail themselves of this contrasted ground, in order to break a young dog from "chasing." They hunt him, as long as he continues fresh, where there are no hares ; and when he becomes tired, they take him to the Lowlands, where they are plentiful. By then killing a good many over him, and severely punishing him whenever he attempts to follow, a cure is often effected in two or three days. In the yet higher ranges, the mountain-hares,* from possessing a peculiarly strong scent, and not running to a distance, are a severe trial to the steadiest dog.

In the autumn they are nearly blue ; in the winter white ; and in some counties are now found in marvellous quantities. The greater pains taken of late years to destroy all kinds of vermin, has much tended to their increase. A few seasons ago a party at Lord M———d's, in Perthshire, killed seven hundred in one day. The plan adopted was for a large body of men and boys to surround a hill at its base, and beating slantingly upwards, to drive all the hares before them. The sportsmen, who formed part of the ascending

---

* The ears of young hares tear readily ; and there is a gristly substance, larger than half a pea, at the end of the shank-bone of the fore-leg, just above the joint, which departs with youth. Their smooth, close, sharp claws disappear afterwards ; and when quite old their jaw-bones become so strong as not to yield and crack to the strongest pressure of your fingers.

When you observe that the carving knife performs the part of curling-tongs, prefer a help from the birds at the top of the table.

Ditto, ditto, in all particulars, with regard to rabbits.

cordon, obtained many shots; but the principal slaughter was reserved for the guns previously posted on the top. There is, however, little sport or fun in such stationary, wholesale butchery, beyond the excitement of competition, and not being able to load fast enough. The doomed animals, being solely attentive to the movements of their assailants below, come trooping upwards, and are mostly knocked over whilst sitting on their haunches, listening to the unusual sounds made by the approaching beaters.

339. Killing a sitting hare to your dog's point will wonderfully steady him from chasing; but do not fire until he has remained stanch for a considerable time. This will show him that puss is far more likely to be bagged by *your* firing, than by *his* pursuing.

340. For the same object,—I mean, to make your young dog stanch,—I would recommend your killing a few birds on the ground to his point, were it not that you rarely have the opportunity.

341. When you have made your dog perfectly steady from chasing, you may (supposing you have no retriever at hand), naturally enough, inquire how you are to teach him to follow any hare you may be so unlucky as merely to wound. I acknowledge that the task is difficult. I would say, at once resolve to give up every wounded hare during his first season.* The following year, provided you find that he remains quite steady, on your wounding an unfortunate wretch, encourage your dog to pursue it by running yourself after it. When he gets hold of it, check him if he mauls it, and take it from him as quickly as possible. As I cannot suppose that you are anxious to slaughter every hare you see, let the next two or three go off without a shot. This forbearance will re-steady him, and after a while his own sagacity and nose (545) will show him that the

---

* This appears extremely cruel; remember, however, that I entreated you to abstain entirely from shooting hares; but if you would not make this sacrifice, at least "only to fire at those which you were likely to kill outright" (332).

established usage was departed from solely, because puss was severely struck.

342. As you wish to flog your dog as little as possible, never go out without your whip, paradoxical as this may appear. The dog's salutary awe of the implement which he sees in your possession, like a horse's consciousness of your heel being armed with a spur, will tend to keep him in order. If the dog is a keen ranger, you may much spare the whip by making him crouch at your feet for several minutes after he has committed a fault. The detention will be felt by him, when he is all anxiety to be off hunting, as a severe punishment. If he is a mettlesome, high-couraged animal, he will regard, as a yet severer punishment, his being compelled to follow at your heels for half-an-hour, while the other dogs are allowed the enjoyment of hunting.

343. Captain W——l, (son of the celebrated shot), was in the stubbles in '50 with some friends, who were anxious to see how their own dogs hunted. He, therefore, had his favourite pointer taken up and led by an attendant. This first-rate animal, who is passionately devoted to the sport, struggled so violently to get free, that he actually foamed at the mouth. After a time he was uncoupled; when, instead of hunting as usual, he raced over the field, quartering his ground most systematically, and designedly springing all the birds. Quite useless was every halloo and threat, whether of voice or whip;—stop he would not, as long as there was a feather in the field. Satisfied then with the mischief he had done, he sat down by the hedge, quietly awaiting any punishment that might be awarded him. His master, however, feeling persuaded that the dog had only acted from the impulse of momentary passion, and with the intention of avenging the unusual indignity to which he had been subjected, merely reproached him for his misconduct, and allowed him to hunt the next field, which he did as steadily as ever. This was somewhat similar to "Captain's" behaviour (492).

344. Excess of punishment has made many a dog of good promise a confirmed blinker; and of far more has it quenched that keen ardour for the sport, without which no dog can be first-rate. For this reason, if not from more humane motives, make it a rule to

give but few cuts; let them, however, be tolerably severe. Your pupil's recollection of them, when he hears the crack of the whip, will prevent the necessity of their frequent repetition.

345. I knew of a young fellow's purchasing a pointer of an excellent breed from a gamekeeper for a *few shillings* merely, as the animal had become so timid from over-chastisement, that she not only blinked her game, but seldom quitted the man's heels.

The lad had the good sense to treat the bitch, at all times, with the greatest kindness; and in order to induce her to hunt, he used to break off the feet* of every bird he killed, and give them to her to eat along with the sinews. The plan succeeded so well that she eventually became an unusually keen and fast ranger. This would be a hazardous step to take with a dog wanted to retrieve. There are few, if any dogs who may not be tempted by hunger to eat game. A gentleman told me, that, to his great astonishment, he one day saw an old tender-mouthed retriever, that he had possessed for years, deliberately swallow a partridge. Before he could get up to the dog even the tail-feathers had disappeared. On inquiry it turned out that, through some neglect, the animal had not been fed.

346. Some argue that blinking arises from a defective nose, not from punishment; but surely it is the injudicious chastisement following the blunders caused by

* Thus greatly improving it for table. The cook who first thought of breaking the legs of birds, and dragging out the sinews, ought to be immortalized. The first person I saw practising the feat was an admirable black man-cook, in the West Indies: he was preparing turkeys for a large supper; and, to my great surprise, I saw him take up each bird, cut the skin in front of and about the middle of its legs, crack the bone across that part with a blow of the knife; then stick the sinews of the foot on a hook fixed high against the wall, seize firm hold of the thigh of the turkey, give a sudden powerful pull, and leave the lower part of the leg, with a large body of sinews, perfectly stripped of all flesh, suspended on the hook.

a bad nose that makes a dog, through fear, go to "heel" when he winds birds. A bad nose may lead to a dog's running up birds from not noticing them, but it cannot *naturally* induce him to run away from them. Possibly he may be worthless from a deficiency in his olfactory powers; but it is hard to conceive how these powers can be improved by a dread of doing mischief when he finds himself near game. Some dogs that have been unduly chastised do not even betray themselves by running to "heel," but cunningly slink away from their birds without giving you the slightest intimation of their vicinity. I have seen such instances. When a young dog, who has betrayed symptoms of blinking, draws upon birds, *head* him, if you can, before you give him the order to "toho:" he will then have such a large circuit to make, that he will feel the less tempted to run to your heels.

347. Obedience and intelligence are, as I have already remarked, best secured by judicious ratings and encouragements, — scoldings for bad conduct, — praise, caresses, and rewards for good. Never forget, therefore, to have some delicacy in your pocket to give the youngster whenever he may deserve it. All dogs, however, even the most fearful, ought to be made able to bear a little punishment. If, *unfortunately*, your dog is constitutionally timid (I cannot help saying *unfortunately*, though so many of the sort have fine noses), the whip must be employed with the greatest gentleness, the lash being rather laid on the back than used, until such forbearance, and many caresses before his dismissal, have gradually banished the animal's alarm, and ultimately enabled you to give him a very slight beating, on his misconducting himself, without any danger of making him blink. By such means, odd as

it may sound, you *create* courage, and with it give him self-confidence and range.

348. A judiciously-educated dog will know as well as you do whether or not he has earned a chastisement, and many a one is of so noble a nature that he will not wish to avoid it if he is conscious that he deserves it. He will become as anxious for good sport as you are, and feel that he ought to be punished, if from his own misconduct he mars it. Indeed, he will not have much opinion of your sagacity if you do not then give him a sound rating, or let him have a taste of the lash, though it matters not how slight. Clearly this feeling, which it will be right to foster, must have arisen from his belief that you are always conscious of his actions (383); therefore never check him for coming towards you on his committing any unseen error. Moreover, when he has been but a little shot to, you will find that if you abstain from firing at a bird which through his fault he has improperly flushed, although in its flight it affords you an excellent shot, you will greatly vex him; and this will tend to make him more careful for the future.

349. Mr. C——s R——n (286) had a pointer who would at once give up hunting if he was not properly chastised on committing a fault;—but what is far more extraordinary, and strongly shows the varied, and occasionally *odd* dispositions of dogs, he would never hunt keenly until from birds rising wildly (or from some other cause) an *excuse* arose for giving him a flogging. After receiving the punishment he would start off in the greatest spirits, and range with uncommon ardour and perseverance. An excuse was, however, quite indispensable; for, if from a good-humoured desire to gratify his apparent longings he was favoured beforehand with a thrashing, he would consider himself imposed on, and forthwith run home.

350. When, after a few weeks, you perceive that the youngster has confidence in himself, and is likely to hunt independently, not deferentially following the footsteps of an older companion, take out a well-broken

dog with him, that you may have the opportunity of teaching him to "back." Be careful to choose one not given to make false points; for if he commit such mistakes, your pupil will soon utterly disregard his pointing. Select also one who draws upon his birds in a fine, determined attitude; not one to whose manner even *you* must be habituated to feel certain he is on game. Be watchful to prevent your dog ever hunting in the wake of the other, which, in the humility of canine youth, he probably will, unless you are on the alert to wave him in a different direction, the moment you observe him inclined to seek the company of his more experienced associate. By selecting a slow old dog, you will probably diminish the wish of the young one to follow him; for it is likely that the youngster's eagerness will make him push on faster, and so take the lead.

351. The example for a *few* days (but only for a few days) of a good stanch dog who is not a hedge-hunter, —has no bad habits, and does not require being called to,—will be advantageous to your inexperienced animal; —as an instance:

352. On one occasion, when I was abroad, I lent a favourite dog to a young friend who had requested the services of the animal for his kennel, not the field. I much objected to any person's shooting over the dog except myself, particularly as it was only his second season. Therefore, very knowingly as I thought, I sent him on a Saturday evening, having obtained a promise that he should be returned to me early on Monday morning—and so he was; the lad, however, had done me; for he confessed, many months afterwards, that he could not resist the temptation of taking out my pointer snipe-shooting on the intermediate Sunday along with his little liver-coloured bitch;—and with a glowing countenance he observed that he never had been so enchanted, for his young lady seeing her fond companion drop instantly the gun was fired, and remain immoveable until "hied on," sedulously imitated him throughout the day. It was the making of her,—but as it was the first time in her young life she had ever behaved steadily, there was a great risk of my pointer's being much injured; for, alas! like poor

mortals, dogs are more prone to follow a bad example* than a good one. We are, however, wandering.

353. On the old dog's pointing, catch the eye of the young one. If you cannot readily do so, and are not afraid of too much alarming the birds, call to the old fellow by name, and desire him to "toho." The order will make the young one look round, and awaken him to a suspicion of what is going forward. Hold up your right arm,—stand still for a minute,—and then, carrying your gun as if you were prepared momentarily to fire, retreat, or move sideways in crab-like fashion towards the old dog, continuing your signal to the other to remain steady, and turning your face to him, so that he may be restrained by the feeling that your eye is constantly fixed upon him. He will soon remark the attitude of the old dog, and almost intuitively guess its meaning. Should the old one draw upon his game, still the other dog must remain stationary. If he advance but an inch, rate him. Should he rush up (which is hardly to be expected), at him at once ;—having made him drop, catch hold of him, and drag him to the place at which he should have backed,—there (if you judge such strong measures necessary) peg him down until after you have had your shot and are reloaded. If by heading the birds you can drive them towards the young

---

* A singular evidence of the influence of example was furnished by a favourite charger belonging to the father of the present Lord G——d. As a reward for gallant service, she had been turned out for life, when only seven years old, on the banks of the Shannon. She had a shed to run into, and plenty of hay in winter. It pleased her, in all seasons, daily to have a swim in the river. Year after year colts were turned out on the same grass. All these, following the example set them by the mare, voluntarily took to the water, and gradually became expert swimmers. Until within a short time of her death, and she attained the unusual age of forty-three, she continued to bathe ; and I have heard that she was evidently much puzzled and vexed whenever from the stream being frozen she could not get her plunge. She would walk a little way on the ice, but finding it too slippery, unwillingly return.

dog, do so; and aim at the one most likely to fall near him. Endeavour to make him comprehend that any sign or word to urge on or retard the leading dog, in no way applies to him. This he will soon understand if he has been properly instructed with an associate in the initiatory lesson described in (49). After you have picked up the bird let him sniff at it.

354. It is most important that the dog which first winds birds should be allowed to "road" them to a spring without being flurried, or in any way interfered with by another dog. Few things are more trying to your temper as a sportsman, than to see a self-sufficient cub, especially when birds are wild, creep up to the old dog whom he observes pointing at a distance, or cautiously drawing upon a covey. The young whipper-snapper pays no attention to your most energetic signals: you are afraid to speak lest you should alarm the birds, and before you can catch hold of the presumptuous jackanapes, he not only steals close to the good old dog, but actually ventures to head him; nay, possibly dares to crawl on yet nearer to the birds in the hope of enjoying a more intoxicating sniff.

355. All dogs but the "finder" should stand wholly by sight,—just the reverse of pointing. Your dog's nose ought to have nothing to do with backing. If you permit it, he will get the abominable habit of creeping up to his companions in the manner just described (354), when he observes them to be winding birds; and though he may not presume to take the lead, nay, even keep at so respectful a distance as in no way to annoy the "finder," yet a longing to inhale the "grateful steam" (as that good poet and capital sportsman, Somerville, terms it) will make him constantly watch the other dogs, instead of bestowing his undivided attention and

faculties upon finding game for himself. It is quite enough if he backs whenever you order him, or he accidentally catches sight of another dog either "pointing" or "roading;" and the less he is looking after his companions, the more zealously will he attend to his own duties.

356. If you have any fears that the old dog when he is on birds will not act steadily, should you have occasion to chide the young one, be careful to give the old dog a word expressive of your approval, before you commence to rate the other.

357. When your youngster is hereafter hunted in company, should he make a point, and any intrusive companion, instead of properly backing him, be impertinently pressing on, the youngster should not be induced (however great may be the trial upon his patience and forbearance) to draw one foot nearer to the game than his own knowledge of distance tells him is correct; not even if his friend, or rather, jealous rival, boldly assumes the front rank. Your pupil will have a right to look to you for protection, and to expect that the rash intruder, however young, be *at the least* well rated.

358. It is a matter of little moment whether the "backer" attends to the "down charge," or continues to back as long as the other dog remains at his point. It appears, however, best, that he should "drop," unless he is so near that he winds the game, when he would be rather pointing than backing (and should, consequently, behave as explained in 274); for the fewer exceptions there are to general rules the more readily are the rules observed.

359. Should both dogs make separate points at the same moment, it is clear that neither can back the other.

They must act independently—each for himself. Moreover, your firing over one should not induce the other to "down charge," or in any way divert his attention from his own birds. He ought to remain immoveable as a statue. Some dogs, whose high courage has not been damped by over-correction, will do this from their own sagacity; but to enable you to *teach* them to behave thus steadily, game should be plentiful. When you are lucky enough to observe both dogs pointing at the same time, let your fellow-sportsman (or your attendant) flush and fire at the birds found by the older dog, while you remain stationary near the young one, quietly but earnestly cautioning him to continue firm. When your companion has reloaded and picked up his game (and made the other dog "back"), let him join you and knock over the bird at which your pupil is pointing. It will not be long before he (your young dog) understands what is required of him, if he has been practised (as recommended in 274) not to "down charge" when pointing unsprung birds. In short, it may be received as an axiom, that *nothing ought to make a dog voluntarily relinquish a point so long as he winds birds; and nothing but the wish to continue his point should make him neglect the "down charge" the instant he hears the near report of a gun.*

360. "Dove," (the setter spoken of in 102, who invariably stands at her point,) on one occasion in the season of '50 dropped as usual on her master's firing at some distance from her; but, instead of "seeking dead" as ordered when he had reloaded, she remained immoveable at the "down charge," although repeatedly coaxed and called to. The sportsman thought that birds must be near, and after much perseverance, he succeeded in *walking* up a brace that were lying close to her. We must allow that this was a prettily *conceived* piece of caution on the part of Mrs. "Dove;" but how far more usefully would she have acted had she been taught the inferiority of the "down charge" to the *continued* point, followed by the "road" to successive birds.

P

CHAPTER XIII.

HINTS TO PURCHASERS. PRICE OF DOGS.—SHEEP KILLING.

331. The "back" being taught—young Dog again hunted alone.—362. Breakers hun too many together. Why injudicious.—363. One hour's Instruction alone, better than a day's in company.—364. Horse's value little dependent on Education Dog's greatly. Many good points in Dog, similar to those in Horse; in Note, Frame of Pony studied. Arab proverbs. Admirable receipt for putting hard flesh on Horse. Hoof Ointment.—365. Hints to Dog-purchasers. Tenderness of Nose, how judged of.—366 to 368. Instance of great superiority of Nose in Pointer on bad scenting Day.—369. Ditto in Setter.—370. In Breeding, Nose sought for in both parents.—371. Good Dog, like good Horse, not suited to all countries.—372. Purchasing a Brace of Dogs, before buying shoot over.—373. Case in Point.—374. Rushing in to "dead," how cured.—375. Dogs shot over "single-handed." Jealousy decreases with intimacy. Independence and self-reliance, how imparted.—376. Good Breeding and Breaking command good Prices.—377 to 379. Great Sums realized at Tattersall's for thirteen highly-bred Pointers.—380. Small sums unknown Dogs fetch.—381. Mr. C——t's Dogs' half a sovereign each.—382. Immense price given for stanch Setter.—383. Best Dogs; summary of rules for making, concisely given. The best will make mistakes.—384. Companionship with man makes Dog useful servant.—385. Tweed-side Spaniel and blind man.—386. Dog that always ran riot when out of sight.—387. Killing Sheep; cure attempted.—388. Another plan.—389. Third attempt at Remedy.—390. Sir H——n S——d's recipe.—391. Muzzle Dog likely to worry Sheep.—392. Killing Fowls; the cure.

361. WHEN your dog has been properly taught the "back," fail not to recommence hunting him alone, if it is your object to establish a perfect range.

362. Professional dog-breakers, I have remarked, almost invariably hunt too many dogs together. This arises, I suppose, from the number which they have to train; but the consequence is, that the younger dogs are spectators rather than actors, and, instead of ranging independently in search of game, are watching the manœuvres of their older associates.

363. A glimmering of knowledge may be picked up in this way; but no one will argue that it is likely to create great excellence. Doubtless the young ones will be good backers; and to the inexperienced a troop of perhaps a dozen dogs, all in chiselled form, stanchly backing an old leader, is a most imposing sight, but if the observer were to accompany the whole party for a few hours, he would remark, I will bet any money, that the same veterans would over and over again find the birds, and that the "*perfectly*" broken young ones in the rear would do nothing but "back" and "down charge." What can they know of judicious quartering? Of obeying the signals of the hand? Of gradually drawing upon the faintest token of a scent (only perceptible to a nose carried high in the air) until they arrive at a confident point? Of perseveringly working out the foil of a slightly winged bird, on a hot still day, to a sure "find?" Nothing, or next to nothing,—nearly all is to be taught; and yet the breaker will show off those raw recruits as perfectly drilled soldiers. Would they not have had a much better chance of really being so, if he had given a small portion of his time each day to each? He well knows they would; but the theatrical display would not be half so magnificent. If he had truly wished to give his pupils a good systematic range, without a doubt he would have devoted one hour in the field exclusively to each dog, rather than many hours to several at once—and not have associated any together in the field until he had gained full command over each separately. And this he would have done (*because it would have tended to his interest*), had he supposed that his dog's qualifications would be investigated by judges, —by those who would insist on seeing a dog hunted singly (in order to observe his method of ranging), or

with but one companion, before they thought of definitively purchasing.

364. The good qualities of a horse being principally derived from nature, a judge can pretty accurately discover his general capabilities simply by a glance at his make and action ;—but the good qualities of a sportsman's dog are chiefly derived from art ; consequently, though his movements may be light and springy,—his countenance intelligent,—his nostrils wide,—his cerebral development large,—his forehand deep,—his ribs round and full,—his elbows well detached from them, not tied in,—his shoulders high, and slanting backwards,—his loins muscular and arched,—his quarters lengthy, and sinewy,—his legs bony, and straight,—his feet small and round, pointing direct to the front,—his tail taper to the finest point from a strong root,* yet if he has been improperly shot over as a young-

---

* The continuation of the vertebræ of the back, and clearly, therefore, an indication of their substance. *Query*—Was it because our grandfathers knew that a tail naturally short was a pledge of stamina, that they endeavoured to imitate it by docking their horses and pointers? Curiously enough, the points named in 364 as desirable in a dog are considered good in a horse. In portraits of the useful old English hunter, you never see a feeble, flexible neck,—it is desirable that it should be arched,—a dog's neck also should be sufficiently strong, and put on high. Neither horse nor dog should have large fleshy heads,—and a full bright eye is in both a sign of spirit and endurance. The canon bone in a horse should be short, so ought the corresponding bone of a dog's leg; and every joint ought to be large, yet clean ; and (without a bull) the *short* ribs in both animals should be *long*. There are hardy horses whose flesh you cannot bring down without an amount of work that is injurious to their legs,—there are also thrifty dogs which are constantly too fat, unless they are almost starved, and common sense tells us they cannot be so starved without their strength being much reduced. The analogy does not hold with respect to ears, for it is generally considered that the dog's should be soft and drooping, lying close to his head—not short and ever in motion. Moreover, most men would wish his muzzle to be broad as well as long.

Our eye is so accustomed to the sight of weeds,—animals bred for short-lived speed, not for endurance,—that we no longer look for, and possibly do not properly appreciate, the short back (though long body), with scarcely room for a saddle ; and *the width between the upper part of the shoulder-blades* (as well as the lower)—the indication of space within—upon which points our forefathers justly set great value. We forget its being mentioned of Eclipse, whose endurance is as undeniable as his speed, that he had a "shoulder broad enough to carry a firkin of butter,"—and that Stubb's portraits of winners (of races four and occasionally six miles long !) show that they possessed powerfully muscular, as well as slanting shoulders. The frame of a clever Welsh, or New Forest pony, if his head is set on at a considerable angle with his neck, is perfection.

ster he may never be worth his keep. Therefore, though a man may in five minutes decide upon purchasing the horse, he would act very imprudently if he ventured upon buying the dog before he had seen him hunted ; * unless indeed he feels well-justified confidence in the ability of the party who broke him in, and is also satisfied with the character, as a sportsman, of the person who has since shot over him.

365. No dog can be worth a large sum, or should be considered *perfectly made*, that cannot be hunted in perfect silence,—that is not good at finding dead or wounded birds, and that is not sure to point them when found. If in his transverse range he keep his head to windward it is a good sign, for it evinces his consciousness that it is in the breeze he should seek for an intimation of the vicinity of game. As to the excellence of his nose, this can only be fully ascertained by experience, and by comparing him in the field with other dogs ; but some opinion may be formed by observing whether on first winding game he confidently walks up to his point

It might with profit be studied by any youngster wishing to form his eye, and know what, on an enlarged scale, should be the build of a real hunter,—an animal fitted for every kind of work. The Arabs so much prize a short back and lengthy quarters, that they have a proverb to the effect that a horse which measures the same from the hip-bone to the end of his croupe, that he does from the hip-bone to the withers, is a blessing to his master. Another assertion of theirs is, that all their fastest horses measure less from the middle of the withers to the setting on of the tail, than they do from the middle of the withers to the extremity of the nose, or rather extremity of the upper lip. This measurement is supposed to be taken along the crest of the neck, over the forelock, and between the eyes.

It is sometimes so difficult to get a horse into condition, and the following recipe, given me by an old cavalry officer who is an excellent stable-master, is so admirable, that I need not apologize for inserting it :—

"Give three[1] ounces of cold drawn linseed-oil in a cold mash every alternate night for a fortnight. If you judge it advisable, repeat the same after an interval of a fortnight. The good effects of the oil are not immediately visible, but in about a month the horse's coat will become glossy, and he will commence putting up good *hard* flesh."

The daily rubbing in a portion of the following ointment into a horse's hoof (especially after exercise in moist ground, and on removal of wet bandages, *before any evaporation can take place*,) will prevent, indeed cure, brittleness— that constant precursor of contracted feverish feet :—

Tar (not Coal Tar).
Soft Soap.
Soap Cerate.
Hog's Lard.
½ lb. of each well mixed together over a very slow fire.

* Amidst sheep too.

---

[1] 20 oz. = 1 imperial pint.

with a high head, or is shuffling in an undecided manner to the right and left (perhaps even pottering with his nose near the ground), before he can satisfy himself respecting the exact locality of the birds. There are favourable days when any dog can wind game, when finding many birds will far more depend upon "range" than nose. The surest way to test the olfactory powers of different dogs is to take them out directly after mid-day in sultry weather, or when a north-easterly wind has been blowing for some days. If their condition, &c. is then alike, you may be certain that the dog who winds most birds has the finest (or most cautious?) nose. On such a day chance will but little assist him.

366. On an extremely bad scenting day in October, 1838, a cold dry wind blowing from the east, the Hon. F—— C——, Baron A. and Sir F. H——, then partridge-shooting at C——n, in Staffordshire, saw a liver-coloured pointer take every point from three setters of some celebrity belonging to a very sporting baronet. The setters did not make a single "set" throughout the day, but ran into the birds as if they had been larks. The pointer's nose was, however, so good that the party, notwithstanding the badness of the scent, bagged thirty-five brace.

367. The keeper who brought out the setters was obliged to own, that he could not otherwise account for the apparent singularity of their behaviour, than by admitting the superiority of the pointer's nose; yet, judging from the engraving, he did not carry his head well.

368. A stiffish price had been given for the dog, but I need hardly say that it was not considered unreasonable, after the exhibition of scenting-powers so unusual, fairly tested in the field with competitors of established character.

369. In this instance it was a pointer that evinced singular tenderness of nose; but in the following, a setter bore off the palm in a contest with good pointers. Mr. Q——r, of F——w (county of Suffolk), who is an enthusiast about shooting, three years ago took out his favourite dog, a heavy, large-limbed, liver-coloured setter, on a cold, raw, bad-scenting day, together with a brace of pointers of high character belonging to another Suffolk sportsman, Mr. W——s. The latter had expressed rather a contemptuous opinion of the setter, whose appearance was undeniably not very prepossessing; but to the gentleman's astonishment, and perhaps somewhat to his mortification, the lumbering dog found plenty of birds, though there was so little scent that the vaunted pointers were nearly useless. I was told, that at that moment Mr. Q——r would not have taken two hundred guineas for the animal.

370. What a pity it is that more pains are not taken to link in matrimonial chains dogs of the rare excellence of nose described in the preceding paragraph, and in 182, 204, and 289, instead of being satisfied with marked superiority in one parent only! In a setter or pointer sensitiveness of nose is the most valuable *natural* quality sought for;—correctness of range the most valuable *artificial* quality.

FASHIONABLE (ENGLISH) SETTER, AND OLD-FASHIONED POINTER.

"He did not carry his head well."—Par. 367.

371. Few horses, however good, are fitted to hunt in all countries, nor are many dogs; and as in selecting a hunter a man ought to consider the kind of work for which he is wanted, so ought he when he is purchasing a dog to be influenced by the kind of country in which the animal is to perform. A slow dog, however good, would weary your heart out on the moors with his perpetual seesaw, ladylike canter; and a fast one, *unless wonderfully careful*, on enclosed lands alive with game, would severely test your self-control over tongue and temper.

372. If a purchaser be in search of a brace of dogs, assuredly he ought not to give a large figure for them, if they do not traverse their ground separately. What is the use of two dogs if they hunt together? Both are engaged in doing what would be better done by one, for there would be no undue excitement, or jealousy, or withdrawal of attention. Not only ought a purchaser to see how dogs quarter their ground, but, if the time of the year will permit, he should even kill a bird to them,—for though they may once have been good, if an ignorant or careless sportsman has shot over them but for a few days, they may be spoiled (end of 364).

373. At the beginning of a partridge season, I unexpectedly wanted to purchase a dog. An old gamekeeper,—one on whose judgment I could rely, and who, I knew, would not willingly deceive me,—saw a setter in the field that he thought would please, and accordingly sent it to my kennel. I greatly liked the looks of the animal. He quartered his ground well—was obedient to the hand—carried a high and apparently tender nose—pointed, backed, and down-charged steadily. Unquestionably he had been well broken. I thought myself in great luck, and should not have hesitated to complete the purchase, but that fortunately I had an opportunity of shooting a bird over him, when to my horror, he rushed at it with the speed of a greyhound. As in spite of all my remonstrances, shouted in the most determined manner, he repeated this manœuvre whenever a bird fell, I returned him. I afterwards heard he had just been shot over by a party on the moors, who, no doubt, had spoiled him by their ignoble, pot-hunting propensities.

374. Had I chosen to sacrifice my shooting in order to reclaim him (which I must have done, had I too hastily concluded the purchase), I ought to have sent home the other dogs, and proceeded, but with greater severity, much in the manner described in 321 and 323. I ought not, however, to have gone after him when first he bolted; I ought merely to have endeavoured to check him with my voice, for it would have been most important to set him a good example by remaining

immoveable myself; he might have misconstrued any hasty advance on my part into rivalship for possession of the bird; in short, into a repetition of one of the many scrambles to which he had recently been accustomed, and in which I feel sure he must invariably have come off victorious. I ought, when loaded, to have walked calmly up to him, and, without taking the slightest notice of the disfigured bird, have dragged him back, while loudly rating him, to the spot where he should have "down charged." After a good flagellation, a protracted lecture, and a long delay, (the longer the better,) I ought to have made him cautiously approach the bird; and by a little scolding, and by showing him the wounds he had inflicted, have striven to make him sensible and ashamed of his enormities. Probably, too, had the birds lain well, the moment he pointed I should have employed the checkcord * with a spike, giving him a liberal allowance of slack line (335). Had I thus treated him throughout the day, I have little doubt but that he would have become a reformed character; though an occasional outbreak might not unreasonably have been expected. (See 302 to 305.)

375. If you purchase a dog who has been much shot over single-handed by a tolerably good sportsman, you have the satisfaction of knowing that the animal must necessarily have great self-reliance and experience. On the other hand, you will see reason to distrust his forbearance and temper when he is hunted with a companion. Of the usual run of dogs, it probably would be better to purchase two which have been shot over singly, and then associate them in

---

* I am glad to say I never had occasion to adopt so severe a remedy as the following; but I have heard of an otherwise incorrigible taste for blood being cured by a partridge pierced transversely with two knitting-pins being *adroitly* substituted for the fallen bird which the dog had been restrained by a checkcord from bolting. The pins were cut to a length somewhat less than the diameter of its body, and were fixed at right angles to one another. Several slight wires would, I think, have answered better.

the field, than to buy a brace which had been broken in together. You would, I think, find it more difficult to give independence to the latter, than to cure the jealousy of the former. Jealousy in the field would, however, decrease with their increasing intimacy in the kennel.

To create a feeling of self-dependence, obviously there is no better plan than for a considerable time to take out the dog by himself, and thus force him to trust for sport to his own unaided powers; and when he is at length hunted in company, never to omit paying him the compliment of attending to every indication he evinces of being upon birds, even occasionally to the unfair neglect of confirmed points made by the other dogs.

376. Confidence, however, in good breeding and breaking often induces sportsmen to give large sums for young dogs without seeing them in the field.

377. In July, 1848, thirteen pointers were sold at Tattersall's, which brought the large sum of two hundred and fifty-six guineas, though only two of them had ever been shot over.

378. The following description of each was advertised before the sale. I have prefixed to it the prices they severally realized. Such sums mark how highly the public appreciate the qualifications of the breaker who lives with Mr. Moore, of Derbyshire, and ought to stimulate others to increased exertions.

379. To be Sold by Auction,
AT MESSRS. TATTERSALL'S,
On Monday, July 3d, 1848,
FOURTEEN SUPERIOR BRED POINTERS.

Prices realized at the Sale.	Lot.	Name.	When Pupped.	Sire.	Dam.
Gns. 15	1	Nelson	Nov. 1st, 1846.	Bounce, own brother to Bloom.	Bloss, by the late Mr. Edge's Rake, out of his Bess, by Capt. White's Don out of Deuce.
16	2	Nell			
13	3	Drab..	June 18th, 1847.	Bounce......	Rev. J. Cooper's Dido, out of Mr. Marriott's Bitch by Capt. White's Don.
5	4	Buzz..	April 13th, 1847.	Bounce......	Mab, by a Dog of Major Bilbie's, by the late Mr. Edge's Nelson.
16	5	Rake..	June 11th, 1847.	Mr. Hurt's Rake, out of his Nance.	Die, by Rock out of Belle, own sister to Bloom.
Dead.	6	Dot ..	May 2d, 1847.	Bang (Lot 14)..	Rue, dam Bess out of the late Mr. Edge's Mink.
21	7	Ben	April 20th, 1847.	Sir Arthur Clifton's Don ...	Dam by the late Mr. Edge's Rake out of Mab, by a son of Mr. Edge's Nelson.
16	8	Belle			
17	9	Czar	May 8th, 1847.	Don, by Rap out of Bess, sister to Bloom ...	Bitch of Sir Robert Wilmot's.
17	10	Crack			
25	11	Swap	Feb. 2d, 1847.	J. Newton's, Esq. Duke, by Capt. White's Don .	Bloom (sold at the late Mr. Edge's sale for 80 Guineas), by Rake out of Mink.
25	12	Snake			
24	13	Rock..	Two years old.	Rap (sold at the late Mr. Edge's sale for 53 Guineas), by a Dog of Dale Trotter's, Esq. of Bishop Middleham	Bitch of H. K. Fenton's, Esq. by Lord Mexborough's Romp.
46	14	Bang..	Three years old.	Bounce (Sire of Lots 1, 2, 3, and 4)	The late Mr. Edge's Bess, by Captain White's Don out of Deuce, sister to Die the Dam of Rake.
256					

THE ABOVE POINTERS ARE THE PROPERTY OF A GENTLEMAN, AND HAVE BEEN BRED WITH THE GREATEST CARE.

⁎ *The first twelve Lots are well broke, but have not been shot over. Lots 13 and 14 have been shot over both in England and Scotland, and are in every respect superior Pointers.*

IRISH RED SETTER.—"Steadily pointing." Par. 382.

380. In marked contrast to such high prices, are those often realized at Laing's and at Wordsworth's stables, in Edinburgh, where sometimes a batch of pointers and setters are sent for unreserved sale, of whose previous history and education no one can tell anything, except perhaps, the party sent by the vendor,—naturally considered a prejudiced if not an interested witness.

381. The Mr. C——t named in 289 boasts, that he never gives more than half a sovereign for any dog, and that he has some of the best in Scotland. He attends at Laing's and Wordsworth's, when dogs are advertised for sale by auction, and buys all those that are decent-looking, and fetch no higher bid than ten shillings,—a frequent occurrence where their characters are quite unknown. He takes his bargains to the moors. Those that show any promise he keeps for further trial; the rest he at once shoots, leaving their bodies unhonoured by any other burial than the purple heather that blooms around them.

382. A red setter brought the largest price that I ever knew paid for a dog. After mid-day he came upon a covey basking in the sun. His owner very knowingly told the shooting party that they might go to luncheon; that he would leave the dog, and accompany them, engaging that they should find him still steadily pointing on their return. The promise was faithfully redeemed by the stanch setter. One of the sportsmen was so struck with the performance, that he could not resist buying at a tremendous figure, and he soon regained, I believe, much of the purchase-money from some incredulous acquaintance, by backing the animal to perform a similar feat. It was, however, no great test of excellence.

383. I conceive those dogs must be considered the *best*, which procure a persevering sportsman most shots in a season, and lose him fewest winged birds.* If you are anxious for your pupil to attain this superlative excellence (I will repeat it, at the risk of being accused of tautology), you must be at all times consistently strict, but never severe. Make him, as much as you can, your constant companion; you will thereby much develop his intelligence, and so render him a more efficient assistant in the field, for he will understand your manner better and better, and greatly increase in affection as well as observation. Many men would like so faithful an attendant. *Teach* obedience at home—to *obtain* it in the field. Consider the instantaneous "drop,"

* And if hares are shot to him, fewest wounded hares.

the moment he gets the signal, as all-important,—as the very key-stone of the arch that conducts to the glorious triumphs of due subordination. Notice every fault, and check it by rating, but never punish with the whip unless you judge it absolutely necessary. On the other hand, following Astley's plan (10), reward, or at least praise, every instance of good behaviour, and you will be surprised to find how quickly your young dog will comprehend your wishes, and how anxious he will be to comply with them. Remember that evil practices, unchecked until they become confirmed habits, or any errors in training committed at the commencement of his education, cannot be repaired afterwards without tenfold—nay, twentyfold trouble. Never let him hunt from under your eye. Unceasingly endeavour to keep alive in him as long as possible his belief that you are intuitively aware, as fully when he is out of sight as within sight, of every fault he commits, whether it arise from wilfulness or mere heedlessness. This is a very important admonition. Remember, however, that the best dogs will occasionally make mistakes when they are running down wind (especially if it blows hard), and that there are days when there is scarcely any scent. (Note to 174.)

384. I said, "Make him," (your pupil,) "as much as you can, your constant companion." Many breakers seem not to consider, or, at least, seem not to be sufficiently influenced by the consideration, that it is companionship with us, *through successive generations*, which alone has led to the dog's becoming the useful servant we find him. In his wild state he may have as much sagacity as when domesticated ; but this he displays in a manner in no way advantageous to us ;—it is shown in the mode in which he procures his food, avoids his enemies, &c. We hear much of the different degrees of "natural sagacity" evinced in different breeds ;—of the wonderful intelligence of collies, &c.: but surely it is chiefly association with man that awakened that apparently greater intelligence; or, to speak more correctly, that gave them the greater habit of observation,—of watching their master's looks,—of listening to his

voice, &c. : whence comes their readier comprehension of his wishes and orders—often termed sagacity.

385. When recently salmon-fishing on the upper part of the Tweed, I occasionally met on its banks a totally blind man, and who, in spite of this great disqualification, continued a keen and successful trout-angler. He had been for some years entirely sightless, and was led about by a large brown Tweed-side spaniel, of whose intelligence wonderful stories are told. M——r travelled much round the country ; and it is certain, for he would frequently do so to show off the dog's obedience, that on his saying (the cord being perfectly slack), " Hie off to the Holmes," or, " Hie off to Melrose," &c., &c., the animal would start off in the right direction without an instant's hesitation. Now, this Tweed spaniel was not born with more brains than other Tweed spaniels, but he was M——r's *constant* companion, and had, in consequence, acquired a singular facility of comprehending his orders, and doubtless from great affection was very solicitous to please.

386. Attend most carefully to the injunction not to let your dog hunt out of sight. It is essential that you do so.

I once possessed a pointer who behaved admirably while he was under my eye, but who, if he could cunningly contrive to get on the other side of rising ground, would invariably, instead of pointing, make a rush at any game he came across,—determined, as my Irish companion used to say, "to take his diversion :" and it was most curious to remark how immediately his pace would slacken, and how promptly he would resume a cautious carriage, the moment he perceived I again had the power of observing him. His proceedings displayed so much sagacity, that though I was extremely vexed, I could hardly find it in my heart to punish him as he deserved.

387. Notwithstanding Beckford's capital story of the hounds making a dinner of the old ram which his lordship had left in their kennel to intimidate them, if your dog be unhappily too fond of mutton or lamb of his own killing, perhaps no better cure can be *attempted*, provided you superintend the operation, than that of muzzling him, and letting a strong ram give him a butting at the time that you are administering the lash, and hallooing out " Ware " or " Sheep." But, unfortunately, this too often fails.

388. If you do not succeed, you must hang or drown

Q

him, (the latter is probably the less painful death, but a charge of shot well lodged behind the ear in the direction of the brain would be yet better.) Therefore you will not mind giving him another chance for his life, though confessedly the measure proposed is most barbarous. Procure an ash-pole about five feet long. Tie one extremity of the pole to a strong ram, by the part of the horns near the forehead. To the opposite extremity of the pole attach a strong spiked collar, and strap it round the dog's throat, to the audible tune of "Ware" or "Sheep." (To prevent the possibility of the cord slipping, through each end of the pole burn a hole.) The continued efforts of the ram for some hours either to free himself from his strange companion, or to attack him, will possibly so worry and punish the dog as to give him a distaste ever afterwards for anything of a woolly nature. The pole will so effectually separate these unwilling (but still too intimate) associates, that you need not muzzle the dog.

389. There is yet another remedy, which I will name as it sounds reasonable, though I cannot speak of its merits from personal observation, never having seen it tried.

Wrap a narrow strip of sheep-skin, that has much wool on it, round the dog's lower jaw, the wool outwards, and fasten it so that he cannot get rid of it. Put this on him for a few hours daily, and there is a chance that he will become as thoroughly disgusted, as even you could wish, with every animal of the race whose coat furnished such odious mouthfuls; but prevention being better than cure, pay great attention to your dog's morals during the lambing season. Dogs not led away by evil companionship rarely commence their depredations upon sober, full-grown sheep. In ninety-nine cases out of a hundred,* they have previously yielded to the great temptation of running down some frisking lamb, whose animated gambols seemed to court pursuit.†

* In the remaining odd case (one out of a hundred) the propensity may be traced to the animal belonging to a vicious stock,—in short, to hereditary instinct.

† Mr. C. B——y, who has written so cleverly and usefully under the name of "Harry Hieover," supports (in "Practical Horsemanship") an argument respecting the breaking of horses, by describing with such good judgment the manner in which he would proceed to gradually wean a dog from worrying sheep (much on the principle of taking him to a rabbit-warren, 337), that I think some of my readers may peruse it with profit:—

"I suppose myself to have a dog addicted to chasing sheep. He must be cured of that. If I depute a servant to do this, I know how he will set about it. He will take the dog on a common, where sheep are running at large. The moment they see the dog they begin running. This is just what the man wished they might do. The dog, of course, immediately sets off after them, and the man after the dog. Probably after the latter has ceased chasing, he is caught; and at a moment when he is not in fault he is most brutally thrashed, knowing or not knowing what he is thrashed for. He is cowed for the day, and sore for three or four afterwards, when he forgets the beating; and the next time he sees the sheep, he feels the same excitement and propensity, and away he goes after them; so probably it would be as long as he lives.

"I now take the dog in hand, and as sedulously avoid taking him where he has a chance of seeing sheep running, as the other sought for a place where he should; for I know, with his present habits, the temptation will be too strong for the dog to resist. I put a collar round his neck, with a chain to hold him by, and a good dog-whip in my hand. I take him to a sheep-fold: here the sheep cannot run: and not being wild, the utmost they can do on seeing the dog is to huddle all together. On entering the fold I cry in a warning voice, 'Ware sheep, Don.' The dog looks up. 'Ware sheep,' I cry again. If he appears in the least elated or fidgety, 'Ware sheep,' I cry in a voice of anger. If he attempt to make any hasty advance towards them, a smart stroke or two of the whip makes him find 'Ware sheep' must be attended to. If after this he pulls towards, or jumps at them, I give him a good flogging, he deserves it, for he knows he is doing wrong, and has not over-excitement as an excuse. In a day or two, more or less, as he is more or less incorrigible, he will cease not only to jump at the sheep, but will walk quietly among them. He has learned perfectly one lesson, which is, that he must not touch sheep standing still. Probably, being now cowed by the warning 'Ware sheep,' if I took him on the common, he would, if he saw sheep running, stop at being halloed to (if not too far off); but it would be highly injudicious to trust him, for if he broke away, my three or four days' lesson would go for nothing:—he would be nearly as bad as ever.

"I now take him where sheep are wild, but never get near enough to set them running. But sup-

390. A full admiral (Sir H――n S―― d), as well known in the field as in the ballroom, and whose exhilarating society is coveted alike by young and old, had many years ago a valuable retriever named "Lion," bred between a setter and a Newfoundland, fast and high-couraged, but which had not been properly trained.

His condemnation had been pronounced by his owner, the late Sir J――s D――n H――y, in the hearing of the admiral, who at once asked for and obtained the dog. Sir J――s' keeper (P――n) had put a ring upon one of the animal's fore feet to prevent his travelling too fast. This the admiral immediately removed, and by making "Lion" his companion, and feeding him himself, he soon brought him into tolerable obedience, but he had the vexation of finding that the retriever always showed a great longing to chase sheep, and more than once had pulled one down in spite of all threats and admonitions.

One fine summer's morning the cheery admiral, who is an excellent piscator, had started at sunrise across the moors to fish a distant loch. "Lion" quietly followed behind the dog-cart, but on getting sight of some sheep he started off and overturned one.

The admiral hurried up in time to save its life. Although alone, he managed to tie its legs securely together. Ditto "Lion's," and then he laid the two helpless animals nearly side by side. With his driving-whip he belaboured "Lion" most severely, endeavouring to make him comprehend why he was punished, and in the intervals of the flagellation caressing the poor sheep.

This occurred about 6 A.M. and the admiral did not return to his captives until the same hour in the evening. After repeating his powerful admonitions he released both the animals, determined to give up the dog as incorrigible should he ever repeat the offence,— but he never did. He turned out an admirable retriever, and a faithful, attached friend. He seemed ever after ashamed to look a sheep in the face. On catching sight of one, he would slink to heel.

Be assured that the *truly* gallant admiral's is an excellent recipe for giving a dog a higher relish for cooked than for uncooked mutton.

---

pose they were to do so, I am prepared, for I have him in a cord some twenty yards long. This length gives him something of a feeling of liberty. If he looks towards the flock, 'Ware sheep' reminds him of his lessons. In a day or two I approach them; they begin to run: Don gets fidgety, but the warning and showing him the whip most probably controls him; if it does not, and he breaks away, I let him reach the end of the cord, and with a stentorian 'Ware sheep,' I pull him head over heels, haul him up, and getting hold of him, give him a second thrashing—a lesson or two more, and he, in nine cases in ten, will be broken of the habit. But if without the cord to check him he had got in full career, flaying the poor brute alive would not have prevented his doing it again; but his propensity having been diminished gradually, moderate reflection will reform him, which it would not have done while that propensity was in full force."— Page 171.

391. If ever you have fears that you may be unable to prevent a dog's breaking away to worry sheep, hunt him in a muzzle * of a size that will not interfere with his breathing, and yet effectually prevent the wide extension of his jaws.

392. The killing of fowls is more easily prevented. The temptation, though equally frequent, is not so great —he will only have tasted blood, not revelled in it. Take a dead fowl—one of his recent victims if you can procure it,—and endeavour, by pointing to it, while you are scolding him, to make him aware of the cause of your displeasure. Then secure him to a post, and thrash him about the head with the bird, occasionally favouring his hide with sundry applications of a whip, and his ears with frequent repetitions of the scaring admonition, " Ware fowl," " Fowl—fowl—fowl." Whenever you afterwards catch him watching poultry, be sure to rate him.

* A muzzle is the best recipe for keeping a howling dog quiet at night—from what is commonly called " baying the moon." It should invariably be employed whenever any oiutment is applied to his skin for mange, &c.

CHAPTER XIV.

A REST BEYOND "HALF-WAY HOUSE." ANECDOTES OF DOGS ON
SERVICE AT HOME.

393. A Halt sounded; present Position considered; Refinements or extra Accomplishments easily taught.—394. Excellent Snipe-shot who never used Dog.—395. Dog employed by another.—398. Which Sportsman had the best of it.—399. Squire O——n's and Mr. C——d's Match,—396. Snipe killed off.—397. Woodcocks become attached to undisturbed Covers; Mr. S——t's.—400. Partridges cut off from Place of Refuge.—401. Turnip-Field ridden round.—402. After Wind and Rain, hunt driest places; late in season, beat uncultivated lands. —403. In hot weather, give marked birds time to run.—404. Advantage of killing Old Birds; protects young Breeders.—405 to 407. Old Hen Pheasants shot; case in point; in Note, Pheasants reared under barn-door hen require meat; so do Fowls. Cantelo's method. Pheasantries, Mr. Knox. (See Appendix). Oak-bark a tonic. Cross with China Pheasant.—408. Sportsmen urged to break in their own Dogs.—409. Shooting conducive to Health.—410, 411. Mr. W——n and the old crippled Scotch Sportsman.—412. Instructing Dogs improves temper; not an ungentlemanly recreation. — 413. "Beckford's" opinion.—414. "Munito" selecting cards.—415. Shepherds' Dogs in France.—416. Collie Dogs.—417. "Fairy" ringing bell.—418, 419. "Médor's" fetching house-keys. Installed as their keeper.—420. "Sultan's" keeping the key in his larder.—421. Mr. A——n's "Taffy" knowing by name every member of family.—422. "Taffy" proves himself a first-rate Watch-Dog.—423. "Taffy" understands why he is borrowed.—424. "Taffy" an able Poacher.—425. "Taffy" being insulted bides his time to avenge the affront.—426. "Taffy" "turns the tables" upon workman who tries to impose upon him.—427. "Taffy" purloins for his master when ordered.—428. "Taffy" betrayed into momentary weakness purloins for himself.—429. "Taffy's" birth and education revealed; but his parentage a mystery.—430. "Taffy's" dam shipwrecked on the Needles.—431. Jesse's opinion of Dogs; in Note, Lord Brougham's—cunning of Fox—of Dog —of Monkey.—432. Exhibition of jealousy.—433. Lost Child fed by Dog.—434. "Philax" and "Brac" playing Dominos.—435 to 441. Showman's Dogs in Paris. Tricks with Cards and Numbers. Fortune-telling. Playing Dominos. —442. How assisted by Showman.—443. Our attention to be confined to Sporting Dogs.

393. WE have now arrived at a good halting-station, far beyond the half-way house; for any dog educated as I have described may fairly be considered well-broken. Shall we here part company, or will you proceed with me to what I termed "refinements" in breaking? I did so, as I mentioned at the time, in deference to general opinion, for many would call it superfluous breaking. It may be—but the additional excellence is easily attainable by perseverance in the system which I have detailed, and but little

extension of it. Why then should we not strive to reach it? It must, however, be granted that so finished an education is not absolutely necessary, for many killing dogs never attain it: indeed, many good sportsmen have never witnessed it. And this is probably the reason why such a number abjure the aid of a dog in snipe-shooting.

394. Years ago, when I was in County Wexford, I knew, by sight, a capital snipe-shot, though he constantly wore spectacles, who loathed the idea of letting a dog accompany him. This he would not have done, had he known to what perfection the animal could be brought. But certainly our spectacled friend had less occasion for canine assistance than any man I ever saw. He knew every rushy spot for miles around. If there was a snipe in a field, he would point to within a few feet where it was lying. He walked very fast; was indefatigable; without waiting for loading picked up every bird the moment it was knocked over; kept relays of ammunition at several farm-houses; and nearly always came home with his capacious pockets (for he carried no bag) well filled. I heard an anecdote of him, more in praise of the correctness of his eye than the make of his leg, that on one occasion, after he had stuffed his pockets full of snipe, he proceeded actually to cram more birds into the tops of his boots.

395. An officer whom I knew well in Canada came for a few days to Isle Aux Noix. He paddled himself and a favourite dog to the opposite shore. The dog made nineteen separate points at snipe—of which my friend bagged seventeen,—and he thinks he did not see above three more birds. He admits that the day was hot,* and that in consequence the snipe lay well; but he certainly would not have obtained so many shots without the assistance of his intelligent companion. He was, however, beautifully broken. I do not suppose that my friend had once occasion to use his voice. And the sagacious animal would creep across wind as stealthily as a cat on the right hand being slightly raised, as described in XII. of 141.

396. My friend's sport caused a laugh in the little garrison at the expense of its Fort Adjutant, by no means a first-rate shot, who complained that his favourite, though confessedly very small, preserve was destroyed for the season; and I rather think it was; for my experience leads me to believe, contrary to what is generally supposed, that snipe, when once they have had time to settle in a spot, become attached to it, and do not much shift their ground. At least I have known many places in which snipe having been killed off early in the season, none appeared the same season in their stead, although in preceding years birds had been plentiful during the whole winter.

397. Woodcocks also consider themselves permanently established in localities where they have been long undisturbed (82). Mr.

---

* A dark day with a good breeze would be preferred with us.

S——t of C——n, on the west coast of Ireland, was so fully impressed with this opinion that he would not allow a gun to be fired in his covers until after Christmas,—asserting that not a bird would then leave them before the regular period of migration, but merely, when flushed, remove from one part of the woods to another. It is hard to think that he reasoned incorrectly, for he had when I was in his neighbourhood,—and may have to this day for aught I know to the contrary,—nearly the best, if not undeniably the best, woodcock-shooting in Ireland until the very end of the season. This, too, is saying a "big word," for woodcock-shooting in the emerald isle is the cream of sport.

398. Now our spectacled acquaintance (394), capital sportsman as he was, owed his numerous shots solely to his great pedestrian powers, and the large development of his organ of locality. It is sometimes difficult enough, even with a clever dog, to spring a jack snipe, and you will not tell me that he (not master "Jack," but the gentleman) would not have bagged more birds, and have had to walk over less ground, had he possessed as good an animal as that which helped to destroy the Fort Adjutant's preserve. And do you think that our friend with the barnacles, who was in no way of a misanthropical disposition, would not thus have more enjoyed his day's sport? He might have been assured that birds, if they would not lie for a good-nosed dog, who hunted as cautiously as the officer's, would not lie for his walking them up. And if on a boisterous day he chose to shoot down wind (as snipe fly against it), why should he not call his companion in to "heel," and afterwards employ him when re-hunting the same ground up-wind? An *experienced* old dog, would rarely, however, when beating down-wind, pass by many birds without noticing them.

399. We often hear of sportsmen shooting against each other for considerable sums in our best partridge-counties, where the game is so abundant that they consider it most advisable to employ no dog, save one or two retrievers. I at once admit that they act judiciously in not hunting any ordinary animal, but I am confident that the competitor who used such a cautious dog as the officer's (395), would not only get more shots than his opponent, but be able to kill to a greater certainty, because better prepared for every rise. The quantity of game would not have confused that first-rate dog,—his nose was too discriminating. He would have walked quietly,—almost crept,—up to every bird, and I will venture to say would not have sprung one out of shot, that would not have risen as readily had he been left in his kennel. In the match that came off in October, '50, at Lord L——h's, R——d Hall, between the Squire O——n and Mr. C——d,—both good performers—so many birds would not have been missed had the sportsmen been warned to look out for most of their shots by a careful dog's drawing upon the birds. Victory would have sided with the party thus aided.

400. I said (398), "An experienced old dog would rarely, however, even when beating down-wind, pass by many birds without noticing them:" and most fortunate is it that this is the case, for

otherwise you would seldom get a shot to a point at partridge when the ground is wet, and the birds have taken to running ahead along a furrow—or, as is frequently the case, are all making off in one direction, probably seeking the shelter of some well-known friendly cover. Should you think this likely to happen, you must, without minding what quarter the wind blows from, commence your beat by traversing the ground that lies between them and their place of refuge. Even then you will often find that they will rather face you, than be diverted from their original design.

401. In large turnip-fields you would do well when birds are wild to hunt the outer parts first, and so gradually work round and round towards the centre. Then return to the outer parts, and again work round the borders. The birds thus finding themselves headed in every direction are much more likely to lie than if you had not so manoeuvred. On such occasions the great advantages of caution in dogs, and of their prompt obedience to the hand are made manifest. I heard of a man who, in order to make birds lie close in turnips, used to direct his little boy to trot his pony round and round the field. The plan was very successful. The birds seemed quite bewildered, especially when time had been allowed for the boy to complete the circuit before the dogs were permitted to enter. I remember a good sportsman telling me that he had more than once succeeded in making wild birds lie by attaching soft-sounding bells to the collars of his pointers. The novel sound appeared to arrest the attention of the partridges. This seems opposed to what is said in 74 about bells used in cover scaring game.

402. High winds and rain greatly disturb birds; and if you are a tyro in partridge-shooting you should thank me for recommending you, if you are ever so anxious to get a few shots, to wait for the first hour of sunshine after such weather,* and then to hunt the *driest* grounds, where you probably will find the birds *not feeding*, but quietly reposing, after the knocking about they have undergone. But, my *young* friend, I should like to give you another hint. When it is late in the season, instead of constantly beating the denuded stubbles, try the wild uncultivated lands (if there are any in your neighbourhood) where it is likely the birds will be found searching for the common grass-seeds which they neglected when more palatable grain could be easily obtained. Wind without wet sometimes makes wild birds lie,—probably because they do not hear the sportsman's footsteps.

403. After you have sprung a covey, and succeeded in killing the old pair, should the scent be bad, give the young birds time to run a little before you let your dogs hunt for them. Late in the season, in hot, dry weather, such delay is frequently productive of much

---

* But there is this to be said in favour of your perpetually shooting in wind and wet:—you will be acting a most friendly part by your less persecuting neighbour, for under the two-fold annoyance of the gun and such weather, the birds will fly to great distances to seek for quiet shelter.

good, for partridges will often at such times not move an inch from the spot where they first pitched; thereby emitting so little scent that an ordinary dog will not be able to find them, however accurately you may have marked the place where they *opened their wings* preparatory to dropping.

404. If, when first a covey rose, the old pair was knocked over, the young ones would lie singularly close, awaiting the accustomed, unspellable, unpronounceable parental call. But there is a yet stronger reason why the precedence and attention usually given to age should not in the present instance be withheld. *Old birds, whether breeding or barren, drive off the younger ones during the breeding season.* Some sportsmen, I am aware, deem this opinion a vulgar prejudice; but, if it be well founded, common sense bids us kill the old birds, that the young ones may have undisturbed possession of their ground. They must be unusually small squeakers if they cannot shift for themselves early in September, particularly if the weather be warm. They will come to no harm, where the keeper has done his duty as a trapper. On estates infested with vermin, they will, of course, suffer from the absence of the warning parental cry. There are country gentlemen who go so far as to have the old birds shot in August (when they can readily be distinguished even in the most forward coveys), well knowing that a jealous old pair of partridges will take possession of as much ground in spring, as would suffice for nearly half-a-dozen young couples; especially if the latter belong to the same covey, and are therefore accustomed to associate together; for, contrary to the general laws of nature, these birds breed in and in.

405. Old hen pheasants should also be killed off:—they are barren, and are accused of sucking the eggs of the younger birds. They may be readily distinguished by their deeper and more brilliant plumage. As a case in point,—

406. I know of a gentleman going to the North to reside on a small property, where the game had not been preserved for years. He at once engaged a clever keeper, who joined him immediately after the conclusion of the shooting season. In a few days the latter requested to see his master.

"Well, George, I fear you don't find much game."

The other replied, in broad Yorkshire dialect, "No-o, sir, no—nŏt mutch. 'A' been thruff (through) t' covers, and seen some auld budds—and, please, sir, I'd loike to shūt 'em."

The gentleman started. "Shoot them! That's an odd way of preserving them, unless indeed you intend to stuff them. Are you mad? There may be only a few birds, but I suppose a few are better than none."

"No-o, sir, no—they beant. A few auld budds is wuss than none."

"How's that? What do you mean?"

"Well, I tell'e, sir—t' auld uns be so stŭpid—jealous *verrē* (very)—t' missis is sŭm*tímes* (sometimes) ees verrē—I sure she is. They *fight* t' young uns, and *can't do* with strangers no how. Folks say

—folks say a barren hen, if she foĭnd (find) a nest, 'ill brak all t' eggs. A don't k*n*ow about that ; perhaps they brak 'em i' t' fighting, but they be brukken sure en*aef.* So ye see, sir, 'spose we have *no* budds here, then t' young 'uns, when t' auld 'uns fight 'em in neighbours' covers, coom in here to uz—and foĭnd 'emselves quite coomfortuble and *bide.* And b'sides they'll knōw-thĕy-'ve-nŏ-rīght —thĕy'll knōw-thĕy-'ve-nŏ-rīght thĕmsĕlves, and so *they* wunt fight t' new comers. There be sŭm gentlemen as shŭts doon one-third of their estate every year, clean right away—and then t' pheasants and t' partridge coom in like-o-o-o. Quite many of them ; yes, they do like t' settlars in 'Merika, as á' do hear say."

407. This homely reasoning of the honest Yorkshireman * prevailed, and a good show of game the following season satisfactorily established the soundness of his views.

408. But we have been astray on the stubbles and in cover, instead of attending to our friend (394, 398) snipe-shooting in the marshes, and determining (for our own satisfaction, if not for his) whether the companionship of a good dog would not have greatly added to his enjoyment. Doubtless it would ; for I appeal to you, if you are a devotee to the double detonator, whether it be not a magnificent thing to witness brilliant performance in fine dogs—to watch their prompt obedience—their graceful action—the expression of their intelligent countenances—to hope at the first feathering at a haunt—to participate in the nervous start on a closer touch— to share in the exciting alternation of 'the cautious " road," and the momentary stop—to exult in the certainty of a sure find—to hesitate in the expectation of a sudden rise,—and, finally, to triumph in the fall of the noble old bird you have been steadily following through all his wiles and stratagems ? If we have travelled over the past pages together, I hope you will further agree with me in thinking, that should you shoot over well-educated dogs of your *own making,* instead of to dogs broken by others, your gratification would be as greatly increased as would have been our Irish acquaintance's, had he shot to really killing dogs, instead of possessing none at all. I firmly believe that more than half the pleasure a sportsman derives from shooting, consists in watching the hunting of wellbroken dogs, and that his gratification is nearly doubled if the dogs are of his own training. It was this persuasion that, on our introduction to each other (3), made me so strongly urge you to break in your dogs yourself.

409. I might urge you to do so from yet another motive. What can you name besides glorious hunting that will keep you in strength and prime condition so long as shooting ? Is not an autumnal excursion to the wild mooŕs, or even homely stubbles, far more invigorating than a saunter at the most salubrious watering-place ? And would not continued, though it may be diminished, zest for the sport induce you to take air and exercise at a time of life

---

* This note about rearing pheasants, &c., is so long that the printer has placed it in an Appendix. See page 335.

when little else would lure you from the fire-side? That shooting, then, may not pall upon you as years creep on, surely you would do well to make the healthy recreation as attractive as possible; and hunting dogs of your own breaking would undeniably lend it not only a great but an enduring charm.

410. A fondness for the beauties of nature, a sense of freedom while one is inhaling the pure mountain breezes, and it may be a consciousness of power, have made men bordering on four-score continue to love their guns with a feeling somewhat akin to the fervour of their first love, as is well exemplified in an aged tenant of Mr. W——n of Edinburgh, to whom I have been occasionally indebted for a capital day's sport.

411. Mr W——n visiting one of his farms, found the old man, who had been a keen sportsman all his life, labouring under chronic rheumatism (caught by injudicious exposure in the discharge of his agricultural duties), so severe as to be obliged to go about on crutches. After the usual salutations, at meeting, the farmer began:—

"May be ye'll think the place negleckit-like, but I'm no able to look after the wark noo."

"Keep a good heart," said Mr. W——n; "things are looking well enough. I suppose you are pining after the shooting—you can get no sport now."

"Ye may weel think that," replied the farmer, adding in a sort of chuckle and confidential undertone, "the auld gun and me is no parted yet."

"But," rejoined Mr. W——n, "you surely don't mean that you can still kill birds? You can hardly manage that."

"I can manage it fine," observed the other, with some pique; "the cart takes me to the neeps.* The bit callant † helps me oot. I hirple‡ on. When the dog maks a point, doon gang the crutches—the laddie takes haud o' me, and though my legs is neither straught nor steady, my e'e is as true as yer ain."

412. Breaking in dogs is not only an invigorating bodily exercise, but a healthy moral training; for to obtain *great* success, you must have much patience and self-command; and whatever may be your rank or position in life, Beckford—not he of Fonthill, but the man whose memory is held in veneration by all Nimrods for his admirable "Thoughts on Hunting"—will not allow you to plead, as an excuse, for what just possibly may be want of energy or sad laziness, that breaking in dogs for your own gun is an ungentlemanly or unbecoming recreation. I grant he is speaking of instructors of hounds, but his words in their spirit are fully as applicable to the instructors of pupils accustomed to the smell of gunpowder.

413. In his 22d letter he writes, "It is your opinion, I find, that a gentleman might make the best huntsman. I have no doubt that

---

* Neeps, anglicè turnips.   † Callant, anglicè boy.
‡ Hirple, anglicè limp.

he would, if he chose the trouble of it. I do not think there is any profession, trade, or occupation, in which a good education would not be of service; and hunting, notwithstanding that it is at present exercised by such as have not had an education, might without

SCENE FROM 'CRIPPLE-GAIT.'—'GAME' TO THE LAST.—Par. 411.

doubt be carried on much better by those that have. I will venture to say fewer faults would be committed, nor is it probable the same faults would be committed over and over again as they now are. Huntsmen never reason by analogy, nor are they much benefited by experience." I fear we may say the same of the generality of keepers, for decidedly dog-breaking has not kept pace with the manifest improvements in other arts. Few brigades—indeed few dogs are now-a-days broken like Major B——d's (251), or Captain J——n's (542). But I do not intend to say it is necessary; all that is merely for show might be advantageously dispensed with.

414. It is hard to imagine what it would be impossible to teach a dog, did the attainment of the required accomplishment sufficiently recompense the instructor's trouble. Most of us have heard of the celebrated dog "Munito," who, at some private signal from his master, quite imperceptible to the spectator, would select from a pack of out-spread cards that which the spectator had named to the master in a whisper, or merely written on a piece of paper.

415. In the unenclosed parts of France, when the young crops are on the ground, you may frequently see a shepherd's dog trusted to prevent the sheep from nibbling the tender wheat growing contiguous to the grass, which he peaceably permits them to crop within a foot of the tempting grain ; but he is keenly watching, ready to dart at the first epicure who cannot resist a bite at the forbidden dainty ; and so ably and zealously does the dog discharge his duties, that even in such trying circumstances will the shepherd leave his sheep for hours together under the charge of their sagacious and vigilant guardian. In a similar manner, a couple of dogs, stationed one at each flank of a large flock, effectually protect the vineyards from their depredations. The latter you will think not so remarkable an instance of discrimination as the former ; for, compared with the difference in appearance between the herbage and the vine, there is but little between the young grain and the adjacent grass.

416. Who has not read with intense delight the tales of the almost incredible intelligence and devotion to their duties of the Scotch collie dogs, as related by the Ettrick Shepherd? He mentions one which, when his master was speaking, evidently understood much of what was said.

417. I know a lady who had a small, nearly thorough-bred King Charles. Being one day desired by her mother to ring the bell, she turned to the dog, and said, very energetically, "Fairy, ring the bell." The little dog had no previous training, but she had been observant, and was imitative. She immediately sprung at the bell-rope, and pulled it. "Fairy," indeed, unfortunately pulled with great violence—the rope came down, and so alarmed was she (remember how I have cautioned you never to alarm your pupil), that no subsequent coaxing could induce her to return to the bell. But if she had not been frightened, she might have become as serviceable a bell-ringer as the little dog that preceded her in the office of pet. That predecessor (the mention of a *useful pet*, though a lady was not his instructor, will, I hope, redeem my character with the fair sex) saved his young mistress from many an interruption of work and study, by ringing the bell on command. And "Bob" was discreet in his *spontaneous* ringings. He never rang without a cause ; but if he was unreasonably detained by himself, or a visitor's knock remained too long unanswered, the tardy attendant was warned of his remissness by a loud peal.

418. A French lady, who is fond of animals, at my request committed the following anecdote to paper :—

419. "My dear Médor, a beautiful red and white setter, was remarkable, I am told, for many rare qualities as a sporting dog ; but, of course, none of these could be compared, in *my* eyes, to his faithfulness and sagacity. I looked upon him as a friend ; and I know that our affection was mutual. I could mention several instances of his intelligence, I might say reflection, but one in particular gave me such delight that, though years have since passed away, all the circumstances are as fresh in my memory as if they had occurred but yesterday. I was returning from school at Ver-

sailles, and having rung uselessly for a little time at the front door, I went round to the carriage-gate to have a chat with my silky-haired favourite. He barked anxiously; thrust his cold nose through an opening near the ground; scratched vigorously to increase its size; and in numerous ways testified great joy at again hearing my voice. I put my hand under the gate to caress him, and while he was licking it, I said in jest, but in a distinct, loud voice, 'Dear Médor, I am shut out—go, bring me the keys.' It so happened that the stable where they usually hung was not closed. Médor ran off, and in a few seconds returned and placed them in my hands. I will not attempt to describe *my* gratification at such a striking proof of his intelligence, nor *his* evident pride at seeing me enter the hall; nor yet the fright of the servant at thinking how long the street-door must have been carelessly left open. 'Médor deserves that his life should be written,' said I to my uncle when afterwards telling him the whole story; 'I am sure his deeds are as wonderful as those related of the "Chiens célèbres" by De Fréville.'

"My setter was immediately declared 'Keeper of the Keys,' and forthwith invested with all the rights of office,—nor was this confidence misplaced. He would never give up his charge to any one but to my uncle or myself; and always seemed fully sensible of the dignity and responsibility of his new position."

420. Another anecdote touching keys.

A family residing at Chepstow had a house with a gate leading into the castle-ditch, and they used to pass through it almost daily in order to avoid the bustle of the town. The key of this gate was kept in the kitchen, and a black retriever, Sultan by name, was accustomed to ask the cook for it by pulling her dress until he succeeded in bringing her under the nail on which the key was hung, and he always returned it most honestly when the family had done with it. One day, however, having brought it back as usual, he found the cook too busy to attend to him, and, growing impatient he trotted off with it, and for a whole fortnight it was missing. At length Miss ———, being much inconvenienced by its loss, armed herself with a whip, and, standing by the gate, called the dog, and said in a very determined tone, "Now, Sultan, bring me that *key directly.*" Off he went to a gooseberry-bush, scratched up the key, and brought it to her. He had, probably, found the same spot a safe depository for many a bone.

421. Mr. A——n, with whom I was slightly acquainted,—a man of great originality, and singular shrewdness and intelligence,—had a dog called Taffy, who had a remarkable aptitude for comprehending whatever was told him. He knew by name every member of Mr. A——n's family, though composed at least of ten individuals. On his master's saying, "Taffy, give so-and-so a grip," the dog would to a certainty take hold of the right person. "Harder, Taffy,—give a harder grip;" the dog would bite more firmly. At the third order, "Harder, my boy,—yet harder," the party assaulted would be too glad to *sue* for mercy; for no one dared to *strike* Taffy excepting Mr. A——n. Even to him the animal never submitted quietly, but

kept growling and snarling whenever he was being punished—indeed, on more than one occasion he fought for the mastery, but unsuccessfully, for few men are more resolute than was Mr. A——n.

422. Taffy was an admirable watch-dog, and fully sensible of the responsible duties that devolved upon him. It happened that, in a violent storm, late one evening, when Mr. A——n was from home, the force of the wind drove in the front door. Taffy forthwith commenced a search from the bottom of the house to the top, apparently to ascertain that no stranger had entered, and he then went downstairs. Next morning he was found lying across the door-mat, where evidently he had remained the whole night, although the cold and wet had been most severe.

423. Taffy's character was so established as a sagacious, faithful guardian, that Mr. A——n's sister-in-law, feeling nervous at her husband's being obliged to leave home, begged the loan of Taffy for a few nights. Mr. A——n consented, and ordered Taffy, manifestly to his great annoyance, to remain at the house. Four days afterwards he reappeared at home, when Mr. A——n, in the belief that he had run away, was about to beat him, but was persuaded to suspend the punishment until it was ascertained whether Mrs. —— had not brought him into the neighbourhood. About an hour afterwards she arrived to make inquiries about the dog, who, she said, had left her house the moment her husband put his foot' withinside the door.

424. Taffy was also a sporting character,—I fear I ought to say a *poaching* character,—for he was a peculiar dog, he had peculiar ideas—would that such ideas were more *peculiar*—on the subject of game, and fancied all means lawful that insured success. In the Isle of Wight there once were (probably the spot is now drained) ten or twelve acres of marsh-land, nearly surrounded by water, much in the shape of a horse-shoe. It was a favourite resort for hares, as Taffy well knew. His bulk prevented his ever having a chance of catching any in a fair run ; he used, therefore, to dodge about between them and the outlet, and would so worry and distress them, that he was pretty certain of eventually carrying off one as a prize.

425. We all remember the story of the unfortunate tailor deluged with a shower of dirty water by the indignant elephant whose proboscis he had imprudently insulted in the morning by pricking it with his needle, instead of presenting the expected delicacy. It would appear as though Taffy had heard and understood the anecdote. He was once pelted with stones by some boys from behind a wall : having then no means of retaliating, he seemed to take the affront quietly, but he did not forget it ; he patiently bided his time, and, as opportunities offered, avenged himself upon each successively by knocking them down in the dirt ; nor did he allow one to escape unpunished, though some of them avoided him for three weeks or a month. There were six offenders, and he made all the six expiate their offences in a dirty kennel.

426. Indeed, Taffy would *never* allow anybody, young or old, to

play tricks upon him with impunity. On one occasion, when the labourers had left off work to take their dinners, one of them amused himself by offering Taffy a piece of bread stuck on the end of a knife, and by suddenly turning it over, managed to give the dog a rap on the nose with the handle, on his attempting to seize the proffered gift. Taffy bore the joke patiently for some time ; but at length, thinking that his good-nature was unduly taxed, and perceiving also that the loaf was fast decreasing, he determined to turn the tables. Bristling up, therefore, he jumped, open-mouthed, at the man, and so alarmed him, that in his fright he dropped the bread, and Taffy quietly walked off with it, much to the delight of the bystanders.

427. Though Taffy's natural parts were so great, they were doubtless improved by education. If Mr. A——n ever called the dog's attention to a thing by pointing at it, the dog would, to nearly a certainty, bring it to him when he had got well out of sight, and was, therefore, not likely to be suspected of participating in the robbery. Many a time has Taffy run off with the *finest* fish from the side of the unsuspecting angler, who, until he was enlightened upon the subject on its safe restoration, may in his bewilderment have gravely considered whether, under very favouring circumstances, it would be possible for a trout to possess the same vitality and power of locomotion as an eel. It always tended to the maintenance of the piscator's proverbial reputation for patience and equanimity, that he should not detect Taffy in the commission of the theft ; for the dog would constantly show fight rather than give up the prize. He evinced yet greater adroitness in securing pigeons. On numerous occasions bets have been laid, and rarely lost, that he would bring home the *particular* one indicated to him out of a large flock feeding on the ground ; for he would patiently crouch,—perhaps affecting to be asleep,—until it incautiously afforded him the opportunity of seizing it ; but so careful was he of his charge, that he invariably delivered it up to his master, perfectly uninjured.

428. With all his cunning and eccentricities, Taffy was "passing honest," and seldom purloined on his own account ; but I regret to say it is recorded of him, that in a moment of weakness and hunger he yielded to temptation, The instance was this.—Taffy observed a woman seated at a cottage-door feeding her child. He earnestly begged for a share, but in vain. Remarking, however, that she frequently turned round to dip the spoon into something, he contrived to creep behind her without her perceiving him, when to his satisfaction he discovered a basin of pap on the floor. It was too hot to gobble up at once ; so waiting quietly until her attention was drawn away, he cautiously took up the crock and trotted off with it—to the good woman's dismay, who was wondering what had become of her dear baby's dinner—and, without spilling any of the contents, carried it to a convenient distance, where he leisurely ate up all the carefully-prepared food, leaving the basin perfectly undamaged, and as clean as if it had been washed by the most praiseworthy housewife.

R

429. Other stories could be told of Taffy's sagacity, but these you will probably think more than sufficient. However, you would perhaps like to hear how he was bred. No one can tell you more than that, judging from his appearance, he must have had a strain of the Newfoundland in him, for the circumstances attending his birth and parentage are nearly as singular as his character.

430. A ship was lost in a storm off the Needles, in 1811. Nothing was saved, not a plank whereon was a letter to indicate to what country she belonged. For some weeks afterwards, a farmer in the Isle of Wight found that regularly every night one of his sheep was destroyed. A watch was set. The culprit was at length discovered to be a strange, savage-looking dog, supposed to have escaped from the wreck. For many, many nights it baffled its pursuers, but was at length wounded, and tracked by its blood to a cave, where it was killed. Three young pups were found. One of them, the said Taffy, was saved, and brought up by hand by Mr. A——n, who became so fond of it that their attachment might almost be said to be mutual. Taffy lived admired and honoured beyond the term of life usually assigned to the canine race.

431. Jesse * narrates many instances similar to the foregoing, in

---

* Lord Brougham, in his "Dialogues on Instinct," gives anecdotes showing the great sagacity of animals. He writes — "The cunning of foxes is proverbial ; but I know not if it was ever more remarkably displayed than in the Duke of Beaufort's country ; where Reynard, being hard pressed, disappeared suddenly, and was, after strict search, found in a water-pool up to the very snout, by which he held on to a willow-bough hanging over the pond. The cunning of a dog, which Serjeant Wilde tells me of as known to him, is at least equal. He used to be tied up as a precaution against hunting sheep. At night he slipped his head out of the collar, and returning before dawn, put on the collar again to conceal his nocturnal excursions."

All animals are more or less cunning. The cunning of monkeys —I do not quite like using that word : it hardly does them justice —is nearly as proverbial as the cunning of foxes—but it is not so generally admitted that the monkey has an innate sense of the ludicrous ; and it would surprise many to be told that its mischievous propensities frequently arise, not from a spirit of wanton destructiveness, but from a consciousness of fun—from a feeling of enjoyment at thinking of, or witnessing the embarrassments created by its pranks. Yet it is so. Captain H——e, when in the 7th Fusiliers, mentioned to me that the sailors of the ship in which he returned from the Mediterranean had two pet monkeys on board. The older one not being so tame as the smaller, a belt with a short rope was fastened round his waist, in order that he might be occasionally tied up, and as this belt had chafed him he greatly disliked its being touched. One hot day when the monkeys were lying beside each other on the deck, apparently asleep, H——e observed the little one raise himself softly, look at his companion, and feeling assured that he was asleep, sink down quietly, close his eyes, and give the obnoxious belt a sudden twitch. The other instantly sprang up,—perceiving, however, nothing near

his amusing work on Dogs—a book likely to convince the most sceptical, that few among us give the canine race credit for half the sagacity and intelligence with which they are really endowed. He asserts, and I, for one, fully agree with him, "that there is not a faculty of the human mind, of which some evident proof of its existence may not be found in dogs. Thus," he says, "we find them possessed of memory, imagination, curiosity, cunning, revenge, ingenuity, gratitude, devotion or affection, and other qualities."

432. To this list he ought to have added jealousy: only this year I heard of a stronger instance of it than I could have imagined possible. Walking near Devonport, I met a man with two small dogs; one was evidently a foreigner. Apologising for the abruptness of the question, I inquired from what country the animal came. "From Japan." I then asked whether he had ever bred from the other dog, a most varmint-looking, wiry little terrier; he replied that she was three years old, and had never had but one pup, which, because he was fondling it, she had deliberately killed that very morning, although it was six weeks old, and she was still nursing it. I cannot say that she manifested either sorrow for its

him but the little fellow (seemingly) in a deep slumber, he laid himself down to continue his siesta. After a while the young tormentor cautiously peered round; when satisfied that his friend was again in the arms of "Mr. Murphy," he repeated the disagreeable twitch with yet greater success,—the old chap becoming this time delightfully puzzled.

A third time the little rascal, after the same precautions as before, endeavoured to play off his trick,—but he was foiled at his own weapons. The old gentleman suspecting him, had cunningly pretended to be asleep; and on the small paw quietly approaching his sensitive loins, he jumped up— seized the culprit in the very fact, and forthwith gave him a drubbing that taught him more respectful manners during the remainder of the voyage.

But to return for a moment to foxes. A story is told in the family of Mr. C——s R——n (286) of the sagacity of these animals, to which he gives implicit credence. Adjacent to their old family house stands a yet older high tower, the summit of which commands an extensive view of the surrounding country, and consequently of the several rides leading to the building. From this elevated position his grandfather was one morning watching the hounds drawing some neighbouring covers, when he saw a fox steal away unobserved, and hide himself in a few furze-bushes. The pack passed by at some distance from him, and Monsieur Reynard must have begun congratulating himself upon his escape, when to his horror he perceived two lagging skirters approaching his place of concealment. Instead of breaking away in an opposite direction, he at once went forth to greet them,—lay down, playfully wagging his tail,—and gave them a pressing, and doubtless sincere, invitation to join in a game of romps. The ruse was successful. The hounds came up, paid him the compliment of sniffing at him as he rolled on his back humbly admitting his inferiority, and then cantered off to join their companions. Upon this, Pug at once retreated to his first covert.

loss, or repentance of her unnatural conduct; on the contrary her joyous gambols seemed to evince her delight at having removed from her path a dreaded rival in the affections of her master.

433. We must all admit that they have much reflection, or they would not evince the good judgment they so frequently display in unusual circumstances—circumstances in which mere instinct could in no way assist them.* An industrious couple, who lived high on the side of one of the romantic Ennerdale Hills, (Cumberland) in a cottage which had descended through several generations from father to son, used to gather fuel in a neighbouring wood. They often took their little daughter with them; but one evening, whilst hunting for wild flowers, she strayed beyond their sight or hearing. They searched unceasingly for their lost darling as long as the waning light permitted them to distinguish objects amidst the thick foliage; and then, with heavy hearts, turned towards home, the father endeavouring to cheer the mother with the hope he could not himself entertain that the little girl might have wandered to her accustomed haunts; but they had the grief of finding that she had not returned; and fruitless also was the anxious search renewed by torchlight. The poor mother mechanically spread out the frugal supper, thinking it possible that her husband might partake of the food she could not taste. It would, however, have remained on the board untouched had not the old dog seized a large slice of the loaf and rushed out of the cottage. The father quietly observed, "I never knew the dog to thieve before." Ere the day had fully dawned, they were again hunting the wood; but they could discover no trace of their child. At breakfast-time the dog, as on the preceding evening, purloined a piece of bread. The man was about to strike the depredator, but his wife, her countenance radiant with hope, stopped him with the exclamation, "I am sure he knows where Agnes is." They ran down hill after him, and at length found him near the edge of the lake, lying on the child to keep her warm. She appeared quite satisfied with her position, and extremely pleased with her shaggy companion. In her small fat fingers she grasped the stolen bread, together with many flowers she had gathered.

434. You may have seen the account of the marvellous tricks which Monsieur Leonard, by kindness and perseverance, taught his dogs Philax and Brac. That a dog could be tutored into playing as good a game of dominos as a man, may sound preposterously unreasonable, but the respectability of the writer compels us to give credence to the recital.

435. I, also, had once the honour of playing a game of dominos with a learned dog, whose celebrity, however, was far inferior to that acquired by M. Leonard's clever pupil. It thus happened. As I was crossing the *Place St. Sulpice*, at Paris, I saw a large crowd collected in a circle of considerable diameter round a man

---

* Is not the capability of forming a good judgment in unusual circumstances more dependent upon the exercise of the reasoning than the instinctive faculties?

who was exhibiting tricks with dogs. He had a great variety. Six were yoked in pairs to a light carriage. On the roof sat a terrier dressed up most fantastically, and who with difficulty retained his elevated position when the carriage was in motion. Two others,— one an extremely small animal, called the "petit Caporal,"—were favoured with places in the interior. There were, also, two slight greyhounds and a Russian poodle. Total, a dozen. It may be worthy of note that all, with, I believe, only one exception, were of the masculine gender. They were miserably thin, but I must admit that they appeared attached to their master.

DOMINI AND 'DOMINOS.'—Par. 434.

436. When I joined the group, the showman was making a dog, dressed in a petticoat and smart cap, dance a minuet. Then a greyhound leaped, of course gracefully, through a hoop held by a boy over his head; and afterwards trotted, as ungracefully, on three legs, affecting extreme lameness on each alternately. The man then promised numerous surprising feats if he could but collect as many as twelve sous. On summing up the coppers thrown to him, there appeared to be thirteen. This he averred to be such an unlucky number that he dare not proceed unless some benevolent, Christian-like person would break the charm by adding another sou. His demand was immediately complied with.

In order to increase the size of the arena—at least, such I conceived to be the reason, it certainly had the effect—he drove the car fast round the circle. He then spread ten cards on the four sides of an old cloth, about five feet long, and of nearly the same width. Each card bore a legibly-written number from 0 to 9. He invited the spectators to ask for whatever number they pleased, provided it did not hold doublets, nor contain more than four of the cyphers ; asserting that his dogs, without the least assistance from him, would bring, in regular order, the several cards representing the required number ; and to create, as it seemed to me, the impression that it was a matter of perfect indifference what dog he took, he unyoked one of the leaders,—a close-cropped, small Dane,—and called him to the centre. I begged a lady who was leaning on my arm, and whose eyes are generally sharp enough, to watch the man most carefully. Some one demanded 1824. The dog went round and round the cloth as if examining every card separately, and lifted, in regular succession (carrying them one by one to his master), the several numbers composing 1824. The dog committed no blunder ; and did not long hesitate in making his selection. Another person in the crowd called out for 29, when the dog was equally successful ; and on neither occasion could the lady or myself perceive that the man gave the slightest sign. At one time I thought I had detected that he took a short step forward, as if to receive the card, when the dog was about to grasp the right one ; but I was soon aware that I had only found a "mare's nest."

437. When reharnessing the Dane to the carriage, the showman gave out that, if duly paid, he could exhibit before the "respectable and discriminating company" the feats of a far more wonderful animal. He collected what satisfied him ; and producing two similar packs of common playing cards (say a dozen in each), he bade the Russian come forth and astonish the public. The man distributed one pack along the borders of the cloth ; and handing round the other pack, he begged as many of the company as pleased, to take a card. Five or six did so. The man then showed what cards remained in his hands to the poodle, desiring him to point out those that had been taken. The dog walked round and round the cloth, and one by one fetched the corresponding cards.

438. The showman still more astonished the gaping crowd by assuring them that this dog's intellect was so extraordinary and wonderful, that he could read their most secret thoughts ; and to prove the truth of his assertion, whilst telling a good-humoured fiacre-driver, well known to many of them, to think of a card, he successfully *forced** one upon his sight : and after coachee had,

---

* So adroitly obtruding (or forcing) a particular card of an outspread pack upon the notice of an unsuspecting party, that he unhesitatingly selects that identical card. This trick is performed very effectively, having previously concealed the eight of a suit, by temporarily converting the seven into the eight by lightly sticking on a bit of paper cut into proper shape, and of the same colour as the suit. The metamorphosed card is forced upon one of the audience, and the exhibitor manages unperceived to remove the deception with his little finger when reshuffling the cards.

agreeably to the showman's desire, whispered to a neighbour what it was, the dog, without taking much time for reflection, selected the true card from among those lying on the cloth.

439. The expressions of admiration and bewilderment this feat elicited having somewhat subsided, the showman again laid out those cards on which the numbers were written. There was a large public clock easily visible from the *Place:* he held the dog's head towards it; requested him to look at it attentively, and tell the gentlemen and ladies the exact time,—first the hours, then the minutes. It was a quarter-past two. The dog brought 2 for the hours, and then 1 and 5 for the minutes.

440. Having now sufficiently worked upon the imagination and credulity of the observers, the showman drew forth a quantity of small folded papers of various colours; and having spread them along the edges of the cloth, he solemnly protested that the dog would tell the fortune of any of his hearers who would first give him a sou. As a guarantee for the dog's ability, he told them they might compare the several fortunes written on the papers selected for them by the dog, however numerous they might be, when it would be found that, without a single exception, the canine magician would have foretold to each what could only happen to an individual of his or her sex. The charlatan reaped a plentiful harvest, for the temptation was strong—to female curiosity especially; and no one could prove that the dog was ever in error.

441. After a laughable exhibition of several of the dogs marching in procession, which he called "the carnival of Venice," he affected suddenly to discover that none of the dogs had been allowed a game of dominos. He again unyoked the Dane, and asked if any one was willing to become his antagonist. As no one would step forward, whether from bashfulness or fear of necromancy I cannot say, I avowed my willingness to play. There were fourteen dominos. I drew seven. The others were arranged for the dog on the cloth, far apart from one another. He had the double six, and he immediately took it up to begin the game. I followed; and we alternately played a piece in the most orderly and regular manner—the dog carrying the dominos to the man to place for him; wagging his short stump when he found (from his master's manner), that he was right; and, to do him justice, he never made a mistake.

442. Although I was now close to the showman, I could not remark that he gave the least signal by look, or by motion of hand or foot: but I fancied—this, however, may be only another "mare's nest," though I cannot think it was—that I heard him make a slight chuckling sound* (with his tongue against the roof of his mouth), whilst the dog was walking round from domino to domino, which ceased when he approached the right domino, leaving the man at liberty to jest and talk nonsense for the amusement of the crowd.

---

* This would account for the showman's wish to increase the size of the circle (436), and keep his audience at a respectable distance, well out of hearing.

He had evidently a long string of ready-prepared witticisms. He laughed at the dog for being so long in making up his mind as to what it would be most judicious to play ;—told him that he had been so hospitably treated by the good Parisians, that it was evident his brains were not so clear as they ought to be, &c., &c. : all which verbiage I suspect the dog took as a confirmation that he was making the selection his master wished. The man promised to call upon me ; but I was obliged to leave Paris sooner than I had expected, and I never saw him again.

443. Our attention, however, perhaps you will think, ought to be confined to instances of intelligence and high education in sporting-dogs. Well, then, in the next Chapter I will speak of what some dogs of that class do in this, and some are *trained* to do in other countries ;—facts for the truth of which I can vouch, and I hope the account will induce you to believe I am not unreasonable in asserting that we have a right to require greater excellence in our sporting-dogs than what is now regarded by most of us as satisfactory.

CHAPTER XV.

ANECDOTES OF DOGS ON SERVICE ABROAD. RUSSIAN SETTERS.

444. Dogs for Hunting Bears in India.—445. Polygar Dogs for Hunting Wild Hog in India.—446. Beaters in India; the greater utility of Dogs.—447. Mongrel Pointer in India which proved of great value.—448. Cross between Pointer and Indian Dog recommended; in Note, Arab Greyhounds.—449. Coolness necessary in attacking large Game.—450 to 457. K——g's critical encounter with Elephant.—458. Sketch of Scene.—459, 460. Wounded Elephant.—461. Pot shot at Bear to be potted.—462. Skull of Indian and African Elephant differs.—463 to 467. M——e bearding Lion in Den.—468. Hindu's estimate of courage of Europeans. Encounter with Wild Boar.—469. Strong Greyhounds for killing Kangaroos in Australia.—470. Greyhound hunted with Falcon.—471. The Creole Sportsman and admirable little Cur.—472. His good generalship with Wild Hog. —473. The moral of the Story; in Note, Guinea chicks; Guinea birds' eggs, how taken. Cross with Muscovy Drake.—474, 475. Quantity of fish at Newfoundland. Dog Fishing.—476. Sir H——d D——s.—477 to 480. Newfoundland fetching back Fox.—481. Sir George B——k, R.N.—482 to 488. His Terrier "Muta" leading him to Musk Bull.—489. His Sketch of the Scene.—490. Lord M——f; the dogs "Captain" and "Suwarrow."—491. Dot-and-go-one, with his old Pointer.—492. How fairly done by "Captain."—493. Breakers, not dogs, in fault; they could be taught anything.—494. "Rap" (a Pointer) hunting covers with Springers and Terriers.—495. "Shot" (a Pointer), on alternate days, hunting with Hounds and standing at Birds.—496. How accounted for.—497. Affection an incentive to exertion; Dropper alternately pointing Grouse and Snipe; Grouse-dog to be rated when noticing Snipe. – 498. Capital Dropper from Russian Setter; difficulty of procuring Russian Setters.—499. Bet respecting superiority of two Keepers in the Highlands; how decided.—500. High-priced dogs ought to be highly broken.

444. BEARS of the common species which we often see led about, are very numerous in the hilly districts of some parts of India. In rocky, nearly inaccessible places, the natives hunt them with a strong-set wiry dog. This dog is trained to watch for his opportunity, and leap very high upon the chest of the bear, and seize his throat. You would, perhaps, think this the most disadvantageous position which the dog could select, enabling Bruin to crush him in his powerful embrace. Not so. The well-instructed creature draws himself up so high that the bear, in lieu of crushing his ribs, merely presses his hips,—and the bear's arms, instead of injuring his opponent are often his best protection; for the animals frequently come rolling together to the foot of the hill, where the hunters despatch poor Bruin with their spears.

445. In other parts of India the natives chase the wild hog with

a coarse dog of the Polygar breed. The dog is taught to seize the hog between the hind legs when he has turned his head to meet some other assailant, and to retain the hold until the hunters come up.

446. Talking of India, however, I cannot help digressing. Why should not more Europeans residing in that country, have dogs as well-trained for *birds* as the Natives have for the bear and hog? I have often thought what much finer sport I should have enjoyed, when I was serving there, if I had then gained as much experience in dog-breaking as I now have. As too many young fellows, belonging both to the Queen's and Company's service, frequently complain of their inability to kill time—(time which so soon kills them!)—it is a pity more of them do not take to the innocent amusement of dog-breaking. The broiling sun * makes all game lie so close in India (except very early in the morning, and towards the close of day) that the best beaters, unless the number be unusually great, leave nearly a dozen head of game behind them for every one that is sprung, especially in jungly ground. The evil is partially, I allow, but very partially, remedied in grass-land, by attaching numerous little bells to the long cord carried by the line of beaters. I have heard of this plan being pursued in England in the absence of dogs, or when the scent was unusually bad.

447. The object at that time of my especial envy was a nondescript belonging to an officer of the Company's service, with whom I used occasionally to shoot near Belgaum. The animal had, I fancy, some cross of pointer in his composition; so little, however, that he never pretended to point. He used just to "feather" feebly when he happened to get near any game; and as he was a wretchedly slow potterer, and never strayed (for hunting it could not be called) far from his master, all that he did put up was well within gun-range. His owner thus got nearly twice as many shots as any of his companions. How much his sport would have been increased had he possessed a good dog!

448. Now there are some native dogs † in India with not a bad nose (those, for instance, which are employed to hunt the porcupine at night), and a breed from them with an European pointer ‡ would,

---

* We speak not of the delightful Neilgherry hills, nor the valleys of the magnificent Himalaya mountains.

† The really wild dogs of India,—the Dhole,—hunt by nose, and in packs.

‡ Pointer rather than setter, not only on account of his shorter coat, but because his nose seems better suited to a hot climate. This cross would be hardy; and prove extremely useful when the grain fields are cut; but in high grass and strong jungle a team of Clumbers would be invaluable. They could not, however, be kept healthy in the low, hot lands. We must naturally expect that in the cool parts of India the true English pointer (or setter) would be found more serviceable than the best cross. For those who are fond of coursing in India what a pity it is that it should be so difficult to procure good Arab-greyhounds. Whilst

doubtless, prove extremely useful. Their strength of constitution would compensate for acknowledged inferiority in every other respect. A cross with the Spanish Don would probably be the best, and the easiest broken in, as he is so steady and full of point. But the Hidalgo would be of little service out of the kennel. From his natural inactivity and weight, he would soon knock up under an Indian sun. Three or four pups would be enough for the dam to rear. Those most like the sire should be preserved; and they might be kept in good health, if they were occasionally treated to a *little* calomel overnight, with castor oil in the morning, and allowed full liberty to run about for an hour every morning and evening. I knew some greyhounds of a purely English breed, but born in the country, which were thus maintained in capital health. They belonged to the only litter that the mother ever had. The climate, which is generally fatal to England-born dogs, killed both the parents within a year after their arrival in India. It is best that the pups should be whelped in the latter part of the year, as they would then acquire some strength before the setting in of the hottest weather, and be of an age to commence hunting at the beginning of the following cool season. The companionship of dogs in the jungle adds much to the security of the pedestrians. A timid yelp or a clamorous bark gives timely notice of the vicinity of every disagreeable, dangerous neighbour, and enables the sportsman to take a cool deliberate aim, instead of having to make a hurried snapshot at some stealthy panther or tiger, or the far more formidable foe, a solitary buffalo. The habit of placing the fore-finger alongside the stock, and not letting it touch the trigger, until the moment of firing, proves very valuable in these critical circumstances. Many a barrel has gone off, even in the hands of an old sportsman, before he properly covered some vital part of his first royal tiger. The certainty of ignition afforded by a detonator gives great confidence to the present generation of sportsmen. Even in the wettest weather, the waterproof caps manufactured by Eley and others, seem to insure an instantaneous fire.

449. Great presence of mind in moments of unforeseen, sudden peril is undoubtedly a gift; but calmness and self-possession, fortunately for sportsmen seeking "large game" (burrah shicar), as it is technically termed in India, can be acquired by reflection and habit.

450. A friend and old fellow-passenger of mine, one of the Colonels K——g,—a name that will long be remembered at Hythe —evinced in 1816 as much coolness as I ever heard of. He was

I was in the country, but I speak of many years ago, I never saw a decent one. A far better description of dog, and one which would keep healthy in the hottest weather, might be imported (if expense was no consideration) from the upper parts of Arabia, where an admirable, short-coated greyhound is reared for different kinds of coursing. The best dogs are greatly valued, and it is a question whether our noble breed is not originally derived from this stock.

then on the staff at Ceylon, and used, while accompanying the Governor on his annual tour throughout the island, to have magnificent sport in places rarely visited by Europeans. Indeed, his character as a slayer of elephants was so fully established that he was often called "elephant-king."

451. On the party arriving one morning within the Mahagampattoo district, the Governor said to K——g, "Surely you will not attack the desperate brute that lately killed those villagers and the two letter-carriers?" The sportsmen modestly replied, "I cannot say, sir; perhaps I may." Now it is well known that a rogue-elephant is always a formidable animal; but one *recently* driven from a herd by a stronger bull is particularly dangerous. In his malignant rage he often wantonly attacks whatever he sees; and there are several instances of his having displayed extraordinary patience in waiting for imprisoned men who had climbed into trees, or retreated into caves, to avoid his fury.

452. The elephant the Governor referred to was, at that time, the terror of the surrounding neighbourhood; for when maddened by jealousy and rage at being expelled after a severe conflict from the harem, and smarting from the blows and wounds inflicted by his more powerful rival, he had ventured to attack an unfortunate labourer, and finding how slight was the resistance offered, he had since sought opportunities for wreaking his vengeance on man, of whom he had now lost all his former instinctive dread.

453. About four o'clock, as the Governor, Lady B——g, and the staff, &c., were seated at dinner, which was nearly over, a message that caused some excitement among the hearers was delivered to K——g. The Governor inquired about it. K——g explained that the Shircarree set as a watch had reported that the much dreaded "Rogue" had just left the jungle and appeared upon the plain. K——g asked leave to attack him. Lady B——g begged that, escorted by a few gentlemen, she might be allowed to watch his proceedings from some safe spot. This K——g acceded to, but stipulated that he was then to be left entirely to himself. On getting a view of the low ground, and observing several herds of elephants scattered over the extensive plain, her ladyship became nervous, and returned to the encampment. Her brother, Mr. B——t and Mr. G. (now living in London) remained; and K——g placed them in a secure position amidst some trees standing too close together to admit of the elephant's forcing his large body through, should he be merely wounded, and perchance take that direction.

454. After carefully examining the localities, K——g made a détour to prevent the "Rogue" from winding him. There was some brushwood, but no trees, to cover his approach. The vindictive solitary animal was apparently brooding over his wrongs in an open space rich with the luxuriant vegetation consequent on tropical rains. He began to feed, striking the ground with each fore-foot alternately, in order to loosen the grass from the soil. He then collected the herbage with his trunk; but before carrying the mass to his

mouth, shook it carefully to free the roots from earth. This gave K——g the opportunity, stealthily and creeping low, to get undetected about twenty paces in rear of him. There he knelt and anxiously awaited the turn of the head that should expose some spot not completely protecting the brain.

455. Long did he watch, for the elephant, when not engaged in feeding, stood motionless, save an occasional whisk of his cord-like tail, or the flopping of his huge ears. At times, however, he would slightly bend his head when with his proboscis scattering sand over his body, in order to drive off some troublesome insect; at which moment the hopeful sportsman would noiselessly cock his piece, but only to again half cock it in disappointment.

456. Messrs. B. and G. became impatient. They fancied the elephant must have stolen away; and a peacock happening to fly over their heads, they fired at it. On hearing the noise, the elephant wheeled, and perceived K——g. He curled his trunk under his neck, lowered his head, and charged. The most vulnerable spot was thus presented. K——g's barrel was deliberately poised,—a cool aim taken, and the trigger pulled;—but it yielded not! K——g felt, he told me, "a choking sensation"—certain death was before him; but instantly remembering that he had replaced the piece on half-cock, he brought it from his shoulder—full-cocked it—raised it again to level—and with unshaken nerve, and unerring precision, a second time covered the vulnerable spot. Down with a tremendous crash dropped the ponderous brute, first on his knees, then on his chest; and with such speed was he charging that he almost made a complete somerset in the act of falling stone dead near the feet of his comparatively puny conqueror—vanquished by skill and cool intrepidity.

457. The party on descending found K——g endeavouring to climb up the enormous carcass. They feared the animal might be only stunned, but K——g satisfied them by probing to its brain with his ramrod in the direction the bullet had taken.

458. Colonel W. (the Q. Master General), who was of the party, made a spirited sketch of the scene. I have more than once admired it. It is admirably done in red chalk. K——g is seen standing upon the prostrate elephant, and a number of the natives are represented in their picturesque costumes, making grateful salaams to the "bravo sahib" who had slain their formidable enemy. Underneath the sketch is written "The Mighty King."

459. My friend's nerves were so little affected by his narrow escape that he killed two more elephants the same evening, and wounded another. It was a long shot across the river. The animal was feeding. K——g waited to aim until he could bring its temple so low as to align with the elbow, when the head would be in a favourable position for a well-directed ball to penetrate to the brain. But the two oz. bullet missed the temple; it, however, struck the elbow and fractured the bone. Darkness was gradually coming on,—the river was full of alligators,—there was no bridge,—and K——g was unwillingly compelled to defer despatching the

poor creature until daylight the next morning. He left it ineffectually endeavouring to make use of the fractured limb by frequently lifting it with his trunk and placing it in front.

THE MIGHTY KING.—Par. 458.

460. Colonel W., whose artistic sketch shows that he was an undeniable hand at the pencil, whatever he might be with the rifle, was ambitious of being able to say he had killed an elephant. He, therefore, begged leave to give the wounded animal its *coup de grace*. It was found wallowing in an adjacent buffalo hole. Colonel W. got within twelve yards of it, but bespattered by the mud the disabled beast threw over him—the novel and only defence it could make—his aim was so uncertain, that, after all, K——g had to put the sufferer out of its misery.

461. Colonel W.'s ambition recals to my mind a singular advertisement, though I cannot think that even he would have answered it had he been in London at the time. It appeared in the papers many years ago, but was too ludicrous not to be still in the recollection of many. A perfumer in Bishopsgate Street Without, gave notice in conspicuous characters " to SPORTSMEN," that a splendid Bear was to be killed on his premises, at which they might have a shot by paying,—I now forget what exact sum.

462. I am told that an examination of the skulls of the Asiatic and African elephants would show a marked difference between the two, and explain why the latter animal cannot be instantaneously killed. In the Asiatic elephant there is a spot about the size of a man's hand between and somewhat above the eyes, where a bullet

COOL AS A CUCUMBER.

Made the Caffre boy behind him pull the deadly trigger."—Par. 464.

can easily penetrate to the brain when the head is carried low; whereas the brain, it is said, of the African elephant is as effectually guarded on the forehead as elsewhere. This might be inferred from a perusal of Gordon Cumming's exciting book. Murray would not print many of the startling anecdotes related in the manuscript, fearing they might throw discredit upon the work. But it is, I think, to be regretted that he did not trust more to the discernment of the public; and to the strong internal evidence of truthfulness afforded in the descriptions given of the habits of the various beasts which the author had singular opportunities of observing.

463. The mention of Gordon Cumming's name, which is naturally associated with feats of cool daring, leads one to speak of an old fellow-sportsman of his at the Cape of Good Hope. Doubtless there are men of whom it may be almost averred that they know not the sensation of fear. Of this number was Gordon Cumming's friend Captain G. B. M——e of the 45th. Alas! we must say "was," for that brave heart has ceased to beat.

464. Whilst quartered with his regiment at the Cape, M——e took constant opportunities of encountering single-handed the real lords of the forest in their own wild domain; and numerous are the stories told by his brother officers of his hair-breadth escapes. Gordon Cumming and he often shot together; and I have heard it said that at a time when his left arm was so much injured as to be perfectly useless, he went close up to a lion, which was standing over Cumming's prostrate body, and with his right hand aiming at the animal's heart made the Caffre boy behind him pull the deadly trigger. And does not the little fellow's heroic conduct, who placed such implicit confidence in his master's address and nerve, claim much of our admiration!

465. M——e's courage was reckless. Having more than once failed in getting a shot at a formidable lion which had committed great ravages, and was reported to be of immense size, he determined upon tracking the beast to his rocky fastness, and forcing him to a hand-to-hand combat in his very den. One morning a recent spoor * enabled him to find the cave he sought, the entrance of which was so contracted that in order not wholly to exclude the light, he was compelled to lie down and crawl in upon his elbows. Pushing the muzzle of his gun before him, slowly, inch by inch he crept on, expecting every moment to see the large, glaring, cat-like eye-balls, or to hear the menacing growl. His sight becoming more accustomed to the gloom, he was enabled to scan every crevice, and was satisfied that the master of the habitation could not have yet returned from his nocturnal rambles. Bones of large size were strewn about, as well as others whose suspicious appearance prompted the involuntary reflection that the absent animal was in very truth the dreaded "man-eater" who had so long baffled all pursuit.

---

* Impression of feet.

Nothing daunted, but rather aroused by the thought to an increased determination to destroy the monster, M——e resolved quietly to await his return.

466. Hour after hour passes. The shades of evening fall. The bark of the jackal and the howlings of the hyæna, showing the advance of night, meet his ear,—but not the longed-for roar of the expected lion. Surely he will again seek his lair while the bright moon yet favours the intrepid sportsman. No—he comes not. Complete darkness sets in—darkness intense in that deep recess ;—but ere long the discordant screams of the peacock announce the early dawn, and after a while the hot beams of the sun again hush all into silence, save the busy hum of innumerable insects. Horrible suspense ! The weary hours drag on—still he returns not ; and there still sits M——e, but not the man he was. Anxious excitement—want of sleep—and, above all, the deprivation of bodily stimulants, have done their work. He was agitated and unnerved. To quote his own words when afterwards recounting the adventure, he " would have given worlds to have been away, or to have had a flask of brandy." What madness, he thought, could have tempted him to seek such certain destruction ? Had the taint of his feet raised the animal's suspicions ? Was his presence detected ? And was the shaggy monster watching outside, crouching low, ready to spring when his victim should be forced by hunger to emerge ? Quit he dare not ; yet to remain with nerves unstrung was terrible. In his diseased state of mind imagination conjured up awfully harrowing scenes in which man in his feebleness had succumbed ;—and was it really decreed that his crushed bones should mingle unhonoured and unnoticed with the heap around him ? Hours that seemed days of torture passed away—again the sun reached the zenith—again it sets—and again it shines upon the remains of huge limbs, and upon those of slighter mould that bear a fearfully close resemblance to his own ! The sun has sunk behind the summit of the distant hills, already the short twilight commences. Can he survive another night of horrors, or shall he, risking ˏall, rush forth.

467. Suddenly a deep and angry growl is heard. It acts as music upon his soul—his nerves are at once restored to their pristine firmness—strong is his pulse—steady his hand ; his countenance lights up with hope and animation ; and as the cave is darkened by the entrance of its legitimate but no longer dreaded owner, the favourite barrels are deliberately levelled with the accustomed deadly aim.

468. The Hindoos, who are naturally an inoffensive timid race, have an almost fabulous reverence for the courage of Europeans, whom they often term fighting devils—an epithet applied in no disparaging way, but, on the contrary, as the highest of compliments. The Assistant-surgeon (B——h) and a Lieutenant (D——n), of a regiment to which I once belonged on the Indian establishment, were travelling up the country. On arriving early one morning at their breakfast tent (which had been sent forward as usual the

A REGULAR BORE.

"Dropped upon his right knee,—brought his firelock to the charging position."—Par. 468.

preceding evening), they were met by the Cutwal and principal men of the small village, bearing a trifling present of fruit. After many salaams, the deputation said that the villagers were in the greatest distress,—that an enormous wild boar and a sow had taken up their abode in the neighbouring sugar plantation,—that the crop was fully ripe, but that whenever the labourers ventured in to cut the canes they were driven out by a charge of the swine ; that the whole body, women as well as men, had united more than once in an attempt to alarm the intruders with the noise of tomtoms, cholera horns, firing of matchlocks, &c., but that the unclean brutes would not leave, and that the inhabitants had nearly resigned all hope of saving the crop, when they had the happiness of hearing that an English officer was expected, who, as a matter of course, could have no objection to shoot the vicious animals. D——n and B——h willingly consented to start directly after breakfast. The former was a keen sportsman, but the latter had never fired a gun ; however, he said he would do his best ; and being furnished with an old musket, he sallied forth "at fixed bayonets." Almost the moment they entered the cover a crashing noise warned them to be on their guard. The boar, without an instant's hesitation, rushed at the invaders, making a special selection of the individual least accustomed to arms. B——h, in no way daunted, dropped upon his right knee,—brought his firelock to the charging position,—and calmly waited to pull trigger until the formidable beast was so close upon the bayonet, that he knocked the piece out of B——h's grasp, and sent him spinning heels over head. On regaining his feet, B——h found that his formidable adversary was already dead ; the bayonet, much bent in the encounter, was buried deep in his huge chest ; and subsequent examination showed that the ball had severed his heart into two nearly equal portions. The sow had apparently quickly become aware of the mischance that had befallen her mate, for she ignominiously fled from the field at her best pace. In reply to the thanks, congratulations, and encomiums bestowed upon the worthy Assistant-surgeon for his success and admirable coolness, he quietly observed, that all was well that ended well ; that it was an awful beast ; and that he would take precious good care never voluntarily to encounter such another ;—that he had had his first shot, and fervently hoped it would be his last.

469. To hark-back, however, to our subject. Greyhounds of a large rough kind are trained in some parts of Australia to course the kangaroo. A kangaroo when he is brought to bay* would disable a great number of dogs, however bold and strong they might be, should they incautiously attack him in front : for while he is sitting upon his hind quarters, or standing upright, he can by one blow, or rather strike of his hind-leg, which is furnished with huge claws, tear open the strongest greyhound from the chest downwards ; and many dogs have been thus killed. As soon, therefore, as a large kangaroo is seen, a *well-educated* brace of greyhounds are

---

* In general he knowingly places his back against a tree.

slipped. For some time, by a succession of enormous bounds, the animal keeps far ahead of his pursuers—especially when running up hill, where he is as much favoured by his long hind-legs as a hare is by hers,—and all are soon lost to the sight of unmounted hunters. When he has been overtaken and brought to bay, one of the trained dogs keeps him there; and this he does barking round and round him, threatening every moment to fly at him. The other dog returns to the hunters, and leads them to the spot where his companion is detaining the kangaroo: and so completely does the noisy assailant engage the attention of the unfortunate beast, that the hunters are frequently enabled to approach unperceived, and stun him with a blow over the head. An old kangaroo is there termed by the hunters "an old man;"* the flesh of a young one is, however, by many considered very delicate eating. A powerful dog will kill a small kangaroo single-handed; and if properly taught, will then seek for his master, and conduct him to the body.

470. In Persia and many parts of the East greyhounds are taught to assist the falcon in the capture of deer. When brought within good view of a herd the bird is flown, and at the same moment the dog is slipped. The rapid sweep of the falcon soon carries him far in advance. It is the falcon who makes the selection of the intended victim,—which appears to be a matter of chance,—and a properly-trained greyhound will give chase to none other, however temptingly close the alarmed animals may pass him. The falcon is instructed to aim at the head only of the gazelle, who soon becomes bewildered; sometimes receiving considerable injury from the quick stroke of its daring adversary. Before long the gazelle is overtaken by the greyhound. It is not always easy to teach a dog to avoid injuring the bird, which is so intent upon its prey as utterly to disregard the approach of the hound. Death would probably be the penalty adjudged to him for so heinous an offence; for a well-trained falcon is of great value. You can readily imagine that neither it nor the greyhound could be properly broken unless the instructor possessed much judgment and perseverance. The sport is very exciting; but the spectator must be well-mounted, and ride boldly who would closely watch the swift, varying evolutions of the assailing party, and the sudden evasions of the helpless defendant. The education of this falcon is conducted on the same principle as that of the cheeta.—(Note to 284.) The lure is a stuffed gazelle. It is placed at gradually increased distances. The raw meat is fixed between its eyes, and the concluding lessons terminate with the sacrifice of a few tame or maimed deer; a portion of whose warm flesh is given to the bird as a reward for his aid in recapturing the unfortunate creatures.

471. An officer, quartered at Antigua, used occasionally to obtain permission to shoot on an island called Barbuda, in the possession of Sir Bethel Codrington. It is a strange spot,—a coral rock just

---

* The North American trappers apply the same term to an old beaver.

THERE ARE BOUNDS TO SPORT.

"By a succession of enormous bounds, the animal keeps far ahead."—Par. 469

emerging from the sea, its highest point being no more than one hundred and twenty feet above the water. The horses, cattle, and everything on the island are wild, save the manager and two overseers, its only white inhabitants. The former (I speak of the year 1835) was a splendidly built man, not very refined, but full of energy, an excellent shot, and an indefatigable sportsman. No Indian had a keener eye for a trail. A turned leaf or a broken twig told him the path, and almost the distance, of the hog or deer which he was pursuing through the dark intricacies of stunted trees, cactus, and long grass, with which the island is, in a great measure, covered. A small mangy-looking mongrel, with a long thin muzzle, and lanky body, always accompanied him. The sagacity of this brute, and his powers of scenting game, were most remarkable. He generally walked about ten yards in front of his master, and suddenly throwing his nose high in the air, would quicken his pace, and trot up wind. Gradually again his pace would slacken,—the trot was changed to a walk, the walk to stealthy creeping, when he would raise each foot with the greatest caution, putting it down as noiselessly as though shod with velvet, most carefully avoiding the crisp leaves and dry twigs, for fear of making the slightest sound. Presently he would stand stock-still (the inclination to point is, I think, more general among dogs than many men suppose) and look at his master; but he never did this unless the game was well within shot. His master would now peer closely round, and his eagle-eye never failed to detect the tip of a horn, or a dappled spot, showing where a fallow-deer was feeding. If there was a flock of Guinea-birds,* (which are numerous in Barbuda,) the sagacious

---

* Guinea-birds being much prized in such of the islands as possess but little game, many are reared at the farms of the planters. The negroes dig up ants' nests, which are disagreeably numerous, and on bringing one into the yard, dash it violently upon the ground, when the chicks eagerly scramble for the contents, — the insects *and* the eggs. By the bye, much is said about the difficulty of taking eggs from Guinea-birds without making them abandon their nests. The would-be purloiner, in answer to his inquiries, is often recommended to keep as far as possible from the nest; and, that it may in no way be contaminated by his touch, to remove the eggs during the absence of the birds with an iron or silver spoon, having a long stick attached to it as a handle;—but it is seldom told him,—and therein lies the real secret,—that, in addition to such precautions, he never ought to rob a nest without leaving *at the least* three eggs. It is surprising how many may in this way be taken. I know of a single pair of guinea-birds being thus robbed in one spring of no less than eighty-four.

Having got into a Creole's poultry-yard, I am unwilling to quit it without observing, that few better birds are reared than his cross between common ducks and a Muscovy drake. It is found necessary carefully to guard against the ungainly gentleman's having any rival of the ordinary breed in the neighbourhood, for if the opportunity were afforded them, the ladies would to a certainty forsake their cumbrous lord for

little creature would wait until the gun was close to him, and then, to prevent their running, would dash in and spring them.

472. If a hog was in the wind, the cur dashed off immediately, following the animal until it stopped at bay, when a shrill bark

WARM GREETING OF A GREAT 'BORE.'—Par. 472.

warned the sportsman of the scene of action. The tiny animal had many a scar on his rugged hide, cut by hogs, with whose ears and heels he frequently took liberties; but, up to the time that the officer left that part of the world, the dog had escaped serious injury by his good generalship and activity. He certainly had a very just estimate of his own physical powers, for with young porkers he stood on little ceremony, rushing into them at once, and worrying and holding them until the hunter came to his assistance.

473. You might draw a useful moral from this long story by considering for a moment what kind of sport our Creole acquaintance would have had, and what number of Guinea-birds, wild hogs, and deer (capital shot as he was) he would have killed in the year, had

the more active commoner. Although the true Muscovy is very coarse eating, the Hybrid is as much an improvement upon the flavour as it is upon the size of the common duck. I have known the birds to be reared in this country, and often wondered that the plan was not more generally pursued.

he been obliged to *speak* to the little cur when hunting. The calculation, I fancy, would not be found difficult from the number of figures employed in the enumeration.

474. You may think the foregoing a tough yarn, but I have now in my mind an instance of sagacity in a Newfoundland, apparently so much less entitled to credence, that I should be afraid to tell it (though the breed is justly celebrated for its remarkable docility and intelligence), if its truth could not be vouched for by Capt. L——n, one of the best officers in the navy; and who, when I had the gratification of sailing with him, commanded that noble ship, the "Vengeance."

475. At certain seasons of the year the streams in some parts of North America, not far from the coast, are filled with fish to an extent you could scarcely believe, unless you had witnessed it—and now comes the Munchausen story. A real Newfoundland, belonging to a farmer who lived near one of those streams, used, at such times, to keep the house well supplied with fish. He thus managed it:— He was perfectly black, with the exception of a white fore-foot, and

INVITATION TO A "WHITE-BAIT" DINNER.—Par. 475.

for hours together he would remain almost immoveable on a small rock which projected into the stream, keeping his white foot hanging over the ledge as a lure to the fish. He remained so stationary that it acted as a very attractive bait; and whenever curiosity or hunger tempted any unwary fish to approach too close, the dog plunged in, seized his victim, and carried him off to the foot of a neighbouring tree; and, on a successful day, he would catch a great number.

476. I have another anecdote of a young Newfoundland, told me by General Sir H——d D——s, to whose scientific attainments the two sister-services, the army and the navy, are both so greatly indebted. He bred the dog in America, having most fortunately taken the dam from England; for, to her address in swimming, and willingness to "fetch," he and his surviving shipwrecked companions were, under Providence, chiefly indebted for securing many pieces of salt pork that had drifted from the ill-fated vessel, and which constituted their principal food during their six weeks' miserable detention on an uninhabited island.

477. At a station where he was afterwards quartered as a subaltern, in '98, not far from the falls of Niagara, the soldiers kept a tame fox. The animal's kennel was an old cask, to which he was attached by a long line and swivel. The Newfoundland and the fox soon scraped an acquaintance, which, in due course, ripened into an intimacy.

478. One day that Sir H——d went to the barracks, not seeing anything of the fox, he gave the barrel a kick, saying to a man standing by, "Your fox is gone!" This sudden knock at the back-door of his house so alarmed the sleeping inmate, that he bolted forth with such violence as to snap the light cord. Off he ran. The soldiers felt assured that he would return, but Sir H——d, who closely watched the frightened animal, had the vexation of observing that he made direct for the woods.

479. Sir H——d bethought him to hie on Neptune after Reynard, on the chance of the friends coming back together in amicable converse. It would, however, appear that the attractions of kindred (more probably of freedom) had greater influence than the claims of friendship; for, instead of the Newfoundland's returning with Pug as a *voluntary* companion, after a time, to the surprise and delight of many spectators, the dog was descried, with the end of the rope in his mouth, forcibly dragging along the disappointed fox, who was struggling, manfully but fruitlessly, against a fresh introduction to his military quarters.

480. "Nep" was properly lauded and caressed for his sagacity; and Sir H——d was so satisfied that he would always fetch back the fox perfectly uninjured and unworried, however much excited in the chase, that the next day, after turning out Reynard, he permitted the officers to animate and halloo on the dog to their utmost. When slipped, though all eagerness for the fun in hand, "Nep" took up the trail most accurately, hunted it correctly, and in due course, agreeably to his owner's predictions, dragged back the poor prisoner in triumph, having, as on the previous occasion, merely seized the extremity of the cord.

BRINGING HOME THE BRUSH.

"The dog was descried, with the end of the rope in his mouth, forcibly dragging along the disappointed fox."—Par. 479.

481. For the following anecdote I am indebted to Sir G——e B——k, the intrepid and scientific navigator, whose name will be mentioned as long as British deeds of the present century are cited, descriptive of bold daring and perseverance in surmounting the greatest difficulties.

482. " On the 8th of September, 1834, after a laborious morning spent in ascending a part of the Thlew-ĕe-chōh-dezeth, or Back River, we were detained by the portage of the 'Cascades.' While the men were actively employed in carrying the things across, I was equally busy in the tent, working a series of observations which had just been obtained for longitude, &c.

483. " A little dog, a species of terrier, called 'Muta' from her silent, quiet habits, was my only companion. She had been the faithful follower of my party to the polar sea, and, independently of her value as a good watch, was not only a pet of mine, but had managed to become a great favourite with all the others.

484. " Muta had left the tent for upwards of an hour, but returned in great haste, bustled about inside, rubbed against me, and with eyes bright and eager stood looking in my face. Finding I paid no attention to her, she rushed out—came back, however, quickly; and standing over the gun, which was near me, again looked imploringly at me. Once more she sprung outside, and barked anxiously.

485. " Still I continued my calculations; and perhaps twenty minutes might have elapsed when Muta, warm and panting, leapt upon me—ran to the gun—then to the opening of the tent, and evinced such very unusual restlessness that I could not help fancying something must be wrong. Being alone, I thought it well to be prepared, and accordingly put a ball into my second barrel,—there always was one in the first,—and followed her out.

486. " Her joy was unbounded, and perfectly noiselessly she led me such a distance that I thought she was deceiving me, and I chidingly told her so; but she still persisted in going forward, pleased though excited. I walked on a little further, when conceiving I was but losing my time I turned back. She ran round to intercept me, and so earnestly resisted my attempts to retrace my steps, that I yielded to the appeal, and again consented to accompany her.

487. " She brought me to the edge of a gully, fully half-a-mile from the tent, partly sheltered by willows. Here she stopped. Thinking she had tricked me, I began to reproach her, on which she darted like lightning into the underwood, barking furiously, when, to my great surprise, out rushed a large musk bull, which unluckily I only wounded, to Muta's manifest disappointment, and my own great annoyance.

488. " Poor Muta's sad fate is recorded in the 462d page of my Narrative of the Arctic Land Expedition of 1833-4-5, and she may be seen in the mouth of the white wolf that killed her, safely housed in a glass case within the walls of the United Service Institution."

489. At my request, Sir G——e kindly drew the spirited sketch, which I have had engraved, of the scene he so vividly described.

SCENE ON THE 'THLEW-EE-CHOH-DEZETH.'—Par. 487.

490. Dining one day at the hospitable board of Lord M——f, he told me, that many years ago an uncle of his, an excellent sportsman, lent him a brace of short-haired English dogs, yclept "Captain" and "Suwarrow,"—martial names! yet not inappropriate, you will think, when you hear some of their feats of strategy. "Captain," moreover, had other warlike propensities; he was a close-knit, powerful dog, and there was no peace in any kennel he ever entered until its boldest inmates had conceded to him all the privileges of commander-in-chief.

491. Lord M——f and a friend had obtained permission to shoot on a considerable part of an extensive valley in Perthshire, lying at the foot of "Schichallion;" but unfortunately they had not the sole right,—a similar favour had been granted to a lame man, but no *lame* sportsman, who for some days greatly annoyed them. Start when they would, and take what line they might, Dot-and-go-one with his old pointer was sure to be on the heather before them.

492. "Captain" and "Suwarrow" bore this for some time with greater *apparent* patience than the gentlemen. On one occasion, however, when the inferiority of the ground they were compelled to take was more than usually obvious, "Captain's" blood was fairly

roused,—he could stand it no longer. Leaving his companion, he crossed at full speed to the other side of the valley,—not, as might possibly be surmised, to wreak his vengeance upon the old pointer, —but, strange to say, to hunt at his best pace the good ground in front of his rival, and *raise*, not *point*, every grouse he could find. When he conceived he had done enough mischief, or perhaps thought he had driven a fair proportion of birds to Lord M——f's side of the valley, he quietly returned to his usual duties—duties which, be it remarked, he always performed most steadily. As an evidence —on the evening of that very day, instead of *pointing*, as was his wont, he *dropped*, on unexpectedly getting into the midst of a pack, and did not stir an inch until all the birds had successively risen. You will surely think *his* right to be considered a first-rate tactician is fully proved:—when you read 530, you will perhaps allow that "Suwarrow" has an equally good, if not superior, claim to the title.

493. And will not these evidences of great sagacity and, except in the few last cases, instances of good breaking—and they might be multiplied, I was nearly saying, *ad infinitum*, [for every sportsman could furnish some—convince you, that it is our own fault, if our high-bred pointers, setters, and retrievers (which can scarcely be surpassed in docility and intelligence), are indifferently educated? It is not that *they* cannot understand, but that *we*, either for want of patience or reflection, cannot make ourselves understood. The fault is *ours*, not *theirs*. They might, indeed, almost be taught anything —even things quite opposed to their nature—if we did but act more reasonably, and were not in most cases supinely content to stop so very far short of perfection, apparently grudging a little additional trouble.

494. In the "Sporting Magazine" for May, 1834, a likeness is given of an admirable pointer named "Rap," of whom it is recorded that "he often hunted in the woods with springers and terriers, all which time he played in both characters, and in both excelled. No sooner, however, had he returned to his especial occupation, as a pointer, than he became as steady as ever."

495. I knew intimately an excellent shot (T. F——e, of the 76th), who, some years ago, during one of the many disturbances in County Tipperary, was quartered with a detachment of men at a gentleman's house, in rather a wild part of the country. The proprietor kept a small scratch-pack of harriers, with which the officer's pointer, called Shot, became very intimate. When the hunting season commenced, Shot accompanied them to the field, joined in the chase, and performed uncommonly well; indeed, he frequently led the pack, and yet, singular to say, he continued as steady as possible when he was shot to. As you may well suppose, it was a source of much fun and laughter to the Nimrods to see, regularly hunting with their harriers, a dog which possibly had stanchly pointed at birds the preceding day.

496. Though I had bred and educated him myself,—he was the dog of which I spoke (139) as behaving so well on the Galtee moun-

T

tains when first shown game,—no one could be more surprised than I was at hearing of so novel a display of intelligence. It is partly to be accounted for by the fact, that none of his high animal spirits and self-confidence had been destroyed by severity in breaking. I can conscientiously aver that I do not think I whipped him more than twice in the whole course of his training, and I am certain not once harshly; and his next owner was equally kind,—I might more correctly say, equally judicious.

497. As a dog that loves you, and possesses proper self-confidence, —though, at the same time, he entertains due respect for your authority,—will always exert himself to the best of his abilities to please, it remains but for you to direct those abilities aright. "Shot," you see, *pointed* and *hunted* on alternate days. A little bitch, that I knew, would, on the same day, set alternately different kinds of game, according to the wishes of her master. She belonged to a Mr. B———e, near Templemore, and, with the exception that she had no established judicious range, was one of the most killing dogs to be met with in a long drive. She was an ugly, short-tailed dropper; in appearance not worth three half-crowns. She was capital on snipe; but on the bogs, if you were in expectation of meeting with grouse, and, in consequence, refused to fire at one or two snipes, and slightly scolded her for pointing them, she would immediately leave off noticing them, confining herself entirely to hunting for grouse. If you shot a snipe, and showed it to her, she would immediately recommence seeking for the long-bills. But this would be a dangerous lesson to teach a dog ever likely to be required on the moors. A dog trained for grouse should invariably be rated whenever he notices snipe; lest, after toiling up the side of a mountain on a broiling day, in expectation of hearing the exciting "Whirr-r whirr-r," you be only greeted with the disappointing "Skeap, skeap." On the other hand, if you live in the lowlands, and think you may hereafter wish to take your dog out snipe-shooting, make him occasionally point one in the early part of his education. It is often difficult to bring a partridge-dog to notice snipe, whereas a snipe-dog will readily acknowledge partridge on account of the stronger scent.

498. Many sportsmen are of opinion that droppers inherit more of the bad than the good qualities of their parents; but occasionally one of a litter, like Mr. B———e's bitch, turns out an admirable dog, and proves a valuable exception to the supposed rule. Some time since I heard an officer of the Eng'neers expatiating upon the excellent qualities of a dropper (by his pointer "Guy") out of a Russian setter, which, as he said, belonged to me many years ago: but he was mistaken. I never possessed one. I wish I had; for I hear the breed is capital,—that they are very easily broken,—are very intelligent,—have excellent noses, and great endurance, but not much speed,—and never forget what has been once taught them: in this respect more resembling pointers than our setters, which are often wild at the beginning of a season. Could we, by judicious crossing, improve them half as much as we did the old heavy

RUSSIAN SETTER.

"Difficult to procure even in Russia of a pure breed."—Par. 498.

Spanish pointer,* what glorious dogs we should possess! It is, however, very difficult to procure them even in Russia of a pure breed; for so few sportsmen in that country think of shooting according to our system, that but little attention is paid to their fine setters.

499. If your patience is not exhausted, you shall hear (as told me by an old commanding officer of mine, Major S——n) how, many years ago, a bet was decided in the Highlands, as to the perfection in dog-breaking attained by two rival keepers. It was in the month of August, and there was plenty of game. The dogs produced by the two competitors performed so brilliantly,—were hunted so noiselessly,—quartered their ground so systematically and independently, —and worked so zealously, yet cautiously, that the awarding of the palm seemed to be a difficult matter. At length one of the keepers obtained the decision of the umpires in his favour by the following feat. He made his three dogs, in obedience to a low whistle and a sign, at a moment when all three were separately setting, retreat from their several points without flushing any of the birds, and take up each other's points, each dog remaining stationary until he was individually shot over. This great command, I suppose, but I cannot assert it positively, must have been gained by much such kennel discipline as is described in 30. It would appear, too, as if a distinct whistle or note had been employed for each dog (505).

500. I only advocate instruction that is really useful; therefore, I merely mention this instance of excellent breaking as another evidence of the great perfection to which our well-bred dogs *can* be brought: and as it is certain they can reach such perfection, I think you will admit that every *high-priced dog* ought to be far better educated than is customary. Indeed, I trust, if you are an enthusiast on the subject, that you will not only agree with me in requiring that he be as fully made as I have described, and as I am of opinion is absolutely necessary (393), but that occasionally you will wish him to be yet further instructed in some of the still higher accomplishments or refinements which, if you are willing, we will now proceed to consider.

---

* Improved as regards shape and action, but not as to stanchness and nose.

CHAPTER XVI.

DISTINGUISHING WHISTLES. "BACKING" THE GUN. RETREAT FROM AND RESUMPTION OF POINT. RANGE UNACCOMPANIED BY GUN. HEADING RUNNING BIRDS.

501. A DISTINGUISHING WHISTLE FOR EACH DOG; disadvantage of employing but one Whistle for several Dogs; supposed Case.—502. Another Case. 503. Third Case.—504. Reader will admit correctness of reasoning.—505. Dissimilar Whistles, or distinct notes on one whistle.—506. Boatswain's Whistle almost a musical instrument.—507. Railway Whistles; Porteous': general Rule for whistling.—508. Porteous' newly-invented Dog Whistles.—509. DOG TO BACK THE GUN; how taught; it creates Caution: in Note, sagacity of Fawn Antelope in concealing itself; want of like sagacity in Pea-fowl. Portable rest for Rifle.—510. Advantage of Dog backing the Gun.—511. American Woodduck.—512. DOG TO RETREAT FROM POINT AND RESUME IT.—513. How taught.—514. Shows dog object for which he is hunted.—515. Not taught too early.—516. Dog's Consciousness of its Object.—517. Pointer doing it spontaneously.—518. Setter which was taught to do it.—519. Surprising author by volunteering the feat.—520. Irish Setter retreating from, and resuming point at Hare.—521. Bitch that barked when pointing and hid in cover.—522. DOG TO HUNT FROM LEEWARD TO WINDWARD, UNACCOMPANIED BY GUN; how taught.—523. A *careful* Dog running down wind would not spring birds.— 524. The great Advantages of the Accomplishment.—525. DOG TO HEAD RUNNING BIRDS; could be taught.—526. Tolfrey's "Sportsman in France." —527. Instance of Dog's spontaneously heading, and thus intercepting, red-legged Partridges.—528, 529. M——l's "Albert" volunteering to head Guinea birds.—530. Lord M——f's "Snwarrow" spontaneously heading running Grouse; then keeping his stern towards them.—531. How accounted for.— 532. Not so extraordinary had the Dog been taught to hunt "unaccompanied by Gun."—533. The accomplishment taught by "lifting;" not commenced first season. In Note, "Niger's" spontaneously running to further side of hedge to drive birds to this side.—534. Could be taught as easily as Shepherds' Collies are instructed.—535. Particularly useful where the red-legged Partridge is found. Shooting in Africa.

A DISTINGUISHING WHISTLE FOR EACH DOG.

501. THOUGH you may have only begun to shoot last season, have you not often wished to attract the attention of one of your two dogs, and make him hunt in a particular part of the field, but, for fear of alarming the

birds, have been unwilling to call out his name, and have felt loth to whistle to him, lest you should bring away at the same time the other dog, who was zealously hunting exactly where you considered him most likely to find birds.

502. Again: have the dogs never been hunting close together instead of pursuing distinct beats; and has it not constantly happened, on your whistling with the view to separate them, that *both* have turned their heads in obedience to the whistle, and *both* on your signal changed the direction of their beat, but still the *two together?* And have you not, in despair of ever parting them by merely whistling and signalling, given the lucky birds (apparently in the most handsome manner, as if scorning to take any ungenerous advantage) fair notice of the approach of the guns by shouting out the name of one of the dogs.

503. Or, if one dog was attentive to the whistle, did he not gradually learn to disregard it from observing that his companion was never chidden for neglecting to obey it?—and did not such laxity more and more confirm both in habits of disobedience?

504. I believe several of my readers will be constrained to answer these questions in the affirmative; and, further, I think their own experience will remind them of many occasions, both on moor and stubble when birds were wild, on which they have wished to attract the notice of a particular dog (perhaps running along a hedge, or pottering over a recent haunt; or hunting down wind towards marked game) by *whistling* instead of calling out his name, but have been unwilling to do so, lest the other dogs should likewise obey the shrill sound to which all were equally accustomed.

505. Now, in breaking young dogs, you could, by

using whistles of dissimilar calls, easily avoid the liability of these evils; and by invariably employing a particular whistle for each dog to summon him separately to his food (30), each would distinguish his own whistle as surely as every dog knows his own master's whistle, and as hounds learn their names. Dogs not only know their own names, but instantly know by the pronunciation when it is uttered by a stranger. To prevent mistakes, each dog's name might be marked on his own whistle. You might have two whistles, of very different sound, on one short stock. Indeed, *one* whistle would be sufficient for two dogs, if you invariably sounded the same two or three sharp short notes for one dog, and as invariably gave a sustained note for the other. Nay, the calls could thus be so diversified, that one whistle might be used for even more than two dogs.

506. Whoever has heard the boatswain of a man-of-war piping all hands on deck, must think his whistle, from the variety of its tones, almost a musical instrument; but it could not well be employed for dogs, as they would not understand it when sounded by any one but their master.

507. Railways have led to the introduction of new whistles. Porteous, the band-master at Chelsea College (whose Light Infantry Field Pipe is well-known to military men), has exercised his ingenious talents in making several, but they are too shrill to be of much service to the sportsman. The acorn (or bell pattern) has, however, a much softer tone, yet it, too, makes an awful noise.

But whatever whistle you choose to employ, be sure, both in and out of the field, to sound it softly whenever the dog is near you. Indeed, you would act judiciously to make it a constant rule, wherever he may be, *never to whistle louder than is really requisite*, otherwise (as I think I before remarked) he will, comparatively speaking, pay little attention to its summons, when, being at a distance, he hears it but faintly.

508. I wrote to Mr. Porteous, explaining how much a whistle was wanted that might be used by the most unmusical person, yet

give distinct unvarying sounds, so that no dog could mistake his own whistle, let it be blown by whom it might. He at once understood what was required, and has invented one with a slide that answers well for two dogs. He told me that he was making further improvements, and expected to contrive one which would answer for as many as three or four dogs. Messrs. Stevens, Darlington Works, Southwark-bridge Road, are the manufacturers.

TO BACK THE GUN.

509. In shooting, especially late in the season, you will often mark down a bird, and feel assured that you stand a better chance of getting a shot at it if the dogs cease hunting whilst you approach it. You can teach your dog to do this by holding up your right hand *behind* you when you mark down a bird, saying at the same time, "Toho," in an earnest, quiet voice, and carrying your gun as if you were prepared to shoot. He will soon begin, I really must say it, to *back you,*— for he actually will be backing you, ludicrous as the expression may sound. After a few times he will do so on the signal, without your speaking at all; and he will be as pleased, as excited, and as stanch, as if he were backing an old dog. Making him "drop" will not effect your object; for, besides that it in no way increases his intelligence, you may wish him to follow at a respectful distance, while you are stealing along the banks of some stream, &c. Ere long he will become as sensible as yourself that any noise would alarm the birds, and you will soon see him picking his steps to avoid the crisp leaves, lest their rustling should betray him. I have even heard of a dog whose admirable caution occasionally led him, when satisfied that his point was observed, to crawl behind a bush, or some other shelter, to screen* himself from the notice of the birds.

* On one occasion, shooting in India, I saw an instance of an animal's endeavouring to hide itself, that always struck me as

510. The acquisition of this accomplishment—and it is easily taught to a young dog previously made steady in backing another (it should not be attempted before)—will often secure you a duck, or other wary bird, which the dog would otherwise, almost to a certainty, spring remarkable from the youth of the creature, and the fact that its usual instincts lead it to seek safety, not in concealment, but in flight. I was looking for a small kind of grouse commonly called there rock-pigeon, when, crowning a small eminence, I unexpectedly came upon a young antelope, about a hundred yards off, that apparently had lost its dam. The country was open and bare, with here and there a few stunted bushes. It instantly ran behind one of these, and there remained while I drew the shot, and had nearly rammed down one of the balls (enclosed in greased cloth) that I constantly carried in my pocket ready for immediate use. I was almost prepared, when off it went. As the ball was nearly home, I forced it down, not liking the trouble of extracting it, and took a random chance shot at the little animal. I could not perceive that it winced, and it was not until it fell that I was aware I had struck it. The ball had passed through its body a little too far behind the shoulder, and somewhat too high—a common fault. It was so thin and poor that it must have been separated for some time from its mother. The want of sagacity evinced by peafowl, when hiding themselves, is strongly contrasted with the intelligence displayed by the fawn. I have known these birds, when alarmed, run their heads into a crevice, leaving the whole of their bodies exposed, and then fancy themselves so effectually protected, as to remain immoveable, until the sportsman got close to them.

When you are hunting, rifle in hand, for large game on an open prairie, or where it is unlikely that you will find a convenient rest, you can carry in your waistcoat pocket, until the moment you require it, not a very bad substitute, in the shape of a piece of string looped at both ends. This string will have been carefully adjusted to exactly such a length that when one loop is slipped over your left foot, and the other loop over the end of the ramrod (near the muzzle), on your bringing up your rifle to the poise, the pull of the string will restrain you from unduly elevating it while taking aim. An ordinary rest prevents your *lowering* the muzzle when in the act of firing—the resistance of the string opposes your *raising* it. The string, however, will not wholly hinder the muzzle from diverging to the right or left,—but in reality it will much prevent such unsteadiness, by permitting your left hand to press strongly upwards against the rifle. In the new drill for firing with the Enfield, the soldier is taught a position which gives him a firm rest for his musket. It is to sit on his right heel (the right knee carried well to the right, and resting on the ground), and to place his left elbow on his left knee. He is taught to take aim a little below the object, and to raise the muzzle very slowly—and to pull the moment he covers the object, having previously well considered what allowance he should make for the influence of the wind.

TELL ME MY HEART (HART) IF THIS BE LOVE.

"And took a random chance shot."—Par. 509, Note.

out of gun-shot. If you should "soho" a hare, and wish to kill one, you will have an excellent opportunity of practising this lesson.

511. In America there is a singular duck, called, from its often alighting on trees, the Wood-duck. I have killed some of these beautiful, fast-flying birds, while they were seated on logs overhanging the water, which I could not have approached within gun-shot had the dog not properly backed the gun when signalled to, and cautiously crept after me, still remaining far in the rear.

TO RETREAT FROM A POINT AND RESUME IT.

512. Amidst coppices, osiers, or broom—indeed, sometimes on a rough moor—you will occasionally lose sight of a dog, and yet be unwilling to call him, feeling assured that he is somewhere steadily pointing; and being vexatiously certain that, when he hears your whistle, he will either leave his point, not subsequently to resume it, or (which is far more probable) amuse himself by raising the game before he joins you. There are moments when you would give guineas if he would retreat from his point, come to you on your whistling, lead you towards the bird, and there resume his point.

513. This accomplishment (and in many places abroad its value is almost inappreciable) can be taught him, if he is under great command, by your occasionally bringing him to heel from a point when he is within sight and near you, and again putting him on his point. You will begin your instruction in this accomplishment when the dog is pointing quite close to you. On subsequent occasions, you can gradually increase the distance, until you arrive at such perfection that you can let him be out of sight when you call him. When he is first allowed to be out of your sight, he ought not to be far from you.

514. You may, for a moment, think that what is here

recommended contradicts the axiom laid down in 359; but it is there said, that nothing ought to make a dog "*voluntarily*" leave his point. Indeed, the possession of this accomplishment, so far from being productive of any harm, greatly awakens a dog's intelligence, and makes him perceive, more clearly than ever, that the sole object for which he is taken to the field is to obtain shots for the gun that accompanies him. When he is pointing on your side of a thick hedge, it will make him understand why you call him off;—take him down wind, and direct him to jump the fence : he will at once go to the bird, and, on your encouraging him, force it to rise on your side.

515. You will practise this lesson, however, with great caution, and not before his education is nearly completed, lest he imagine that you do not wish him always to remain stanch to his point. Indeed, if you are precipitate, or injudicious, you may make him blink his game.

516. After a little experience, he will very likely some day satisfactorily prove his consciousness of your object, by voluntarily coming out of thick cover to show you where he is, and again going in and resuming his point.

517. I was once shooting in Ireland with a friend (Major L——e), late in the season, when we saw a very young pointer do this solely from his own intelligence. Unperceived by either of us he had broken fence, and was out of sight. In vain we whistled and called. At length we saw him on the top of a bank (in that country usually miscalled "ditch"); but the moment he perceived that we noticed him, down he jumped. We went up, and to our great satisfaction found him steadily pointing a snipe. I need not say that he received much praise and many caresses for the feat.

518. I was partridge-shooting a few seasons back with an intimate friend, who was anxious to give me a good day's sport, when I observed him beckoning to me from a distance. He told me, when I came up to him, that some birds were immediately before him. I was puzzled to conceive how he could know this, for his white setter was alongside of him rolling on her back. He signalled to her to go forward, and sure enough she marched on, straight as an arrow's flight, to a covey lying on the stubble. In answer to my

inquiries, my friend, who seemed to attach no value to the feat, but to take it as a matter of course, told me that he had called the bitch away from her point lest her presence should alarm the birds, and make them take wing before I could come up.

519. As my friend was obliged to return home early, he left the lady with me. I had marked some partridges into the leeward-side of a large turnip-field. I could not get her to hunt where I wished ; I, therefore, no longer noticed her, but endeavoured to walk up the birds without her assistance. After a time she rejoined me, and ranged well and close. I then proceeded to beat the other part of the field—the part she had already hunted contrary to my wishes. Instead of making a cast to the right or left, on she went, directly ahead, for nearly three hundred yards. I was remarking to my attendant that she must be nearly useless to all but her master, when I observed her come to a stiff point. I then felt convinced that I had done her great injustice,—that she must have found and left this covey, whilst I was hunting far to leeward,—and that she had gone forward to resume her point, as soon as my face was turned in the right direction. On my mentioning all this to her owner, he said he had no doubt but that such was the case, as she would often voluntarily leave game to look for him, and again stand at it on perceiving that he watched her movements.

520. An *old* Kentish acquaintance of mine, though he is still a *young* man, has an Irish setter that behaved in a very similar manner. F——r, having severely wounded a hare in cover, put the dog upon the scent. He immediately took it up, but "roaded" so fast as to be soon out of sight. After a fruitless search for the setter, F——r was obliged to whistle two or three times, when he showed himself at the end of a ride, and by his anxious looks and motions seemed to invite his master to come on. This he did. The sagacious beast, after turning two corners, at each of which he stopped until F——r came up, went into cover and resumed the point, which my friend feels satisfied the dog must have left on hearing the whistle, for the wounded hare, whose leg was broken, was squatted within a yard of him. Such instances of a voluntary relinquishment and resumption of a point, must lead us to think that this accomplishment cannot be very difficult to teach dogs who have been accustomed to the gratification of always seeing their game carefully deposited in the bag.

521. In a capital little treatise on field diversions, written by a Suffolk sportsman upwards of seventy years ago, it is recorded that a pointer bitch, belonging to a Doctor Bigsbye, used to give tongue if she found in cover and was not perceived, and that she would repeatedly bark to indicate her locality until she was relieved from her point.

TO HUNT REGULARLY FROM LEEWARD TO WINDWARD WITHOUT THE GUN.

522. In paragraph 201 I observed, that when you are obliged, as occasionally must be the case, to enter a field to windward with your pupil, you ought to go down to the leeward side of it, keeping him close to your heels, before you commence to hunt. After undeviatingly pursuing this plan for some time, you can, before you come quite to the bottom of the field, send him ahead (by the underhand bowler's swing of the right hand, IV. of 141), and, when he has reached the bottom, signal to him to hunt to the right (or left). He will be so habituated to work under your eye (176) that you will find it necessary to walk backwards (up the middle of the field), while instructing him. As he becomes, by degrees, confirmed in this lesson, you can sooner and sooner send him ahead (from your heel),— but increase the distances very gradually,—until at length he will be so far perfected, that you may venture to send him down wind to the extremity of the field (before he commences beating), while you remain quietly at the top awaiting his return, until he shall have hunted the whole ground, as systematically and carefully as if you had accompanied him from the bottom. By this method you will teach him, on his gaining more experience, invariably to run to leeward, and hunt up to windward (crossing and re-crossing the wind) whatever part of a field you and he may enter. What a glorious consummation! and it can be attained, but only by great patience and perseverance. The least reflection, however, will show you that you should not attempt it until the dog is perfected in his range.

523. A careful dog, thus practised, will seldom spring birds, however directly he may be running down wind. He will pull up at the faintest indication of a scent, being at all times anxiously on the look-out for the coveted aroma.

524. Not only to the idle or tired sportsman would it be a great benefit to have a field thus beaten, but the keenest and most indefatigable shot would experience its advantages in the cold and windy weather customary in November, when the tameness of partridge-shooting cannot be much complained of; for the birds being then ever ready to take wing, surely the best chance, by fair means, of getting near them would be to intercept them between the dog and yourself. The manœuvre much resembles that recommended in 284, but in this you sooner and more directly head the birds.

525. Here the consideration naturally arises, whether dogs could not be *taught* (when hunting in the ordinary manner with the dog in rear)

TO HEAD RUNNING BIRDS.

Certainly it could be done. There have been many instances of old dogs *spontaneously* galloping off, and placing themselves on the other side of the covey (which they had pointed) as soon as they perceived that it was on the run,—and by good instruction you could develop, or rather excite, that exercise of sagacity.

526. Tolfrey (formerly, I believe, of the 43rd) gives, in his "Sportsman in France," so beautiful an instance of a dog's untutored intelligence, leading him to see 'the advantage of thus placing running birds between himself and the gun, that I will transcribe it, although I have already mentioned (end of 206) Grouse's very similar behaviour.

527. "On gaining some still higher ground, the dog drew and stood. She was walked up to, but to my astonishment we found no birds. She was encouraged, and with great difficulty coaxed off

her point. She kept drawing on, but with the same ill-success. I must confess I was for the moment sorely puzzled; but knowing the excellence of the animal, I let her alone. She kept drawing on for nearly a hundred yards—still no birds. At last, of her own accord, and with a degree of instinct amounting almost to the faculty of reasoning, she broke from her point, and dashing off to the right made a *détour*, and was presently straight before me, some three hundred yards off, setting the game whatever it might be, as much as to say, ' I'll be ****** if you escape me this time.' We walked steadily on, and when within about thirty yards of her, up got a covey of red-legged partridges, and we had the good fortune to kill a brace each. It is one of the characteristics of these birds to run for an amazing distance before they take wing; but the sagacity of my faithful dog baffled all their efforts to escape. We fell in with several coveys of these birds during the day, and my dog ever after gave them the double, and kept them between the gun and herself."

528. Mr. M——i, an officer high in the military store department, wrote to me but last Christmas (1863) almost in the following words:—

529. "When stationed in Jamaica, quail and the wild guinea-fowl were the only game I ever hunted for. The latter are very difficult to approach, as they run for hours through the long grass and brushwood, and will not rise unless hard pressed; but when once flushed, they spread through the cover, and lie so close, that one may almost kick them before without raising them. My dog, 'Albert,' was broke on grouse before I had him out from home. A steadier or better dog you will rarely see. The first time we went out after guinea-fowl he set to work as though hunting for grouse, pointing, and roading cautiously when he came on the run of the birds, but, from their pace through the cover, never coming up with them. This occurred the first two or three mornings, and annoyed him greatly. At last one day, as soon as he found that the birds were running through the bush, he halted, turned round, and looked up at me as much as to say : 'My poking after these fellows is all nonsense; do let me try some other dodge.' So I told him to go on, when he instantly started off, making a wide cast until he headed his game, when he commenced beating back towards me, driving the birds before him until they were sufficiently near me, when he dashed suddenly in amongst them, forcing the whole pack to take wing. They spread through the surrounding grass and cover, and 'Albert' and his mother, 'Peggy,' went to work, picking up the birds singly or in pairs as they lay. Old mother 'Peggy' was far too sedate and stanch to follow her son in the chase; she remained with me until he had brought back, and flushed the birds, and then she vied with him in finding them.

From this time I never had any difficulty in getting shots at these wary birds, for the very moment they commenced running, 'Albert' was off until he headed them, drove them back, and flushed them, as above described.

When looking for quail, 'Albert' behaved quite differently,

working steadily and cautiously, and never attempting to run into or spring his game until I came close up to him."

530. Grouse were unusually on the run one misty day, when the able Judge mentioned in 490 was shooting over "Captain's" companion, "Suwarrow." The dog "roaded" a pack for some time very patiently, but suddenly darted off for a considerable distance to the right and dropped into a long hag, through the mazes of which Lord M——f followed as fast as the nature of the ground would permit him. Every now and then the dog just raised his head above the heather to satisfy himself that his Lordship was coming. Where the hag ceased, and "Suwarrow" could no longer conceal his movements, he commenced a very curious system of tactics, travelling, after a most extraordinary fashion, *sideways* on the arc of a circle, constantly keeping his stern towards its centre. At length he wheeled about, and stood stock-still at a fixed point, as if inviting Lord M——f to approach. He did so,—raised a large pack, and had a capital right and left.

531. It would appear that the "Marshal" soon perceived that he had no chance of being enabled by a regular pursuit to bring his artillery to bear upon the retreating party ; he, therefore, resorted to a novel strategy to lull them into fancied security, and induce them to halt. He at once made a feint of abandoning the pursuit, and moved off to the flank. He made a forced *concealed* march in the hag ; and when it would no longer mask his plans and he was compelled to show himself, he merely let them see his *rear* guard, that they might still think he was retiring, and did not show any front until he had fairly entangled them between himself and his guns. It was a feat worthy of " Wellington " or " Napoleon," let alone "Suwarrow." By the bye, it explains why Lord M——d's dog (295) faced about whenever he perceived that his presence alarmed the birds.

532. If "Grouse" (206), Tolfrey's bitch, "Albert," and "Suwarrow" had been taught to "hunt from leeward to windward without the gun" (522), they would have been habituated to seeing game intercepted between themselves and their masters,—and then their spontaneously heading running birds (though undeniably evincing great intelligence) would not have been so very remarkable. They would but have reversed matters by placing themselves to windward of the birds while the gun was to leeward. This shows that the acquisition of that accomplishment (522) would be a great step towards securing a knowledge of the one we are now

considering. Indeed, there seems to be a mutual relation between these two refinements in education, for the possession of either would greatly conduce to the attainment of the other.

533. This accomplishment—and hardly any can be considered more useful—is not so difficult to teach an intelligent dog as one might at first imagine; it is but to lift him, and make him act on a larger scale, much in the manner described in 309 and 544. Like, however, everything else in canine education—indeed, in all education—it must be effected gradually; nor should it be commenced before the dog has had a season's steadying; then practise him in heading every wounded bird, and endeavour to make him do so at increased distances. Whenever, also, he comes upon the "heel" of a covey which is to leeward of him,—instead of letting him "foot" it,—oblige him to quit the scent and take a circuit (sinking the wind), so as to place himself to leeward of the birds. He will thereby *head the covey*, and you will have every reason to hope that after a time his own observation and intellect will show him the advantage of thus intercepting birds and stopping them when they are on the run, whether the manœuvre places him to leeward or to windward of them.*

534. If you could succeed in teaching but one of your dogs thus to take a wide sweep when he is ordered, and head a running covey before it gets to the extremity of the field (while the other dogs remain near you), you would be amply rewarded for months of extra trouble in

---

* A reverend and *very enthusiastic* dog-breaker in Cornwall (R. R. W——t), who took to the art late in life, had an admirable dog named Niger, who practised a peculiar self-taught dodge. He had a capital nose, and when he winded birds on the other side of a hedge, he would make a circuit, and coming behind them would drive them over to his master. This was all innate talent. In no way did it result from tuition.

training, by obtaining shots on days when good sportsmen, with fair average dogs, would hardly pull a trigger. And why should you not? Success would be next to certain, if you could as readily place your dog exactly where you wish, as shepherds do their collies (143). And whose fault will it be if you cannot? Clearly not your dog's, for he is as capable of receiving instruction as the shepherd's.

535. Manifestly it would be worth while to take great pains to teach this accomplishment, for in all countries it would prove a most killing one when birds become wild; and, as Tolfrey shows (529), it would be found particularly useful wherever the red-legged partridge abounds,*—which birds you will find do not lie badly when the coveys are, by any means, well headed and completely broken. But there are other accomplishments nearly as useful as those already detailed; the description of them, however, we will reserve for a separate Chapter.

---

* Unless they are very young they are little prized at table; and they afford such bad sport to the gun that, notwithstanding their beauty, great pains are now taken in Norfolk and Suffolk to exterminate the breed. Their nests are sought for to be destroyed; and when the snow is on the ground, the old birds are killed in great numbers. It is observed that in proportion as they increase, so do the common partridge decrease. The stronger bird, according to the general law of nature, drives off the weaker congener. Mr. L——d, A——r's keeper (of H——n Hall), told me he had on several occasions seen the young red-legged Frenchmen perseveringly attack and eventually kill a whole covey of the less active English squeakers. The late Marquis of Hertford has the credit (?) of having been the first to turn out a few of the strangers. This was nearly fifty years ago at Sudbourn Hall, his seat in Suffolk, whence they have spread over that county and Norfolk, and are fast invading the northern parts of Essex.

CHAPTER XVII.

SETTER TO RETRIEVE. BLOODHOUNDS. RETRIEVERS TO "BEAT."
WOUNDED WILD FOWL RETRIEVED BEFORE THE KILLED.

536. SETTER TO RETRIEVE; obtain thereby in one dog the services of two; necessity of having some Dog that retrieves.—537. Predilection for Setters confessed; Reason given; in Note, Setters daily becoming more valuable than Pointers; Partridges netted by Poachers, also by Keepers, to make birds wary: Bloodhounds to track Poachers; Education of Bloodhounds; Education of Keeper's night dog. (See Appendix).—538. Retrieving not to be taught first season.—539. Value of retrieving instanced in Pointer.—540. One Dog only to retrieve; Dog that bolted Partridge because interfered with by companion; Birds kept cool.—541. Let "retrieving" be done by "Finder."—542. Captain J——n's three Dogs that alternately retrieved as ordered.—543. Such an Education could be given, but unnecessary.—544. Seeking Dead with two Dogs; Winged Bird searched for in direction of covey's flight.—545. Scent differs of wounded and unwounded birds.—546. Three dead Snipe lifted in succession; Setter that stood fresh birds while carrying a dead one; Pointer that pointed Partridge while carrying a hare; Retriever refusing to relinquish chase of wounded Hare; *wounded* Woodcock walked up to, not "set" by Dog.—547. "Venus" tracking winged Partridge through Pheasants and Rabbits.—548. Injudiciousness of *retrieving* Setter pointing dead. —549. Argument against employing retrieving Setters holds against using regular Retrievers. —550. REGULAR RETRIEVERS TO BEAT; its Advantages; one Dog does the duty of two.—551. Instance of Retriever doing so spontaneously.—552. Retriever that never disturbed fresh ground.—553. WATER RETRIEVERS (OR WATER SPANIELS) TO RETRIEVE CRIPPLED BEFORE PICKING UP DEAD WILD FOWL; how taught.—554. None of these Accomplishments so difficult to teach as a good range.—555. Might be taught by your Gamekeeper but not to be expected of regular Breaker.

SETTER TO RETRIEVE.

536. UNDENIABLY there is some value in the extra number of shots obtained by means of highly-broken dogs; and nearly as undeniable is it that no man, who is not over-rich, will term that teaching superfluous which enables him to secure in one dog the services of two. Now, I take it for granted (as I cannot suppose you are willing to lose many head of killed game), that you would be glad to be always accompanied in the

field by a dog that retrieves. Unless you have such a companion, there will be but little chance of your often securing a slightly winged bird in turnips. Indeed, in all rough shooting, the services of a dog so trained are desirable to prevent many an unfortunate hare and rabbit from getting away to die a painful, lingering death; and yet, if the possession of a large kennel is ever likely to prove half as inconvenient to you as it would to me, you would do well, according to my idea of the matter, to dispense with a regular retriever, provided you have a highly-broken setter who retrieves well.

537. I say setter rather than pointer, not on account of his more affectionate, and perhaps more docile disposition (for certainly he is less liable to sulk under punishment), but because, thanks to his long coat, he will be able to work in any cover, and that from nature he "roads" quicker.

I must, however, plead *guilty* (for many good sportsmen wil think I evince bad taste) to a predilection for setters—meaning always *cautious* setters—a partiality, perhaps, attributable to having shot more over wild, uncertain ground than in well-stocked preserves. Doubtless, in a very enclosed country, where game is abundant, pointers are preferable, far preferable, more especially should there be a scarcity of water; but for severe and fast work, and as a servant of all work, there is nothing, I humbly conceive, like the setter.* He may be, and generally is, the more difficult to break; but when success has crowned your efforts, what a noble, enduring, sociable, attached animal you possess. I greatly, too, admire his long, stealthy, blood-like action,—(for I am not speaking of the large heavy sort before which in old days whole coveys used to be nettled), and the animated waving of his stern, so strongly indicative of high breeding; though, strange to say, in gracefulness of carriage the fox, when hunting, and actually on game, far excels him. But we are again getting astray beyond our proper limits; let us keep to the subject of dog-breaking.

---

* This note on setters, poachers, keepers, bloodhounds, night-dogs, &c., is so long, that the printer has placed it in an Appendix. See page 344.

538. As it will be your endeavour, during your pupil's first season, to make him thoroughly stanch and steady, I cannot advise you (as a general rule liable, of course, to many exceptions—one of which is named in 317), to let him retrieve,—by retrieve I always mean fetch,—until the following year. There is another advantage in the delay. His sagacity will have shown him that the design of every shot is to bag the game—when, therefore, he has once been permitted to pick up a bird, he will be desirous of carrying it immediately to you, and will resist the temptation to loiter with it, mouthing and spoiling it; and however keenly he may have heretofore "sought dead," he will henceforth search with redoubled zeal, from the delight he will experience in being permitted to carry his game. Moreover, the season's shooting, without lifting, will have so thoroughly confirmed him in the "down charge," that the increased * inclination to bolt off in search of a falling bird will be successfully resisted. If he has been taught while young to "fetch" (107, 109, &c.), he will be so anxious to take the birds to you, that instead of there being any difficulty in teaching him this accomplishment, you will often, during his first season, have to restrain him from lifting when he is "pointing dead." The least encouragement will make him gladly pick up the birds, and give them, as he ought, to no one but yourself.

539. Suppose you possess no regular retriever—if, instead of lifting your game yourself, you accustom one of your pointers or setters to do so, you will occasionally, in some odd manner, bag a bird which you would otherwise inevitably lose. In 97 is given such an instance; and in Scotland, no later than last season, I saw another. An outlying cock-pheasant rose out of stubble. It was a long shot, but he was knocked over, falling into an adjoining piece

---

* "Increased:" the gratification of carrying being far greater than that of merely "pointing dead."

of turnips. After the "down charge," a pointer bitch accustomed to retrieve, was sent to fetch him. The moment she approached the bird, up he got, apparently as strong as ever, and flew over some rising ground, but whither, I had no idea, further than suspecting that he was making for a distant cover on *forbidden* ground. I, therefore, at once gave him up as lost. The dog, however, was more sanguine, for, to my great surprise, off she started in pursuit, clearly imagining it was quite a mistake of the pheasant's. I soon lost sight of her, but, to my great gratification, I observed her, some little time afterwards, topping the hillock with the bird in her mouth. If she had been young, her chase after the pheasant might only have shown sad unsteadiness and wildness; but as she was a stanch sober old lady, it manifestly evinced nothing but,—it will be safest to say,—much intelligence and discrimination, lest *you* cavil at the words reason or reflection. I must own *I* should not.

540. You need hardly be cautioned not to let more than one dog retrieve the same bird. With more dogs

"With more dogs than one the bird would, almost to a certainty, be torn."

than one the bird would, almost to a certainty, be torn : and if a dog once becomes sensible of the enjoyment he would derive in pulling out the feathers of a bird, you will find it difficult to make him deliver it up before he has in some way disfigured it.

A bitch that retrieved admirably, known to an acquaintance of mine, was on one occasion so annoyed at being interfered with by her companion, that, in a fit of jealousy, she actually bolted the partridge she was carrying lest "Jack" should come in for a nibble. I must confess I think it of much importance that a dog who retrieves should be tender-mouthed, for I own I like to put my birds by smooth and tidy, and, if I want them to keep long, take care to observe the old rule of hanging them (by their heads rather than their feet, that rain may not saturate the feathers) on the loops outside the game-bag until they are quite cool, before I allow them to become inside passengers; but I generally have their bodies placed within the netting, as for want of this precaution many a bird has been decapitated in the scramble through a thick hedge. Game, whether cool or warm, kept in a close *Mackintosh* bag, soon becomes unfit to send to any distance.

541. If you shoot with several dogs that retrieve, be careful always to let the dog who finds the game be the one to bring it. It is but fair that he should be so rewarded, and thus all will be stimulated to hunt with increased diligence.

542. Captain J——n, R.N., of Little B——w, Essex (well-known for the gallantry and skill he displayed when risking his own life to save that of many stranded on the Kentish coast), used to break in his own dogs, and required them to show yet greater obedience and forbearance while retrieving. At one period he was in the habit of taking two pointers and a little spaniel into the field to hunt together,—the latter so small that he often carried it in his pocket when it was fatigued. The following kind of scene constantly occurred. One of the pointers would stand,—the other back,—so also would the spaniel. Captain J——n, after killing his bird and loading, probably said, "Don, go fetch it." Don went forward to obey. "Stop, Don." Don halted. "Carlo, fetch the bird." Carlo advanced. "Stop, Carlo." Carlo obeyed. "Tiny, bring it." The little creature did as ordered, and placed it in her master's hand, the pointers meanwhile never moving.

543. I am not urging you to give up the time requisite to educate dogs so highly as this, but you see it can be done.

544. If the dog that found the covey be not able to wind the bird you have shot, make one of the other

dogs take a large circuit. The latter may thus, without interfering with the first dog, come upon the bird, should it have run far. Send him in the direction the covey has taken—the chances are great that the bird is travelling towards the same point. By pursuing this plan, obviously there will be much less chance of your losing a bird than if you allow the dogs to keep close together while searching. (See also 115.)

545. Do not think that by making your setter lift (after his first season), instead of "pointing dead," there will be any increased risk of his raising unsprung birds. The difference between the scent of dead or wounded game, and that of game perfectly uninjured, is so great that no steady, experienced dog will fail to point any fresh bird he may come across whilst seeking for that which is lost.

As a proof of this I may mention that,
546. In North America I once saw three snipe lying on the ground, which a pointer, that retrieved, had regularly set one after the other, having found a couple on his way to retrieve the first, and which he afterwards brought in succession to his master, who had all the time governed the dog entirely by signs, never having been obliged to use his voice beyond saying in a low tone, "Dead," or "Find." I remember, also, hearing of a retrieving setter that on one occasion pointed a fresh bird, still retaining in her mouth the winged partridge which she was carrying,—and of a pointer who did the same when he was bringing a hare; there must, too, be few sportsmen who will not admit that they have found it more difficult to make a dog give up the pursuit of a wounded hare than of one perfectly uninjured. I know of a sportsman's saying he felt certain that the hare his retriever was coursing over the moors must have been struck, although the only person who had fired stoutly maintained that the shot was a regular miss. The owner of the dog, however, averred that this was impossible, as he never could get the discerning animal to follow any kind of unwounded game; and, on the other hand, that no rating would make him quit the pursuit of *injured* running feather or fur. The retriever's speedy return with puss, conveniently balanced between his jaws, bore satisfactory testimony to the accuracy of both his own and his master's judgment. In December, '49, a woodcock that was struck hard took a long flight. A setter-bitch I have often shot over came,

quite unexpectedly to herself, on the scent of the bird when it was at such a distance from her that the party who had shot it felt sure she was on other game. Instead, however, of "setting," the bitch, who, be it observed, is particularly steady, drew on, and after deliberately walking up to the woodcock, gave it a touseling, for she is not broken into "pointing dead." It is certain that her olfactory nerves plainly told her there was no chance of its rising.

547. In corroboration of the correctness of the opinion I have just expressed, respecting the difference between the scent of injured and uninjured birds, I am glad to be permitted to make the following extract from a letter I lately received from Colonel T——y, spoken of in 99. He writes, "When shooting at Alresford, in Essex, last year, I had a singular instance of Venus' sagacity in detecting the scent of wounded game. I was returning home, and while walking through a field of turnips a covey of birds got up near the fence. I winged one, which fell in the midst of some rabbits and pheasants feeding near the edge of the cover on the opposite side. Of course, they all bolted at the appearance of such an unwelcome visitor as the retriever—the rabbits into their burrows,—the pheasants into cover. My servant brought the bitch up to the place where I thought the bird had fallen. After puzzling about for some time, she took the trail about thirty yards down by the side of the fence, and then 'set' at a rabbit-hole. Thinking she was mistaken, I rated her and tried to get her away, but she stuck to her point. Determining, therefore, to ascertain the facts, we dug up the top part of a narrow fence, and bolted a couple of rabbits out of the hole, at the further end of which we found my wounded bird, an old Frenchman."*

548. Some good sportsmen maintain that a retrieving setter (or pointer) on finding a dead bird ought to point it until directed to lift it. This training they hold to be advisable, on the ground that it conduces to the dog's steadiness by diminishing his wish to run forward on seeing a bird fall; but the plan has necessarily this evil consequence, that should the setter, when searching for the dead bird, come across and point, *as he ought*, any fresh game, on your telling him to fetch it (as you naturally will), he must spring it if he attempt to obey you. Surely this would tend more to unsteady him than the habit of lifting his dead birds as soon as found? Your dog and you ought always to work in the greatest

* A red-legged partridge.

harmony—in the mutual confidence of your, at all times, thoroughly understanding each other—and you should carefully avoid the possibility of ever perplexing him by giving him any order it is out of his power to obey, however much he may exert himself. Moreover, if you teach your retrieving setter to "point dead," you at once relinquish—surely unnecessarily ?—all hope of ever witnessing such a fine display of sagacity and steadiness as has just been related in the first part of 546.

549. If you object to a setter's being taught to lift on the ground, that it will make the other dogs jealous, pray remember that the argument has equal force against the employment of a regular retriever in their presence.

REGULAR RETRIEVER TO BEAT.

550. We all have our prejudices,—every Englishman has a right to many. One of mine is to think a *regular* retriever positively not worth his keep to you for general shooting *if one of your setting dogs will retrieve well*—but what an all-important "if" is this ! However, if you shoot much in cover, I admit that a regular retriever which can be worked in perfect silence, never refusing to come in when he is merely signalled to, or, if out of sight, softly whistled to, is better * (particularly when you employ beaters), but even then he need not be the idler that one generally sees,—he might be broken in to hunt close to you, and give you the same service as a mute spaniel. I grant this is somewhat difficult to accomplish, for it much tends to unsteady him, but it can be effected, —I have seen it,—and being practicable, it is at least worth trying; for if you succeed, you, as before (536), make one dog perform the work of two ; and, besides its

---

* Of course, a regular retriever is absolutely necessary when a team of spaniels is hunted, none of which are accustomed to retrieve (78).

evident advantage in thick cover, if he accompany you in your every-day shooting, you will thus obtain, in the course of a season, many a shot which your other dogs, especially in hot weather, would pass over. If, too, the retriever hunts quite close to you, he can in no way annoy his companions, or interfere with them, for I take it for granted he will be so obedient as to come to "heel" the instant he gets your signal.

551. Many regular retrievers take spontaneously to beating. Two brothers, named W———e, living at Grewell, in Hampshire, termed by the village wags, not inappropriately, "Watergruel" (there is good snipe and duck-shooting in the surrounding marshes), have a ranging-retriever (a Newfoundland), still young, now called "Nelly," though, as a puppy, christened "Nelson" by the girls of the family. *Miss* Nelly, as if to give further proof of the impropriety of her original name, is remarkably timid, and therefore has been allowed to follow, unchecked, her own devices in the field. In imitation of her companions, she took to beating and pointing; and, after the "down-charge," would retrieve as zealously and efficiently as if she had never been allowed to "quit heel," except for that express purpose. I have myself, when in the north, killed game to the voluntary point of "Sambo," a black regular-retriever, who was permitted to range close to the keeper. I have also shot to the point of "Bang," a very handsome animal, a cross between a Newfoundland and a setter. Dogs so bred often, when ranging, take to pointing for a short period before dashing in; or can easily be made to do so,—thereby giving the gun a very acceptable caution.

552. The sire of "Venus"—honourable mention is made of her in 99—a very celebrated dog, had an invaluable quality as a retriever, though the very opposite of the range I have been recommending. He disturbed as little ground as possible during his search, and *no fresh ground returning*. After running with the greatest correctness a wounded pheasant through a large cover, he would invariably return upon the same track he had taken when first sent from "heel." I confess I cannot see how this admirable habit could be taught by any one but Dame Nature. Is it not a beautiful instance of sagacity? But you will observe that, singularly good as was this regular-retriever, he would have sprung the snipe at which the retrieving-pointer stood (546). For instructions regarding regular land retrievers, see 112 to 130.

EXAMPLE BETTER THAN PRECEPT.

"Accoutred as I was I plunged in and bade him follow."—Pars. 276 and 553.

WATER RETRIEVERS (or WATER SPANIELS)

TO RETRIEVE WOUNDED, BEFORE PICKING UP KILLED WILDFOWL.

553. This a knowing old dog will often do of his own accord; but you must not attempt to teach a young one this useful habit, until you are satisfied that there is no risk of making him blink his birds. You can then call him off when he is swimming towards dead birds, and signal to him to follow those that are fluttering away. If the water is not too deep, rush in yourself, and set him a good example by actively pursuing the runaways; and until all the cripples that can be recovered* are safely bagged, do not let him lift one of those killed outright. If very intelligent, he will before long perceive the advantage of the system, or at least find it the more exciting method, and adhere to it without obliging you to continue your aquatic excursions. (For advice about water retrievers, see 90 to 95.) I have placed this paragraph among the "refinements" in breaking; but I ought, perhaps, to have entered it sooner; for if you are fond of duck-shooting, and live in a neighbourhood where you have good opportunities of following it, you should regard this accomplishment as a necessary part of your spaniel's education.

554. In your part of the country none of these extra, or, as some will say, always superfluous accomplishments may be required; but if you consider that a pupil of yours attaining any one of them would be serviceable, be not deterred from teaching it by the idea that you would be undertaking a difficult task. Any one of them, I was nearly saying all of them, could be taught

* In deep water diving birds will of course beat the most active dog.

x

a dog with far greater ease, and in a shorter time, than a well-established, judicious range.

555. It would be quite unreasonable to expect a regular breaker ("mark," I do not say your gamekeeper) to teach your dog any of these accomplishments. He may be fully aware of the judiciousness of the system, and be sensible of its great advantages, but the many imperious calls upon his time would preclude his pursuing it in all its details. At the usual present prices it would not pay him to break in dogs so highly.

CHAPTER XVIII.

BECKFORD. ST. JOHN. CONDITION. INOCULATION. VACCINATION
CONCLUSION.

556. Reflect on what is said.—557. Not to rest content with bad dogs.—558. Beckford's opinion of the education that could be given to Dog.—559. Education of the Buckhound.—560, 561. St. John's opinion. The old Show-woman's learned dog.—562. Hunting to be Dog's principal enjoyment.—563. While young, not to have run of kitchen. To be in kennel; not tied up; chain better than rope. —564. When older, more liberty allowed, but never to "self-hunt;" old Dogs spontaneously take *judicious* liberties. Easier to teach accomplishments than cure faults. "Self-hunter's" example most dangerous.—565. Fine range and perseverance attained. Irish red setters.—566. Good condition; exercise on road; attention to feet. In Note, Claws sometimes too long; Claws of Tigress that ran into feet.—567. Diet to be considered; muscle wanted; fat detrimental, except to Water Retrievers. In Note, recipe for waterproofing boots.—568. Indian-corn meal; Mr. Herbert's opinion of; feed of an evening.—569. Beefsoup brings Mange in hot climates: Mutton better—meat necessary to prevent disgusting habits.—570. Good condition of Nose most material; Kennels.— 571. Warmth necessary; Winter pups.—572. Pups inoculated for Distemper.— 573 to 575. Vaccinated for Distemper.—577. Blaine and Colonel Cook thought it useless.—577. Old prejudice against Vaccination.—578. Colonel Hawker advocates it.—579. Salt for Distemper.—580. Easy to give medicine.—581. The method.—582. If force is necessary.—583. Castor oil lapped up with milk.— 584. Dog not to be lent.—586. In Note, old sportsman's advice about choosing a Keeper.—588. Education gradual; taught from the A, B, C. In Note, Query, do Keepers find time to break in dogs of strangers, while their masters' remain unfinished? Advantage of young Dog's accompanying Keeper when he goes his rounds by day. "Snap" daily visiting the traps for his master.—585 to 589. The Conclusion.

556. WE have come to the concluding division (dignified by the name of Chapter) of this little Work; for I have at length nearly finished my prosing about dog-breaking. But reflect upon what I have said. The more you do, the more, I think, you will be of opinion that I have recommended only what is reasonable, and that but little attention beyond the trouble usually bestowed, *if directed by good judgment*, is required to give a dog the education which I have described.

557. I wish I could animate you with but a quarter of the enthusiasm which I once felt on the subject. I am not desirous of making you dissatisfied with anything that you possess, excepting your dogs, such as, I fear, they most probably are, and that only

X 2

because, if they are young, a little judicious extra-exertion on your part will add as much to their usefulness as to your own enjoyment. And I do not wish them, or anything you have, or have not, to make you discontented ; I only pray you not to be supine. If you can get no more alluring drink than cold water, reflect on its wholesomeness, and enjoy it, if you can, with all the relish of a parched Arab ; but I entreat you not to be contented with a disorderly *noise-exciting* cur, when a trifling addition to your pains will ensure you an obedient, well-trained animal,—one that will procure you twice as many shots as the other. It will, indeed. Believe me, I am not too extravagant in my conception of a perfect dog. You may not consider it worth your while to take the trouble of giving him such an education ; but it seems hardly reasonable to say it could not be imparted. Naturally enough you may distrust my judgment, but you cannot doubt the experience of the reflecting, discriminating Beckford ; and what does he say on the subject of canine education ?

558. "The many learned dogs and learned horses that so frequently appear and astonish the vulgar, sufficiently evince what education is capable of ; and it is to education I must attribute the superior excellence of the buckhound, since I have seen high bred fox-hounds do the same under the same good masters.

559. "Dogs that are constantly with their masters acquire a wonderful degree of penetration, and much may be done through the medium of their affections. I attribute the extraordinary sagacity of the buckhound to the manner in which he is treated. He is the constant companion of his instructor and benefactor—the man whom he was first taught to fear he has since learned to love. Can we wonder that he should be obedient to him ? Oft have we viewed with surprise the hounds and deer amusing themselves familiarly together on the same lawn,—living, as it were, in the most friendly intercourse ; and with no less surprise have we heard the keeper give the word, when instantly the very nature of the dog seemed changed ; roused from his peaceful state, he is urged on with a relentless fury, which only death can satisfy—the death of the *very* deer he is encouraged to pursue. The business of the day over, see him follow, careless and contented, his master's steps, to repose on the same lawn where the frightened deer again return, and are again indebted to *his* courtesy for their wonted pasture. Wonderful proofs of obedience, sagacity, and penetration ! "

560. If you have at hand St. John's "Tour in Sutherlandshire" (he is the author of that most interesting work, "Wild Sports and Natural History of the Highlands"), pray turn to the part in the second volume, where he describes the old show-woman's learned dog. I would transcribe the whole of the amusing account, were not this little book already swollen to undue proportions—but I must quote the concluding observations, as his opinion respecting the aptitude of dogs for instruction so fully coincides with Beckford's.

561. "The tricks consisted of the usual routine of adding up figures, spelling short words, and finding the first letter of any town

named by one of the company. The last trick was very cleverly done, and puzzled us very much, as we—*i.e.* the grown-up part of the audience—were most intently watching not him but his mistress, in order to discover what signs she made to guide him in his choice of the cards ; but we could not perceive that she moved hand or foot, or made any signal whatever. Indeed, the dog seemed to pay but little regard to her, but to receive his orders direct from any one who gave them. In fact, his teaching must have been perfect, and his intellect wonderful. Now I dare say I shall be laughed at for introducing an anecdote of a learned dog, and told that it was 'all trick.' No doubt it was 'all trick,' but it was a very clever one, and showed how capable of education dogs are—far more so than we imagine. For here was a dog performing tricks so cleverly that not one out of four or five persons, who were most attentively watching, could find out how he was assisted by his mistress."

562. In following Beckford's advice respecting your making, as far as is practicable, your dog your "constant companion," do not, however, forget that you require him to evince great diligence and perseverance in the field ; and, therefore, that his highest enjoyment must consist in being allowed to hunt.

563. Now, it seems to be a principle of nature,— of canine as well as human nature,—to feel, through life, most attachment to that pursuit, whatever it may be, which is most followed in youth. If a dog is permitted as a youngster to have the run of the kitchen, he will be too fond of it when grown up. If he is allowed to amuse himself in every way his fancy dictates, he will think little of the privilege of hunting. Therefore, the hours he cannot pass with you (after you have commenced his education), I am sorry to say it, but I must do so, he ought to be in his *kennel*—loose in his kennel,* not tied up ; for straining at his collar would throw out his elbows, and so make him grow up bandy-legged. If, however, he must be fastened, let it

* Twice a day he should be allowed to run out, that he may not be compelled to adopt habits wholly opposed to his natural propensities. If he has acquired the disagreeable trick of howling when shut up, put a muzzle on him.

be by a chain. He would soon learn to gnaw through a cord, especially if a young puppy, who, from nature, is constantly using his teeth, and thus acquire a trick that some day might prove very inconvenient were no chain at hand. You would greatly consult his comfort by having the chain attached, with a loose ring and swivel, to a spike fixed a few paces in front of his kennel, so that he could take some exercise by trotting round and round.

564. When your dog has attained some age, and hunting has become with him a regular passion, I believe you may give him as much liberty as you please without diminishing his zeal,—but most carefully prevent his ever hunting alone, technically called " self-hunting." At that advanced time of life, too, a few occasional irregularities in the field may be innocuously permitted. The steadiest dogs will, at times, deviate from the usual routine of their business, sagaciously thinking that such departure from rule must be acceptable if it tends to obtain the game ; and it will be advisable to leave an experienced dog to himself whenever he evinces great perseverance in spontaneously following some unusual plan. You may have seen an old fellow, instead of cautiously "roading" and "pointing dead," rush forward and seize an unfortunate winged bird, while it was making the best use of its legs after the flight of the rest of the covey—some peculiarity in the scent emitted having probably betrayed to the dog's *practised* nose that the bird was injured. When your pup arrives at such years of discrimination, you need not so rigorously insist upon a patient "down charge," should you see a winged cock-pheasant running into cover. Your dog's habits of discipline would be, I should hope, too well confirmed by his previous course of long drill for such a

temporary departure from rule to effect any permanent mischief; but, oh! beware of any such laxity with a *young* pupil, however strongly you may be tempted. In five minutes you may wholly undo the labour of a month. On days, therefore, when you are anxious, *coûte qui coûte*, to fill the game-bag, pray leave him at home. Let him acquire any bad habit when you are thus pressed for birds, and you will have more difficulty in eradicating it than you would have in teaching him almost any accomplishment. This reason made me all along keep steadily in view the supposition, that you had commenced with a dog unvitiated by evil associates, either biped or quadruped; for assuredly you would find it far easier to give a thoroughly good education to such a pupil, than to complete the tuition (particularly in his range) of one usually considered broken, and who must, in the natural order of things, have acquired some habits more or less opposed to your own system. If, as a puppy, he had been allowed to self-hunt and chase, your labour would be herculean. And inevitably this would have been your task, had you ever allowed him to associate with any dog who "self-hunted." The oldest friend in your kennel might be led astray by forming an intimacy with the veriest cur, if a "self-hunter." There is a fascination in the vice—above all, in killing young hares and rabbits,—that the steadiest dog cannot resist when he has been persuaded to join in the sport by some vagabond of a poacher possessing a tolerable nose, rendered keenly discerning by experience.

565. I hope that by this time we too well understand each other for you now to wonder why I think that you should not commence hunting your young dog where game is abundant. Professional breakers prefer such ground, because, from getting plenty of points, it enables

them to train their dogs more quickly, and *sufficiently well* to ensure an early sale. This is *their* object, and they succeed. *My* object is that you shall establish *ultimately* great perseverance and a fine range in your young dog, let birds be ever so scarce. If you show him too many at first, he will subsequently become easily dispirited whenever he fails in getting a point.

It is the general paucity of game in Ireland (snipe and woodcock excepted) that makes dogs trained in that country show so much untiring energy and indomitable zeal when hunted on our side of the Channel. But the slight wiry Irish red setter (whom it is so difficult to see on the moor from his colour), is naturally a dog of great pace and endurance. There is, however, a much heavier sort.

566. Many dogs, solely from want of good condition, greatly disappoint their masters at the beginning of the season. You could not expect your hunter to undergo a hard day's work without a previous course of tolerably severe exercise; and why expect it of your dog? A couple of hours' quiet exercise in the cool of the morning or evening will not harden his feet, and get him into the wind and condition requisite for the performance you may desire of him some broiling day in the middle of August or early in September. If you do not like to disturb your game, and have no convenient country to hunt over, why should you not give him some gallops before the beginning of the shooting-season, when you are mounted on your trotting hackney? Think how greyhounds are by degrees brought into wind and hard meat before coursing commences. Such work on the road will greatly benefit his feet,* particularly if, on his return home in wet weather, they are bathed with a strong solution of salt and water. When the ground is hard and dry, they should be washed with warm water and soap, both to soothe them

---

* Claws of dogs kept on boarded floors, or not exercised, occasionally become so long, that unless they are filed or pared down, they cause lameness. In the menagerie at the Cape of Good Hope I saw a fine tigress, the claws of whose fore-feet had grown so far beyond her power of sheathing that they had penetrated deep into the flesh, and it was under consideration how to secure her so that the operator should incur no risk while sawing off the ends. She was very tame and sociable, and would rub against the bars when she was approached by visitors to invite their caresses; but it was quite distressing to see her raising each leg alternately, really to ease it of her weight, but apparently as if soliciting relief. The blessings of chloroform were then unknown. No tiger while under its drowsy influence had ever had an injured limb amputated, as was once successfully managed at the Surrey Zoological Gardens.

and to remove all dust and gravel. They might afterwards be gradually hardened by applying the salt and water. When they are inflamed and bruised, almost a magical cure might be effected by their being sponged with a solution of arnica—ten parts of water to one of arnica. Should the dog lick the lotion, dissolve a little aloes in it. If, by the bye, you would make it a rule personally to ascertain that attention is always paid to your dogs after a hard day's work, and not leave them to the tender mercies of an uninterested servant, you would soon be amply repaid for your trouble by their additional performance. Many men make it a rule to send their dogs to the mountains a week or two before the grouse shooting; but they seldom even then get sufficiently exercised, and their mettle is slacked (confessedly a temporary advantage with half-broken, *wild* dogs), instead of being increased, by finding that, however many points they may make (at squeakers under their nose), they never secure a bird. A month's road-work, with alterative medicine, is far better.

567. Dogs severely worked should be fed abundantly on a nutritious diet. Hunters and stage-coach horses have an unlimited allowance, and the work of eager setters and pointers (in a hilly country particularly) is proportionately hard; but the constitutions of dogs vary so greatly that the quantity as well as quality of their diet should be considered; for it must be your aim to obtain the largest development of muscle with the least superfluity of flesh,— that enemy to pace and endurance in dog as surely as in horse and man. Yet this remark does not apply to a water retriever: he should have fat. It is a warm, well-fitting great coat, more impervious to wet than a *Mackintosh*,—furnished by Providence to whales, bears, and all animals that have to contend with cold; and obviously your patient companion will feel the benefit of one when he is shivering alongside you while you are lying *perdu* in a bed of damp rushes.*

---

* It will tend to your comfort and health to have your boots made waterproof, and you will not easily get a better preparation, when well rubbed into the leather, for effecting your object, than the following. It is an admirable one for rendering all kinds of leather pliable, and for *preserving* them in that state—and how often in the beginning of a season have you found your water-boots as hard as a board!

To one ounce of India-rubber (the old bottle-shaped gum) cut into very small pieces, and dissolved in only as much spirits of naphtha as will convert the rubber into a thick fluid, add not more than one pint of oil; linseed oil, or neat's foot oil is, I am told, the best.

For waterproofing cloth :—
2 lbs. alum,
1 lb. sugar of lead,
20 quarts spring water.

Strain off to clear. Let garment soak 48 hours. Hang up until dry. Well brush afterwards. Inexpensive yet effective!

When you catch cold, do not too hastily blame our climate, our enviable climate, which preserves longer than any other the bloom of its women and the vigour of its men, where the extremes of cold and

568. Having mentioned condition, I am led to observe, that in America I saw a pointer, which, from being hunted, I may say daily, Sundays excepted, could not be kept in condition on oatmeal and greaves, but which was put in hard flesh, and did his work admirably, when Indian-corn meal was substituted for the oatmeal. I have not seen it used in this country, but I can fancy it to be a heating food, better calculated for dogs at regular hard work than when they are summering.* It is well known that no food should be given in a very hot state,—not of a higher temperature than milk-warm; and that evening is the proper feeding time, in order that the dogs may sleep immediately afterwards, and not be full when they are taken out for their morning's work.

569. In India, I remember complaining to an old sportsman that I had much difficulty in keeping my dogs free from mange. He at once asked if I did not give them beef-tea with their rice. I acknowledged that I did. He said it was of too heating a nature. I tried mutton-broth, agreeably to his recommendation. Every vestige of mange vanished, but yet I could hardly believe it attributable to so slight a change in their diet, for very little meat was used. As the mutton was much dearer, I again tried the beef. It would not do. The mange reappeared. I was, therefore, obliged to return to the mutton, and continue it. The teeth of dogs show that flesh is a natural diet; and if they are wholly deprived of it when they are young, they will acquire most revolting habits,—feeding upon any filth they may find, and often rolling in it. The meat should be cooked.

570. The good condition of a dog's nose is far from being an immaterial part of his conditioning, for on the preservation of its sensitiveness chiefly depends your hope of sport. If it be dry from being feverish, or if it be habituated to the villanous smells of an impure kennel, how are you to expect it to acknowledge the faintest taint of game—yet one that, if followed up by

and heat are equally unknown, in which you can take with advantage exercise every day in the year, and need never suffer annoyance from mosquitoes, sandflies, fleas, and other abominations, from which few countries are free. When heated by labour, are we not too apt to throw off some article of apparel in order to get cool? whereas the Turk, more sensibly, puts on additional clothing, and sits out of a draught until he loses all the extra heat he acquired from exercise.

* Since the publication of the first edition of this book, I have had the gratification of reading Mr. Herbert's "Field Sports in the United States, &c.," and find that he does not consider Indian-corn to possess any injurious qualities—on the contrary, he strongly recommends its adoption in kennels.

olfactory nerves in high order, would lead to a sure find? Sweetness of breath is a strong indication of health. Cleanliness is as essential as a judicious diet; and you may be assured, that if you look for excellence, you must always have your youngster's kennel clean, dry, airy, and yet sufficiently warm. The more you attend to this, the greater will be his bodily strength and the finer his nose.

In India the kennels are, of course, too hot; but in the best constructed which fell under my observation, the heat was much mitigated by the roofs being thickly thatched with grass. In England, however, nearly all kennels—I am not speaking of those for hounds—are far too cold in winter.

571. There must be *sufficient* warmth. Observe how a petted dog, especially after severe exercise, lays himself down close to the fire, and enjoys it. Do you not see that instinct teaches him to do this? and must it not be of great service to him? Why, therefore, deny him in cold weather, after a hard day's work, a place on the hearth-rug? It is the want of sufficient heat in the kennels, and good drying and brushing after hard work, that makes sporting dogs, particularly if they are long-coated ones, suffer from rheumatism, blear eyes, and many ills that generally, but not necessarily, attend them in old age. The instance given in 226 is a proof of this.

Winter pups, you are told, are not so strong as those born in summer. They would be, if they were reared in a warm room. The mother's bodily heat cannot warm them; for after a while, they so pull her about and annoy her, that she either leaves them for a time, or drives them from her.

572. As I have casually touched on puppies, I will take the opportunity of recommending, according to the plan adopted by some sportsmen, and of which I have experienced the advantage, that you have a whole litter, soon after it has been weaned, (provided it be in a healthy state), inoculated for the distemper,— a small feather, previously inserted in the nose of a diseased dog, being for an instant put up the nostrils of the puppies. It will be

necessary to keep them unusually warm,* and feed them high, while they are suffering from the effects of this treatment. It is not likely that you will lose any; but if you should, the loss will be small compared with that of an educated dog at a mature age. The extent of the mischief will probably be a slight cough, with a little running at the nose for a few days.

573. Having heard that vaccination would greatly mitigate the distressing symptoms of distemper, if not entirely remove all susceptibility to infection, I endeavoured to possess myself with the facts of the case. Circumstances were thus brought to my knowledge which appear so interesting, that a brief detail of them may not be unacceptable to some of my readers. It would seem that vaccination might be made as great a blessing to the canine race as it has proved to mankind:—that is to say, many experienced men are still of that opinion. All that I heard of material import is nearly embodied in letters I received, some years ago, from Mr. L——e, of Neat's Court, Isle of Sheppey, an intelligent sportsman, much attached to coursing. As I am sure he will not object to my doing so, I will quote largely from his notes. He writes nearly *mot-à-mot*.

574. "It is with pleasure that I answer yours of this morning, and give you what little information I can respecting the vaccination of my puppies. Mr. Fellowes, who resided about eight years since at 34, Baker Street, was the first person from whom I learned anything on the subject. He was a great breeder of bull-dogs, of all the canine race the most difficult to save in distemper, greyhounds being, perhaps, the next on the list.† He told me that in twelve years he had lost but two puppies, and those not, he believed, from distemper, and yet he had regularly bred every year.

575. "I went to town purposely to see him operate upon a clutch. The method is very simple. Take a small piece of floss silk, and draw the end through a needle. On about the middle of the silk place some matter (when in a proper state) extracted from a child's arm. Unfold (throw back) the ear so as to be able to see the interior part near the root. You will then perceive a little projecting knob or kernel almost detached from the ear. With the needle pierce through this kernel. Draw the silk each way till the blood starts. Tie the ends of the silk, and the process is completed. You may let the silk remain there: it will drop off after a time. The object is to deposit the matter by this method, instead of employing a lancet. I have great faith in the efficacy of the plan, simple as it appears. With me it has never failed. For some years in succession I dropped a clutch of greyhounds and two litters of setters, and not a single pup had the distemper more severely than for the disease to be just perceptible. A little opening medicine then

---

* In all diseases of dogs—inflammatory, of course, excepted—warmth is recommended.

† There is a hardy breed of pointers that rarely take it,—especially if they are liberally fed, and lie warm while young.—W. N. H.

quickly removed that slight symptom of illness. Perhaps the best age to operate upon puppies is when they are well recovered from their weaning."

576. The balance of testimony and experience is, in my opinion, quite in favour of vaccination; but there are authorities of weight who think that no good results from it. It is, however, certain that it cannot be productive of harm. Blaine writes that, as far as his experience went, "vaccination neither exempts the canine race from the attack of the distemper, nor mitigates the severity of the complaint." He adds, however, that the point was still at issue.

577. It appears right to observe that Blaine and Jenner were contemporaries at a period when the medical world was greatly opposed to the vaccination of children. It is not surprising, therefore, that there should have been an unjust prejudice against the vaccination of puppies. Youatt is altogether silent on the subject, although he quotes Dr. Jenner's description of distemper. Colonel Cook, in his observations on fox-hunting, &c., says, "Vaccination was tried in some kennels as a preventive, but it failed, and was abandoned." Mayhew* does not allude to it.

578. Not until after the foregoing remarks on vaccination were written, was I aware that Colonel Hawker recommended the plan, or, of course, I should, in former editions, have quoted such high authority. Speaking in 1838, he observes, "I have ever since adopted the plan of vaccination; and so little, if any, has been the effect of distemper after it, that I have not lost a dog since the year 1816."—"This remedy has been followed with great success both here and in the United States. The plan adopted is to insert a small quantity of vaccine matter under each ear, just as you would do in the human arm."

579. I know of many dogs in the south of England having been cured of a regular attack of distemper by a lump of salt, about the size of a common marble, being occasionally forced down their throats; say, for a grown-up pointer, half a dozen doses, with an interval of two or three hours between each. The salt acts as an emetic. Nourishing food and warmth are very requisite.

580. To some few of my readers it may possibly be of use to observe, that with a little management, it is very easy to trick a dog into taking medicine.

581. If your patient is a large animal, make a hole in a piece of meat, and having wrapped the physic in thin paper, shove it into the hole. Throw the dog one or two bits of meat, then the piece containing the medicine, and the chances are that he will bolt it without in the least suspecting he has been deceived. A pill, enveloped in silver paper, emits no smell. If a powder is well

---

* "Dogs, their Management," published by Routledge,—a work evidently written by a kind-hearted man of reflection, experience, and judgment; one who dares think for himself, not servilely treading in the footsteps of his predecessors.

rubbed up with butter, and a little at a time of the mixture be smeared over the animal's nose, he will lick it off and swallow it. Powders can also be placed between thin slices of bread and butter, and be so administered. If you are treating a small pampered favourite, probably a little previous starvation will assist you.

582. Should you fail in your stratagems, and force be necessary, it will be best to lay the dog on his back, or place him in a sitting posture between your knees, with his back towards you. In either position his legs are useless to him, as they have no fulcrum. While you are making him open his mouth, if you do this by forcing your thumb and fingers between his grinders, you can effectually protect yourself from a bite by covering them with the dog's own lips—any powders then placed far back on the tongue near the throat must be swallowed on the dog's mouth being firmly closed for a few seconds. He will not be able to eject them as they will adhere to his moist tongue. If given with a little dry sugar they will be the less nauseous, and therefore the dog will be less disposed to rebel when next you have occasion to act the part of a doctor.

583. Castor oil is a valuable medicine for dogs; and it is a good plan to let a pup occasionally lap milk into which a little of this oil is poured, as then he will not in after life dislike the mixture.

584. I have still one very important direction to give: *NEVER LEND YOUR DOG.* It may seem selfish, but if you make him a really good one, I strongly advise you never to lend him to any one not even to a brother, unless, indeed, his method of hunting be precisely the same as your's. If you are a married man, you will not, I presume, lend your wife's horse to any one who has a coarse hand; you would at least do it with reluctance; but you ought (I hope she will forgive my saying so) to feel far more reluctance and far more grief, should you be obliged to lend a good dog to an ignorant sportsman or to one who shoots for the pot.

CONCLUSION.

585. GENTLE Reader, according to the courteous phraseology of old novels, though most probably I ought to say, Brother Sportsman;—if you have had the patience to attend me through the preceding pages, while I have been describing the educational course of a dog from almost his infancy, up to maturity, I will hope that I may construe that patience into an evidence that they have afforded you some amusement and, perhaps, some useful instruction.

586. Though I may have failed in persuading you to undertake the instruction of your dogs yourself, yet I trust I have shown you how they ought to be broken in;* and if you are a novice in the field, I hope I have clearly explained to you in what manner they ought to be shot over,—a knowledge which no one can possess by intuition, and which you will find nearly as essential to the preservation of the good qualities of well-tutored dogs, as to the education of uninformed ones.

587. I believe that all I have said is perfectly true, and, as the system which I have described advocates kind treatment of man's most faithful companion, and his instruction with mildness rather than severity, I trust that you will be induced to give it a fair trial, and if you find it successful, recommend its adoption.

588. I dare not ask for the same favour at the hands of the generality of regular trainers—I have no right to expect such liberality. They, naturally enough, will not readily forgive my intruding upon what they consider exclusively their own domain,— and, above all, they will not easily pardon my urging every sportsman to break in his own dogs. They will, I know, endeavour to persuade their employers that the finished education which I have described is useless, or quite unattainable, without a great sacrifice of time;† and that, therefore, the system which I advocate is a bad

---

* A right good sportsman, in days long gone by, gave this advice to his son—"a true chip of the old block,"—" Don't get an experienced keeper wedded to his own customs and prejudices; but engage a young man fond of sport. Break *him* to your mind; and then, and not until then, will you have *dogs* broken to your mind."

† Is it quite certain that the keepers who plead their inability to devote more time to the improvement of their masters' dogs have never found time to break in dogs belonging to strangers? If a keeper would but make it a rule while he is going his rounds by day (to examine his traps, &c.) to allow each of his pupils in turn to

one. They will wish it to be forgotten—that I advise a gradual advance, step by step, from the A, B, C;—that accomplishments have only been recommended *after* the acquisition of essentials—never at the expense of essentials;—that at any moment it is in the instructor's power to say, "I am now satisfied with the extent of my pupil's acquirements, and have neither leisure nor inclination to teach him more;"—and that they cannot suggest quicker means of imparting any grade of education, however incomplete; at least they do not—I wish they would ; few would thank them more than myself.

589. Greatly vexed at the erroneous way in which I saw some dogs instructed in the north by one, who from his profession should have known better, I promised, on the impulse of the moment, to write. If I could have purchased any work which treated the subject in what I considered a judicious and perspicuous manner, and, above all, which taught by what means a *finished* education could be imparted, I would gladly have recommended the study of it,—have spared myself the trouble of detailing the results of my own observations and experience,—and not have sought to impose on any one the task of reading them. When I began the book, and even when I had finished it, I intended to put it forth without any token by which the writer might be discovered. Mr. Murray, however, forcibly represented that unless the public had some guarantee

to accompany him in fine weather, and avail himself of that opportunity to give the young dogs an occasional out-door lesson, they would all be brought under good subjection, and be taught to obey implicitly every signal of the hand —which is half the battle—without taking him from his other occupations, and without his having devoted more than a few hours exclusively to their preparatory education. If a keeper feels no pride in the conduct of his dogs—if he is not animated with a spark of the enthusiasm that incites the huntsman to such willing exertion in the education and performance of his hounds, he (the keeper) had better change his profession. He may attain to eminence in another, he certainly never will in his present position.

As I have just talked about a keeper "going his rounds" to examine his traps, it would be wrong not to mention the serviceable "Snap," a white, short-haired terrier belonging to a game-keeper of Mr. R——es, who for many years has sat as member for Dover. The little animal's personal qualities are far inferior to his mental, for even his master, with all his well-known partiality for his petted companion, cannot call him handsome; but he has a right to quote in the dog's favour the old saying, "Handsome is as handsome does." Besides other ways of rendering himself useful, "Snap" willingly considers it a standing rule that he is to start off alone every morning after breakfast to take the tour of all the traps. On his return to the lodge, if he has no report to make, he maintains a discreet silence; but if any of them are sprung, by vermin or otherwise, he loudly proclaims the fact, and leads the keeper, whose time and legs he has thus cleverly saved, direct to any spots requiring his personal attention.

CAUSE OF AUTHOR'S WRITING. 321

for the fidelity of the details, there would be no chance of the little work being circulated, or proving useful; therefore, having written solely from a desire to assist my brother sportsmen, and to show the injudiciousness of severity, with a wish that my readers might feel as keen a zest for shooting as I once possessed, and with a charitable hope that they might not be compelled to seek it in as varied climates as was my lot, I at once annexed my address and initials to the manuscript, but with no expectation that my pen could interest the public half as much as it would a favourite Skye terrier, well known in Albemarle Street.

UNITED SERVICE CLUB,
    PALL MALL.

BRISK.

POSTSCRIPT

TO THE SECOND EDITION, REPRINTED IN THIS.

Sometime after the foregoing sheets were numbered and prepared for the press, I received a letter on the subject of dogs and dog-breaking from Mr. L——g (spoken of in 183).

I had long ago requested him freely to make remarks upon my book, assuring him that as I had only written from a wish to be serviceable, I could not but take all his comments in good part, however much they might be opposed to my pre-conceived ideas. I further promised to mention his criticisms for the benefit of my future readers, if I considered them judicious.

Every man is fully entitled to form an opinion for himself: and as there are minor points—though on most we are fully agreed—in which Mr. L——g and myself slightly differ, I think it the fairest plan to let him explain his own views in his own way, and I have the less hesitation in doing so as, to most sportsmen, a letter from a clever sportsman on his favourite subject must always be more or less interesting. He writes nearly word for word as follows:—

"7, Haymarket, January, 1850.

"Sir,—On perusing your book on dog-breaking I really find little, if anything, to say that will assist you in your new edition; but I must observe that I think you would be doing a service to the community, if you would lend a helping hand to improve the breed of pointers; or rather to get up a sort of committee of sportsmen (thorough judges) to investigate into the pedigree of dogs, and express their opinion of the make, nose, durability, &c., of the several animals submitted to them; that prizes might be awarded, or stakes hunted for; and books kept of the pedigree of the several competitors, much in the same way as such matters are managed with greyhounds.

"It is of no consequence how fast a dog travels who is wanted for the moors, or how wide he ranges; but such a dog would be worse than useless in the south, and in all small enclosures. I feel assured that dogs which are first-rate on grouse are not fitted for partridge. My experience tells me that not one dog in twenty is worth keeping,—that the generality do far more harm than good,—this I see almost every day that I am out. There seem to be now-a-days no recognised thorough-bred pointers, but those obtained from one or two kennels in Yorkshire. I have shot over many north-country dogs, but found there was too much of the fox-hound blood in them for the south,—they are too high couraged, and range much too far. After the first fortnight of partridge-shooting you want quiet, close rangers who will never move until told. In the turnip fields in Norfolk you will get among lots of birds, and you may then fill your bag any day, provided you can hunt the field in perfect quiet; but with a rattling, blustering dog you will hardly get a shot,—yet you want a dog that shall be neither too large nor too heavy.

"Not one dog in fifty of the many I see, properly hunts his ground. The reason is this. The keepers in the north,—yet none understand their duties better,—take out a lot of dogs along with an old one; off they all start like oiled lightning—some one way, the others just the contrary : one gets a point, they all drop and stop. The keepers say, is not that beautiful?—is it not a picture for Landseer? I have followed the party on the moors over the self-same ground a dozen of times, and obtained with my brace of close rangers and good finders double the number of shots that they did, and three times the amount of game; for I was walking at my ease, and giving my dogs time to make out the birds—which is very essential in the middle of the day, when there is a scorching sun.

"I recollect one instance in particular. Some years ago I had just arrived at the top of a very stiff hill on the Bradfield Moors (in Yorkshire), and was making for a certain spring where I had forwarded my luncheon, and a fresh supply of ammunition, when I saw, immediately before me, two gentlemen with their keepers, and four very good-looking setters, hunting the precise ground I had to take to get to my point—about a mile off. I therefore sat down for a quarter of an hour to let them get well ahead. They found several straggling birds; but there was such a noise from the keepers rating and hallooing to the dogs, that, although they got five or six shots, they only bagged one brace of birds. When they reached the spring, they observed me coming over the very ground they had beat only a quarter of an hour before. I got ten shots, every one to points, and killed nine birds. I was highly complimented on the beautiful, quiet style of my dogs, &c., and was offered a goblet of as fine old sherry as man ever drunk. I need not observe that I much relished it after my morning's walk. The gentlemen said, that if I felt disposed to take the dogs to the Tontine Inn, Sheffield, when I had done with them, I should find fifty guineas there awaiting me; but I declined the offer, as on several occasions I had repented having yielded to the temptation of a long price for favourite dogs. The brace I refused to sell were young setters, bred by Tom Craddas, keeper to — Bowes, Esq., near Barnard Castle, Durham. I subsequently found them very unfitted for the style of work required in small fields and indifferent stubble, and I was well beaten in a trial with them against a brace of Russian setters. I afterwards procured the latter by exchanging my Englishmen for them. For two years I was much pleased with the foreigners, and bred some puppies from them; they did not, however, turn out to my satisfaction. I then tried a cross with some of the best dogs I could get in England and from Russia, but could never obtain any so good as the original stock. I have now got into a breed of red and white pointers from the splendid stock of the late

Sir Harry Goodrich, and many and many another hundred head of game should I have killed,—and in much greater comfort and temper should I have shot,—had I possessed so perfect a breed twenty years ago.

"As a proof of what can be done with dogs, I will mention that I broke in a spaniel to hunt (with my setters) in the open as well as in cover, and made him 'point,' 'back,' and 'drop to charge,' as perfectly as any dog you ever saw; and he would, when ordered, retrieve his game; the setter, meanwhile, never moving until desired. I shot over them for two years. They were a very killing pair, but had not a sporting look. In September, '38, I took them with me to that excellent sportsman, Sir Richard Sutton. The old Squire Osbaldiston, was there. They were both much pleased with the dogs. By letting my poor pet 'Dash' run about, he was bitten by a mad dog in the neighbourhood. Of course I lost him.

"Speaking of spaniels, I must say I think that there is no kind of dog that retrieves birds so well in thick turnips, where so much dead and wounded game is frequently left unbagged. With 'Dash' I seldom lost a feather in the strongest turnips in the course of a whole day; but I now rarely go out with sportsmen but that I see two or three birds lost,—sometimes more,—from what are *said* to be the best breed of retrievers in the country. The constant loss of wounded birds is one of the drawbacks to the Norfolk shooting, where, without doubt, the finest shooting in England is to be obtained. Gentlemen there go out, some four, five, or six in a line, with only one or two retrievers, and a man to each to pick up the killed game. The sportsmen never stop to load, for each has generally a man by his side with a spare gun ready charged. If a bird is winged, or a hare wounded, the dogs go in at once to fetch it. Were the sportsmen to divide into distinct parties, each party taking one or two steady, close-ranging dogs, what much more true sport and pleasure they would have!—and kill, too, quite as much game.

"You ask me wherein I differ from you in what you have written? Certainly in very little,—and I have sent several gentlemen to Murray's for copies of your book; but in page 3, you say that 'dog-breaking does not require much experience.' There I cannot agree with you,—for how is it that there are so few who understand it? Not one keeper or gentleman in a thousand, in my opinion. The reason is that they have not sufficient practice and experience.*

"In another point I differ with you. I have seen some of the best rangers I ever shot over made by being allowed to follow their mother in the field, or some very old dog,†—what some people would term a worn-out potterer. But I think it a yet better plan to attach a lay cord of about forty yards in length to the collar of the young dog, and let a man or boy hold the other end. You will give a slight

---

* The reason in my opinion is, that they have not been properly taught—how to teach.— W. N. H.

† An expeditious method, as is admitted in 191, but there, I think, all praise ceases. —W. N. H.

whistle when he gets to the extremity of his range, and a wave of the hand to turn him forward or back.* By such means I have seen dogs, with a few days' constant shooting, made perfect in that,—the *most essential* thing in all dog-breaking.

"I observe that you condemn the check-collar † *in toto*. I think you are wrong. I have seen dogs cured by it who would not drop to shot, but would perpetually rush in, especially if a wounded bird was fluttering near them, and who had been most unmercifully licked, to no useful purpose. I recollect orders being given to destroy a dog that appeared utterly incorrigible. As he was a beautiful 'finder,' I begged that he might be allowed one more trial. I sent to town for a check-collar, and in a few hours he was pulled head over heels half-a-dozen times. He then found out what he was punished for, squatted down accordingly, and never afterwards attempted to rush forward, unless he was over-fresh. You speak of hares not annoying your dogs in Scotland. I have been sadly annoyed by them when grouse-shooting there. In one part, from hares jumping up every five minutes, I had great difficulty in restraining my dogs from chasing; and on this occasion I found the check-collar quite a blessing,—for had I used the whip I should have been thrown off my shooting, and the noise would have disturbed the birds. I had at the time two of the best shots in England shooting against me, and I should to a certainty have been beaten had I not been so prudent as to take out the collar.

"I remember selling to a young officer a brace of my puppies, or rather young dogs (for they were eighteen months old), for twenty-five guineas. They were well broken, but had not been shot over. He had not been an hour on the moors before up started one of the small Scotch sheep. Both the dogs gave chase, and on their return the keeper was directed to give them a good dressing. One of them would not hunt for them again, and became so timid that the officer desired the keeper to get rid of it. It was given to a gentleman in the neighbourhood, who knew he could not be far away in accepting it, as it had been bred and sold by me. He took it out a few times and soon found out its value. The other dog the officer sold for 10*l*., and then wrote a very angry letter to me, complaining of my having sold him such a brace as well broken. A fortnight after this he invited the gentleman who had become possessor of the shy puppy to come and shoot with him. The gentleman made his appearance with, what he termed, his 'shy friend.' After many protestations against

---

* Doubtless a good plan; perhaps the best plan with a bold dog whose initiatory education has been neglected—and who, in consequence, will not watch for your signals, nor yet look to you on your whistling; but the cord might be longer, and the boy should follow the dog to allow of his range being more extended.— W. N. H.

† Meaning the spike collar described in 300 of this, and 136 of first edition. No mention was made in that edition of the milder collar now spoken of in 301.— W. N. H.

taking out such a brute, it was agreed that it should be done on the gentleman's offering to bet 5*l*. that his 'shy friend' would get more points than either of the dogs they proposed hunting; and another 5*l*. that he should prove himself the best broken of the dogs, and never during the whole day offer to chase hare or sheep. The bets were not made, but to show you the esteem in which his late master afterwards held the animal, he offered fifty guineas to get her back, but the money was refused. His brother also turned out a magnificent dog—so much for want of patience.

"It is just possible that all I have written may be of no use,—but should you find it of any, it is quite at your service. Since I last saw you I have had many more opportunities of observing the extraordinary nose of the dog I showed you—a quality in which I fancy forty-nine out of fifty dogs are deficient. I sent him down to Hickfield-place, Hants, for the Speaker, who is an excellent sportsman, to use for a few times to see if he was not superior to his dogs. He returned the dog with a very handsome basket of game, saying he was one of the finest dogs he had ever seen hunted, and he begged me to get him a brace of the same kind against next season; stating that the price would be no consideration if they proved as good as mine. I have tried him against many other old dogs, *said* to be 'the best in England,' but not one of them had a shadow of a chance against him. I have refused a very long price for him. For beauty, style, symmetry, nose, durability, and good-temper (a great thing), none can beat him. I should like to increase his breed for the sake of the shooting community; yet I have no wish to keep him publicly as a sire, nor to send him away. I think I should be doing a general benefit, if I gave it out that his services could be obtained for three guineas : and that the sums thus obtained were to be set aside as a prize for the best dog, to be contended for by competitors who should give 3*l*. or 5*l*. each. Something of this kind, could, I think, be managed, and it would greatly tend to improve our breed of pointers. I bought a bitch with the view of getting some pups by him. She had nine, but not one like the father, grandfather, or great-grandfather—so I sold her, puppies and all. I have just purchased another; she comes of an excellent stock, and has good shape. I shall see what luck I have with her. She is a far more likely dam.

"I should have written to you long ago, had I not expected to meet the person I term my Yorkshire breeder. He is *the best breaker I ever saw*, and a man you can depend upon. He and his father, for sixty years, have borne as high a character for honesty, as for excellence in breaking. Many a time has he contended, and always come off victor, against Mr. Edge's dogs—a good trial kennel, but the breed have savage dispositions, bad tempers, and are very unmanageable when young. I have tried many of them myself, and have no faith in them.

"On the moors, when the work is excessively fatiguing, and plenty of water is generally to be found, you may with advantage employ setters: but in a hot September, in England, when no water could be procured, I have known some of the best setters I ever saw do nothing but put up the birds. In mid-day, when there was but little scent, their nasal organs seemed quite to fail them, and being fast they constantly ran into coveys before they could stop themselves.

"I was once asked to be umpire in a match between a pointer and a setter. It was to be decided by which of the dogs got most points in the day. As this was the agreement, I was obliged to abide by it and decide accordingly: but that is not the test by which the superiority of dogs ought to be determined. I presume what is really wanted in a dog is *usefulness to his master in killing game*. If so, that dog ought to be considered best which gets his master most shots within a rise not exceeding forty yards.* The setter being faster and taking a much wider range, got by far the most points, therefore I was compelled to award him the prize; but the pointer made twenty-two points to which the party got twenty-one shots. The setter got thirty points, but only sixteen of them could be shot to, and he put up thrice as many birds as the pointer. I could mention twenty other similar instances of trials between pointers and setters, but I should fill half-a-dozen more sheets and not interest you. It is getting dark, so I will conclude my long yarn.

"I am, Sir,
"Your obedient servant,
(Signed) "JOSH. LANG."

* In the correctness of this reasoning I fully concur.—W. N. H.

APPENDIX.

NOTE TO 65.—*Covers.—Shooting.—Loading.*

WHAT convenient covers they are—and what excellent shelter they furnish for game, when planted with holly, laurel, and other evergreens!—especially if the proprietor, in a moment of sporting enthusiasm, has consented to his keeper's request, and had some of the trees half-felled, so that the branches lying on the ground live and grow, deriving nourishment from the sap still flowing through the uncut bark. Perhaps gorse forms the best ground cover for the preservation of game; but it is far from being the most agreeable to shoot in. It has, however, a great merit—it is much disliked by poachers. There should be good roosting-trees; and the different kinds of fir—spruce particularly—give most security, their thick, spreading branches affording much concealment at all seasons of the year. They are, too, of quick growth. But the most favourably planted covers will prove unattractive unless there is a constant supply of water within a reasonable distance. An old brother officer of mine, who has property in Suffolk, argues,—and most will think correctly,—that for the preservation of game, beltings should not run round the external part of an estate (as is often the case,) but lie well within it, and at some distance from a high road.

Talking of beltings and pheasants, as some sporting Griffin (to use an Indian expression) may come across this book, I may as well, for his sake, mention, that pheasants are generally prevented from running to the further end of a belting, and then rising in one dense cloud, by a man sent ahead striking two sticks together, or making some other slight noise which, without too much alarming the birds, yet prevents their running past him. As the guns approach him he gets further forward and takes up another position, keeping wide of the cover whilst he is on the move. Should the Griffin make one of the shooting-party, he is advised to bear in mind that the guns should keep close to the hedge (or rails), that any game on the point of "breaking" may not so readily observe them, and in consequence beat a retreat. By the bye, my young friend, should you wish your host to give you another invitation to his covers never let him see you carrying your barrels horizontally. If you are a bit of a soldier you will know what I mean when I say that, combining due preparation for prompt action with security to him who may be skirmishing near, your gun can be conveniently borne across the open at the " Slope arms " of the sergeant's fusil. When you are in cover (or your dog draws upon game), it might be carried much in the position of " Port arms." At the moment you level, following the example of the best pigeon shots, place your left hand well in advance of the poise. If you have any fears of the barrels bursting, leave them at home. Your steadiest position is with the elbow held nearly perpendicularly under the gun: whereas your right elbow ought to be almost in a horizontal line with your shoulder, thus furnishing a convenient hollow for the reception of the butt. The firmer you grasp the stock the less is the recoil. That amusing fellow Wanostrocht, in his work on cricketing ("Felix on the Bat"), writes, "The attitude of *en garde* of the left-handed swordsman is the attitude of *play* for the right-handed batsman,"—and you, my supposed Griffin, may rest assured that it is the best position your feet and legs can take on a bird's rising, but the right foot might be with advantage a little more to the right. Wanostrocht continues, "The knees are bent; and the body, well balanced, is prepared," you may add, "to turn steadily to the right or left according to the flight of the bird." In nine cases out of ten the common advice to "keep both eyes open" when firing is extremely judicious. But some men are "left-eyed;" a matter you have probably little thought about; and yet it is of consequence, for if you are "left-eyed," your aim from the right shoulder (both eyes being open) cannot be correct. To determine whether or not you are "right-eyed," look steadily, with both eyes open, at any small object near you,—rapidly raise a finger (of either hand) perpendicularly, endeavouring to cover the object. Instantly close the left eye. If you find that your finger lies in the direct line between the object and your right eye, you will have the satisfaction of knowing that you are "right-eyed;" but if your finger, instead of intercepting the object, is wide of the mark, at once close the right eye and open the left, when you will, in all probability, perceive that that your finger lies directly between your left eye and the object, thereby showing that you are "left-eyed." I hope it may not be so, as, unless you can shoot from the left shoulder, you ought to close the left eye when bringing your gun to the poise, until from practice you become "right-eyed." The odds are in favour of your being right-legged as well as right-eyed, which important point will be settled, I hope to your satisfaction, should you ever be under the disagreeable necessity of having to kick an impertinent fellow downstairs. Never shoot in a hurry. Strive to acquire coolness—in other words, strive to acquire such a command over your trigger-finger that it shall never bend until so ordered by your judgment. Your eye will inform your reason of the exact moment when you ought to pull, and your finger, submissive to reason, ought to wait for that precise moment, and not yield to any nervousness. Look with the *greatest intensity* at the bird as it rises, and coolly observe its line of flight while deliberately bringing the barrels to your shoulder. Steadiness will be increased by your not removing the gun from your shoulder the instant you have fired. Never fire when your shot can be of no more advantage than a single bullet. If you have a bet about killing a jack snipe, seize the favourable moment for pulling the trigger when the pellets will be spread over a disk of more than a yard in diameter. He will then be zigzagging some thirty-five or forty yards from you; and if your aim is taken at this moment a full foot in advance of his *general*

line of flight, there is little chance of his escaping unpeppered (and one grain will suffice), however adroitly he may turn and twist. For any kind of bird flying at that distance rapidly down-wind and crossing you, your gun ought to be pitched *much* further forward. A still greater allowance should be made if the distance be considerable: and greater elevation should be then given to the barrels, as the grains of shot will become deflected. The same rule holds with birds rising. Aim must be taken above them. There is always more fear of your firing too much to the rear and too low, than too much to the front and too high. Fancy that hares and rabbits have only heads—and get into the habit of looking at no other part,—nay, of looking yet further ahead. The best cover-shot I know says, that he aims at a rabbit rushing through gorse or underwood a yard in front of the spot where he last caught a glimpse of it. Rabbits halt for a moment the instant they get hidden by cover—not so hares. That their hands and eyes may work in unison, novices have been recommended to hang on the flight of swallows with an unloaded gun. It would be better practice to hang on a full foot or more in front of the birds. To save your locks use snap caps, and pull the very instant you think your aim is correct. No second aim can be so effective as the first. The more you thus practise (and at game especially, in order to overcome any nervous sensation occasioned by birds rising) before you commence using powder, the more certain is it that you will eventually become a cool, steady shot. After having commenced the campaign in right earnest, should you be shooting unsteadily or nervously, you would do well to have the philosophy to go up a few times to your dog's point with uncapped nipples, and by taking (long after the birds are on the wing, but yet within shot) a deliberate aim reassure yourself of the folly of all hurry and precipitancy. Lest you should (as often happens in spite of every previous resolution) involuntarily pull the trigger sooner than you intend, keep your finger off it until the very instant you wish to fire.*
If you shoot with a muzzle loader and carry one of Sykes's spring-shot pouches—at present in such general use—by having its nozzle lengthened (some few are made long),—I mean by having a cylinder of nearly three inches in length welded to its end,—you will be able to load quicker than most of your fellow-sportsmen—particularly if you use a loading-rod: the best are of cane, because the material is light and tough. You can make the long nozzle of the shot-pouch (its end being cut square, *i.e.* at a right angle to its length) force the wad over the powder so far down the barrel before you press the pouch-spring to pour in the charge of shot, that you need not draw your ramrod to drive home until after you have inserted the shot-wad. Using a long nozzle has also this great advantage, that the shot is packed more densely than the powder. In the new German copper-cap musket (whose long range is now, 1854, much spoken of,) to keep the powder loose when the charge is rammed home, a thick peg, nearly one and a half inches long, is fixed longitudinally in the

---

* See end of 448.

centre of the chamber,—I mean, in the direction of the axis of the bore. This cylindrical peg, which is much like the *tige* invented by Colonel Touvenin in 1828, arrests the *jagged* bullet at the precise moment when the powder is sufficiently pressed to remove all chance of the *slightly* six-grooved barrel's bursting; and yet not so much pressed as to interfere with the complete ignition of *every* grain. These lie loose round the peg. The want of this complete ignition (owing to the rapidity of explosion not giving time for all the particles of closely-wedged powder being fired) has been the only valid objection yet offered to the detonating system. For strong shooting, the wad over the powder should be *much* thicker than the wad placed over the shot. The several waddings now sold greased with some mercurial preparation undeniably retard leading—a great gain. If the long nozzle of the shot-pouch fits close within the barrel, on unloading your gun you can easily return the shot into the pouch without losing a grain. As a concluding piece of advice let me recommend you, my young friend, to make but a light breakfast whenever you expect a heavy day's work,—take out, however, a few sandwiches for luncheon.

NOTE TO 283.—*Trapping.—Owl as decoy.—Hen Harrier.—Keeper's Vermin dogs.—Stoats.*

A good book for gamekeepers on trapping is still a great desideratum. It should be written by a practical man who is a bit of a naturalist ; for no trapper can be very successful unless he is well acquainted with the haunts and habits of the many kinds of vermin it is his business to destroy. Mr. C——e's gamekeeper, at R——n, Perthshire, who was well aware of the great importance of diligently searching for their nests in the breeding season, was at length amply repaid for often watching the proceedings of a hen-harrier frequently seen hovering over a small wood not far from his cottage. He could never perceive that she alighted on any of the trees ; but from the time of year, and her so perseveringly returning to the spot, he felt convinced that her nest was not far off. Ineffectual, however, was every search. At length, one morning he was lucky enough to remark that something fell from her. He hunted close in that direction,—found the nest, and the young ones regaling on a snipe whose remains were still warm ; evidently the identical bird she had most adroitly dropped from a considerable height into the middle of her hungry brood. It would have been very interesting to have observed how she managed on a windy day. Probably she would have taken an easy shot by sweeping close to the trees. In Germany much winged vermin is destroyed with the aid of a decoy horned owl. The keeper having selected a favourable spot on a low hillock where the bird is likely to be observed, drives an upright post into the ground, the upper part of which is hollowed. The bird is placed on a perch much shaped like the letter **T**. A string is attached to the bottom of the perpendicular part, which is then dropped into the hollow or socket. The armed keeper conceals himself in a loopholed sentry-box, prepared of green boughs, at a suitable distance, amidst sheltering foliage. His pulling the string raises the perch. The owl, to preserve its balance, flutters its wings. This is sure to attract the notice of the neighbouring magpies, hawks, crows, &c. Some from curiosity hover about, or, still chattering and peering, alight on the neighbouring trees (of course, standing invitingly within gun-shot); others, having no longer any reverence for the bird of Wisdom in his present helpless condition, wheel round and round, every moment taking a sly peck at their fancied enemy, while their real foe sends their death-warrant from his impervious ambuscade.

Talking of vermin, I am reminded that J——s H——d, an old gamekeeper with whom I am acquainted, avers that one of his craft can hardly be worth his salt unless he possesses "a regular good varmint of a dog." It should be of a dark colour, not to betray so readily the movements of his master to interested parties. He says he once owned one, a bull-terrier, that was, to again quote the old man's words, "worth his weight in gold to a gamekeeper;" that it was incredible the quantity of ground-vermin, of every kind, the dog killed, which included snakes and adders—destroyers of young birds of every sort, and it is said of eggs (but this it is difficult to conceive, unless we imagine them to be crushed in the same manner as the boa-constrictor murders his victims, a supposition without a shadow of proof—small eggs, however, might be swallowed whole),—that he was perpetually hunting, but never noticed game—had an excellent nose, and, on occasions when he could not run into the vermin, would unerringly lead his master to the hole in the old bank, tree, or pile of fagots where it had taken refuge; when, if it was a stoat or weasel, and in a place where the report of a gun was not likely to disturb game, the keeper would bring him into "heel," wait patiently awhile, and then, by imitating the cry of a distressed rabbit, endeavour to entice the delinquent to come forth and be shot. If this *ruse* failed, H——d quickly prepared a trap that generally sealed the fate of the destructive little creature. As the dog retrieved all he caught, the old barn-door was always well covered with *recent* trophies. Old trophies afford no evidence of a keeper's diligence.

The dog invariably accompanied his master during his rounds at night, and had great talents for discovering any two-legged intruder. On finding one he would quietly creep up, and then, by running round and round him as if prepared every moment to make a spring, detain him until joined by the keeper; all the while barking furiously and adroitly avoiding every blow aimed at his sconce.*

---

* If you are attacked by a dog when you have the good fortune to be armed with a shilelagh, do not hit him across the head and eyes; bear in mind that the front part of his fore legs is a far more vulnerable and sensitive spot. One or two well applied blows upon that unprotected place will generally disable the strongest dog. Consider how feelingly alive your own shins are to the slightest rap. I have in India seen a vicious horse quite cowed under such discipline, and a really savage nag in that country is, to use an expression common among the natives, a fellow who would

He was moreover (but this has little to do with his sporting habits), a most formidable enemy to dogs of twice his power; for he would cunningly throw himself upon his back if overmatched, and take the same unfair advantage of his unfortunate opponent which Polygars are trained to do when they are attacking the wild hog (445).

I relate this story about H——d and his bull terrier because few men ever were so successful in getting up a good show of game on a property. It was a favourite observation of his that it was not game,—it was vermin, that required looking after; that these did more injury than the largest gang of poachers, as the depredations of the latter could be stopped, but not those of the former. There are few who, on reflection, will not agree with the old keeper. Stoats are so bloodthirsty, that if one of them come across a brood of young pheasants he will give each in succession a deadly gripe on the back of the neck close to the skull, not to make any use of the carcasses, but in the epicurean desire to suck their delicate brains. All who are accustomed to "rabbiting" know that even tame ferrets evince the same murderous propensities, and commit indiscriminate slaughter, *apparently* in the spirit of wanton destructiveness.

From all, however, that I have seen and heard, I fancy no animal so much prevents the increase of partridges and pheasants, as the hooded crow.

An intelligent man, C——s M——n (an admirable dresser of salmon-flies), whose veracity I have no reason to distrust, assured me that he had seen about the nest of a "hoodie" (as he called the bird), the shells of not less than two hundred eggs, all nearly of the partridge and pheasant. He told me that he once had an opportunity of observing the clever proceedings of a pair of these marauders, bent on robbing the nest on which a hen-pheasant was actually sitting. One of the depredators by fluttering round her, and slily pecking at her unprotected stern, at length so succeeded in irritating her, that she got up to punish him. By a slow scientific retreat, he induced her to pursue him for a few steps, thus affording his confederate, who

"eat one to the very turban." They will sometimes cure a biter by letting him seize a leg of mutton burning hot off the fire— not so expensive a remedy as you may think, where sheep, wool, or rather hair and all, are constantly sold at 2*s.* each,—I will not describe how poor,—I have lifted them up, one in each hand, to judge of their comparative weight. A country bred horse may be conquered by harsh means; but a true Arab never. It is rare to find one that is not sweet-tempered; but when he is vicious,

his high spirit and great courage make him quite indomitable.

With a stout stick, a better defence than you may at first imagine can be made against the attack of a vicious bull. Smart blows struck on the *tip* of his horns seem to cause a jar painfully felt at the roots. Mr. B——n, of A——n, when he was charged in the middle of a large field by a bull which soon afterwards killed a man, adopting this plan, beat off the savage animal, though it several times renewed its attacks.

had concealed himself, the opportunity of removing certainly one egg, perhaps two. By repetitions of this sham attack and retreat, the adroit pilferers eventually managed to empty the nest.

The above mentioned man had been brought up as a gamekeeper in Cumberland. He became an excellent trapper; and was afterwards employed on an estate near the Cheviot Hills, where, in a short time, he got up a decent stock of game by destroying the vermin. He found the grounds swarming with "hoodies;" but it was not until their breeding season the following spring, when he was favoured in his operations by a frost, that he succeeded in capturing them in considerable numbers. On the ground becoming hard, he, for nearly a fortnight, fed certain spots on the banks of the Teviot with wood pigeons and rabbits, besides any vermin that he contrived to shoot. By that time the "hoodies" habitually resorted, without distrust, to those places for food. He then set his traps baited with all such delicacies,—but he considered a small rabbit, or a pigeon lying on its back with outstretched wings, as the most tempting of his invitations; and it often happened that he had scarcely disappeared before the click of the closing spring apprised him of a capture. When his frequent success had rendered the birds shy, he set his traps in the adjacent stream, covering their sides with grass or rushes,—the attractive bait alone appearing above the surface. For three reasons he regarded the banks of the river as the best situation for his traps—he could, as just mentioned, conceal them in the water on the birds becoming too suspicious—secondly, streams are much resorted to by the "hoodie," who searches diligently for any chance food floating on the water,—and lastly, the rooks, of which there were many in that part of the country, from naturally hunting inland, the reverse of the "hoodie," were the less likely to spring his traps.

From the short, fuller neck,—the head bent peeringly downwards,—but, above all, from the hawk-like movements of the wing, the sportsman will be able to distinguish the hooded-crow from the rook at a moment when he may be too distant to observe the black and more hooked bill,—and never let him spare. He should be suspicious of every bird he sees crossing and recrossing a field,—in reality hunting it with as regular a beat as a pointer's.

M——n killed a great many stoats and weasels with *unbaited* traps. As it is the habit of these little animals, when hunting a hedgerow, to prefer running through a covered passage to turning aside, he used, where the ground favoured him by slightly rising, to cut a short drain, about a foot in breadth, and rather less in depth, parallel and close to the hedge, covering it with the sods he had removed. At the bottom of these drains he fixed his traps, as soon as the animals became accustomed to the run, and rarely failed in securing every member of the weasel family which had taken up its abode in the vicinity. The best description of hutch-trap (which many prefer to the gin-trap) is made entirely of wire, excepting the bottoms. All appears so light and airy that little suspicion is awakened. The doors fall on anything running over the floor. Of

APPENDIX.

food. In a long voyage a bird that dies in a coop is often found by "Billyducks"* half eaten up; and it is questionable whether a sickly companion be not occasionally sacrificed by his stronger associates to appease their natural craving for flesh. In the West Indies the accidental upsetting of an old sugar-cask in a farm-yard, and its scattering forth a swarm of cock-roaches, sets all the feathered tribe in a ferment. The birds that had been listlessly sauntering about, or standing half-asleep in the friendly shade, suddenly seem animated with the fury of little imps,—and, influenced by a taste *in every way* repugnant to our feelings, with outstretched necks and fluttering wings race against each other for possession of

FOUL' FEEDING.

the offensive, destructive insects, evincing in the pursuit an agility and a rapidity of movement of which few would imagine them to be capable.

The keeper just spoken of used to rear his pheasants within doors, or rather in an outhouse, the floor of which was in part covered with sods of turf,—but I think J——s T——n, another of the craft whom I know well, pursues a better and far less trouble-

---

* The common sobriquet of the boy in charge.

some plan. He selects a piece of clover * facing the south, and sheltered from the north and east winds by a contiguous small copse which he feels assured can harbour no destructive vermin. On this grass-plat, if the weather is fine, he places the common barn-door hens,—each with her brood the moment they are hatched,—under separate small coops. Two or three boards run from each coop, forming a temporary enclosure, which is removed in about a week on the little inmates gaining strength. If he has any fear of their being carried off by hawks, &c., he fixes a net overhead. The hens had sat on the eggs in an outhouse.

The first food given to the chicks is soaked bread,—and white of eggs cut up fine. The colour (is not that a bull?) catches their eye, which is the alleged reason for all their food being given to them white. Ants' nests are procured for them,—of the red ant first,—of the larger kind, when the chicks become so strong that the insects cannot injure them—later in the season, wasps' nests. When there is a difficulty in procuring any of these nests, curd is often given; but should it become sour, as frequently happens in hot weather, it is likely to occasion dysentery,† therefore oatmeal porridge made with milk is considered a safer diet. This is eagerly picked up when scattered about, sprinkled as it were,—and the weaker chicks are thus enabled to secure a fair share. T——n breeds a quantity of maggots for them,—and at no expense,—in the adjacent copse. Whatever vermin he kills (whether winged or four-footed) he hangs up under a slight awning as a protection from the rain. On the flesh decaying the maggots drop into the box placed underneath to receive them. The insects soon become clean, if sand and bran is laid at the bottom of the box, and it is an interesting sight to see the excited little birds eagerly hurrying from all quarters to the grass-plat on the keeper striking the tray with his knuckles to invite them to partake of some choice maggots, spread out on sanded boards.

If a piece of carrion is placed under a wire netting near the coops, the chicks will feed with avidity on the flies it attracts.

Change of food is beneficial:—therefore, boiled barley or rice, is often substituted, or oatmeal, or Indian-corn meal,—mixed with the flesh of boiled rabbits.

Saucers of clean water are placed about. Water in a dirty state is very injurious. It is not of any depth, lest the chicks should wet their feathers when standing in it. Occasionally iron saucers are used, ingeniously designed on the ridge and furrow plan. The

---

* Clover does not retain the wet like common grass, and it affords some shade in hot weather to the very young birds.

† Until the young birds recover do not let them have access to any water in which alum is not dissolved in the proportion of a lump about the size of a walnut to half a gallon of water—also mix such a quantity of common salt in their food, that the stimulant therein is quite perceptible to your taste, and feed more sparingly than usual.

Z

ridges are so little apart, that the chicks can insert no more than their heads into the furrows. As cleanliness must in all things be preserved, the coops are shifted a few feet aside twice a day.

The chicks soon quit the hens to roost in the shrubs, which afford welcome shade during the mid-day heat; but the imprisoned matrons are still useful, as their plaintive call prevents the chicks from becoming irreclaimable truants. As they have always the opportunity of running in the grass and copse, where they find seeds and insects, they quickly become independent, and learn to forage for themselves,—yet when fully grown up they are not so likely to stray away as birds who have been more naturally reared, and who have been made wanderers even in their infancy. This is a great advantage.

That the chicks may come upon fresh ground for seeds and insects, the situation of the coops may be occasionally changed. If liable to be attacked by vermin at night, a board can be fixed in front of each coop.

Partridges may be reared by the same means. But instances are rare of their laying while in a state of captivity.

That the young birds may be able to rid their bodies of vermin, they should be provided with small heaps of sand protected from rain, and dry earth, in which they will gladly rub themselves.

If you design rearing pheasants annually, always keep a few of the tame hens and a cock at home. By judicious management these will supply a large quantity of eggs for hatching,—eggs that you can ensure, when in their freshest state, being placed under barn-door hens. Keep the eggs in a cool place. I cannot believe that you will ever be guilty—for it is guilt, great guilt—of the sin of *purchasing* eggs. "Buyers make thieves,"—and one sneaking, watching, unwinged pilferer on two legs would do more mischief in the month of May than dozens of magpies or hooded crows.

Pheasants so soon hunt for their own subsistence, that they are brought to maturity at less expense than common fowls.

Since the publication of the second edition, I have had an opportunity of talking to Mr. Cantelo, the clever inventor of the novel hatching machine, whereby (following nature's principle) heat is imparted only to the upper surface of eggs. He annually rears a large quantity of all kinds of poultry, besides partridges and pheasants, and I believe no one in England is so experienced in these matters.

He found it best not to give food to any kind of chicks for the two first days after they were hatched. As they would not all break the shell together, it is probable that in a state of nature many of them would be for, at least, this period under the hen before she led them forth to feed. To young turkeys and pheasants he gave no food for three days. They would then eat almost anything voraciously, whereas, when fed sooner, they become dainty and fastidious.

He recommends that the lean of raw beef, or any meat (minced fine, as if for sausages) be given to partridge or pheasant chicks, along with their other food,* or rather before their other food; and only in certain quantities; for if they are fed too abundantly on what they most relish, they are apt to gorge themselves, and they will seldom refuse meat, however much grain they may have previously eaten. He said that they should be liberally dieted, but not to repletion,—that once a day they should be sensible of the feeling of hunger.

It certainly is most consonant to nature, that the flesh given to the chicks should not be cooked; and Mr. Cantelo observed that it would be immediately found on trial, that young birds prefer that which is undressed,—nay, that which has a bloody appearance.

He considers maggots (gentles) an admirable diet, and he gave me a valuable hint about them. This is, that they be fattened on untainted meat, placed in the sand-box into which they fall. The pieces of meat will soon be drilled like a honey-comb, and the little crawlers, by becoming in a day or two large and fat, will prove a far more nourishing diet than when given in the attenuated state to which they are commonly reduced, by the present starving process of cleansing.

Mr. Cantelo has remarked that guinea-birds require food at an earlier period after they are hatched than any other sort of chick,—and that they and ducklings eat most meat,—turkey-poultry least.

Wet is injurious to all chickens (the duck-tribe excepted); and when the hen, from being confined, cannot lead her brood astray, they will, of themselves, return to her coop on finding the grass too damp.

Mr. Cantelo is strongly of opinion, that all diseases to which infant birds are liable are contagious. He advises, in consequence, that the moment any one of the brood is attacked with diarrhœa, sore eyes, or sneezing, it be instantly separated from the others.

He considers all chickens safe from ordinary diseases on their gaining their pen-feathers.

He has found that *nest* eggs, not sat on for twelve hours, do not lose their vitality. This shows that eggs taken by mowers should not be hastily thrown away, in consequence of a considerable delay unavoidably occurring before they can be placed under a hen to complete their hatching.

Pheasants sit about five days longer than common fowls.

Mr. Cantelo recommends that eggs sent from a distance be packed in oats. He had succeeded in hatching some he had kept, as an experiment, upwards of two months in a temperate atmosphere, *turning them daily*. This continued vitality is, however, seldom a consideration as regards pheasants; for the earlier in the season the birds can be produced the better. It is a great advantage to have five months' growth and feed in them by the first of October.

---

* Principally Indian corn-meal. When the chickens are older, the grain is merely bruised. To full-grown birds of a large species, it is given whole.

Mr. Knox, in his interesting work on "Game-birds and Wildfowl," has given some good advice about the rearing and preservation of pheasants. I will make some extracts from it, and, I think, many would do well to read the whole book.

With respect to a pheasantry for procuring eggs, he is of opinion that in March,—the time when the cocks begin to fight,—the enclosure containing the stock of birds should be divided, by high hurdles, or wattles, into partitions, so that each cock may be told off with three hens into a distinct compartment. He advises that no harem should be greater in a state of confinement. His opportunities for forming a correct judgment have probably been greater than mine; but I must observe that I have known of ladies, kept in such small seraglios, being worried to death. "The larger the compartments," he says, "the better;" "a heap of bushes and a mound of dry sand in each;" an attendant to visit them once (and but once) a day, to take in the food of "barley, beans, peas, rice, or oats; boiled potatoes, Jerusalem artichokes, and Swedish turnips;"* and to remove whatever eggs may have been laid during the preceding twenty-four hours.

The accidental destruction of the net overhanging Mr. Knox's pheasantry, and the escape of the cocks, led to his ascertaining a fact of much importance; viz. that pinioned hens (one wing amputated at the carpal joint—"the wounds soon healed") kept in an unroofed enclosure, near a cover, into which (what are called) "tame-bred pheasants" have been turned, will always attract sufficient mates—mates in a more healthy state than confined birds,—and that the eggs will be more numerous, and unusually productive.

I can easily imagine that such matrimonial alliances are sure to be formed wherever the opportunity offers; and if I were establishing a pheasantry, I would adopt the plan Mr. Knox recommends, unless withheld by the fear that more than one cock might gain admittance to the hens; for I am aware of facts which incline me to think, that, in such instances, the eggs may be unserviceable. At a connexion's of mine, where the poultry-yard lies close to a copse, hybrid chickens have often been reared—the offspring of barn-door hens and cock-pheasants *not tame-bred*.

Mr. Knox elsewhere observes, that the hen-pheasants kept in confinement should be tame-bred; that is, be "birds which have been hatched and reared under domestic hens, as those which are netted, or caught, in a wild state, will always prove inefficient layers." "About the fourth season a hen's oviparous powers begin to decline, although her maternal qualifications, in other respects, do not deteriorate until a much later period. It is, therefore, of consequence to enlist, occasionally, a few recruits, to supply the place of those females who have completed their third year, and who then may be set at large in the preserves." Of course, not those birds who have had the fore-hand of a wing amputated.

---

* For reasons already given, I think some animal food should be added.—W. N. H.

Talking of ants' eggs, which Mr. Knox terms "the right-hand of the keeper" in rearing pheasant chicks—it is the first food to be given to them—Mr. Knox says, "Some persons find it difficult to separate the eggs from the materials of the nest. The simplest mode is, to place as much as may be required—ants, eggs, and all—in a bag or light sack, the mouth of which should be tied up. On reaching home, a large white sheet should be spread on the grass, and a few green boughs placed round it on the inside, over which the outer edge of the sheet should be lightly turned; this should be done during sunshine. The contents of the bag should then be emptied into the middle, and shaken out so as to expose the eggs to the light. In a moment, forgetting all considerations of personal safety, these interesting little insects set about removing their precious charge—the cocoons—from the injurious rays of the sun, and rapidly convey them under the shady cover afforded by the foliage of the boughs near the margin of the sheet. In less than ten minutes the work will be completed. It is only necessary then to remove the branches; and the eggs, or cocoons, may be collected by handfuls, unencumbered with sticks, leaves, or any sort of rubbish."

Mr. Knox goes on to say, that "green tops of barley, leeks, boiled rice, Emden groats, oatmeal, &c.," are excellent diet for the chicks, but that this kind of food is "almost always given at too early a period. In a state of nature, their food, for a long time, would be wholly insectile." "Now, as it is not in our power to procure the quantity and variety of small insects and larvæ which the mother-bird so perseveringly and patiently finds for them, we are obliged to have recourse to ants' eggs, as easily accessible, and furnishing a considerable supply of the necessary sort of aliment in a small compass."

"When the chicks are about a week or ten days old, Emden groats and coarse Scotch oatmeal may be mixed with the ants' eggs; and curds, made from fresh milk, with alum, are an excellent addition. If ants' nests cannot be procured in sufficient quantities, gentles should occasionally be given."

When more wasps' nests are obtained than are required for immediate use, "it will be necessary to bake them for a short time in an oven. This will prevent the larvæ and nymphs from coming to maturity,—in fact, kill them—and the contents of the combs will keep for some weeks afterwards. Hempseed, crushed and mingled with oatmeal, should be given them when about to wean them from an insect diet. Hard-boiled eggs, also, form a useful addition, and may be mixed, for a long time, with their ordinary farinaceous food."

"Young pheasants are subject to a kind of diarrhœa, which often proves fatal. If the disease be taken in time, boiled milk and rice, in lieu of any other diet, will generally effect a cure. To these chalk may be added, to counteract the acidity which attends this complaint; and should the symptoms be very violent, a small quantity of alum, as an astringent."

This treatment appears reasonable. Many consider rice a judicious diet in such cases; and I know of a surgeon's giving boiled milk with great success, in the West Indies, to patients suffering from diarrhœa.

"But the most formidable disease from which the young pheasant suffers is that known by the name of 'the gapes:'—so termed from the frequent gaping efforts of the bird to inhale a mouthful of air. Chickens and turkeys are equally liable to be affected by it; and it may be remarked, that a situation which has been used, for many successive seasons, as a nursery ground, is more apt to be visited with this plague, than one which has only recently been so employed. Indeed, I have observed that it seldom makes its appearance on a lawn or meadow during the first season of its occupation; and, therefore, when practicable, it is strongly to be recommended, that fresh ground should be applied to the purpose every year: and when this cannot be done, that a quantity of common salt should be sown broadcast over the surface of the earth, after the birds have left it in the autumn." He elsewhere describes the gapes as that "dreadful scourge, which, like certain diseases that affect the human subject, seems to have been engendered and fostered by excessive population within a limited district."

"Dissection has proved that the latent cause of this malady is a minute worm of the genius *fasciola*, which is found adhering to the internal part of the windpipe, or trachea." Then Mr. Knox explains how this worm may be destroyed; (and only by such means,—the most delicate operator being unable to extract it without materially injuring the young bird)—viz. by fumigating with tobacco-smoke, according to the method (which he fully describes) recommended by Colonel Montagu. If the worm is not destroyed, the death of the bird ensues "by suffocation from the highly inflamed state of the respiratory apparatus."

I once kept many guinea-birds when abroad; and I am now convinced that I should have succeeded in rearing a far greater number, had I adopted more closely the mode of feeding, &c., here recommended for young pheasants.

In July, '57, I saw in a large clover field at Sandling, East Kent, 820 pheasant chicks which had been reared by M——n under sixty-six common hens. It was a very interesting sight. I accompanied him round all the coops. They stood about twenty paces apart, and I could not detect a single bird with a drooping wing or of sickly appearance. He told me most positively that he had not lost one by disease, but a few had been trodden under foot by careless, awkward hens, and, what seems curious, some few chicks on quitting the shell had been intentionally killed by the very hens which had hatched them. A hatching hen will sometimes thus destroy ducklings,—but these are far more unlike her natural progeny than are pheasant chicks. M——n found that game-fowls make the best mothers—Cochin-china the worst. He has a prejudice,—how doctors differ! against maggots and ants' nests. However, he has a right to his notions, for he lost hardly any birds in the year '56, out of the 400 and upwards that broke the shell. He devotes himself to what, with him, is a labour of love. He has great, and just pride in his success. He maintains that pheasants can be reared cheaper than barn-door fowls, wherever there are woods, as the chicks find their own food at such an early age. The rearing of the birds that I saw and about fifty partridge-chicks, occupied the whole of his time and that of an assistant. There was also a boy to cook, &c. The chicks were fed every two hours throughout the day with a mixture of hard boiled eggs,* curds, bread-crumbs, rape and canary seed. The shutter of each hutch doing duty as a tray for the food. After the chicks had fed M———n made his rounds, and scraped into a pot all that was not consumed, being careful that nothing was left to get sour. He gave a small portion of these remains to the imprisoned matrons. He feeds the chicks liberally, yet calculates to a great nicety what will be eaten, for on every shutter a portion, but a very small portion of food was left. Water, kept in earthenware pans made with concentric circles on the ridge and furrow system, was placed at intervals between the hutches. Many times a day he moved the several coops a few feet to fresh ground. At night when all the chicks have joined the hens he fastens the shutters, and does not remove them in the morning until the dew is off the grass. How entirely is this practice opposed to the advice of the Yorkshireman given at the commencement of this note! and yet it might be possible to reconcile the contradictory recommendations by supposing that as soon as the young birds have nearly reached maturity they are allowed to search for insects at the earliest dawn. M———n's last location for the hutches would be in the centre of the landlord's property, and they would not be taken away until the hens were quite abandoned by the young pheasants—which in general would be at the end of August. Differing much from Mr. Knox, it was M———n's practice to keep as many as five hens with one cock for the purpose of obtaining eggs. I observed that some hutches possessed a disproportionate number of inmates. This had arisen from the hutches having been placed in too close proximity before the chicks had the sense to know their respective foster-mothers.

Remarking once after a good battue in cover upon the fine condition of the birds spread in a long array on the lawn for the inspection of the ladies, I was told that the keeper greatly attributed their size and weight to keeping ridge and furrow pans near their feeding places constantly filled with bark-water. He used to boil from a quarter to half a pound of oak-bark in two gallons of water until it was reduced to half the quantity. After once tasting it the pheasants become fond of it, their natural instinct telling them the advantages of the tonic. A cross with the true China makes the young birds hardy and wild. The brilliancy of the plumage is much increased but not the size of the birds. However long Chinese pheasants may be kept in confinement they will be alarmed at the sight of strangers.

---

* French eggs, which he purchased cheap in large quantities from an importing house at Folkestone.

NOTE TO 537.—*Setters.—Poachers.—Keepers.—Netting Partridges.—
Bloodhounds.—Night-dogs.*

It is far more easy to get a well-broken pointer than a well-broken setter; but times may change, for clean farming, the sale of game, poaching, and poisoning of seed-grain, are now carried on to such an extent, and the present game-laws are so inefficacious, that, probably, our children will much prefer the hard-working setter to the pointer. What an encouragement to villany is it that poulterers will give a higher price for game that appears perfectly uninjured, than for what has been shot; and *seldom ask questions!* It is a pity that the sale of such game cannot be rendered illegal. The destructive net sweeps off whole coveys at a time. The darkest night affords no protection, for the lantern attached to the dog's neck sufficiently shows when he is pointing at birds. A friend of mine in Kent, some years ago, wanted a partridge in order to break in a young bitch. Under a solemn promise of secrecy he was taken to an attic in an old house, not far from London, where he saw more than a hundred birds, ready for the market against the approaching first of September, running among the sheaves of corn standing in the corners of the room. To prevent the employment of the net, it has been recommended that the fields frequented by partridges should be staked, according to the method successfully followed in some preserved streams: but there are French gamekeepers who adopt a far less troublesome, and more effective plan. They themselves net the coveys at night, as soon as the harvest is collected, and turn them out again on the same ground the next evening, in the fullest confidence that the birds are henceforth safe from the poacher's net: for, however carefully they may have been handled, they will have been so alarmed, that their distrust and wariness will effectually prevent their being again caught napping. Talking of poaching, I am led to observe that one well-trained bloodhound would be more useful in suppressing poaching than half a-dozen under-keepers; for the fear poachers naturally entertain of being tracked to their homes at dawn of day, would more deter them from entering a cover, than any dread of being assailed at night by the boldest armed party. Even as compared with other dogs, the sensitiveness of the olfactory nerves of the bloodhound appears marvellous. Let one of pure breed but once take up the scent of a man, and he will hold it under the most adverse circumstances. No cross scents will perplex him.

At two o'clock on a frosty December morning in '44, when the wind blew bitterly cold from the east, Mr. B——e, of S——d, Warwickshire, was called up by the keepers of a neighbour, Mr W——n, and informed that some poachers were shooting pheasants in a plantation belonging to Mr. B——e, whose keepers were on the look-out

APPENDIX. 345

in a different direction. They and Mr. W——n's had agreed to work in concert, and mutually assist each other.

Mr. B——e instantly dressed, and went out with his brother (Captain B——), and the butler, making a party of eight, including Mr. W——n's keepers. They took with them a couple of trained bloodhounds in long cords, a regular night-dog, and a young bloodhound which had broken loose, and, unsolicited, had volunteered his services.

"One well-trained bloodhound will be more useful."—Page 344.

On entering the plantation, it was found that the poachers, having become alarmed, had made off. Two of the keepers remained to watch. The bloodhounds were laid on the scent. They took it up steadily, and the rest of the party followed in keen pursuit. As the poachers had not been seen, their number was unknown, but it was supposed to be about six from the report of the guns.

Notwithstanding the cold east wind and sharp frost the hounds hunted correctly, for about three miles, across fields, and along footpaths and roads, until they came to a wood of three hundred acres. They took the scent into the heart of it, evincing great eagerness. Here the hunt became most exciting, for the poachers were heard in the front crashing through the branches. A council of war was held, which unluckily ended, as many councils of war do, in coming to a wrong decision. It was resolved to divide forces, and endeavour to head the enemy. Captain B——e, two men and one of the old hounds, turned down a ride towards which the poachers seemed to be inclining; while the others continued the direct chase. The poachers, however, soon broke cover, but had not run across many fields ere they were overtaken. The clear, bright moon showed eight well-armed men,—rather a disproportionate force for the attacking three. A fight ensued. The young hound and the watch-dog were shot. Mr. B——e was lamed, and his two men being a good deal hurt, the poachers triumphed and resumed their flight. On Captain B——e rejoining the baffled party the pursuit was renewed for nine miles,—the dogs carrying the scent the whole way into Coventry, where they were stopped.

It was now half-past seven. Many early risers were about the streets; the police offered to point out the poachers, provided their identity could be sworn to. The hounds were stopped. Two men were apprehended—(a third escaped from the police)—were lodged in jail, and subsequently convicted and sentenced to eighteen months' hard labour. As they had not been seen until the time of the scuffle, which took place fully five miles from Mr. B——e's plantation, the only evidence to prove they had been poaching there was furnished in the undeviating pursuit of the hounds. The remainder of the gang fled the country.

A farmer, several years ago, sent to the same Mr. B——e to say, that a sheep had been killed and carried off in the night. Six hours, to a certainty,—probably many more,—had elapsed since the animal had been stolen before Mr. B——e could put the only hound he had with him on the scent. The dog, which was loose, hunted very slowly to a barn where the hidden skin was found; and afterwards, without any hesitation, held on the scent from the barn to the residence of a respectable person so wholly beyond all suspicion that the hound was called off. It was so late in the day, and along paths so much frequented, that it was thought the dog must have been hunting other footsteps than those of the real culprit. Mr. B——e at that moment was not aware that the respectable householder had taken in a lodger. This lodger, it subsequently appeared, was the thief, and in bed at the house at the time. Did not the Squire get well laughed at in all the adjacent beer-shops for his softness! However, this hunt, and another not very dissimilar under the head-keeper, effectually suppressed sheep-stealing in that neighbourhood.

The principal initiatory lesson for a bloodhound pup is to teach him to " road " well, as described in 43. He should, too, be perfected in following quietly at "heel." When commencing to teach him to follow the footsteps of the runner sent on in advance, it will be your aim to make the dog enjoy the scent and carry it on with eagerness.

Therefore, that the man's shoes may prove attractive, have them lightly rubbed with tainted meat (or blood). The savoury application may be progressively diminished in intensity, until at length the pup is guided only by the natural effluvia escaping from the man's pores. Whenever the dog gets up to him, let it be a rule that he instantly reward the animal liberally with some acceptable delicacy.

After a time the fleetest and most enduring runner should be selected, and the interval between the time of his starting, and the moment when the hound is laid upon the scent, should be by degrees increased, until, at length, an hour and more will intervene.

The first lessons should be given early in the morning, when the dew is not quite off the grass; and the runner should be instructed to take a direction not likely to be crossed by others. Gradually the hound will be made to follow the scent under less favourable circumstances, as respects the state of the ground and the chance of the trail being interfered with.

It will be obvious that the example of an old well-trained hound would be very beneficial to the pup; and, if it can be so managed, he should not be thrown upon his own unaided resources, until he has acquired a tolerable notion of his business.

A young dog that works too fast must be brought to pursue at a pace regulated by your signals (end of IV. of 141). That completes his education.

At night bloodhounds are generally held with a light cord, which restraint appears to lessen their wish to give tongue. Of course, they are checked if they do, that the poachers may not be warned of the pursuit.

A trained bloodhound will seldom endeavour to carry on the scent he has brought into a road, until he has tried the adjacent gates, gaps, and stiles.

Bloodhounds not confined are peaceable and, *apparently*, cowardly. They will rarely attack, unless provoked; but let them be once roused by a blow, and they become extremely savage. They also soon become savage if chained up, when they evince but little affection or obedience. Should they, by accident, get loose, they will more willingly allow a woman or a child to re-chain them than a man.

Bull-dogs have good noses. I have known of the cross between them and the mastiff being taught to follow the scent of a man almost as truly as a bloodhound. The dog I now particularly allude to was muzzled during the day when accompanying the keeper; and the appearance of the formidable-looking animal, and the knowledge of his powers, more effectually prevented egg-stealing than would the best exertions of a dozen watchers. He was the terror of all the idle boys in the neighbourhood. Every lad felt assured that, if once "Growler" were put upon his footsteps, to a certainty he would be overtaken, knocked down, and detained until the arrival of the keeper. The dog had been taught thus:—As a puppy he was excited to romp and play with the keeper's children. The father would occasionally make one of them run away, and then set the pup on him.

After a time he would desire the child to hide behind a tree, which gradually led the pup to seek by nose. An amicable fight always ensued on his finding the boy; and, as the pup grew stronger, and became more riotous than was agreeable, he was muzzled, but still encouraged to throw down the child. It is easy to conceive how, in a dog so bred, the instincts of nature eventually led to his acting his part in this game more fiercely when put upon the footsteps of a stranger.

INDEX.

A.

ACCOMPLISHMENTS or Refinements:—
Distinguishing dog-whistle, 501.
Dog to back the gun, 509.
— to head running birds, 525.
— to hunt without gun, 522.
— to retreat and resume point, 512.
Regular retrievers to beat, 550.
Setter to retrieve, 536.
Water-retriver to fetch cripples, 553.
Affection an incentive, &c., 167, 259, 497, 559.
— gained by first attentions, 167.
Age for education, 15, 62, 132.
Age of game, 7 n. 236 n. 338 n.
Albania, cock-shooting in, 84.
Anecdotes. *See* Instances.
Antelope—sagacity of fawn, 509 n.
Antelopes and cheeta, 284.
Ants' nests, Guinea-chicks, 471 n.
Arnica, lotion for bruises, 566.
Assistant with wild dog, 282.
Australia, kangaroo-hunting, 469.
Author's writing, cause of, 589.
Axioms, 274, 359.

B.

BACK turned brings dog away, 223.
"Backing" how taught, 350, 353.
— initiatory lesson in, 50.
— the gun, 509.
"Bar," for wild dog, 299.
Bark of Oak—tonic for pheasants—end of note to 407.
Barbuda—Creole and cur, 471.
Beagles shot over, 80.
Bear at perfumer's, 461.
Bears killed in India, 444.
"Beat," a, range taught, 132, 133, 171, 175—179.
— bad, hard to cure, 283.
— good, difficult, but invaluable, 189.
— Herbert's opinion, 232.
— without gun, 522.
— of five or six dogs, 245—248.
— of four dogs, 244.
— of three, 242, 243.
— of two, 238—240.
— taught following old dog, 191.
Beaters in India, 446.

Beckford. Education of buckhound, 558, 559.
— Gentlemen hunting hounds, 413.
"Beckon," why useful signal, 37.
— and "Heel," differ, 44.
Beef, heating in hot climates, 569.
Begging, how taught, 149.
Bell rang by dog, 417.
Bells, to rope of beaters in India, 446.
— put on dogs, 63, 74, 401.
Beltings of wood, spaniels, 65.
"Ben," a capital retriever, 121.
Bermuda, militia, 200 n.
Best dogs err, concise hints, 383.
Bird dead, loss of discourages dog, 312.
— dead, seized and torn by dog, 321.
— shot on ground, steadies dog, 340.
— shot, search for, 266, 307, 309, 317, 322, 544.
— shot, signal heel, 269.
— winged, shoot on ground, 308.
Birds, lie well, dog winding them, 186.
— lie, induced to, 401.
— old, cunning of, 220, 232, 236.
— wounded, scent differs, 545.
— wild, intercepted, 384, 400, 525, 533.
— wounded, first retrieved, 553.
— wounded, make off towards covey, 544.
— wounded, found evening, 316.
— wounded, the search for, 266.
— wounded, observed by dog, 113.
Bit for bloodsucker, 117.
Black-cock pointed three times, 289.
— dog drawing on his first, 297.
Black too conspicuous a colour, 93.
Blacksmith shoeing kicker, 60.
Blind man, and Tweed-side spaniel, 385.
Blinking dead bird, 257.
— from punishment, 165, 344.
Blinking, initiatory lessons prevent, 17.
B——k, Sir George, 481.
Bloodhounds, training of; poachers, 537 n. App.
Boar, wild; encounter with, 468.
Brace of dogs, sufficient if good, 137.
Break in dogs yourself, 3, 408, 409.
Breaker, qualifications required, 6.
— one, better than two, 14.
Breakers in fault, not dogs, 493.
— regular, displeased, 598.

Breakers hunt too many, 191, 362.
— idle, dislike bold dogs, 198.
Breakers' accomplishments, 555.
"Breaking fence" prevented, 222.
Breeding and breaking, fetch money, 376.
— in and in, bad, 279.
— superior nose sought, 370.
Brougham's story of fox, of dog, 431 n.
Buck-hound, Beckford's story of, 559.
Bull, strike horns, 283 n. App.
Bull-dogs, keepers, 546 n. App.
— cross with, 137.
Bull-terrier, keeper's, 283 n. App.
Buying dogs. See Purchasers.

C.

CALLING constantly, injudicious, 148.
Cantelo on rearing birds, 407 n. App.
"Captain," Lord M——f's dog, 491.
Cards selected by "Munito," 414, 436.
"Care," signal for, 39.
Carrots, for horses, 10, 11, 33.
"Carrying" and "fetching," differ, 153.
— how taught, 96, 109.
Cats and dogs returning home, 221.
"Caution," taught to fast dogs, 197.
— in excess, 287; cure for, 293
Cautious and wild dog contrasted, 194.
— dog, rarely too fast, 194.
Chain better than rope, 563.
Check-cord, 53, 54, 262, 282.
— spike to, 25, 281, 335.
Cheeta and antelopes, 284.
— how trained, 284 n.
Child lost, fed by dog, 432.
China Pheasant, cross with, end of note to 407, page 343.
Circle wide when heading dog, 265.
Cirque National de Paris, 11.
Claws of dogs pared, 566 n.
Clothes, dog sleeping on, 167 n.
Clumber spaniels, 75.
Cock-shooting, 37, 84, 397.
Cocking, young man's pursuit, 72.
Cockroaches eaten by fowls, 407 n. App.
Collar, a light one on dog, 259.
Collie dogs, 415, 516.
Colours for concealment, 93 n.
Commands given in a low tone, 20.
— understood before seeing game, 16.
Companion, dog to be yours, 18, 383, 384.
— initiatory lessons with, 49, 51.
Condition attended to, 566.
Consistency necessary, 6, 165, 278.
Coolness recommended, 278.
Couple to older dog, 29.
Couples, accustomed to, 48.
Courage created, 135, 347.
Cover, pointers in, 88.
Covers for game, 65 n. App.
Cricket, dogs made fag at, 150.
Cripples first retrieved, 553.
Cunning of old birds, 229.

D.

"DASH," a spaniel, described, 234.
Dead bird, blinking of, 267.
— lifted by you, error of, 98.
— loss of, discourages dog, 312.
— rushing into, 321, 374.
— search for, 266, 307, 309.
— search for, with two dogs, 544.
— the first killed, 265.
— to be pointed, 267; but not by retrieving setter or pointer, 548.
— torn by dog, 322.
Dead, initiatory lesson in, 19, 34.
Diet considered, 567.
Distance, whence birds are winded, 182, 183.
— between parallels, 181.
— dog's knowledge of, 285.
Distemper, pups inoculated for, 572.
— salt for, 579.
— vaccination for, 573, &c.
Diving, how taught, 105.
Dogs, good, cheapest in the end, 137.
— shape, &c. of, 137, 187, 364, 537.
— shepherds', in France, 415.
— slow, beating more than faster, 327.
— unknown, fetch small sums, 380.
— wildest, most energetic, 53, 137. 198.
Dominos played at by dogs, 433, 441.
"Down" see "Drop."
"Down-charge," dog pointing, not to, 359.
— initiatory lesson in, 27,
— ingenious argument against, 316 n.
— why retrievers should, 119.
Draughts, the first to move wins, 158.
"Drop," a better word than "Down," 146.
— dog to, another dropping, 49.
— dog to, game rising, 328.
— initiatory lessons in, 23, 25, 26.
— unnatural, "Toho" natural, 24.
Dropper, pointing grouse or snipe, 497.
— by Russian setter, 498.
Duck emits a goodish scent, 94.
Duck. Wood-duck of America, 511.
Duck-shooting in wild rice, 95.
Ducks, wounded, first retrieved, 553.
Duke of Gordon's dogs, 237.

E.

EARS not pulled violently, 327.
Education, age when commence, 15.
— best conducted by one, 14.
— Beckford's opinion of, 558.
— commenced from A, B, C, 588.
— expeditious, economical, 13.
Elephant, critical encounter with, 450.
— skulls of, 462.
— tricks exhibited, 160.
Energy, wildest dogs have most, 53, 137, 198.
Esquimaux dogs, and women, 169.
— crossed with wolf, 137.

INDEX. 351

Example advantageous, 351; especially to spaniels, 62; yours has influence, 264, 374.
Exercise on the road, 566.

F.

FALCON with Greyhound, 470.
Fastest dogs not *beating* most, 257.
— walkers not *beating* most, 256.
Fasting, initiatory lessons given, 12.
Fat, enemy to endurance, 567.
Fatigued, dog not hunted when, 224.
Faults, punishment expected for, 348.
Fawn, sagacity of, 509 n.
Feeding-time, lessons at, 30.
— pistol fired, 28.
— the evening, 568.
Feet, 187; attended to, 566.
— and loins compared, 137.
— of setter better than pointer's, 187.
— Partridge's, given to dog, 345.
Fence not to be broken, 222.
"Fence," or "Ware fence," initiatory lesson in, 46.
"Fetching" and "carrying" differ, 153.
— evil of not, 235.
— lessons in, 96, 109.
Fields, largest beat, 173.
"Find," initiatory lesson, 34, 35.
"Finder" not to advance, 357.
— retrieves, 541.
Fire, dog to bask before, 225.
First day on game, good conduct of dog, 139; of two dogs, 280.
First good point, 264; first bird killed, 265.
Flapper shooting, 226.
Fleas. Saffron. Gum of aloe, 165 n.
Flesh detrimental to pace, 567.
Flogging, how administered, 323.
— reprobated, 9, 344.
"Flown," initiatory lesson, 45; real, 330.
Food given cool, 568.
"Footing" a scent, 43, 112, 285.
"Forward," initiatory lesson, 36.
Fowls, killing of—the cure, 392.
— require animal food. 407 n.
Fox brought back by dog, 478.
— his sagacity, 431 n.
— graceful when hunting, 537.
Fox-hound, cross gives vigour, 137.
Francoul's Cirque National de Paris, 11.

G.

GAME, age, &c. 7 n. 236 n. 338 n.
— bag, birds looped on, 540.
— lies close in hot weather, 446.
— lies too close in turnips, 193.
— not shown dog soon, 16, 171.
— plentiful. Bad rangers. 255.
— sprung towards gun, 64, 89, 284.
"Gone," initiatory lesson, 45; real, 330.
Gordon, the Duke of, his dogs, 237.
Gorse, spaniels to be habituated to, 61.
Greyhounds, conditioning of, 566.
— with Falcon, 470.
Griffin, hints to, 65 n. 400—403.

Grouse and snipe alternately set, 497.
— best to break dog on, 331 n.
— cunning of old, 229.
— dog for, rated on snipe, 497.
— shot from stooks, 7 n.
— shot with aid of cart, 384.
— spread while feeding, 265.
"Grouse's" portrait, 210.
Guinea-birds' eggs. Chicks, 471 n.
Guinea-birds headed, 528.
Gun, dog to "back" the, 509.
— first over fence, not dog, 222.
— game flushed towards, 64, 89, 284.
— how carried, 65 n.

H.

HAND, bird delivered into, 98.
— rewards taken from, 27.
Hare, chase of, checked, 334, 335.
— heavy, tempts dog to drop, 116.
— killed in form, steadies dog, 339.
— scent of, strong, 333.
— shooting of, condemned, 331.
— white, the mountain, 338.
— wounded, dog may pursue, 341.
Harriers, pointer hunted with, 495.
Hat-brush brought by dog, 156.
Hawker, Colonel, 577.
Haunt, dog brought on, 306; not soon, 330.
Heading birds, 284, 400, 525.
Heading dog making too stanch, 287; circle wide, 265.
Health promoted by shooting, 409.
Heat beneficial to dogs, 571.
Hedge, furthest side hunted, 54.
Hedge-rows not hunted, 175.
"Heel," signal to, on killing, 269, 276.
— the signal to, 37, 44.
Hen-harrier's nest found, 283 n.
Herbert's Field Sports in United States, 241, 568.
Hereditary instincts, 128, 137, 279.
Hog-hunting with native dogs, 445.
Hog, wild, first encounter with, 468.
Hooded crow, 283 n.
Horned owl, a decoy, 283 n.
Horse, memory of, 221, n.
Hoof ointment, 364 n.
Horse, recipe for conditioning, 364 n.
Horse's and dog's points similar, 364.
— biting cured, 283 n.
— leg strapped, 60.
— rushing at his leaps cured, 60.
Horses, how taught by Astley, 10.
— fed on firing, 28.
Hounds, obedience of, 31.
— tuition of, 30, 505.
Hunting, dog's chief enjoyment, 562.
— dog long taking to, 132.
Huntsman for pack bad rangers, 248.
— a gentleman, 413.

I.

IMITATIVE, dogs are, 34, 264.
In-and-in breeding injudicious, 279.

INDEX.

Independence imparted, 375.
India, 444, 446, &c.
Indian-corn meal, 568.
Initiatory lessons, important, 12, 17, 52, 134, 14[?]
Inoculation for distemper, 572 n.
INSTANCE OF breaking highly, 251, 395, 499;—coolness and courage, 449—468;—cunning in grouse, 229; in pheasant, 232, 236; in monkeys, 431 n.;—dog's barking at point, 521;—dog's behaving well first day, 139, 280;—dog's forcing game to gun, 89;—dog's pointing after the shot, 275;—dog's intercepting, 206, 527, 530;—dog's manner showing birds on the run, 295, 530; dog's pointing on his back, 199;—dog's pointing on fence, 200;—dog's detaining with paw, 319;—dog's retreating from and resuming point, 286, 517, 519, 520; dog's retrieving snipe he would not point, 318; dog's retrieving duck, though detesting water, 320;—dog's running riot from jealousy, 343; dog's running riot only out of sight, 386;—dog's running to heel, but not blinking, 195;—dog's slipping off and replacing collar, 431 n.;—dog's stanchness—high price it commanded, 382;—dog's stanchness to excess, point made three times, 289;—dog, though never retrieving, bringing lost bird, 97; dog's walking to mallard from a distance, 93 n.;—dog's walking from a distance to object he seeks, 216;—dogs alternately retrieving as ordered, 542;—dropper's alternately pointing grouse and snipe, 497; example being useful, 352;—good snipe-shot who always used a dog, 395;—good snipe-shot who never used a dog, 394;—longevity and vigour, 226;—old dog proving of great value, 228—Newfoundlands finding their vessels amidst many, 218, 219; pointer's hunting with hounds or standing snipe, 495;—pointer's superior nose, 366;—pointer standing at partridge while carrying hare, 546;—pot-hunting ruining dog, 373;—prices dogs fetch, 137, 237, 254, 379, 382. 500; retriever bolting partridge because interfered with, 540;—retriever losing birds from not delivering into hand, 98;—retriever killing one bird to carry two, 100;—retriever never disturbing fresh ground, 552;—retriever ranging spontaneously, 551;—retriever tracking wounded through other game, 547; retriever running *direct* to hidden object, 216;—"roading" well performed by young dog, 290;—setter facing about, on birds running, 295, 530;—setter's superior nose, 369;—setter's standing fresh birds while carrying dead one, 546;—spaniels pointing, 68, 551;—young dogs behaving well first day shown game, 139, 280.

Instinct and reason contrasted 432.
Instincts hereditary, 128, 137, 279.
Ireland. Snipe, Woodcock, 397, 565.
Isle-aux-Noix, good conduct of dog, 395.

J.

JESSE'S opinion of dogs, 431.

K.

KANGAROOS, Greyhounds, 469.
Keeper, advice in choosing, 586 n.
Keeper, feeding several dogs, 30.
— to teach accomplishments, 555.
Keeper's dogs for vermin and poachers, 283 n. App. 537 n. 588 n.
Keepers dislike this book, 588.
— blameable for bad dogs, 4.
— idle, dislike dogs of energy, 193.
— rival, bet respecting, 499.
Kennel, dog in, when not with you, 563.
Kennels in India and England, 570.
Keys, retrievers taught with, 106.
— "Médor's," bringing, 418.
Killed outright—evil of thinking, 311.
Killing fowls - the remedy, 392.
— sheep—cure attempted, 387, &c.
Kitchen, dog not allowed run of, 563.
Knox on rearing Pheasants, 407 n. App.

L.

LADIES, breaking for gun, 166.
— no control over dogs, 147.
Ladies' Pets pampered, 163.
Learned dog in Paris, 435; St. John's, 561.
Leeward, beat from, 201.
— dog's beat from without gun, 522.
Left hand signals, "Down charge," 24.
— less than right, 142.
Left side of dog, keep on, 285.
"Left," signal for dog to go to, 36.
Lending dog injudicious, 584.
Lesson left off when well repeated, 96.
Lessons, initiatory, reasonable, 12, 17, 52, 134.
— — walking in fields, 131.
"Lifting" a dog, 309, 533, 546.
Lion bearded in his den, 165.
Liver, hard-boiled, 116.
Loins and feet compared, 137.
Longevity and vigour in a setter, 226.
Lord M——'s setter facing about on birds running, 295, 530.

M.

MAJOR B——d's well-broken dogs, 250.
Mange—mutton instead of beef, 569.
Mare making colts swim, 352 n.
Markers used with spaniels, 81.
Meat recommended for dogs, 569.
Medicine, how easily given, 580.
Memory in horse, 221 n.
Militia regiment treeing, 200 n.

Monkeys—their fun, 431 n.
Moors, advantage of, 137.
"Munito" selecting cards, 414.
Muscle wanted, not flesh, 567.
Muscovy drake, the cross, 471 n.
Musk bull found by "Muta," 487.
Mute spaniels, old sportsmen prefer, 83.
Mutton less heating than beef, 569.
Muzzle dogs that worry sheep, 391.

N.

NAMES ending in "o"—dissimilar, 145.
Netting partridges, 537 n. App.
Newfoundland carrying off parasol, 151.
— swimming to ship, 218, 219.
— that fished, 474, 475.
— the true breed, 126.
"Niger's" crossing hedge to drive birds, 533 n.
Night-dogs, 283 n. and 537 n. App.
"No" better word than "Ware," 47.
Noise spoils sport, 7, 20, 172, 473.
Nose carried high, 42, 186.
— condition of, important, 570.
— direction of, shows birds, 284.
— of pointers and setters differ, 174 n.
— of timid dogs often good, 135.
— tenderness of, how judged, 365
"Nosing" allowed, 314.

O.

OATMEAL and Indian corn, 568.
Old birds, cunning of, 229, &c.
— first killed, 404, 405.
Old crippled Scotch sportsman, 411.
Old dog allowed liberties, 564.
— range taught with, 191.
— when good, value of, 227.
"On" initiatory lesson in, 19, 21.
Owl used to decoy vermin, 283 n. App.

P.

PARALLELS, distance between, 181, 184.
Parasol carried off for bun, 151.
Partridges, benefit farmers, 407 n. App.
— how to choose, 7 n.
— netted, 537 n. App.
— old killed first, 404.
— red-legged, 535 n.
— wild, intercepted, 284, 400.
Patience enjoined, 263.
Paw kept on wounded bird by dog, 319.
Pea-fowl wants sagacity, 509 n.
Peg, or spike on check-cord, 281, 335.
Perseverance and range attained, 565.
— cures bad habits, 165.
— in seeking, taught, 313.
Pheasants, benefit farmer, 407 n. App.
— cover for, 65 n. App.
— cunning of old, 231, 236,
— old hens killed off, 404.
— rearing of, 471 n. App.
Physic, how easily given, 580.
Pigeons shot to retriever, 114.

Pike, voracity of, 231 n.
Pincushion, retrievers fetch, 106.
Pistol, horses fed at discharge, 28.
Poachers, dogs for attacking, 283 n. and 537 n. App.
— killing birds, 7 n. 93 n.
— tracked by bloodhounds, 537 n.
Poultry and game reared, Cantelo, 407 n. App.
— killing birds, 7 n. 93 n.
— tracked by bloodhounds, 537 n.
Poultry and game reared, Cantelo, 407 n. App.
"Point dead," to, 266.
Point left and resumed, 512.
— 150 yards from grouse, 183.
— 100 yards from partridge, 182.
— not quitted for "down charge," 274, 359.
— the first good one, 264.
— inclination to, general, 471.
— same, taken three times, 289.
Pointer cross with Indian dog, 448.
Pointer's points, 137, 187, 364, 537.
Pointing, dog not soon, 132, 281, 306.
— dog when, not to down, 359.
— origin of, 24.
Polygar dogs, to hunt hog, 445.
Pony for shooting, how broken in, 32.
Porcupine, dogs for hunting the, 448.
Porteous's whistles, 507, &c.
Pot-hunting sportsmen ruin dogs, 373.
Potato-fields, avoid, 192.
Preparatory lessons important, 12, 17, 52, 134, 141.
Price of dogs, 138, 237, 254, 379, 382, 500.
Punishment avoided by lessons, 17.
— causes blinking, 344, &c.
— decreases, whip carried, 342.
— not shunned by dogs, 348, &c.
— how administered, 323.
— making dog too stanch, 287.
— not inflicted on *suspicion*; 326.
— reprobated, 9, 344.
Pups born in India, 448.
— — in winter, 571.
— inoculated for distemper, 572.
— vaccinated for distemper, 573, &c. 372.
Purchasers of dogs, hints to, 146, 365, 372.
Puzzle peg, saved by word "up," 41.
"Puzzling" with nose to ground, 105.

Q.

QUAIL pointed, dog on fence, 200.
— large in Canada, 277.
Qualities expected in good dog, 8.
Quartering-ground. *See Beat.*

R.

RABBIT-SHOOTING, reprobated, 331.
— with beagles, 80.
Rabbit-warren, visit, hares scarce, 337.
Rabbits, choice and age of, 338 n.

A A

Railway whistles, 507.
"Range." *See* "Beat."
"Rating" dogs, how best done, 188.
Rats, dogs for gun not to kill, 130.
Red-legged partridges, headed, 527.
— destroyed, 535 n.
Red setters, Irish, 565.
Refinements. *See* Accomplishments.
Relays desirable—not a pack, 248.
Requisites in a dog, 8; in a breaker, 6.
Retreat from point, &c. 512.
Retriever, bit for one that mouths, 117.
— evil of assisting, 115.
— "footing" scent, lesson in, 112.
— for water, qualities in, 93.
— made whipper-in, 57.
— observes struck bird, 113.
— (regular), useful with beaters, 550.
— (regular), to "down charge" or not? 119.
Retrievers, shape, &c. of, 125.
— to beat, 550.
— to fetch, taught, 108, &c.
— to pursue faster, 118.
— water, to fetch cripples first, 553.
— how bred, 126.
Retrieving not taught first season, 538.
— setters or pointers not to "point dead," 548.
— setters, not pointers, 536.
Rewards always given, 27, 40.
Rheumatism prevented by care, 571.
Rice; wild lakes, duck-shooting in, 95.
"Richelieu," snipe-shooting, 277.
Rifle, rest for, 509 n.
Right, the signal to go towards, 36.
Right-eyed, 65 n. App.
Right hand, for "Toho" and "Drop," 24.
— signals more than left, 142.
Road, exercise on, good for dogs, 566.
"Roading," instance of fine, 290—292.
— by 6 dogs alternately, 251.
— by "Finder," 354.
Rope to tie dog, bad, 563.
Running bird, firing at, 308.
Rushing in to "dead" cured, 374.
Russian setter, dropper from, 498.

S.

SAFFRON removing fleas, 165 n.
Salt for distemper, 579.
Scent, bad in calm or gale, 174.
— differently recognised by pointers and setters, 174 n.
— of birds, not left for hare, 333.
— "footing" a, initiatory lesson in, 43.
Scent of wounded and unwounded birds differs, 545.
Search "dead," 266; with 2 dogs, 544.
— for wounded bird, when to leeward, 309; when to windward, 307.
Seeking dead, how taught, 313.
"Self-hunting," prevent, 564.

September, dog taken out in, 171.
— day's lesson continued, 259.
Servant useful in field, 262.
Seton proved useful, 123.
Setter, stanch—sum paid for, 382.
— to retrieve, 536; argument against applies to retriever, 549.
Setters crouch more than pointers, 23.
— Duke of Gordon's breed, 237.
— for cover shooting, 87.
Setters, points in, 137, 187, 364, 537.
— red—the Irish breed, 565.
Setters' feet better than pointers', 187.
Severity reprobated, 9, 344.
Sheep, killing of—cure, 387—390.
Sheep-stealing. Bloodhounds, 537 n.
Shepherds' dogs, 143, 163, 415.
— "forward" signal, for water retrievers, 91.
Shooting, excellence in, not necessary in breaker, 5, 253.
— hints to tyros, 65 n. App.
Shot-belt, nozzle lengthened, 65 n. App.
— on spaniels and setters, 60, 329.
Shot over, dog to be, before bought, 372.
Showman's dogs in Paris, 434, &c.
Shy birds intercepted, 284, 400, 525, 533.
Sight, dog not to be out of, 386.
Silence enjoined, 7, 172, 473.
Sinews of legs drawn, 345 n.
Single-handed, shot to, 375.
Sloe, gum of, 165 n.
Slow dog, associate for young one, 350.
— dogs hunting more than faster, 257.
Snipe, condition of, 236 n.
— grouse dog rated noticing, 497.
— killed off, 396.
Snipes, three, lifted in succession, 546.
Snipe-shooting on Richelieu, 277.
Snipe-shot who never used dog, 394; who used one constantly, 395.
Spaniel puppies, keep close, 59.
Spaniels, age when shown game, 62.
— babbling occasionally best, 84.
— hunted in gorse, 61.
— mute, preferred, 83.
— numbers for a team, 74, 77.
— requisites in, 70.
— shot-belt on wildest, 60.
— Sussex, 236.
— that pointed, 68.
— water, how broken in, 90.
Spike-collar, 300, &c.
Spike fastened to check-cord, 281, 335.
Sportsmen to break dogs, 3, 408, 409.
Spring, dogs broken in, 170.
Springing the other birds after pointing one, 373.
Stanch—made too, by heading, 287.
St. John's old woman's dog, 559 n.
Stoat, range of, 283 and n. App.
Stone, error of retrieving, 103.
Summary imparted by lessons, 141.
Sussex spaniel, 236.
"Suwarrow," heading running birds, 530.

T.

"TAFFY," anecdotes of, 421—430.

INDEX. 355

Tattersall's, thirteen pointers at, 379.
Temper in breaker necessary, 6; improved by *successfully* teaching, 409.
Temper hereditary, 128.
Terrier pointing in varied attitudes, 298.
Terriers for covers, 24 *n*.
Tigress' claws running into feet, 566 *n*.
Time given determines education, 2.
— saved by initiatory lessons, 52.
Timidity cured, 135, 345, 347.
"Toho," first good one in field, 264.
— initiatory lesson in, 19, 21, 24.
Traps beat guns for vermin, 283, App.
— visited by terrier, 283 *n*.
Tricks easily taught after first, 136.
— exhibited with effect, 154, 437.
— taught by ladies, 150.
Trout, tame, 164.
— trolling for, 231 *n*. 588 *n*.
Turning back, brings dog away, 223.
Turnip-field ridden round, 401.
Turnips avoided, 192.
— lessons in, 329.
Tweed spaniel, and blind man, 385.
Two dogs, beat of, 238—240.
— steady, first day, 280.

U.

"UP," signal for—initiatory lesson, 41.

V.

VACCINATION for distemper, 573, &c.
Vermin, dogs for, 283 *n*. 588 *n*.
— traps. Decoy owl, 283 *n*. App.
Vigour and longevity in setter, 226.
Vineyards protected by dogs, 415.

W.

WALKERS, fastest, not beating most, 256.
"Ware," not so good word as "No," 47.
Warmth necessary for dogs, 571.
Warren, visit, hares scarce, 337 *n*.
Water, dog taught to plunge into, 104.

Water-proof, recipe for leather, 567 *n*.
— — for cloth, 567 *n*.
Water-retriever, how broken, 90.
— observes struck bird, 113.
— qualities required in, 93.
Whales, Bermuda, 165 *n*.
Whip carried saves punishment, 342.
— to crack loudly, 188.
Whistle low, 20, 507.
— dissimilar notes on one, 505.
— distinguishing, for each dog, 501.
— inattentive to, how punish, 188.
— initiatory lesson in, 19.
Whistles, boatswain's, 506; railway, 507.
Whistling to animate, injudicious, 172; spoils sport, 7.
White dogs, arguments for and against, 187.
White feet, objectionable, 187.
White, too conspicuous a colour, 93.
Wild birds, intercepted, 284, 400, 525, 533.
Wild dog contrasted with cautious, 194.
Wild dogs turning out best, 198.
Wildfowl, wounded, retrieved first, 553.
— reconnoitred with glass, 92.
Winged bird. *See* Bird winged.
Winter pups, 571.
Wolf, cross with Esquimaux dog, 137.
Woodcock-shooting in Albania, 84; in America, 87; in Ireland, 397; in Kent, 82.
Woodcocks attached to covers, 397.
— reflushed, 82.
— small, in Canada, 277.
Wood-duck of North America, 511.
Wounded bird. *See* Bird wounded.

Y.

YEOMEN of Kent, 236.
Yorkshire keeper's advice, 406.
Young dogs steady first day on game, 139, 280.
Youth, game followed in, liked, 69.
— occupation followed in, liked, 563.

THE END.

M. CLAY, SON, AND TAYLOR, PRINTERS, BREAD STREET HILL.

ALBEMARLE STREET, LONDON,
January, 1865.

MR. MURRAY'S

GENERAL LIST OF WORKS.

ALBERT (PRINCE). THE SPEECHES AND ADDRESSES on Public Occasions of H.R.H. THE PRINCE CONSORT; with an Introduction giving some Outlines of his Character. Portrait. 8vo. 10s. 6d.; or Popular Edition, fcap. 8vo, 1s.

ABBOTT'S (REV. J.) Philip Musgrave; or, Memoirs of a Church of England Missionary in the North American Colonies. Post 8vo. 2s.

ABERCROMBIE'S (JOHN) Enquiries concerning the Intellectual Powers and the Investigation of Truth. 16th *Edition.* Fcap. 8vo. 6s. 6d.

―――――――― Philosophy of the Moral Feelings. 12th *Edition.* Fcap. 8vo. 4s.

ACLAND'S (REV. CHARLES) Popular Account of the Manners and Customs of India. Post 8vo. 2s.

ÆSOP'S FABLES. A New Translation. With Historical Preface. By Rev. THOMAS JAMES. With 100 Woodcuts, by TENNIEL and WOLF. 50th *Thousand.* Post 8vo. 2s. 6d.

AGRICULTURAL (THE) JOURNAL. Of the Royal Agricultural Society of England. 8vo. *Published half-yearly.*

AIDS TO FAITH: a Series of Essays. By various Writers. Edited by WILLIAM THOMSON, D.D., Lord Archbishop of York. 8vo. 9s.

CONTENTS.

Rev. H. L. MANSEL—*Miracles.*
BISHOP OF KILLALOE—*Christian Evidences.*
Rev. DR. MCCAUL—*Prophecy and the Mosaic Record of Creation.*
Rev. CANON COOK — *Ideology and Subscription.*

Rev. GEORGE RAWLINSON—*The Pentateuch.*
ARCHBISHOP OF YORK—*Doctrine of the Atonement.*
BISHOP OF ELY.—*Inspiration.*
BISHOP OF GLOUCESTER AND BRISTOL.—*Scripture and its Interpretation.*

AMBER-WITCH (THE). The most interesting Trial for Witchcraft ever known. Translated from the German by LADY DUFF GORDON. Post 8vo. 2s.

ARMY LIST (THE). *Published Monthly by Authority.* 18mo. 1s. 6d.

ARTHUR'S (LITTLE) History of England. By LADY CALLCOTT. 130th *Thousand.* Woodcuts. Fcap. 8vo. 2s. 6d.

ATKINSON'S (MRS.) Recollections of Tartar Steppes and their Inhabitants. Illustrations. Post 8vo. 12s.

AUNT IDA'S Walks and Talks; a Story Book for Children. By a LADY. Woodcuts. 16mo. 5s.

AUSTIN'S (JOHN) LECTURES ON JURISPRUDENCE; or, the Philosophy of Positive Law. 3 Vols. 8vo. 39s.

―――――― (SARAH) Fragments from German Prose Writers. With Biographical Notes. Post 8vo. 10s.

B

ADMIRALTY PUBLICATIONS; Issued by direction of the Lords Commissioners of the Admiralty:—

A MANUAL OF SCIENTIFIC ENQUIRY, for the Use of Travellers. Edited by Sir JOHN F. HERSCHEL, and Rev. ROBERT MAIN. *Third Edition.* Woodcuts. Post 8vo. 9s.

AIRY'S ASTRONOMICAL OBSERVATIONS MADE AT GREENWICH. 836 to 1847. Royal 4to. 50s. each.

—— ASTRONOMICAL RESULTS. 1848 to 1858. 4to. 8s. each.

—— APPENDICES TO THE ASTRONOMICAL OBSERVATIONS.

1836.—I. Bessel's Refraction Tables.
II. Tables for converting Errors of R.A. and N.P.D. } 8s.
    into Errors of Longitude and Ecliptic P.D.
1837.—I. Logarithms of Sines and Cosines to every Ten } 8s.
    Seconds of Time.
II. Table for converting Sidereal into Mean Solar Time.
1842.—Catalogue of 1439 Stars. 8s.
1845.—Longitude of Valentia. 8s.
1847.—Twelve Years' Catalogue of Stars. 14s.
1851.—Maskelyne's Ledger of Stars. 6s.
1852.—I. Description of the Transit Circle. 5s.
II. Regulations of the Royal Observatory. 2s.
1853.—Bessel's Refraction Tables. 8s.
1854.—I. Description of the Zenith Tube. 3s.
II. Six Years' Catalogue of Stars. 10s.
1856.—Description of the Galvanic Apparatus at Greenwich Observatory. 8s.

—— MAGNETICAL AND METEOROLOGICAL OBSERVATIONS. 1840 to 1847. Royal 4to. 50s. each.

—— ASTRONOMICAL, MAGNETICAL, AND METEOROLOGICAL OBSERVATIONS, 1848 to 1862. Royal 4to. 50s. each.

—— ASTRONOMICAL RESULTS. 1848 to 1862. 4to.

—— MAGNETICAL AND METEOROLOGICAL RESULTS. 1848 to 1862. 4to. 8s. each.

—— REDUCTION OF THE OBSERVATIONS OF PLANETS. 1750 to 1830. Royal 4to. 50s.

———————————— LUNAR OBSERVATIONS. 1750 to 1830. 2 Vols. Royal 4to. 50s. each.

———————————— 1831 to 1851. 4to. 20s.

BERNOULLI'S SEXCENTENARY TABLE. *London*, 1779. 4to.

BESSEL'S AUXILIARY TABLES FOR HIS METHOD OF CLEARING LUNAR DISTANCES. 8vo.

——–FUNDAMENTA ASTRONOMIÆ: *Regiomontii*, 1818. Folio. 60s.

BIRD'S METHOD OF CONSTRUCTING MURAL QUADRANTS. *London*, 1768. 4to. 2s. 6d.

—— METHOD OF DIVIDING ASTRONOMICAL INSTRUMENTS. *London*, 1767. 4to. 2s. 6d.

COOK, KING, AND BAYLY'S ASTRONOMICAL OBSERVATIONS. *London*, 1782. 4to. 21s.

ENCKE'S BERLINER JAHRBUCH, for 1830. *Berlin*, 1828. 8vo. 9s.

GROOMBRIDGE'S CATALOGUE OF CIRCUMPOLAR STARS. 4to. 10s.

HANSEN'S TABLES DE LA LUNE. 4to. 20s.

HARRISON'S PRINCIPLES OF HIS TIME-KEEPER. PLATES 1767. 4to. 5s.

ADMIRALTY PUBLICATIONS—*continued.*
HUTTON'S TABLES OF THE PRODUCTS AND POWERS OF NUMBERS. 1781. Folio. 7s. 6d.
LAX'S TABLES FOR FINDING THE LATITUDE AND LONGITUDE. 1821. 8vo. 10s.
LUNAR OBSERVATIONS at GREENWICH. 1783 to 1819. Compared with the Tables, 1821. 4to. 7s. 6d.
MASKELYNE'S ACCOUNT OF THE GOING OF HARRISON'S WATCH. 1767. 4to. 2s. 6d.
MAYER'S DISTANCES of the MOON'S CENTRE from the PLANETS. 1822, 3s.; 1823, 4s. 6d. 1824 to 1835, 8vo. 4s. each.
————— THEORIA LUNÆ JUXTA SYSTEMA NEWTONIANUM. 4to. 2s. 6d.
————— TABULÆ MOTUUM SOLIS ET LUNÆ. 1770. 4to. 5s.
————— ASTRONOMICAL OBSERVATIONS MADE AT GOTTINGEN, from 1756 to 1761. 1826. Folio. 7s. 6d.
NAUTICAL ALMANACS, from 1767 to 1868. 8vo. 2s. 6d. each.
————— SELECTIONS FROM THE ADDITIONS up to 1812. 8vo. 5s. 1834-54. 8vo. 5s.
————— SUPPLEMENTS, 1828 to 1833, 1837 and 1838. 8vo. 2s. each.
————— TABLE requisite to be used with the N.A. 1781. 8vo. 5s.
POND'S ASTRONOMICAL OBSERVATIONS. 1811 to 1835. 4to. 21s. each.
RAMSDEN'S ENGINE for DIVIDING MATHEMATICAL INSTRUMENTS. 4to. 5s.
————— ENGINE for DIVIDING STRAIGHT LINES. 4to. 5s.
SABINE'S PENDULUM EXPERIMENTS to DETERMINE THE FIGURE OF THE EARTH. 1825. 4to. 40s.
SHEPHERD'S TABLES for CORRECTING LUNAR DISTANCES. 1772. Royal 4to. 21s.
————— TABLES, GENERAL, of the MOON'S DISTANCE from the SUN, and 10 STARS. 1787. Folio. 5s. 6d.
TAYLOR'S SEXAGESIMAL TABLE. 1780. 4to. 15s.
————— TABLES OF LOGARITHMS. 4to. 3l.
TIARK'S ASTRONOMICAL OBSERVATIONS for the LONGITUDE of MADEIRA. 1822. 4to. 5s.
————— CHRONOMETRICAL OBSERVATIONS for DIFFERENCES of LONGITUDE between DOVER, PORTSMOUTH, and FALMOUTH. 1823. 4to. 5s.
VENUS and JUPITER: OBSERVATIONS of, compared with the TABLES. London, 1822. 4to. 2s.
WALES' AND BAYLY'S ASTRONOMICAL OBSERVATIONS. 1777. 4to. 21s.
WALES' REDUCTION OF ASTRONOMICAL OBSERVATIONS MADE IN THE SOUTHERN HEMISPHERE. 1764–1771. 1788. 4to. 10s. 6d.

BABBAGE'S (CHARLES) Economy of Machinery and Manufactures. *Fourth Edition.* Fcap. 8vo. 6s.

————— Reflections on the Decline of Science in England, and on some of its Causes. 4to. 7s. 6d.

BAIKIE'S (W. B.) Narrative of an Exploring Voyage up the Rivers
Quorra and Tshadda in 1854. Map. 8vo. 16s.

BANKES' (GEORGE) STORY OF CORFE CASTLE, with documents relating
to the Time of the Civil Wars, &c. Woodcuts. Post 8vo. 10s. 6d.

BARBAULD'S (MRS.) Hymns in Prose for Children. With 112
Original Designs. Small 4to. 5s.

BARROW'S (SIR JOHN) Autobiographical Memoir, including
Reflections, Observations, and Reminiscences at Home and Abroad.
From Early Life to Advanced Age. Portrait. 8vo. 16s.

——— Voyages of Discovery and Research within the
Arctic Regions, from 1818 to the present time. 8vo. 15s.

——— Life and Voyages of Sir Francis Drake. With numerous Original Letters. Post 8vo. 2s.

BATES' (H. W.) Records of a Naturalist on the River Amazons
during eleven years of Adventure and Travel. *Second Edition.* Illustrations. Post 8vo. 12s.

BEES AND FLOWERS. Two Essays. By Rev. Thomas James.
Reprinted from the "Quarterly Review." Fcap. 8vo. 1s. each.

BELL'S (SIR CHARLES) Mechanism and Vital Endowments of the
Hand as evincing Design. *Sixth Edition.* Woodcuts. Post 8vo. 6s.

BERTHA'S Journal during a Visit to her Uncle in England.
Containing a Variety of Interesting and Instructive Information. *Seventh Edition.* Woodcuts. 12mo.

BIRCH'S (SAMUEL) History of Ancient Pottery and Porcelain :
Egyptian, Assyrian, Greek, Roman, and Etruscan. With 200 Illustrations. 2 Vols. Medium 8vo. 42s.

BLUNT'S (REV. J. J.) Undesigned Coincidences in the Writings of
the Old and New Testament, an Argument of their Veracity : containing
the Books of Moses, Historical and Prophetical Scriptures, and the
Gospels and Acts. *8th Edition.* Post 8vo. 6s.

——— History of the Church in the First Three Centuries.
Third Edition. Post 8vo. 7s. 6d.

——— Parish Priest; His Duties, Acquirements and Obligations. *Fourth Edition.* Post 8vo. 7s. 6d.

——— Lectures on the Right Use of the Early Fathers.
Second Edition. 8vo. 15s.

——— Plain Sermons Preached to a Country Congregation.
Second Edition. 3 Vols. Post 8vo. 7s. 6d. each.

——— Essays on various subjects. 8vo. 12s.

BISSET'S (ANDREW) History of England during the Interregnum,
from the Death of Charles I. to the Battle of Dunbar, 1648—50. Chiefly
from the MSS. in the State Paper Office. 8vo. 15s.

BLAKISTON'S (CAPT.) Narrative of the Expedition sent to explore the Upper Waters of the Yang-Tsze. Illustrations. 8vo. 18s.

BLOMFIELD'S (BISHOP) Memoir, with Selections from his Correspondence. By his Son. 2nd Edition. Portrait, post 8vo. 12s.

BOOK OF COMMON PRAYER. Illustrated with Coloured Borders, Initial Letters, and Woodcuts. A new edition. 8vo. 18s. cloth; 31s. 6d. calf; 36s. morocco.

BORROW'S (GEORGE) Bible in Spain; or the Journeys, Adventures, and Imprisonments of an Englishman in an Attempt to circulate the Scriptures in the Peninsula. 3 Vols. Post 8vo. 27s.; or *Popular Edition*, 16mo, 3s. 6d.

———— Zincali, or the Gipsies of Spain ; their Manners, Customs, Religion, and Language. 2 Vols. Post 8vo. 18s.; or *Popular Edition*, 16mo, 3s. 6d.

———— Lavengro ; The Scholar—The Gipsy—and the Priest. Portrait. 3 Vols. Post 8vo. 30s.

———— Romany Rye ; a Sequel to Lavengro. *Second Edition*. 2 Vols. Post 8vo. 21s.

BOSWELL'S (JAMES) Life of Samuel Johnson, LL.D. Including the Tour to the Hebrides. Edited by Mr. CROKER. Portraits. Royal 8vo. 10s.

BRACE'S (C. L.) History of the Races of the Old World. Designed as a Manual of Ethnology. Post 8vo. 9s.

BRAY'S (MRS.) Life of Thomas Stothard, R.A. With Personal Reminiscences. Illustrated with Portrait and 60 Woodcuts of his chief works. 4to.

BREWSTER'S (SIR DAVID) Martyrs of Science, or the Lives of Galileo, Tycho Brahe, and Kepler. *Fourth Edition*. Fcap. 8vo. 4s. 6d.

———— More Worlds than One. The Creed of the Philosopher and the Hope of the Christian. *Eighth Edition*. Post 8vo. 6s.

———— Stereoscope : its History, Theory, Construction, and Application to the Arts and to Education. Woodcuts. 12mo. 5s. 6d.

———— Kaleidoscope: its History, Theory, and Construction, with its application to the Fine and Useful Arts. *Second Edition*. Woodcuts. Post 8vo. 5s. 6d.

BRINE'S (Capt.) Narrative of the Rise and Progress of the Taeping Rebellion in China. Plans. Post 8vo. 10s. 6d.

BRITISH ASSOCIATION REPORTS. 8vo. York and Oxford, 1831-32, 13s. 6d. Cambridge, 1833, 12s. Edinburgh, 1834, 15s. Dublin, 1835, 13s. 6d. Bristol, 1836, 12s. Liverpool, 1837, 16s. 6d. Newcastle, 1838, 15s. Birmingham, 1839, 13s. 6d. Glasgow, 1840, 15s. Plymouth, 1841, 13s. 6d. Manchester, 1842, 10s. 6d. Cork, 1843, 12s. York, 1844, 20s. Cambridge, 1845, 12s. Southampton, 1846, 15s. Oxford, 1847, 18s. Swansea, 1848, 9s. Birmingham, 1849, 10s. Edinburgh, 1850, 15s. Ipswich, 1851, 16s. 6d. Belfast, 1852, 15s. Hull, 1853, 10s. 6d. Liverpool, 1854, 18s. Glasgow, 1855, 15s.; Cheltenham, 1856, 18s.; Dublin, 1857, 15s.; Leeds, 1858, 20s. Aberdeen, 1859, 15s. Oxford, 1860, 25s. Manchester, 1861, 15s. Cambridge, 1862, 20s. Newcastle, 1863.

BRITISH CLASSICS. A New Series of Standard English Authors, printed from the most correct text, and edited with notes. 8vo.

Already Published.

I. GOLDSMITH'S WORKS. Edited by PETER CUNNINGHAM, F.S.A. Vignettes. 4 Vols. 30s.

II. GIBBON'S DECLINE AND FALL OF THE ROMAN EMPIRE. Edited by WILLIAM SMITH, LL.D Portrait and Maps. 8 Vols. 60s.

III. JOHNSON'S LIVES OF THE ENGLISH POETS. Edited by PETER CUNNINGHAM, F.S.A. 3 Vols. 22s. 6d.

IV. BYRON'S POETICAL WORKS. Edited, with Notes. 6 vols. 45s.

In Preparation.

WORKS OF POPE. With Life, Introductions, and Notes, by REV. WHITWELL ELWIN. Portrait.

HUME'S HISTORY OF ENGLAND. Edited, with Notes.

LIFE AND WORKS OF SWIFT. Edited by JOHN FORSTER.

BROUGHTON'S (LORD) Journey through Albania and other Provinces of Turkey in Europe and Asia, to Constantinople, 1809—10. *Third Edition.* Illustrations. 2 Vols. 8vo. 30s.

———— Visits to Italy. 3rd *Edition.* 2 vols. Post 8vo. 18s.

BUBBLES FROM THE BRUNNEN OF NASSAU. By an Old MAN. *Sixth Edition.* 16mo. 5s.

BUNYAN (JOHN) and Oliver Cromwell. Select Biographies. By ROBERT SOUTHEY. Post 8vo. 2s.

BUONAPARTE'S (NAPOLEON) Confidential Correspondence with his Brother Joseph, sometime King of Spain. *Second Edition.* 2 vols. 8vo. 26s.

BURGON'S (Rev. J. W.) Memoir of Patrick Fraser Tytler. *Second Edition.* Post 8vo. 9s.

———— Letters from Rome, written to Friends at Home. Illustrations. Post 8vo. 12s.

BURN'S (LIEUT.-COL.) French and English Dictionary of Naval and Military Technical Terms. *Fourth Edition.* Crown 8vo. 15s.

BURNS' (ROBERT) Life. By JOHN GIBSON LOCKHART. Fifth *Edition.* Fcap. 8vo. 3s.

BURR'S (G. D.) Instructions in Practical Surveying, Topographical Plan Drawing, and on sketching ground without Instruments. *Fourth Edition.* Woodcuts. Post 8vo. 6s.

BUTTMAN'S LEXILOGUS; a Critical Examination of the Meaning of numerous Greek Words, chiefly in Homer and Hesiod. Translated by Rev. J. R. FISHLAKE. *Fifth Edition.* 8vo. 12s.

BUXTON'S (SIR FOWELL) Memoirs. With Selections from his Correspondence. By his Son. Portrait. *Fifth Edition.* 8vo. 16s. *Abridged Edition,* Portrait. Fcap. 8vo. 2s. 6d.

PUBLISHED BY MR. MURRAY. 7

BYRON'S (Lord) Life, Letters, and Journals. By Thomas Moore.
Plates. 6 Vols. Fcap. 8vo. 18s.
———— Life, Letters, and Journals. By Thomas Moore.
Portraits. Royal 8vo. 9s.
———— Poetical Works. Portrait. 6 Vols. 8vo. 45s.
———— Poetical Works. Plates. 10 Vols. Fcap. 8vo. 30s.
———— Poetical Works. 8 Vols. 24mo. 20s.
———— Poetical Works. Plates. Royal 8vo. 9s.
———— Poetical Works. Portrait. Crown 8vo. 6s.
———— Childe Harold. With 80 Engravings. Small 4to. 21s.
———— Childe Harold. With 30 Vignettes. 12mo. 6s.
———— Childe Harold. 16mo. 2s. 6d.
———— Childe Harold. Vignettes. 16mo. 1s.
———— Childe Harold. Portrait. 16mo. 6d.
———— Tales and Poems. 24mo. 2s. 6d.
———— Miscellaneous. 2 Vols. 24mo. 5s.
———— Dramas and Plays. 2 Vols. 24mo. 5s.
———— Don Juan and Beppo. 2 Vols. 24mo. 5s.
———— Beauties. Selected from his Poetry and Prose. Portrait.
Fcap. 8vo. 3s. 6d.

CARNARVON'S (Lord) Portugal, Gallicia, and the Basque
Provinces. From Notes made during a Journey to those Countries.
Third Edition. Post 8vo. 3s. 6d.
———— Recollections of the Druses of Lebanon. With
Notes on their Religion. Third Edition. Post 8vo. 5s. 6d.

CAMPBELL'S (Lord) Lives of the Lord Chancellors and Keepers
of the Great Seal of England. From the Earliest Times to the Death of
Lord Eldon in 1838. Fourth Edition. 10 Vols. Crown 8vo. 6s. each.
———— Lives of the Chief Justices of England. From the
Norman Conquest to the Death of Lord Tenterden. Second Edition.
3 Vols. 8vo. 42s.
———— Shakspeare's Legal Acquirements Considered.
8vo. 5s. 6d.
———— Life of Lord Chancellor Bacon. Fcap. 8vo. 2s. 6d.
———— (George) Modern India. A Sketch of the System
of Civil Government. With some Account of the Natives and Native
Institutions. Second Edition. 8vo. 16s.
———— India as it may be. An Outline of a proposed
Government and Policy. 8vo. 12s.
———— (Thos.) Short Lives of the British Poets. With an
Essay on English Poetry. Post 8vo. 3s. 6d.

CALLCOTT'S (Lady) Little Arthur's History of England.
130th Thousand. With 20 Woodcuts. Fcap. 8vo. 2s. 6d.

CASTLEREAGH (THE) DESPATCHES, from the commencement
of the official career of the late Viscount Castlereagh to the close of his
life. Edited by the MARQUIS OF LONDONDERRY. 12 Vols. 8vo. 14s. each.

CATHCART'S (SIR GEORGE) Commentaries on the War in Russia
and Germany, 1812-13. Plans. 8vo. 14s.

CAVALCASELLE AND CROWE'S New History of Painting in
Italy, from the Second to the Sixteenth Century, from recent researches in the Archives, as well as from personal inspection of the
Works of Art in that Country. With 70 Illustrations. Vols. I. and II.
8vo. 42s.

———————— Notices of the Lives and Works
of the Early Flemish Painters. Woodcuts. Post 8vo. 12s.

CHAMBERS' (G. F.) Handbook of Descriptive and Practical
Astronomy. Illustrations. Post 8vo. 12s.

CHARMED ROE (THE); or, The Story of the Little Brother and
Sister. By OTTO SPECKTER. Plates. 16mo. 5s.

CHURTON'S (ARCHDEACON) Gongora. An Historical Essay on the
Age of Philip III. and IV. of Spain. With Translations. Portrait.
2 Vols. Small 8vo. 15s.

CLAUSEWITZ'S (CARL VON) Campaign of 1812, in Russia.
Translated from the German by LORD ELLESMERE. Map. 8vo. 10s. 6d.

CLIVE'S (LORD) Life. By REV. G. R. GLEIG, M.A. Post 8vo. 3s. 6d.

COLCHESTER (THE) PAPERS. The Diary and Correspondence
of Charles Abbott, Lord Colchester, Speaker of the House of Commons,
1802-1817. Edited by His SON. Portrait. 3 Vols. 8vo. 42s.

COLERIDGE'S (SAMUEL TAYLOR) Table-Talk. *Fourth Edition.*
Portrait. Fcap. 8vo. 6s.

COLONIAL LIBRARY. [See Home and Colonial Library.]

COOK'S (Rev. Canon) Sermons Preached at Lincoln's Inn Chapel,
and on Special Occasions. 8vo. 9s.

COOKERY (MODERN DOMESTIC). Founded on Principles of Economy
and Practical Knowledge, and adapted for Private Families. By a
Lady. *New Edition.* Woodcuts. Fcap. 8vo. 5s.

CORNWALLIS (THE) Papers and Correspondence during the
American War,—Administrations in India,—Union with Ireland, and
Peace of Amiens. Edited by CHARLES ROSS. *Second Edition.* 3 Vols.
8vo. 63s.

COWPER'S (MARY COUNTESS) Diary while Lady of the Bedchamber
to Caroline Princess of Wales, 1714-20. *Second Edition.* Portrait.
8vo. 10s. 6d.

CRABBE'S (REV. GEORGE) Life, Letters, and Journals. By his SON.
Portrait. Fcap. 8vo. 3s.

——————— Life and Poetical Works. Plates. 8 Vols. Fcap.
8vo. 24s.

——————— Life and Poetical Works. Plates. Royal 8vo. 7s.

CROKER'S (J. W.) Progressive Geography for Children.
Fifth Edition. 18mo. 1s. 6d.

—— Stories for Children, Selected from the History of England. *Fifteenth Edition.* Woodcuts. 16mo. 2s. 6d.

—— Boswell's Life of Johnson. Including the Tour to the Hebrides. Portraits. Royal 8vo. 10s.

—— Essays on the Early Period of the French Revolution. 8vo. 15s.

—— Historical Essay on the Guillotine. Fcap. 8vo. 1s.

CROMWELL (OLIVER) and John Bunyan. By ROBERT SOUTHEY. Post 8vo. 2s.

CROWE'S AND CAVALCASELLE'S Notices of the Early Flemish Painters; their Lives and Works. Woodcuts. Post 8vo. 12s.

—————————————— History of Painting in Italy, from 2nd to 16th Century. Derived from Historical Researches as well as inspection of the Works of Art in that Country. With 70 Illustrations. Vols. I. and II. 8vo. 42s.

CUNNINGHAM'S (ALLAN) Poems and Songs. Now first collected and arranged, with Biographical Notice. 24mo. 2s. 6d.

CURETON (REV. W.) Remains of a very Ancient Recension of the Four Gospels in Syriac, hitherto unknown in Europe. Discovered, Edited, and Translated. 4to. 24s.

CURTIUS' (PROFESSOR) Student's Greek Grammar, for the use of Colleges and the Upper Forms. Translated under the Author's revision. Edited by DR. WM. SMITH. Post 8vo. 7s. 6d.

—— Smaller Greek Grammar for the use of the Middle and Lower Forms, abridged from the above. 12mo. 3s. 6d.

—— First Greek Course; containing Delectus, Exercise Book, and Vocabularies. 12mo. 3s. 6d.

CURZON'S (HON. ROBERT) ARMENIA AND ERZEROUM. A Year on the Frontiers of Russia, Turkey, and Persia. *Third Edition.* Woodcuts. Post 8vo. 7s. 6d.

CUST'S (GENERAL) Annals of the Wars of the 18th & 19th Centuries. 9 Vols. Fcap. 8vo. 5s. each.

—— Lives and Characters of the Warriors of All Nations who have Commanded Fleets and Armies before the Enemy. 8vo.

DARWIN'S (CHARLES) Journal of Researches into the Natural History of the Countries visited during a Voyage round the World. Post 8vo. 9s.

—— Origin of Species by Means of Natural Selection; or, the Preservation of Favoured Races in the Struggle for Life. Post 8vo. 14s.

—— Fertilization of Orchids through Insect Agency, and as to the good of Intercrossing. Woodcuts. Post 8vo. 9s.

DAVIS'S (NATHAN) Visit to the Ruined Cities of Numidia and Carthaginia. Illustrations. 8vo. 16s.

DAVY'S (SIR HUMPHRY) Consolations in Travel; or, Last Days of a Philosopher. *Fifth Edition.* Woodcuts. Fcap. 8vo. 6s.

—— Salmonia; or, Days of Fly Fishing. *Fourth Edition.* Woodcuts. Fcap. 8vo. 6s.

DELEPIERRE'S (OCTAVE) History of Flemish Literature. From the Twelfth Century. 8vo. 9s.

DENNIS' (GEORGE) Cities and Cemeteries of Etruria. Plates. 2 Vols. 8vo. 42s.

DERBY'S (EDWARD EARL OF) Translation of the Iliad of Homer into English Blank Verse. 2 Vols. 8vo. 24s.

DIXON'S (HEPWORTH) Story of the Life of Lord Bacon. Portrait. Fcap. 8vo. 7s. 6d.

DOG-BREAKING; the Most Expeditious, Certain, and Easy Method, whether great excellence or only mediocrity be required. By LIEUT.-GEN. HUTCHINSON. *Fourth and Revised Edition.* With additional Woodcuts. Crown 8vo.

DOMESTIC MODERN COOKERY. Founded on Principles of Economy and Practical Knowledge, and adapted for Private Families. *New Edition.* Woodcuts. Fcap. 8vo. 5s.

DOUGLAS'S (GENERAL SIR HOWARD) Life and Adventures; From Notes, Conversations, and Correspondence. By S. W. FULLOM. Portrait. 8vo. 15s.

—————— On the Theory and Practice of Gunnery. *5th Edition.* Plates. 8vo. 21s.

—————— Military Bridges, and the Passages of Rivers in Military Operations. *Third Edition.* Plates. 8vo. 21s.

—————— Naval Warfare with Steam. *Second Edition.* 8vo. 8s. 6d.

—————— Modern Systems of Fortification, with special reference to the Naval, Littoral, and Internal Defence of England. Plans. 8vo. 12s.

DRAKE'S' (SIR FRANCIS) Life, Voyages, and Exploits, by Sea and Land. By JOHN BARROW. *Third Edition.* Post 8vo. 2s.

DRINKWATER'S (JOHN) History of the Siege of Gibraltar, 1779-1783. With a Description and Account of that Garrison from the Earliest Periods. Post 8vo. 2s.

DU CHAILLU'S (PAUL B.) EQUATORIAL AFRICA, with Accounts of the Gorilla, the Nest-building Ape, Chimpanzee, Crocodile, &c. Illustrations. 8vo. 21s.

DUFFERIN'S (LORD) Letters from High Latitudes, being some Account of a Yacht Voyage to Iceland, &c., in 1856. *Fourth Edition.* Woodcuts. Post 8vo. 9s.

DYER'S (THOMAS H.) History of Modern Europe, from the taking of Constantinople by the Turks to the close of the War in the Crimea. 4 Vols. 8vo. 60s.

EASTLAKE'S (SIR CHARLES) Italian Schools of Painting. From the German of KUGLER. Edited, with Notes. *Third Edition.* Illustrated from the Old Masters. 2 Vols. Post 8vo. 30s.

EASTWICK'S (E. B.) Handbook for Bombay and Madras, with Directions for Travellers, Officers, &c. Map. 2 Vols. Post 8vo. 24s.

EDWARDS' (W. H.) Voyage up the River Amazon, including a Visit to Para. Post 8vo. 2s.

ELDON'S (LORD) Public and Private Life, with Selections from his Correspondence and Diaries. By HORACE TWISS. *Third Edition.* Portrait. 2 Vols. Post 8vo. 21s.

ELLIS (REV. W.) Visits to Madagascar, including a Journey to the Capital, with notices of Natural History, and Present Civilisation of the People. *Fifth Thousand.* Map and Woodcuts. 8vo. 16s.

—— (MRS.) Education of Character, with Hints on Moral Training. Post 8vo. 7s. 6d.

ELLESMERE'S (LORD) Two Sieges of Vienna by the Turks. Translated from the German. Post 8vo. 2s.

——————— Campaign of 1812 in Russia, from the German of General Carl Von Clausewitz. Map. 8vo. 10s. 6d.

——————— Poems. Crown 4to. 24s.

——————— Essays on History, Biography, Geography, and Engineering. 8vo. 12s.

ELPHINSTONE'S (HON. MOUNTSTUART) History of India—the Hindoo and Mahomedan Periods. *Fourth Edition.* Map. 8vo. 18s.

ENGEL'S (CARL) Music of the Most Ancient Nations; particularly of the Assyrians, Egyptians, and Hebrews, with Special Reference to the Discoveries in Western Asia and in Egypt. With 100 Illustrations. 8vo. 16s.

ENGLAND (HISTORY OF) from the Peace of Utrecht to the Peace of Versailles, 1713—83. By LORD MAHON (Earl Stanhope). *Library Edition,* 7 Vols. 8vo. 93s.; or *Popular Edition,* 7 Vols. Post 8vo. 35s.

——————— From the First Invasion by the Romans, down to the 14th year of Queen Victoria's Reign. By MRS. MARKHAM. 118*th* Edition. Woodcuts. 12mo. 6s.

——————— (THE STUDENT'S HUME). A History of England from the Earliest Times. Based on the History by DAVID HUME. Corrected and continued to 1858. Edited by WM. SMITH, LL.D. Woodcuts. Post 8vo. 7s. 6d.

ENGLISHWOMAN IN AMERICA. Post 8vo. 10s. 6d.

ESKIMAUX and English Vocabulary, for Travellers in the Arctic Regions. 16mo. 3s. 6d.

ESSAYS FROM "THE TIMES." Being a Selection from the LITERARY PAPERS which have appeared in that Journal. *Seventh Thousand.* 2 vols. Fcap. 8vo. 8s.

EXETER'S (BISHOP OF) Letters to the late Charles Butler, on the Theological parts of his Book of the Roman Catholic Church; with Remarks on certain Works of Dr. Milner and Dr. Lingard, and on some parts of the Evidence of Dr. Doyle. *Second Edition.* 8vo. 16s.

FAMILY RECEIPT-BOOK. A Collection of a Thousand Valuable and Useful Receipts. Fcap. 8vo. 5s. 6d.

FARRAR'S (REV. A. S.) Critical History of Free Thought in reference to the Christian Religion. Being the Bampton Lectures, 1862. 8vo. 16s.

——————— (F. W.) Origin of Language, based on Modern Researches. Fcap. 8vo. 5s.

FEATHERSTONHAUGH'S (G. W.) Tour through the Slave States of North America, from the River Potomac to Texas and the Frontiers of Mexico. Plates. 2 Vols. 8vo. 26s.

FERGUSSON'S (JAMES) Palaces of Nineveh and Persepolis Restored. Woodcuts. 8vo. 16s.

———— History of the Modern Styles of Architecture, completing the above work. With 312 Illustrations. 8vo. 31s. 6d.

FISHER'S (REV. GEORGE) Elements of Geometry, for the Use of Schools. *Fifth Edition*. 18mo. 1s. 6d.

———— First Principles of Algebra, for the Use of Schools. *Fifth Edition*. 18mo. 1s. 6d.

FLOWER GARDEN (THE). By REV. THOS. JAMES. Fcap. 8vo. 1s.

FONNEREAU'S (T. G.) Diary of a Dutiful Son. Fcap. 8vo. 4s. 6d.

FORBES' (C. S.) Iceland; its Volcanoes, Geysers, and Glaciers. Illustrations. Post 8vo. 14s.

FORD'S (RICHARD) Handbook for Spain, Andalusia, Ronda, Valencia, Catalonia, Granada, Gallicia, Arragon, Navarre, &c. *Third Edition*. 2 Vols. Post 8vo. 30s.

———— Gatherings from Spain. Post 8vo. 3s. 6d.

FORSTER'S (JOHN) Arrest of the Five Members by Charles the First. A Chapter of English History re-written. Post 8vo. 12s.

———— Grand Remonstrance, 1641. With an Essay on English freedom under the Plantagenet and Tudor Sovereigns. *Second Edition*. Post 8vo. 12s.

———— Oliver Cromwell, Daniel De Foe, Sir Richard Steele, Charles Churchill, Samuel Foote. *Third Edition*. Post 8vo. 12s.

FORSYTH'S (WILLIAM) Life and Times of Cicero. With Selections from his Correspondence and his Orations. Illustrations. 2 Vols. Post 8vo. 18s.

FORTUNE'S (ROBERT) Narrative of Two Visits to the Tea Countries of China, 1843-52. *Third Edition*. Woodcuts. 2 Vols. Post 8vo. 18s.

———— Third Visit to China. 1853-6. Woodcuts. 8vo. 16s.

———— Yedo and Peking. With Notices of the Agriculture and Trade of Japan and China. Illustrations. 8vo. 16s.

FOSS' (Edward) Judges of England. With Sketches of their Lives, and Notices of the Courts at Westminster, from the Conquest to the Present Time. 9 Vols. 8vo. 114s.

FRANCE (HISTORY OF). From the Conquest by the Gauls to the Death of Louis Philippe. By Mrs. MARKHAM. 56th Thousand. Woodcuts. 12mo. 6s.

———— (THE STUDENT'S HISTORY OF). From the Earliest Times to the Establishment of the Second Empire, 1852. By W. H. PEARSON. Edited by WM. SMITH, LL.D. Woodcuts. Post 8vo. 7s. 6d.

FRENCH (THE) in Algiers; The Soldier of the Foreign Legion— and the Prisoners of Abd-el-Kadir. Translated by Lady DUFF GORDON. Post 8vo. 2s.

GALTON'S (FRANCIS) Art of Travel; or, Hints on the Shifts and Contrivances available in Wild Countries. *Third Edition.* Woodcuts. Post 8vo. 7s. 6d.

GEOGRAPHY (THE STUDENT'S MANUAL OF ANCIENT). By Rev. W. L. BEVAN. Edited by WM. SMITH, LL.D. Woodcuts. Post 8vo. 7s. 6d.

——— Journal of the Royal Geographical Society of London. 8vo.

GERMANY (HISTORY OF). From the Invasion by Marius, to the present time. By Mrs. MARKHAM. *Fifteenth Thousand.* Woodcuts. 12mo. 6s.

GIBBON'S (EDWARD) History of the Decline and Fall of the Roman Empire. *A New Edition.* Preceded by his Autobiography. Edited, with Notes, by Dr. WM. SMITH. Maps. 8 Vols. 8vo. 60s.

——— (The Student's Gibbon); Being an Epitome of the above work, incorporating the Researches of Recent Commentators. By Dr. WM. SMITH. *Ninth Thousand.* Woodcuts. Post 8vo. 7s. 6d.

GIFFARD'S (EDWARD) Deeds of Naval Daring; or, Anecdotes of the British Navy. New Edition. Fcap. 8vo. 3s. 6d.

GOLDSMITH'S (OLIVER) Works. A New Edition. Printed from the last editions revised by the Author. Edited by PETER CUNNINGHAM. Vignettes. 4 Vols. 8vo. 30s. (Murray's British Classics.)

GLADSTONE'S (RIGHT HON. W. E.) Financial Statements of 1853, 60, 63, and 64; also his Speeches on Tax-Bills, 1861, and on Charities, 1863. *Second Edition.* 8vo. 12s.

——— Wedgwood : an Address delivered at Burslem. Woodcuts. Post 8vo. 2s.

GLEIG'S (REV. G. R.) Campaigns of the British Army at Washington and New Orleans. Post 8vo. 2s.

——— Story of the Battle of Waterloo. Post 8vo. 3s. 6d.

——— Narrative of Sale's Brigade in Affghanistan. Post 8vo. 2s.

——— Life of Robert Lord Clive. Post 8vo. 3s. 6d.

——— Life and Letters of Sir Thomas Munro. Post 8vo 3s. 6d.

GORDON'S (SIR ALEX. DUFF) Sketches of German Life, and Scenes from the War of Liberation. From the German. Post 8vo. 3s. 6d.

——— (LADY DUFF) Amber-Witch : A Trial for Witchcraft. From the German. Post 8vo. 2s.

——— French in Algiers. 1. The Soldier of the Foreign Legion. 2. The Prisoners of Abd-el-Kadir. From the French. Post 8vo. 2s.

GOUGER'S (HENRY) Personal Narrative of Two Years' Imprisonment in Burmah. *Second Edition.* Woodcuts. Post 8vo. 12s.

GRAMMAR (THE STUDENT'S GREEK.) For Colleges, and the Upper Forms. By PROFESSOR CURTIUS. Translated under the Revision of the Author. Edited by WM. SMITH, LL.D. Post 8vo. 7s. 6d.

——— (THE STUDENT'S LATIN). For Colleges and the Upper Forms. By WM. SMITH, LL.D, Post 8vo. 7s. 6d.

GREECE (THE STUDENT'S HISTORY OF). From the Earliest Times to the Roman Conquest. By WM. SMITH, LL.D. Woodcuts. Post 8vo. 7s. 6d.

GRENVILLE (THE) PAPERS. Being the Public and Private Correspondence of George Grenville, including his PRIVATE DIARY. Edited by W. J. SMITH. 4 Vols. 8vo. 16s. each.

GREY (EARL) on Parliamentary Government and Reform. A New Edition, containing Suggestions for the Improvement of our Representative System, and an Examination of the Reform Bills of 1859—61. 8vo. 9s.

GREY'S (SIR GEORGE) Polynesian Mythology, and Ancient Traditional History of the New Zealand Race. Woodcuts. Post 8vo. 10s. 6d.

GROTE'S (GEORGE) History of Greece. From the Earliest Times to the close of the generation contemporary with the death of Alexander the Great. Fourth Edition. Maps. 8 vols. 8vo. 112s.

——— PLATO, and the other Companions of Socrates. 3 Vols. 8vo.

——— (MRS.) Memoir of Ary Scheffer. Post 8vo. 8s. 6d.

——— Collected Papers. 8vo. 10s. 6d.

GUIZOT'S (M.) Meditations on Christianity. Containing 1. NATURAL PROBLEMS. 2. CHRISTIAN DOGMAS. 3. THE SUPERNATURAL. 4. LIMITS OF SCIENCE. 5. REVELATION. 6. INSPIRATION OF HOLY SCRIPTURE. 7. GOD ACCORDING TO THE BIBLE. 8. JESUS CHRIST ACCORDING TO THE GOSPELS. Post 8vo. 9s. 6d.

HALLAM'S (HENRY) Constitutional History of England, from the Accession of Henry the Seventh to the Death of George the Second. Seventh Edition. 3 Vols. 8vo. 30s.

——— History of Europe during the Middle Ages. Tenth Edition. 3 Vols. 8vo. 30s.

——— Literary History of Europe, during the 15th, 16th and 17th Centuries. Fourth Edition. 3 Vols. 8vo. 36s.

——— Literary Essays and Characters. Fcap. 8vo. 2s.

——— Historical Works. Containing History of England, —Middle Ages of Europe,—Literary History of Europe. 10 Vols. Post 8vo. 6s each.

——— (ARTHUR) Remains; in Verse and Prose. With Preface, Memoir, and Portrait. Fcap. 8vo. 7s. 6d.

HAMILTON'S (JAMES) Wanderings in North Africa. Post 8vo. 12s.

HART'S ARMY LIST. (Quarterly and Annually.) 8vo. 10s. 6d. and 21s each.

HANNAH'S (Rev. Dr.) Bampton Lectures for 1863; the Divine and Human Elements in Holy Scripture. 8vo. 10s. 6d.

HAY'S (J. H. DRUMMOND) Western Barbary, its wild Tribes and savage Animals. Post 8vo. 2s.

HEAD'S (SIR FRANCIS) Horse and his Rider. Woodcuts. Post 8vo. 5s.

——— Rapid Journeys across the Pampas. Post 8vo. 2s.

——— Bubbles from the Brunnen of Nassau. 16mo. 5s.

——— Emigrant. Fcap. 8vo. 2s. 6d.

——— Stokers and Pokers; or, N.-Western Railway. Post 8vo. 2s.

——— Fortnight in Ireland. Map. 8vo. 12s.

——— (SIR EDMUND) Shall and Will; or, Future Auxiliary Verbs. Fcap. 8vo. 4s.

PUBLISHED BY MR. MURRAY. 15

HAND-BOOK—TRAVEL-TALK. English, German, French, and Italian. 18mo. 3s. 6d.
——————— NORTH GERMANY, HOLLAND, BELGIUM, and the Rhine to Switzerland. Map. Post 8vo. 10s.
——————— KNAPSACK GUIDE TO BELGIUM AND THE RHINE. Post 8vo. (In the Press.)
——————— SOUTH GERMANY, Bavaria, Austria, Styria, Salzberg, the Austrian and Bavarian Alps, the Tyrol, Hungary, and the Danube, from Ulm to the Black Sea. Map. Post 8vo. 10s.
——————— KNAPSACK GUIDE TO THE TYROL. Post 8vo. (In the Press.)
——————— PAINTING. German, Flemish, and Dutch Schools. Edited by DR. WAAGEN. Woodcuts. 2 Vols. Post 8vo. 24s.
——————— LIVES OF THE EARLY FLEMISH PAINTERS, with Notices of their Works. By CROWE and CAVALCASELLE. Illustrations. Post 8vo. 12s.
——————— SWITZERLAND, Alps of Savoy, and Piedmont. Maps. Post 8vo. 9s.
——————— KNAPSACK GUIDE TO SWITZERLAND. Post 8vo. 5s.
——————— FRANCE, Normandy, Brittany, the French Alps, the Rivers Loire, Seine, Rhone, and Garonne, Dauphiné, Provence, and the Pyrenees. Maps. Post 8vo. 10s.
——————— KNAPSACK GUIDE TO FRANCE. Post 8vo. (In the Press.)
——————— PARIS AND ITS ENVIRONS. Map. Post 8vo. 5s.
——————— SPAIN, Andalusia, Ronda, Granada, Valencia, Catalonia, Gallicia, Arragon, and Navarre. Maps. 2 Vols. Post 8vo. 30s.
——————— PORTUGAL, LISBON, &c. Map. Post 8vo.
——————— NORTH ITALY, Piedmont, Liguria, Venetia, Lombardy, Parma, Modena, and Romagna. Map. Post 8vo. 12s.
——————— CENTRAL ITALY, Lucca, Tuscany, Florence, The Marches, Umbria, and the Patrimony of St. Peter's. Map. Post 8vo. 10s.
——————— ROME AND ITS ENVIRONS. Map. Post 8vo. 9s.
——————— SOUTH ITALY, Two Sicilies, Naples, Pompeii, Herculaneum, and Vesuvius. Map. Post 8vo. 10s.
——————— KNAPSACK GUIDE TO ITALY. Post 8vo. 6s.
——————— SICILY, Palermo, Messina, Catania, Syracuse, Etna, and the Ruins of the Greek Temples. Map. Post 8vo. 12s.
——————— PAINTING. The Italian Schools. From the German of KUGLER. Edited by Sir CHARLES EASTLAKE, R.A. Woodcuts. 2 Vols. Post 8vo. 30s.
——————— LIVES OF THE EARLY ITALIAN PAINTERS, AND PROGRESS OF PAINTING IN ITALY, from CIMABUE to BASSANO. By Mrs. JAMESON. Woodcuts. Post 8vo. 12s.

16   LIST OF WORKS

HAND-BOOK—DICTIONARY OF ITALIAN PAINTERS. By
A LADY. Edited by RALPH WORNUM. With a Chart. Post 8vo. 6s. 6d.
——————— GREECE, the Ionian Islands, Albania, Thessaly,
and Macedonia. Maps. Post 8vo. 15s.
——————— TURKEY, Malta, Asia Minor, Constantinople,
Armenia, Mesopotamia, &c. Maps. Post 8vo. (In the Press.)
——————— EGYPT, Thebes, the Nile, Alexandria, Cairo,
the Pyramids, Mount Sinai, &c. Map. Post 8vo. 15s.
——————— SYRIA & PALESTINE, Peninsula of Sinai, Edom,
and Syrian Desert. Maps. 2 Vols. Post 8vo. 24s.
——————— BOMBAY AND MADRAS. Map. 2 Vols. Post
8vo. 24s.
——————— NORWAY, Map. Post 8vo. 5s.
——————— DENMARK, SWEDEN and NORWAY. Maps. Post
8vo. 15s.
——————— RUSSIA, THE BALTIC AND FINLAND. Maps. Post
8vo. 12s.
——————— MODERN LONDON. A Complete Guide to all
the Sights and Objects of Interest in the Metropolis. Map. 16mo.
3s. 6d.
——————— WESTMINSTER ABBEY. Woodcuts. 16mo. 1s.
——————— KENT AND SUSSEX, Canterbury, Dover, Rams-
gate, Sheerness, Rochester, Chatham, Woolwich, Brighton, Chichester,
Worthing, Hastings, Lewes, Arundel, &c. Map. Post 8vo. 10s.
——————— SURREY, HANTS, Kingston, Croydon, Reigate,
Guildford, Winchester, Southampton, Portsmouth, and Isle of Wight.
Maps. Post 8vo. 7s. 6d.
——————— BERKS, BUCKS, AND OXON, Windsor, Eton,
Reading, Aylesbury, Uxbridge, Wycombe, Henley, the City and Uni-
versity of Oxford, and the Descent of the Thames to Maidenhead and
Windsor. Map. Post 8vo. 7s. 6d.
——————— WILTS, DORSET, AND SOMERSET, Salisbury,
Chippenham, Weymouth, Sherborne, Wells, Bath, Bristol, Taunton,
&c. Map. Post 8vo. 7s. 6d.
——————— DEVON AND CORNWALL, Exeter, Ilfracombe,
Linton, Sidmouth, Dawlish, Teignmouth, Plymouth, Devonport, Tor-
quay, Launceston, Truro, Penzance, Falmouth, &c. Maps. Post 8vo.
7s. 6d.
——————— NORTH AND SOUTH WALES, Bangor, Car-
narvon, Beaumaris, Snowdon. Conway, Menai Straits, Carmarthen,
Pembroke, Tenby, Swansea, The Wye, &c. Maps. 2 Vols. Post 8vo.
12s.
——————— CATHEDRALS OF ENGLAND—Southern Divi-
sion, Winchester, Salisbury, Exeter, Wells, Chichester, Rochester,
Canterbury. With 110 Illustrations. 2 Vols. Crown 8vo. 24s.
——————— CATHEDRALS OF ENGLAND—Eastern Divi-
sion, Oxford, Peterborough, Norwich, Ely, and Lincoln. With 90
Illustrations. Crown 8vo. 18s.
——————— CATHEDRALS OF ENGLAND—Western Divi-
sion, Bristol, Gloucester, Hereford, Worcester, and Lichfield. With 50
Illustrations. Crown 8vo. 16s.
——————— FAMILIAR QUOTATIONS. From English Authors.
Third Edition. Fcap. 8vo. 5s.

HEBER'S (BISHOP) Journey through India. *Twelfth Edition.*
2 Vols. Post 8vo. 7s.

————— Poetical Works. *Sixth Edition.* Portrait. Fcap. 8vo. 6s.

HERODOTUS. A New English Version. Edited, with Notes and Essays, historical, ethnographical, and geographical. By Rev. G. RAWLINSON, assisted by SIR HENRY RAWLINSON and SIR J. G. WILKINSON. *Second Edition.* Maps and Woodcuts. 4 Vols. 8vo. 48s.

HESSEY (REV. DR.). Sunday—Its Origin, History, and Present Obligations. Being the Bampton Lectures for 1860. *Second Edition.* 8vo. 16s.

HICKMAN'S (WM.) Treatise on the Law and Practice of Naval Courts-Martial. 8vo. 10s. 6d.

HILLARD'S (G. S.) Six Months in Italy. 2 Vols. Post 8vo. 16s.

HOLLWAY'S (J. G.) Month in Norway. Fcap. 8vo. 2s.

HONEY BEE (THE). An Essay. By REV. THOMAS JAMES. Reprinted from the "Quarterly Review." Fcap. 8vo. 1s.

HOOK'S (DEAN) Church Dictionary. *Ninth Edition.* 8vo. 16s.

————— (THEODORE) Life. By J. G. LOCKHART. Reprinted from the "Quarterly Review." Fcap. 8vo. 1s.

HOOKER'S (Dr. J. D.) Himalayan Journals; or, Notes of an Oriental Naturalist in Bengal, the Sikkim and Nepal Himalayas, the Khasia Mountains, &c. *Second Edition.* Woodcuts. 2 Vols. Post 8vo. 18s.

HOPE'S (A. J. BERESFORD) English Cathedral of the Nineteenth Century. With Illustrations. 8vo. 12s.

HORACE (Works of). Edited by DEAN MILMAN. With 300 Woodcuts. Crown 8vo. 21s.

————— (Life of). By DEAN MILMAN. Woodcuts, and coloured Borders. 8vo. 9s.

HUME'S (THE STUDENT'S) History of England, from the Invasion of Julius Cæsar to the Revolution of 1688. Corrected and continued to 1858. Edited by Dr. Wm. Smith. Woodcuts. Post 8vo. 7s. 6d.

HUTCHINSON (GEN.) on the most expeditious, certain, and easy Method of Dog-Breaking. *Fourth Edition.* Enlarged and revised, with additional Illustrations. Crown 8vo.

HUTTON'S (H. E.) Principia Græca; an Introduction to the Study of Greek. Comprehending Grammar, Delectus, and Exercise-book, with Vocabularies. *Third Edition.* 12mo. 3s. 6d.

c

HOME AND COLONIAL LIBRARY. A Series of Works adapted for all circles and classes of Readers, having been selected for their acknowledged interest and ability of the Authors. Post 8vo. Published at 2s. and 3s. 6d. each, and arranged under two distinctive heads as follows:—

CLASS A.
HISTORY, BIOGRAPHY, AND HISTORIC TALES.

1. SIEGE OF GIBRALTAR. By JOHN DRINKWATER. 2s.
2. THE AMBER-WITCH. By LADY DUFF GORDON. 2s.
3. CROMWELL AND BUNYAN. By ROBERT SOUTHEY. 2s.
4. LIFE OF SIR FRANCIS DRAKE. By JOHN BARROW. 2s.
5. CAMPAIGNS AT WASHINGTON. By REV. G. R. GLEIG. 2s.
6. THE FRENCH IN ALGIERS. By LADY DUFF GORDON. 2s.
7. THE FALL OF THE JESUITS. 2s.
8. LIVONIAN TALES. 2s.
9. LIFE OF CONDE. By LORD MAHON. 3s. 6d.
10. SALE'S BRIGADE. By REV. G. R. GLEIG. 2s.
11. THE SIEGES OF VIENNA. By LORD ELLESMERE. 2s.
12. THE WAYSIDE CROSS. By CAPT. MILMAN. 2s.
13. SKETCHES OF GERMAN LIFE. By SIR A. GORDON. 3s. 6d.
14. THE BATTLE OF WATERLOO. By REV. G. R. GLEIG. 3s. 6d.
15. AUTOBIOGRAPHY OF STEFFENS. 2s.
16. THE BRITISH POETS. By THOMAS CAMPBELL. 3s. 6d.
17. HISTORICAL ESSAYS. By LORD MAHON. 3s. 6d.
18. LIFE OF LORD CLIVE. By REV. G. R. GLEIG. 3s. 6d.
19. NORTH-WESTERN RAILWAY. By SIR F. B. HEAD. 2s.
20. LIFE OF MUNRO. By REV. G. R. GLEIG. 3s. 6d.

CLASS B.
VOYAGES, TRAVELS, AND ADVENTURES.

1. BIBLE IN SPAIN. By GEORGE BORROW. 3s. 6d.
2. GIPSIES OF SPAIN. By GEORGE BORROW. 3s. 6d.
3 & 4. JOURNALS IN INDIA. By BISHOP HEBER. 2 Vols. 7s.
5. TRAVELS IN THE HOLY LAND. By IRBY and MANGLES. 2s.
6. MOROCCO AND THE MOORS. By J. DRUMMOND HAY. 2s.
7. LETTERS FROM THE BALTIC. By a LADY. 2s.
8. NEW SOUTH WALES. By MRS. MEREDITH. 2s.
9. THE WEST INDIES. By M. G. LEWIS. 2s.
10. SKETCHES OF PERSIA. By SIR JOHN MALCOLM. 3s. 6d.
11. MEMOIRS OF FATHER RIPA. 2s.
12. 13. TYPEE AND OMOO. By HERMANN MELVILLE. 2 Vols. 7s.
14. MISSIONARY LIFE IN CANADA. By REV. J. ABBOTT. 2s.
15. LETTERS FROM MADRAS. By a LADY. 2s.
16. HIGHLAND SPORTS. By CHARLES ST. JOHN. 3s. 6d.
17. PAMPAS JOURNEYS. By SIR F. B. HEAD. 2s.
18. GATHERINGS FROM SPAIN. By RICHARD FORD. 3s. 6d.
19. THE RIVER AMAZON. By W. H. EDWARDS. 2s.
20. MANNERS & CUSTOMS OF INDIA. By REV. C. ACLAND. 2s.
21. ADVENTURES IN MEXICO. By G. F. RUXTON. 3s. 6d.
22. PORTUGAL AND GALLICIA. By LORD CARNARVON. 3s. 6d.
23. BUSH LIFE IN AUSTRALIA. By Rev. H. W. HAYGARTH. 2s.
24. THE LIBYAN DESERT. By BAYLE ST. JOHN. 2s.
25. SIERRA LEONE. By a LADY. 3s. 6d.

⁎ Each work may be had separately.

IRBY AND MANGLES' Travels in Egypt, Nubia, Syria, and the Holy Land. Post 8vo. 2s.

JAMES' (Rev. Thomas) Fables of Æsop. A New Translation, with Historical Preface. With 100 Woodcuts by Tenniel and Wolf. Thirty-eighth Thousand. Post 8vo. 2s. 6d.

JAMESON'S (Mrs.) Lives of the Early Italian Painters, from Cimabue to Bassano, and the Progress of Painting in Italy. New Edition. With Woodcuts. Post 8vo. 12s.

JESSE'S (Edward) Gleanings in Natural History. Eighth Edition. Fcp. 8vo. 6s.

JOHNSON'S (Dr. Samuel) Life. By James Boswell. Including the Tour to the Hebrides. Edited by the late Mr. Croker. Portraits. Royal 8vo. 10s.

—————— Lives of the most eminent English Poets. Edited by Peter Cunningham. 3 vols. 8vo. 22s. 6d. (Murray's British Classics.)

JOURNAL OF A NATURALIST. Woodcuts. Post 8vo. 9s. 6d.

KEN'S (Bishop) Life. By A Layman. Second Edition. Portrait. 2 Vols. 8vo. 18s.

—————— Exposition of the Apostles' Creed. Extracted from his "Practice of Divine Love." Fcap. 1s. 6d.

—————— Approach to the Holy Altar. Extracted from his "Manual of Prayer" and "Practice of Divine Love." Fcap. 8vo. 1s. 6d.

KING'S (Rev. S. W.) Italian Valleys of the Alps; a Tour through all the Romantic and less-frequented "Vals" of Northern Piedmont. Illustrations. Crown 8vo. 18s.

—————— (Rev. C. W.) Antique Gems; their Origin, Use, and Value, as Interpreters of Ancient History, and as illustrative of Ancient Art. Illustrations. 8vo. 42s.

KING EDWARD VIth's Latin Grammar; or, an Introduction to the Latin Tongue, for the Use of Schools. Sixteenth Edition. 12mo. 3s. 6d.

—————————————— First Latin Book; or, the Accidence, Syntax, and Prosody, with an English Translation for the Use of Junior Classes. Fourth Edition. 12mo. 2s. 6d.

KIRK'S (J. Foster) History of Charles the Bold, Duke of Burgundy. Portrait. 2 Vols. 8vo. 30s.

KERR'S (Robert) GENTLEMAN'S HOUSE; or, How to Plan English Residences, from the Parsonage to the Palace. With Tables of Accommodation and Cost, and a Series of Selected Views and Plans. 8vo. 21s.

KUGLER'S Italian Schools of Painting. Edited, with Notes, by SIR CHARLES EASTLAKE. *Third Edition.* Woodcuts. 2 Vols. Post 8vo. 30s.

———— German, Dutch, and Flemish Schools of Painting. Edited, with Notes, by DR. WAAGEN. *Second Edition.* Woodcuts. 2 Vols. Post 8vo. 24s.

LANGUAGE (THE ENGLISH). A Series of Lectures. By GEORGE P. MARSH. Edited, with additional Chapters and Notes, by WM. SMITH, LL.D. Post 8vo. 7s. 6d.

LATIN GRAMMAR (KING EDWARD VITH'S). For the Use of Schools. *Sixteenth Edition.* 12mo. 3s. 6d.

———— First Book (KING EDWARD VITH'S); or, the Accidence, Syntax, and Prosody, with English Translation for Junior Classes. *Fourth Edition.* 12mo. 2s. 6d.

LAYARD'S (A. H.) Nineveh and its Remains. Being a Narrative of Researches and Discoveries amidst the Ruins of Assyria. With an Account of the Chaldean Christians of Kurdistan; the Yezedis, or Devil-worshippers; and an Enquiry into the Manners and Arts of the Ancient Assyrians. *Sixth Edition.* Plates and Woodcuts. 2 Vols. 8vo. 36s.

———————————— Nineveh and Babylon; being the Result of a Second Expedition to Assyria. *Fourteenth Thousand.* Plates 8vo. 21s. Or *Fine Paper,* 2 Vols. 8vo. 30s.

———— Popular Account of Nineveh. *15th Edition.* With Woodcuts. Post 8vo. 5s.

LEAKE'S (COL.) Topography of Athens, with Remarks on its Antiquities. *Second Edition.* Plates. 2 Vols. 8vo. 30s.

———— Travels in Northern Greece. Maps. 4 Vols. 8vo. 60s.

———— Disputed Questions of Ancient Geography. Map. 8vo. 6s. 6d.

———— Numismata Hellenica, and Supplement. Completing a descriptive Catalogue of Twelve Thousand Greek Coins, with Notes Geographical and Historical. With Map and Appendix. 4to. 63s.

———— Peloponnesiaca. 8vo. 15s.

———— Degradation of Science in England. 8vo. 3s. 6d.

LESLIE'S (C. R.) Handbook for Young Painters. With Illustrations. Post 8vo. 10s. 6d.

———————— Autobiographical Recollections, with Selections from his Correspondence. Edited by TOM TAYLOR. Portrait. 2 Vols. Post 8vo. 18s.

———————— Life of Sir Joshua Reynolds. With an Account of his Works, and a Sketch of his Cotemporaries. By TOM TAYLOR. Illustrations. 2 Vols. 8vo.

LETTERS FROM THE SHORES OF THE BALTIC. By a LADY. Post 8vo. 2s.

———————————————— MADRAS. By a LADY. Post 8vo. 2s.

———————————————— SIERRA LEONE. By a LADY. Edited by the HONOURABLE MRS. NORTON. Post 8vo. 3s. 6d.

LEWIS' (Sir G. C.) Essay on the Government of Dependencies. 8vo. 12s.

―――― Glossary of Provincial Words used in Herefordshire and some of the adjoining Counties. 12mo. 4s. 6d.

―――― (M. G.) Journal of a Residence among the Negroes in the West Indies. Post 8vo. 2s.

LIDDELL'S (Dean) History of Rome. From the Earliest Times to the Establishment of the Empire. With the History of Literature and Art. 2 Vols. 8vo. 28s.

―――― Student's History of Rome. Abridged from the above Work. 25th Thousand. With Woodcuts. Post 8vo. 7s. 6d.

LINDSAY'S (Lord) Lives of the Lindsays; or, a Memoir of the Houses of Crawfurd and Balcarres. With Extracts from Official Papers and Personal Narratives. Second Edition. 3 Vols. 8vo. 24s.

―――― Report of the Claim of James, Earl of Crawfurd and Balcarres, to the Original Dukedom of Montrose, created in 1488 Folio. 15s.

―――― Scepticism; a Retrogressive Movement in Theology and Philosophy. 8vo. 9s.

LISPINGS from LOW LATITUDES; or, the Journal of the Hon. Impulsia Gushington. Edited by Lord Dufferin. With 24 Plates, 4to. 21s.

LITERATURE (English). A Manual for Students. By T. B. Shaw. Edited, with Notes and Illustrations, by Wm. Smith, LL.D. Post 8vo. 7s. 6d.

―――― (Choice Specimens of). Selected from the Chief English Writers. By Thos. B. Shaw, M.A. Edited by Wm. Smith, LL.D. Post 8vo. 7s. 6d.

LITTLE ARTHUR'S HISTORY OF ENGLAND. By Lady Callcott. 120th Thousand. With 20 Woodcuts. Fcap. 8vo. 2s. 6d.

LIVINGSTONE'S (Rev. Dr.) Popular Account of his Missionary Travels in South Africa. Illustrations. Post 8vo. 6s.

―――― Narrative of an Expedition to the Zambezi and its Tributaries; and of the Discovery of Lakes Shirwa and Nyassa. 1858-64. By David and Charles Livingstone. Map and Illustrations. 8vo.

LIVONIAN TALES. By the Author of "Letters from the Baltic." Post 8vo. 2s.

LOCKHART'S (J. G.) Ancient Spanish Ballads. Historical and Romantic. Translated, with Notes. Illustrated Edition. 4to. 21s. Or, Popular Edition, Post 8vo. 2s. 6d.

―――― Life of Robert Burns. Fifth Edition. Fcap. 8vo. 3s.

LONDON'S (Bishop of) Dangers and Safeguards of Modern Theology. Containing Suggestions to the Theological Student under present difficulties. Second Edition. 8vo. 9s.

LOUDON'S (Mrs.) Instructions in Gardening for Ladies. With Directions and Calendar of Operations for Every Month. Eighth Edition. Woodcuts. Fcap. 8vo. 5s.

LUCAS' (SAMUEL) Secularia; or, Surveys on the Main Stream of History. 8vo. 12s.

LUCKNOW: a Lady's Diary of the Siege. *Fourth Thousand.* Fcap. 8vo. 4s. 6d.

LYELL'S (SIR CHARLES) Elements of Geology; or, the Ancient Changes of the Earth and its Inhabitants considered as Illustrative of Geology. *Sixth Edition.* Woodcuts. 8vo. 18s.

—————— Geological Evidences of the Antiquity of Man. *Third Edition.* Illustrations. 8vo. 14s.

LYTTELTON'S (LORD) Ephemera. Post 8vo. 10s. 6d.

LYTTON'S (SIR EDWARD BULWER) Poems. *New Edition.* Revised. Post 8vo. 10s. 6d.

MAHON'S (LORD) History of England, from the Peace of Utrecht to the Peace of Versailles, 1713—83. *Library Edition.* 7 Vols. 8vo. 93s. *Popular Edition,* 7 Vols. Post 8vo. 35s.

—————— "Forty-Five;" a Narrative of the Rebellion in Scotland. Post 8vo. 3s.

—————— History of British India from its Origin till the Peace of 1783. Post 8vo. 3s. 6d.

—————— Spain under Charles the Second; 1690 to 1700. *Second Edition.* Post 8vo. 6s. 6d.

—————— Life of William Pitt, with Extracts from his MS. Papers. *Second Edition.* Portraits. 4 Vols. Post 8vo. 42s.

—————— Condé, surnamed the Great. Post 8vo. 3s. 6d.

—————— Belisarius. *Second Edition.* Post 8vo. 10s. 6d.

—————— Historical and Critical Essays. Post 8vo. 3s. 6d.

—————— Miscellanies. *Second Edition.* Post 8vo. 5s. 6d.

—————— Story of Joan of Arc. Fcap. 8vo. 1s.

—————— Addresses. Fcap. 8vo. 1s.

McCLINTOCK'S (CAPT. SIR F. L.) Narrative of the Discovery of the Fate of Sir John Franklin and his Companions in the Arctic Seas. *Twelfth Thousand.* Illustrations. 8vo. 16s.

McCULLOCH'S (J. R.) Collected Edition of RICARDO'S Political Works. With Notes and Memoir. *Second Edition.* 8vo. 16s.

MACDOUGALL (COL.) On Modern Warfare as Influenced by Modern Artillery. With Plans. Post 8vo. 12s.

MAINE (H. SUMNER) On Ancient Law: its Connection with the Early History of Society, and its Relation to Modern Ideas. *Second Edition.* 8vo. 12s.

MALCOLM'S (SIR JOHN) Sketches of Persia. *Third Edition.* Post 8vo. 3s. 6d.

MANSEL (REV. H. L.) Limits of Religious Thought Examined. Being the Bampton Lectures for 1858. *Fourth Edition.* Post 8vo. 7s. 6d.

MANSFIELD (SIR WILLIAM) On the Introduction of a Gold Currency into India: a Contribution to the Literature of Political Economy. 8vo. 3s. 6d.

MANTELL'S (GIDEON A.) Thoughts on Animalcules; or, the Invisible World, as revealed by the Microscope. *Second Edition*. Plates. 16mo. 6s.

MANUAL OF SCIENTIFIC ENQUIRY, Prepared for the Use of Officers and Travellers. By various Writers. Edited by Sir J. F. HERSCHEL and Rev. R. MAIN. *Third Edition*. Maps. Post 8vo. 9s. (*Published by order of the Lords of the Admiralty.*)

MARKHAM'S (MRS.) History of England. From the First Invasion by the Romans, down to the fourteenth year of Queen Victoria's Reign. 156th *Edition*. Woodcuts. 12mo. 6s.

——— History of France. From the Conquest by the Gauls, to the Death of Louis Philippe. *Sixtieth Edition*. Woodcuts. 12mo. 6s.

——— History of Germany. From the Invasion by Marius, to the present time. *Fifteenth Edition*. Woodcuts. 12mo. 6s.

——— History of Greece. From the Earliest Times to the Roman Conquest. By Dr. WM. SMITH. Woodcuts. 16mo. 3s. 6d.

——— History of Rome. From the Earliest Times to the Establishment of the Empire. By DR. WM. SMITH. Woodcuts. 16mo. 3s. 6d.

——— (CLEMENTS, R.) Travels in Peru and India, for the purpose of collecting Cinchona Plants, and introducing Bark into India. Maps and Illustrations. 8vo. 16s.

MARKLAND'S (J. H.) Reverence due to Holy Places. *Third Edition*. Fcap. 8vo. 2s.

MARRYAT'S (JOSEPH) History of Modern and Mediæval Pottery and Porcelain. With a Description of the Manufacture. *Second Edition*. Plates and Woodcuts. 9vo. 31s. 6d.

——— (HORACE) Jutland, the Danish Isles, and Copenhagen. Illustrations. 2 Vols. Post 8vo. 24s.

——— Sweden and Isle of Gothland. Illustrations. 2 Vols. Post 8vo. 28s.

MATTHIÆ'S (AUGUSTUS) Greek Grammar for Schools. Abridged from the Larger Grammar. By Blomfield. *Ninth Edition*. Revised by EDWARDS. 12mo. 3s.

MAUREL'S (JULES) Essay on the Character, Actions, and Writings of the Duke of Wellington. *Second Edition*. Fcap. 8vo. 1s. 6d.

MAXIMS AND HINTS on Angling and Chess. By RICHARD PENN. Woodcuts. 12mo. 1s.

MAYNE'S (R. C.) Four Years in British Columbia and Vancouver Island. Its Forests, Rivers, Coasts, and Gold Fields, and Resources for Colonisation. Illustrations. 8vo. 16s.

MELVILLE'S (HERMANN) Typee and Omoo; or, Adventures amongst the Marquesas and South Sea Islands. 2 Vols. Post 8vo. 7s.

MEREDITH'S (MRS. CHARLES) Notes and Sketches of New South Wales. Post 8vo. 2s.

MESSIAH (THE): A Narrative of the Life, Travels, Death, Resurrection, and Ascension of our Blessed Lord. By A Layman. Author of the "Life of Bishop Ken." Map. 8vo. 18s.

MICHIE'S (Alexander) Siberian Overland Route from Peking to Petersburg, through the Deserts and Steppes of Mongolia, Tartary, &c. Maps and Illustrations. 8vo. 16s.

MILLS' (Arthur) India in 1858; A Summary of the Existing Administration. *Second Edition.* Map. 8vo. 10s. 6d.

———— (Rev. John) Three Months' Residence at Nablus, with an Account of the Modern Samaritans. Illustrations. Post 8vo. 10s. 6d.

MILMAN'S (Dean) History of the Jews, from the Earliest Period, brought down to Modern Times. *New Edition.* 3 Vols. 8vo. 36s.

———— Christianity, from the Birth of Christ to the Abolition of Paganism in the Roman Empire. *New Edition.* 3 Vols. 8vo. 36s.

———— Latin Christianity; including that of the Popes to the Pontificate of Nicholas V. *New Edition.* 9 Vols. 8vo 84s.

———— Character and Conduct of the Apostles considered as an Evidence of Christianity. 8vo. 10s. 6d.

———— Life and Works of Horace. With 300 Woodcuts. 2 Vols. Crown 8vo. 30s.

———— Poetical Works. Plates. 3 Vols. Fcap. 8vo. 18s.

———— Fall of Jerusalem. Fcap. 8vo. 1s.

———— (Capt. E. A.) Wayside Cross. A Tale of the Carlist War. Post 8vo. 2s.

MILNES' (R. Monckton, Lord Houghton) Poetical Works. Fcap. 8vo. 6s.

MODERN DOMESTIC COOKERY. Founded on Principles of Economy and Practical Knowledge and adapted for Private Families. *New Edition.* Woodcuts. Fcap. 8vo. 5s.

MOORE'S (Thomas) Life and Letters of Lord Byron. Plates. 6 Vols. Fcap. 8vo. 18s.

———— Life and Letters of Lord Byron. Portraits. Royal 8vo. 9s.

MOTLEY'S (J. L.) History of the United Netherlands: from the Death of William the Silent to the Synod of Dort. Embracing the English-Dutch struggle against Spain; and a detailed Account of the Spanish Armada. Portraits. 2 Vols. 8vo. 30s.

MOUHOT'S (Henri) Siam, Cambojia, and Lao; a Narrative of Travels and Discoveries. Illustrations. 2 vols. 8vo. 32s.

MOZLEY'S (Rev. J. B.) Treatise on Predestination. 8vo. 14s.

———— Primitive Doctrine of Baptismal Regeneration. 8vo. 7s. 6d.

MUNDY'S (GENERAL) Pen and Pencil Sketches in India.
Third Edition. Plates. Post 8vo. 7s. 6d.

———— (ADMIRAL) Account of the Italian Revolution, with Notices of Garibaldi, Francis II., and Victor Emmanuel. Post 8vo. 12s.

MUNRO'S (GENERAL SIR THOMAS) Life and Letters. By the REV. G. R. GLEIG. Post 8vo. 3s. 6d.

MURCHISON'S (SIR RODERICK) Russia in Europe and the Ural Mountains. With Coloured Maps, Plates, Sections, &c. 2 Vols. Royal 4to.

———— Siluria; or, a History of the Oldest Rocks containing Organic Remains. *Third Edition.* Map and Plates. 8vo. 42s.

MURRAY'S RAILWAY READING. Containing:—

WELLINGTON. By LORD ELLESMERE. 6d.
NIMROD ON THE CHASE. 1s.
ESSAYS FROM "THE TIMES." 2 Vols. 8s.
MUSIC AND DRESS. 1s.
LAYARD'S ACCOUNT OF NINEVEH. 5s.
MILMAN'S FALL OF JERUSALEM. 1s.
MAHON'S "FORTY-FIVE." 3s.
LIFE OF THEODORE HOOK. 1s.
DEEDS OF NAVAL DARING. 3s. 6d.
THE HONEY BEE. 1s.
JAMES' ÆSOP'S FABLES. 2s. 6d.
NIMROD ON THE TURF. 1s. 6d.
ART OF DINING. 1s. 6d.

HALLAM'S LITERARY ESSAYS. 2s.
MAHON'S JOAN OF ARC. 1s.
HEAD'S EMIGRANT. 2s. 6d.
NIMROD ON THE ROAD. 1s.
CROKER ON THE GUILLOTINE. 1s.
HOLLWAY'S NORWAY. 2s.
MAUREL'S WELLINGTON. 1s. 6d.
CAMPBELL'S LIFE OF BACON. 2s. 6d.
THE FLOWER GARDEN. 1s.
LOCKHART'S SPANISH BALLADS. 2s. 6d.
TAYLOR'S NOTES FROM LIFE. 2s.
REJECTED ADDRESSES. 1s.
PENN'S HINTS ON ANGLING. 1s.

MUSIC AND DRESS. By a LADY. Reprinted from the "Quarterly Review." Fcap. 8vo. 1s.

NAPIER'S (SIR WM.) English Battles and Sieges of the Peninsular War. *Third Edition.* Portrait. Post 8vo. 10s. 6d.

———— Life and Letters. Edited by H. A. BRUCE, M.P. Portraits. 2 Vols. Crown 8vo. 28s.

———— Life of General Sir Charles Napier; chiefly derived from his Journals and Letters. *Second Edition.* Portraits. 4 Vols. Post 8vo. 48s.

NAUTICAL ALMANACK. Royal 8vo. 2s. 6d. (*By Authority.*)

NAVY LIST. (*Published Quarterly, by Authority.*) 16mo. 2s. 6d.

NEW TESTAMENT (THE) Illustrated by a Plain Explanatory Commentary, and authentic Views of Sacred Places, from Sketches and Photographs. Edited by ARCHDEACON CHURTON and REV. BASIL JONES. With 110 Illustrations. 2 Vols. Crown 8vo.

NEWDEGATE'S (C. N.) Customs' Tariffs of all Nations, collected and arranged up to the year 1855. 4to. 30s.

NICHOLLS' (SIR GEORGE) History of the English, Irish and Scotch Poor Laws. 4 Vols. 8vo.

———— (Rev. H. G.) Historical Account of the Forest of Dean. Woodcuts, &c. Post 8vo. 10s. 6d.

———— Personalities of the Forest of Dean, its successive Officials, Gentry, and Commonalty. Post 8vo. 3s. 6d.

NICOLAS' (Sir Harris) Historic Peerage of England. Exhibiting the Origin, Descent, and Present State of every Title of Peerage which has existed in this Country since the Conquest. By WILLIAM COURTHOPE. 8vo. 30s.

NIMROD On the Chace—The Turf—and The Road. Reprinted from the "Quarterly Review." Woodcuts. Fcap. 8vo. 3s. 6d.

O'CONNOR'S (R.) Field Sports of France; or, Hunting, Shooting, and Fishing on the Continent. Woodcuts. 12mo. 7s. 6d.

OXENHAM'S (Rev. W.) English Notes for Latin Elegiacs; designed for early Proficients in the Art of Latin Versification, with Prefatory Rules of Composition in Elegiac Metre. *Fourth Edition*. 12mo. 3s. 6d.

PARIS' (Dr.) Philosophy in Sport made Science in Earnest; or, the First Principles of Natural Philosophy inculcated by aid of the Toys and Sports of Youth. *Ninth Edition*. Woodcuts. Post 8vo. 7s. 6d.

PEEL'S (Sir Robert) Memoirs. Edited by EARL STANHOPE and MR. CARDWELL. 2 Vols. Post 8vo. 7s. 6d. each.

PENN'S (Richard) Maxims and Hints for an Angler and Chessplayer. *New Edition*. Woodcuts. Fcap. 8vo. 1s.

PENROSE'S (F. C.) Principles of Athenian Architecture, and the Optical Refinements exhibited in the Construction of the Ancient Buildings at Athens, from a Survey. With 40 Plates. Folio. 5l. 5s.

PERCY'S (John, M.D.) Metallurgy of Iron and Steel; or, the Art of Extracting Metals from their Ores and adapting them to various purposes of Manufacture. Illustrations. 8vo. 42s.

PHILLIPP (Charles Spencer March) On Jurisprudence. 8vo. 12s.

PHILLIPS' (John) Memoirs of William Smith, the Geologist. Portrait. 8vo. 7s. 6d.

—————— Geology of Yorkshire, The Coast, and Limestone District. Plates. 4to. Part I., 20s.—Part II., 30s.

—————— Rivers, Mountains, and Sea Coast of Yorkshire. With Essays on the Climate, Scenery, and Ancient Inhabitants. *Second Edition*, Plates. 8vo. 15s.

PHILPOTT'S (Bishop) Letters to the late Charles Butler, on the Theological parts of his "Book of the Roman Catholic Church;" with Remarks on certain Works of Dr. Milner and Dr. Lingard, and on some parts of the Evidence of Dr. Doyle. *Second Edition*. 8vo. 16s.

POPE'S (Alexander) Life and Works. *A New Edition*. Containing nearly 500 unpublished Letters. Edited with a NEW LIFE, Introductions and Notes. By REV. WHITWELL ELWIN. Portraits. 8vo. (*In the Press*.)

PORTER'S (Rev. J. L.) Five Years in Damascus. With Travels to Palmyra, Lebanon and other Scripture Sites. Map and Woodcuts. 2 Vols. Post 8vo. 21s.

—————— Handbook for Syria and Palestine: including an Account of the Geography, History, Antiquities, and Inhabitants of these Countries, the Peninsula of Sinai, Edom, and the Syrian Desert. Maps. 2 Vols. Post 8vo. 24s.

PRAYER-BOOK (The Illustrated), with 1000 Illustrations of Borders, Initials, Vignettes, &c. Medium 8vo. 18s. cloth; 31s. 6d. calf; 36s. morrocco.

PRECEPTS FOR THE CONDUCT OF LIFE. Extracted from the Scriptures. *Second Edition.* Fcap. 8vo. 1s.

PUSS IN BOOTS. With 12 Illustrations. By OTTO SPECKTER. Coloured, 16mo. 2s. 6d.

QUARTERLY REVIEW (THE). 8vo. 6s.

RAMBLES in Syria among the Turkomans and Bedaweens. Post 8vo. 10s. 6d.

RAWLINSON'S (REV. GEORGE) Herodotus. A New English Version. Edited with Notes and Essays. Assisted by SIR HENRY RAWLINSON and SIR J. G. WILKINSON. *Second Edition.* Maps and Woodcut. 4 Vols. 8vo. 48s.

———— Historical Evidences of the truth of the Scripture Records stated anew. *Second Edition.* 8vo. 14s.

———— Five Great Monarchies of the Ancient World. Illustrations. 4 Vols. 8vo. 16s. each.
Vols. I.—II., Chaldæa and Assyria. Vols. III.—IV., Babylon, Media, and Persia.

REJECTED ADDRESSES (THE). By JAMES AND HORACE SMITH. Fcap. 8vo. 1s., or *Fine Paper*, Portrait, fcap. 8vo. 5s.

RENNIE'S (D. F.) British Arms in Peking, 1860; Kagosima, 1862. Post 8vo. 12s.

———— Pekin and the Pekinese: Narrative of a Residence at the British Embassy. Illustrations. 2 Vols. Post 8vo.

REYNOLDS' (SIR JOSHUA) His Life and Times. Commenced by C. R. LESLIE, R.A., and continued by TOM TAYLOR. Portraits and Illustrations. 2 Vols. 8vo.

RICARDO'S (DAVID) Political Works. With a Notice of his Life and Writings. By J. R. M'CULLOCH. *New Edition.* 8vo. 16s.

RIPA'S (FATHER) Memoirs during Thirteen Years' Residence at the Court of Peking. From the Italian. Post 8vo. 2s.

ROBERTSON'S (CANON) History of the Christian Church, from the Apostolic Age to the Concordat of Worms, A.D. 1123. *Second Edition.* 3 Vols. 8vo. 38s.

ROBINSON'S (REV. DR.) Biblical Researches in the Holy Land. Being a Journal of Travels in 1838 and 1852. Maps. 3 Vols. 8vo. 45s.

———— Physical Geography of the Holy Land. Post 8vo. 10s. 6d.

ROME (THE STUDENT'S HISTORY OF). FROM THE EARLIEST TIMES TO THE ESTABLISHMENT OF THE EMPIRE. By DEAN LIDDELL. Woodcuts. Post 8vo. 7s. 6d.

ROWLAND'S (DAVID) Manual of the English Constitution; Its Rise, Growth, and Present State. Post 8vo. 10s. 6d.

———— Laws of Nature the Foundation of Morals. Post 8vo

RUNDELL'S (MRS.) Domestic Cookery, adapted for Private Families. *New Edition.* Woodcuts. Fcap. 8vo. 5s.

RUSSELL'S (J. RUTHERFURD, M.D.) Art of Medicine—Its History and its Heroes. Portraits. 8vo. 14s.

RUXTON'S (GEORGE F.) Travels in Mexico; with Adventures among the Wild Tribes and Animals of the Prairies and Rocky Mountains. Post 8vo. 3s. 6d.

SALE'S (SIR ROBERT) Brigade in Affghanistan. With an Account of the Defence of Jellalabad. By REV. G. R. GLEIG. Post 8vo. 2s.

SANDWITH'S (HUMPHRY) Siege of Kars. Post 8vo. 3s. 6d.

SCOTT'S (G. GILBERT) Secular and Domestic Architecture, Present and Future. *Second Edition.* 8vo. 9s.

——— (Master of Baliol) University Sermons Post 8vo. 8s. 6d.

SCROPE'S (G. P.) Geology and Extinct Volcanoes of Central France. *Second Edition.* Illustrations. Medium 8vo. 30s.

SELF-HELP. With Illustrations of Character and Conduct. By SAMUEL SMILES. 50th Thousand. Post 8vo. 6s.

SENIOR'S (N. W.) Suggestions on Popular Education. 8vo. 9s.

SHAFTESBURY (LORD CHANCELLOR); Memoirs of his Early Life. With his Letters, &c. By W. D. CHRISTIE. Portrait. 8vo. 10s. 6d.

SHAW'S (T. B.) Student's Manual of English Literature. Edited, with Notes and Illustrations, by DR. WM. SMITH. Post 8vo. 7s. 6d.

——— Choice Specimens of English Literature. Selected from the Chief English Writers. Edited by WM. SMITH, LL.D. Post 8vo. 7s. 6d.

SIERRA LEONE; Described in Letters to Friends at Home. By A LADY. Post 8vo. 3s. 6d.

SIMMONS on Courts-Martial. *5th Edition.* 8vo. 14s.

SMILES' (SAMUEL) Lives of British Engineers; from the Earliest Period to the Death of Robert Stephenson; with an account of their Principal Works, and a History of Inland Communication in Britain. Portraits and Illustrations. 3 Vols. 8vo. 63s.

——— George and Robert Stephenson; the Story of their Lives. With Portraits and 70 Woodcuts. Post 8vo. 6s.

——— James Brindley and the Early Engineers. With Portrait and 50 Woodcuts. Post 8vo. 6s.

——— Self-Help. With Illustrations of Character and Conduct. Post 8vo. 6s.

——— Industrial Biography: Iron-Workers and Tool Makers. A companion volume to "Self-Help." Post 8vo. 6s.

——— Workmen's Earnings—Savings—and Strikes. Fcap. 8vo. 1s. 6d.

SOMERVILLE'S (MARY) Physical Geography. *Fifth Edition.* Portrait. Post 8vo. 9s.

——— Connexion of the Physical Sciences. *Ninth Edition.* Woodcuts. Post 8vo. 9s.

SOUTH'S (JOHN F.) Household Surgery; or, Hints on Emergencies. *Seventeenth Thousand.* Woodcuts. Fcp. 8vo. 4s. 6d.

SMITH'S (Dr. Wm.) Dictionary of the Bible; its Antiquities, Biography, Geography, and Natural History. Illustrations. 3 Vols. 8vo. 105s.
——— Greek and Roman Antiquities. 2nd Edition. Woodcuts. 8vo. 42s.
——————————— Biography and Mythology. Woodcuts. 3 Vols. 8vo. 5l. 15s. 6d.
——————————— Geography. Woodcuts. 2 Vols. 8vo. 80s.
——— Classical Dictionary of Mythology, Biography, and Geography, compiled from the above. With 750 Woodcuts. 8vo. 18s.
——— Latin-English Dictionary. 3rd Edition. Revised. 8vo. 21s.
——— Smaller Classical Dictionary. Woodcuts. Crown 8vo. 7s. 6d.
——————————— Dictionary of Antiquities. Woodcuts. Crown 8vo. 7s. 6d.
——————————— Latin-English Dictionary. 12mo. 7s. 6d.
——— Latin-English Vocabulary; for Phædrus, Cornelius Nepos, and Cæsar. 2nd Edition. 12mo. 3s. 6d.
——— Principia Latina—Part I. A Grammar, Delectus, and Exercise Book, with Vocabularies. 6th Edition. 12mo. 3s. 6d.
——————————— Part II. A Reading-book of Mythology, Geography, Roman Antiquities, and History. With Notes and Dictionary. 3rd Edition. 12mo. 3s. 6d.
——————————— Part III. A Latin Poetry Book. Hexameters and Pentameters; Eclogæ Ovidianæ; Latin Prosody, &c. 2nd Edition. 12mo. 3s. 6d.
——————————— Part IV. Latin Prose Composition. Rules of Syntax, with Examples, Explanations of Synonyms, and Exercises on the Syntax. Second Edition. 12mo. 3s. 6d.
——— Student's Greek Grammar. By Professor Curtius. Post 8vo. 7s. 6d.
——————————— Latin Grammar. Post 8vo. 7s. 6d.
——————————— Latin Grammar. Abridged from the above. 12mo. 3s. 6d.
——— Smaller Greek Grammar. Abridged from Curtius. 12mo. 3s. 6d.
STANLEY'S (Dean) Sinai and Palestine, in Connexion with their History. Map. 8vo. 16s.
——————— Bible in the Holy Land. Woodcuts. Fcap. 8vo. 2s. 6d.
——————— St. Paul's Epistles to the Corinthians. 8vo. 18s.
——————— Eastern Church. Plans. 8vo. 12s.
——————— Jewish Church. Vol. 1. Abraham to Samuel. Plans. 8vo. 16s.
——————————————— Vol. 2. Samuel to the Captivity. 8vo. 16s.
——————— Historical Memorials of Canterbury. Woodcuts. Post 8vo. 7s. 6d.
——————— Sermons in the East, with Notices of the Places Visited. 8vo. 9s.
——————— Sermons on Evangelical and Apostolical Teaching. Post 8vo. 7s. 6d.
——————— Addresses and Charges of Bishop Stanley. With Memoir. 8vo. 10s. 6d.

WELLINGTON'S (THE DUKE OF) Despatches during his various Campaigns. Compiled from Official and other Authentic Documents. By COL. GURWOOD, C.B. 8 Vols. 8vo. 21s. each.

———————— Supplementary Despatches, and other Papers. Edited by his SON. Vols. I. to XII. 8vo. 20s. each.

———————— Selections from his Despatches and General Orders. By COLONEL GURWOOD. 8vo. 18s.

———————— Speeches in Parliament. 2 Vols. 8vo. 42s.

WILKINSON'S (SIR J. G.) Popular Account of the Private Life, Manners, and Customs of the Ancient Egyptians. *New Edition*. Revised and Condensed. With 500 Woodcuts. 2 Vols. Post 8vo. 12s.

———————— Handbook for Egypt.—Thebes, the Nile, Alexandria, Cairo, the Pyramids, Mount Sinai, &c. Map. Post 8vo. 15s.

———————— (G. B.) Working Man's Handbook to South Australia; with Advice to the Farmer, and Detailed Information for the several Classes of Labourers and Artisans. Map. 18mo. 1s. 6d.

WILSON'S (BISHOP DANIEL) Life, with Extracts from his Letters and Journals. By Rev. JOSIAH BATEMAN. *Second Edition*. Illustrations. Post 8vo. 9s.

———————— (GEN^{L.} SIR ROBERT) Secret History of the French Invasion of Russia, and Retreat of the French Army, 1812. *Second Edition*. 8vo. 15s.

———————— Private Diary of Travels, Personal Services, and Public Events, during Missions and Employments in Spain, Sicily, Turkey, Russia, Poland, Germany, &c. 1812-14. 2 Vols. 8vo. 26s.

———————— Autobiographical Memoirs. Containing an Account of his Early Life down to the Peace of Tilsit. Portrait. 2 Vols. 8vo. 26s.

WORDSWORTH'S (CANON) Journal of a Tour in Athens and Attica. *Third Edition*. Plates. Post 8vo. 8s. 6d.

———————— Pictorial, Descriptive, and Historical Account of Greece, with a History of Greek Art, by G. SCHARF, F.S.A. *New Edition*. With 600 Woodcuts. Royal 8vo. 28s.

WORNUM (RALPH). A Biographical Dictionary of Italian Painters: with a Table of the Contemporary Schools of Italy. By a LADY. Post 8vo. 6s. 6d.

BRADBURY AND EVANS, PRINTERS, WHITEFRIARS.

www.ingramcontent.com/pod-product-compliance
Lightning Source LLC
Chambersburg PA
CBHW030424300426
44112CB00009B/833